Study Guide

Jessica Herrmeyer
Hawkeye Community College

Sociology
A Down-to-Earth Approach

Eleventh Edition

James M. Henslin

PEARSON

Boston   Columbus   Indianapolis   New York   San Francisco   Upper Saddle River
Amsterdam   Cape Town   Dubai   London   Madrid   Milan   Munich   Paris   Montreal   Toronto
Delhi   Mexico City   Sao Paulo   Sydney   Hong Kong   Seoul   Singapore   Taipei   Tokyo

© 2012 by PEARSON.
Upper Saddle River, New Jersey 07458

10 9 8 7 6 5 4 3 2 1

ISBN 10: 0-205-09658-1
ISBN 13: 978-0-205-09658-9

Table of Contents

CHAPTER 1
THE SOCIOLOGICAL PERSPECTIVE

LEARNING OBJECTIVES

After reading Chapter 1, you should be able to:

1. Understand what is meant by the broader social contexts that underlie human behavior, and how and why sociologists study these broader social contexts. (4)

2. Explain the sociological perspective: what it is, what it offers, and why C. Wright Mills referred to it as "the intersection of biography (the individual) and history (the social factors that influence the individual)." (4)

3. Define and discuss science as application (the systematic methods used to obtain knowledge) and product (the knowledge and/or information that are obtained by those methods). (5-8)

4. Identify, understand, and make distinctions between the natural sciences and the social sciences. (5-8)

5. Understand how sociology views and studies human behavior, and how its particular areas of focus are similar to and different from each of the other social sciences. (6-7)

6. Discuss the social changes and the changing social conditions that fostered the development of sociology as a distinct academic discipline in the middle of the nineteenth century. (8-9)

7. Identify and critique the sociological contributions of the following mid- to late-nineteenth and early twentieth century European thinkers: Auguste Comte, Herbert Spencer, Karl Marx, Emile Durkheim, and Max Weber. (9-14)

8. Understand how and why levels of social integration affect rates of suicide and how Emile Durkheim's nineteenth century study of suicide helped to demonstrate the ways in which social integration affects people's behaviors. (11-13)

9. Explain the role of values in social research as prescribed by Max Weber and the ensuing controversies over whether sociological research can be and/or should be value free. (14-15)

10. Distinguish between *Verstehen*, as envisioned by Max Weber, and "social facts," as defined by Emile Durkheim; explain how, despite their differences, both approaches can be combined when conducting social research. (15)

11. Trace the history of sociology in North America from the late 1800s to the present while identifying the sociological contributions of the following American sociologists: Albion

Small, George Herbert Mead, Ernest Burgess, Robert E. Park, Talcott Parsons, W.E.B. Du Bois, and C. Wright Mills. (16-24)

12. Discuss the current state of American sociology as it relates to the debate between social reform and social analysis, and the role applied sociology plays in this debate. (21-24)

13. Discuss "public sociology." Do you think that social reform, rather than social science, has become the more dominant goal of sociology? (23)

14. Define the word "theory" and explain why theory is an important part of sociology. (24)

15. Identify the three major theoretical perspectives in sociology—symbolic interactionism, functional analysis, and conflict theory—and describe the particular level of analysis, characteristics, viewpoints, and concerns associated with each. (24-30)

Chapter Outline

I.   The Sociological Perspective
  A.   This perspective is important because it provides a different way of looking at familiar worlds. It allows us to gain a new vision of social life.
  B.   This perspective stresses the broader social context of behavior by looking at individuals' social location—employment, income, education, gender, age, and race— and by considering external influences—people's experiences—which are internalized and become part of a person's thinking and motivations. We are able to see the links between what people do and the social settings that shape their behavior.
  C.   This perspective enables us to analyze and understand both the forces that contribute to the emergence and growth of the global village and our unique experiences in our own smaller corners of this village.

II.   Sociology and the Other Sciences
  A.   Science is the systematic methods used to obtain knowledge and the knowledge obtained by those methods. It can be divided into the natural sciences and the social sciences. Sociology is defined as "the scientific study of society and human behavior."
  B.   The natural sciences attempt to comprehend, explain, and predict events in our natural environment.
  C.   Social sciences attempt to objectively study the social world. Like the natural sciences, the social sciences are divided into specialized fields based on their subject matter.
    1.   Anthropology is the sister discipline of sociology that attempts to understand culture (a people's total way of life) by focusing primarily on tribal people. This is giving way though, to the study of groups in industrialized settings.
    2.   Economics analyzes the production, distribution, and allocation of the material goods and services of a society.

2

3. Political science focuses on politics or government.
4. Psychology concentrates on processes that occur within the individual.
5. Sociology is similar to the other social sciences in some ways, but it is distinct because it looks at all social institutions, focuses on industrialized societies, and looks at external factors that influence people.

D. All sciences have certain goals.
1. The first goal is to explain *why* something happens.
2. The second goal is to make generalizations by looking for patterns, recurring characteristics, or events.
3. The third goal is to predict what will happen in the future, given current knowledge.

E. To achieve these goals, scientists must move beyond common sense and rely on conclusions based on systematic study.

III. Origins of Sociology

A. Sociology developed in the middle of the nineteenth century when European social observers began to use scientific methods to test their ideas. The following four factors led to its development:
1. The social upheaval in Europe as a result of the Industrial Revolution, which led to changes in the way people lived their lives;
2. The political revolutions in America and France, which encouraged people to rethink their ideas about social life;
3. The development of imperialism—as the Europeans conquered other nations, they came in contact with different cultures and began to ask why cultures varied;
4. The success of the natural sciences, which created a desire to apply scientific methods in order to find answers for the questions being raised about the social world.

B. Auguste Comte coined the term "sociology" and suggested the use of positivism—applying the scientific approach to the social world—but he did not utilize this approach himself. Comte believed that this new science should not only discover sociological principles, but should then apply those principles to social reform.

C. Herbert Spencer viewed societies as evolutionary, coined the term "the survival of the fittest," and became known for social Darwinism. Spencer was convinced that no one should intervene in the evolution of society and that attempts at social reform were wrong.

D. Karl Marx, whose ideas about social classes and class struggle between the bourgeoisie and the proletariat were the foundation of the conflict perspective, believed that class conflict was the key to human history. Marx believed that the conflict and struggle would end only with a revolution by the working class.

E. Emile Durkheim played an important role in the development of sociology.
1. One of his primary goals was to get sociology recognized as a separate academic discipline.

2. He was interested in understanding the social factors that influence individual behavior; he studied suicide rates among different groups and concluded that social integration—the degree to which people are tied to their social group—was a key social factor in suicide.

3. Durkheim's third concern was that social research be practical; sociologists should not only diagnose the causes of social problems but should also develop solutions for them.

F. Max Weber was one of the most influential of all sociologists, raising issues that remain controversial even today. Disagreeing with Karl Marx, Weber defined religion as a central force in social change (i.e., Protestantism encourages greater economic development and was the central factor in the rise of capitalism in some countries).

1. The Protestant belief system encouraged its members to embrace change.

2. Protestants (specifically Calvinists) sought "signs" that they were in God's will; financial success became a major sign. The more money they made, the more secure they were about their religious standing.

3. Weber called this behavior the *Protestant ethic*; he called their readiness to invest capital in order to make more money the *spirit of capitalism*.

IV. Values in Sociological Research

A. Weber advocated that sociological research should be value free (personal values or biases should not influence social research) and objective (totally neutral).

1. Sociologists agree that objectivity is a proper goal, but acknowledge that no one can escape values entirely.

2. Replication is when a study is repeated to see if the same results are found. It is one means to avoid the distortions that values can cause.

B. Although sociologists may agree that research should be objective, the proper purposes and uses of sociology are argued among sociologists, with some taking the position that the proper role of sociology is to advance understanding of social life, while others believe that it is the responsibility of sociologists to explore harmful social arrangements of society.

C. On the one side are those who say that understanding social behavior is sociology's proper goal and that the knowledge gained through research belongs to the scientific community and can be used by anyone for any purpose. On the other side are those who say the goal of sociological research should be to investigate harmful social conditions and that sociologists should lead the way in reforming society.

V. *Verstehen* and Social Facts

A. Weber argued that sociologists should use *Verstehen* ("to grasp by insight") in order to see beyond the social facts to the subjective meanings that people attach to their own behavior.

B. Durkheim believed that social facts, patterns of behavior that characterize a social group, reflect underlying conditions of society and should be used to interpret other social facts.

C. Social facts and *Verstehen* fit together because they reinforce each other; sociologists use *Verstehen* in order to interpret social facts.

VI. Sociology in North America

A. The first departments of sociology in the United States were at the University of Kansas (1890), the University of Chicago (1892), and Atlanta University (1897); the first in Canada was at McGill University (1922).
   1. Albion Small, founder of the department of sociology at the University of Chicago, also established the *American Journal of Sociology.*
   2. The department of sociology at the University of Chicago dominated North American sociology. Other early sociologists from the University of Chicago were Robert E. Park, Ernest Burgess, and George Herbert Mead.
B. In the early years of sociology, the field was dominated by men because rigidly defined social roles prevented most women from pursuing an education.
   1. Women were supposed to devote themselves to the four K's: *Kirche, Küchen, Kinder, und Kleider* (church, cooking, children, and clothes).
   2. At the same time, a few women from wealthy families managed to get an education. A few even studied sociology, although the sexism in the universities stopped them from earning advanced degrees, becoming professors, or having their research recognized.
C. Harriet Martineau studied social life in both Great Britain and the United States, publishing *Society in America* decades before Durkheim and Weber were even born. While her original research has been largely ignored by the discipline, she is known for her translations of Comte's ideas into English.
D. African American professionals also faced problems.
   1. W. E. B. Du Bois was the first African American to earn a Ph.D. from Harvard. He conducted extensive research on race relations in the United States, publishing one book a year on this subject between 1896 and 1914.
   2. Despite his accomplishments, he encountered prejudice and discrimination in his professional and personal life. When he attended professional sociologists' meetings, he was not permitted to eat or stay in the same hotels as the white sociologists.
   3. Frustrated at the lack of improvements in race relations, he turned to social action, helping to found the National Association for the Advancement of Colored People (NAACP) along with Jane Addams, Florence Kelley, and others from Hull-House.
   4. Until recently, his contributions to sociology were overlooked.
E. Jane Addams is an example of a sociologist who was able to combine the role of sociologist with that of social reformer.
   1. In 1889, she founded Hull-House, a settlement house for the poor, and worked to bridge the gap between the powerful and powerless.
   2. Sociologists from nearby University of Chicago visited Hull-House frequently.
   3. She is the only sociologist to have won the Nobel Peace Prize; she was awarded this in 1931.

F. Many other early North American sociologists combined the role of sociologist with that of social reformer. For example, University of Chicago sociologists Park and Burgess studied many urban problems and offered suggestions on how to alleviate them. By the 1940s, as sociologists became more concerned with establishing sociology as an academic discipline, the emphasis shifted from social reform to social theory.

    1. Talcott Parsons developed abstract models of society to show how the parts of society harmoniously work together.

    2. Countering this development was C. Wright Mills, who urged sociologists to get back to social reform. He saw the emergence of the *power elite* as an imminent threat to freedom.

G. The debate over what should be the proper goals of sociological analysis—analyzing society vs. reforming society—continues today.

    1. Applied sociology exists between these two extremes. One of the first attempts at applied sociology was the founding of the NAACP.

    2. Today, applied sociologists work in a variety of settings, from business and high-tech organizations to government and not-for-profit agencies.

    3. Applied sociology is the application of sociological knowledge in some specific setting, rather than an attempt to rebuild society. Both sociologists who focus on social reform and those who emphasize basic sociology reject applied sociology.

    4. The American Sociological Association (ASA) is promoting public sociology. The ASA wants the public, especially politicians and policy makers, to make use of sociological data in order to better understand how society works.

VII. Theoretical Perspectives in Sociology

A. Theory is a general statement about how some parts of the world fit together and how they work; it is an explanation of how two or more facts are related to one another. Sociologists use three different theoretical perspectives to understand social behavior.

B. Symbolic interactionism views symbols, things to which we attach meaning, as the basis of social life.

    1. Through the use of symbols, people are able to define relationships to others, to coordinate actions with others, thereby making social life possible, and to develop a sense of themselves.

    2. A symbolic interactionist studying divorce would focus on how the changing meanings of marriage, family, and divorce have all contributed to the increase in the rate of divorce in U.S. society.

C. The central idea of functional analysis is that society is a whole unit, made up of interrelated parts that work together.

    1. To understand society, we must look at both structure (how the parts of society fit together to make up the whole) and function (how each part contributes to society).

    2. Robert Merton used the term *function* to refer to the beneficial consequences of people's actions to keep society stable and *dysfunction* to refer to consequences

that undermine stability. Functions can be either manifest (actions that are intended) or latent (unintended consequences).

  3. In trying to explain divorce, a functionalist would look at how industrialization and urbanization both contributed to the changing function of marriage and the family.

D. According to conflict theory, society is viewed as composed of groups competing for scarce resources.

E. Karl Marx focused on struggles between the bourgeoisie (the small group of capitalists who own the means of production) and the proletariat (the masses of workers exploited by the capitalists).

  1. Contemporary conflict theorists have expanded this perspective to include conflict in all relations of power and authority.

  2. Just as Marx stressed conflict between capitalists and workers, many feminists stress a similar conflict between men and women.

  3. Divorce is seen as the outcome of the shifting balance of power within a family; as women have gained power and try to address inequalities in their relationships, men resist.

  4. The perspectives differ in their level of analysis. Functionalists and conflict theorists provide macro-level analysis because they examine the large-scale patterns of society. Symbolic interactionists carry out micro-level analysis because they focus on the small-scale patterns of social life.

F. Each perspective provides a different and often sharply contrasting picture of the world. However, sociologists often use all three perspectives because no one theory or level of analysis encompasses all of reality.

VIII. Trends Shaping the Future of Sociology

A. To understand the tension between social reform and social analysis, sociologists have found it useful to divide sociology into three phases.

  1. In the first phase, the primary concern of sociologists was making the world a better place.

  2. During the second phase, from the 1920s until World War II, sociologists sought to establish sociology as a respected field of knowledge, emphasizing basic, or pure, sociology.

  3. In the third (current) phase, there has been an attempt to merge sociological knowledge and practical work with the development of applied sociology. This trend has gained momentum in recent years.

  4. Despite being able to identify three phases, each of which has been characterized by a different position on reform vs. analysis, there has never been complete consensus on which approach is better.

B. Globalization is a second major trend destined to leave its mark on sociology.

  1. Globalization is the breaking down of national boundaries because of advances in communications, trade, and travel.

2. Globalization is likely to broaden the scope of sociological analysis as sociologists look beyond the boundaries of the United States in considering global issues.
C. Globalization is one of the most significant events in world history. This book stresses the impact of globalization on our lives today.

Chapter Summary

Sociology offers a perspective, a view of the world. The sociological perspective opens a window into unfamiliar worlds and offers a fresh look at familiar worlds. Sociologists study the broader social contexts that underlie human behavior. These include the social groups that influence human behavior and the larger society that organizes it.

The sociological perspective is an approach to understanding human behavior by placing it within its broader social context. C. Wright Mills referred to the sociological perspective as the intersection of biography (the individual) and history (social factors that influence the individual).

Sociology is one of several disciplines referred to as a "social science." As the term implies, social sciences address the social world. The natural sciences, on the other hand, are the intellectual and academic disciplines designed to explain and predict the events in the natural environment. The other social sciences include anthropology, economics, political science, and psychology.

As a scientific discipline, sociology seeks to explain why something happens, attempts to make generalizations that can be applied to a broader group or situation, and predicts what will happen based on the knowledge received. Sociology specifically seeks to explain the causes of human behavior and to recognize the patterns of human behavior. It also seeks to predict the future behavior of people. Although sociologists usually do not make decisions on how society should be changed or people treated, sociologists provide valuable research data that can be used by authorities who do make such decisions.

Sociology grew out of the social, political, economic, and technological revolutions of the eighteenth and nineteenth centuries. The Industrial Revolution, in particular, eroded old traditions and necessitated new ways of perceiving and examining the social world. With the success of the natural sciences serving as a model for the social sciences, sociology emerged in Western Europe as a distinct discipline in the mid-1800s.

Auguste Comte, Herbert Spencer, Karl Marx, Emile Durkheim, and Max Weber were early thinkers in the development of sociology. The idea of applying the scientific method to the social world, known as positivism, was first proposed by Auguste Comte. Based on this innovation and Comte's effort to apply the scientific method to social life, he is credited as being the founder of sociology. Herbert Spencer, one of the most dominant and influential English sociologists, is often called the "second founder of sociology." Spencer's concept of social Darwinism suggested that societies evolve from primitive to civilized and that the "fittest" societies evolve and survive, while unfit societies become extinct.

Max Weber advocated *Verstehen,* the German term for "grasp by insight," to understand why people act as they do. In contrast, Emile Durkheim believed that sociologists should focus primarily on uncovering social facts—the objective social conditions that influence people's behaviors. *Verstehen* and social facts are not mutually exclusive types of social research. Contemporary sociologists often employ both approaches to examine and understand the social contexts that underlie human behavior.

The early history of sociology in North America was characterized by a debate over whether sociology should analyze or reform society. Early sociology programs were initiated at the University of Kansas in 1890, the University of Chicago in 1892, and Atlanta University in 1897. Albion Small, George Herbert Mead, Robert E. Park, and Ernest Burgess were among the first academicians to dedicate their professional careers to the development of sociological theory. W.E.B. Du Bois, the first African American to earn a doctorate from Harvard University, was a social critic and dedicated his life to analyzing and writing about social injustice.

During the 1940s, the emphasis in American sociology shifted from social reform to social theory. "Grand theorists," such as Talcott Parsons, developed detailed, abstract models of how the complex parts of society harmoniously functioned together. Although this helped to legitimize sociology as a "science," it did little to critique, reform, and/or help to change the social injustices in society. C. Wright Mills' influential analysis of "the power elite"—a small group of business, political, and military leaders whose monopoly on power threatens freedom—helped to shift sociology back toward social reform in the 1960s and 1970s.

Many sociologists continue to disagree over the proper uses of social research. Some sociologists practice basic (or pure) sociology, while others practice applied sociology. Whether one practices basic or applied sociology, a primary goal of social research is to separate fact from fiction, while examining the links between what people do and the social settings that help shape their behavior. The current state of sociology encompasses social analysis and social reform, with a growing emphasis on applied sociology—a sort of middle ground that, rather than focusing on large and/or radical social change, uses sociological analysis to help solve problems in a specific setting.

In an effort to pursue a social reform agenda, the American Sociological Association is now promoting "public sociology" with the goal of influencing politicians, public officials, and policy makers.

Central to the study of any science is the development of theory. A theory is a general statement about how parts of the world fit together, relate to one another, and affect each other. Sociologists use three major theories—symbolic interactionism, functional analysis, and conflict theory—to observe and interpret social contexts, relationships, and realities in distinct ways. Symbolic interactionism analyzes how people use symbols to develop and share their view of the world. Focusing on the micro level, it studies the different ways that individuals and small groups create, disseminate, and/or interpret "reality" through their everyday, face-to-face interactions. Functional analysis examines how the various parts of society work together to fulfill their respective functions and, consequently, create a harmonious society.

Focusing on the macro level, it also looks at how parts of society occasionally dysfunction, negatively affecting other parts of society and, consequently, contributing to a more unstable society. Conflict theory views the social world in terms of competing groups struggling over scarce resources. Also focusing on the macro level, conflict theory examines how groups of people with power maintain and/or impose their power, and how groups of people without power work to acquire power.

As the world becomes more globally connected, American sociology is likely to expand its current horizons: incorporating new perspectives and worldviews that include—and encompass—global issues and concerns.

KEY TERMS
After studying the chapter, review the definition for each of the following terms.

applied sociology: the use of sociology to solve problems—from the micro level of family relationships to the macro level of crime and pollution (21)

bourgeoisie: Karl Marx's term for capitalists, those who own the means to produce wealth (11)

class conflict: Marx's term for the struggle between the proletariat (workers) and the bourgeoisie (capitalist) (11)

common sense: those things that "everyone knows" are true (8)

conflict theory: a theoretical framework in which society is viewed as composed of groups competing for scarce resources (28)

functional analysis: a theoretical framework in which society is viewed as composed of various parts, each with a function that, when fulfilled, contributes to society's equilibrium; also known as functionalism and structural functionalism (26)

generalization: a statement that goes beyond the individual case and is applied to a broader group or situation (8)

globalization: the extensive interconnections among nations due to the expansion of capitalism (31)

globalization of capitalism: capitalism (investing to make profits within a rational system) becoming the globe's dominant economic system (31)

macro-level analysis: an examination of large-scale patterns of society (29)

micro-level analysis: an examination of small-scale patterns of society (29)

natural sciences: the intellectual and academic disciplines designed to comprehend, explain, and predict events in our natural environment (5)

nonverbal interaction: communication without words through gestures, space, silence, and so on (30)

objectivity: total neutrality (14)

patterns of behavior: recurring characteristics or events (7)

positivism: the application of the scientific approach to the social world (9)

proletariat: Marx's term for the exploited class, the mass of workers who do not own the means of production (11)

public sociology: sociology being used for the public good; especially the sociological perspective (of how things are related to one another) guiding politicians and policy makers (23)

pure or basic sociology: sociological research whose only purpose is to make discoveries about life in human groups, not to make changes in those groups (21)

replication: repeating a study in order to check its findings (14)

science: the application of systematic methods to obtain knowledge and the knowledge obtained by those methods (5)

scientific method: the use of objective, systematic observations to test theories (9)

social facts: Durkheim's term for a group's patterns of behavior (15)

social integration: the degree to which people feel a part of social groups (12)

social interaction: what people do when they are in one another's presence (29)

social location: the group memberships that people have because of their location in history and society (4)

social sciences: the intellectual and academic disciplines designed to understand the social world objectively by means of controlled and repeated observations (6)

society: a term used by sociologists to refer to a group of people who share a culture and a territory (4)

sociological perspective: understanding human behavior by placing it within its broader social context (4)

sociology: the scientific study of society and human behavior (10)

subjective meanings: the meanings that people give to their own behavior (15)

symbolic interactionism: a theoretical perspective in which society is viewed as composed of symbols that people use to establish meaning, develop their views of the world, and communicate with one another (24)

theory: a general statement about how some parts of the world fit together and how they work; an explanation of how two or more facts are related to one another (24)

value free: the view that a sociologist's personal values should not influence social research (14)

values: ideas about what is good or worthwhile in life; attitudes about the way the world ought to be (14)

Verstehen: a German word used by Weber that is, perhaps, best understood as "to have insight into someone's situation" (15)

KEY PEOPLE

Review the major theoretical contributions or findings of these people.

Jane Addams: Addams was the founder of Hull-House—a settlement house in the immigrant community of Chicago. She invited sociologists from the nearby University of Chicago to visit. In 1931 she was a winner of the Nobel Peace Prize. (19-21)

Auguste Comte: Comte is often credited with being the founder of sociology, because he was the first to suggest that the scientific method be applied to the study of the social world. (9-11, 19, 26)

Charles Horton Cooley: One of the founders of symbolic interactionism, a major theoretical perspective in sociology. (24)

Lewis Coser: Coser pointed out that conflict is likely to develop among people in close relationships because they are connected by a network of responsibilities, power and rewards. (29)

W. E. B. Du Bois: Du Bois was the first African American to earn a doctorate at Harvard University. For most of his career, he taught sociology at Atlanta University. He was concerned about social injustice, wrote about race relations, and was one of the founders of the National Association for the Advancement of Colored People (NAACP). (18, 20)

Emile Durkheim: Durkheim was responsible for getting sociology recognized as a separate discipline. He was interested in studying how individual behavior is shaped by social forces and in finding remedies for social ills. He stressed that sociologists should use social facts—patterns of behavior that reflect some underlying condition of society. (11-13, 15, 26)

Harriet Martineau: An Englishwoman who studied British and U.S. social life, Martineau published *Society in America* decades before either Durkheim or Weber were born. She is known primarily for translating Auguste Comte's ideas into English. (18-19)

Karl Marx: Marx believed that social development grew out of conflict between social classes; under capitalism, this conflict was between the bourgeoisie—those who own the means to produce wealth—and the proletariat—the mass of workers. His work is associated with the conflict perspective. (11, 28-29)

George Herbert Mead: Mead was one of the founders of symbolic interactionism, a major theoretical perspective in sociology. (16, 24)

Robert Merton: Merton contributed the terms *manifest* and *latent functions* and *dysfunctions* to the functionalist perspective. (26)

C. Wright Mills: Mills suggested that external influences (a person's experiences) become part of his or her thinking and motivations and explain social behavior. As the emphasis in sociology shifted from social reform to social theory, Mills urged sociologists to get back to their roots. He saw the emergence of the power elite composed of top leaders of business, politics and the military as an imminent threat to freedom. (4, 21)

William Ogburn: As early as 1933, Ogburn noted that personality was becoming more important in mate selection; this supported the symbolic interactionists' argument that there was a fundamental shift in the symbolic meaning of U.S. marriages. (25)

Talcott Parsons: Parsons' work dominated sociology in the 1940s and 1950s. He developed abstract models of how the parts of society harmoniously work together. (21)

Albion Small: Small was the founder of the sociology department at the University of Chicago and the *American Journal of Sociology.* (16)

Herbert Spencer: Another early sociologist, Spencer believed that societies evolve from barbarian to civilized forms. He was the first to use the expression "the survival of the fittest" to reflect his belief that social evolution depended on the survival of the most capable and intelligent and the extinction of the less capable. His views became known as *social Darwinism.* (10-11, 26)

Max Weber: Weber's most important contribution to sociology was his study of the relationship between the emergence of the Protestant belief system and the rise of capitalism. He believed that sociologists should not allow their personal values to affect their social research; objectivity should become the hallmark of sociology. He argued that sociologists should use *Verstehen*—those subjective meanings that people give to their behavior. (13-15, 18)

SELF-TEST

MULTIPLE CHOICE QUESTIONS

1. _____ serves as the lens through which we see how our social experiences shape who we are. (4)
    a. *Verstehen*
    b. The sociological perspective
    c. Common sense
    d. Generalization

2. Sociologists consider occupation, income, education, gender, age, and race as (4)
    a. insignificant aspects of social life.
    b. constant features of individual well-being.
    c. influential in shaping society.
    d. dimensions of social location.

3. In what way(s) are the social sciences like the natural sciences? (5-6)
    a. Both attempt to study and understand their subjects objectively.
    b. The relationships that create order in their respective worlds are not immediately obvious but must be discovered through controlled observation.
    c. Both are divided into many specialized fields.
    d. All of the above are ways in which the social sciences are like the natural sciences.

4. Going beyond individual cases and making statements that apply to broader groups or situations is called (8)
    a. objectivity.
    b. *Verstehen.*
    c. generalization.
    d. social facts.

5. Which of the following was *not* important to the development of sociology? (8-9)
    a. the Industrial Revolution
    b. the British revolution
    c. imperialism
    d. the development of the scientific method

6. The application of the scientific approach to the social world is known as (9)
    a. ethnomethodology.
    b. sociobiology.
    c. natural science.
    d. positivism.

7. Which of the following statements *best* reflects Herbert Spencer's views on charity? (10-11)

a. The poor are the unfortunate victims of capitalism and should be helped by the government.

b. The poor will eventually unite in revolution and throw off their chains of bondage.

c. Sociologists should study the poor so that they can learn the best strategies to help them.

d. The poor are the weakest members of society and if society intervenes to help them, it is interrupting the natural process of social evolution.

8. According to Karl Marx, capitalists, who own the means of production, exploit the (11)
   a. bourgeoisie.
   b. proletariat.
   c. masses.
   d. peasants.

9. What did Durkheim identify as the key to explaining patterns of suicide? (11-13)
   a. the individual mental state of the person committing suicide
   b. the degree to which individuals are integrated into their social groups and feel a sense of attachment
   c. the strength of religious beliefs regarding the importance of life
   d. the influence of seasonal factors like the amount of sunlight or the temperature

10. Max Weber's research on the rise of capitalism identified _____ as the key. (13-14)
   a. ownership of property
   b. political reforms
   c. religious beliefs
   d. class conflict

11. Weber argued that sociology should be value free. In order to avoid biased research findings, Weber wanted _____ to be the hallmark of social research. (14)
   a. objectivity
   b. subjectivity
   c. replication
   d. validity

12. Social facts and *Verstehen* (15)
   a. have no relationship to each other.
   b. have been disproved.
   c. go hand-in-hand.
   d. were both concepts developed by Durkheim.

13. Which of the following statements about the experiences of North American women in sociology is *incorrect*? (16-18)
   a. In the early years of sociology, the situation of women in North America was similar to that of European women—they were largely excluded and their work ignored.

b. Unlike the situation in Europe, many North American women found that there were few barriers and they were able to train in sociology and receive faculty appointments.

c. Many early women sociologists in North America turned to social activism.

d. Many male sociologists who worked as professors denied female sociologists the title of sociologist, preferring to call them social workers.

14. Jane Addams won the Nobel Prize for (20-21)
    a. her literary work, *Society in America.*
    b. her contributions to the founding of the NAACP.
    c. her role in the British Revolution.
    d. working on behalf of poor immigrants.

15. Which of the following North American sociologists wrote extensively on race relations, experienced prejudice and discrimination personally and professionally, and helped found the NAACP? (18, 20)
    a. Wright Mills
    b. Talcott Parsons
    c. W. E. B. Du Bois
    d. Jane Addams

16. Which of the following is *not* an accurate description of a theory? (24)
    a. a general statement about how some parts of the world fit together
    b. using objective, systematic observations
    c. a formula of concepts that explain how two or more "facts" are related to one another
    d. an explanation of social occurrences

17. The theoretical perspective that views society as composed of symbols that we use to establish meaning, develop our views of the world, and communicate with one another is (24-26)
    a. functionalism.
    b. symbolic interactionism.
    c. dramaturgical theory.
    d. conflict theory.

18. According to Robert Merton, an action that has an unintended consequence that can hurt a system's equilibrium is a (26)
    a. manifest function.
    b. latent function.
    c. dysfunction.
    d. latent dysfunction.

19. Industrialization and urbanization have undermined the traditional purposes of the family, according to theorists using _____ analysis. (28)
    a. conflict
    b. exchange

c.   symbolic interaction

d.   functional

20. Karl Marx first asserted that _____ was inherent in all relations that have authority. (28)

    a.   conflict

    b.   symbolic interaction

    c.   nonverbal interaction

    d.   subjective meaning

21. Conflict theorists might explain the high rate of divorce by looking at (29)

    a.   the changing meanings associated with marriage and divorce.

    b.   society's basic inequalities between males and females.

    c.   changes that have weakened the family unit.

    d.   the loss of family functions that held a husband and wife together.

22. Which theorists focus on the macro level of analysis? (29)

    a.   functionalists and conflict theorists

    b.   functionalists and symbolic interactionists

    c.   conflict theorists and symbolic interactionists

    d.   functionalists only

23. According to your text, which theoretical perspective is best for studying human behavior? (30)

    a.   the functionalist perspective

    b.   the symbolic interactionist perspective

    c.   the conflict perspective

    d.   a combination of all of the above

24. The first phase of sociology in the United States was characterized by (31)

    a.   a concern with establishing sociology as a social science.

    b.   a focus on establishing sociology as a respectable field of knowledge.

    c.   an interest in using sociological knowledge to improve social life and change society.

    d.   a broad acceptance of women and racial minorities within the discipline.

25. What trend does the author of your text suggest is likely to transform the scope and focus of U.S. sociology in the future? (31)

    a.   race, class, and gender inequalities

    b.   cultural diversity

    c.   technology

    d.   globalization

TRUE-FALSE QUESTIONS

1. _____Herbert Spencer believed that human societies evolve like those of animal species. (10-11)
2. _____Karl Marx thought that a classless society eventually would exist. (11)
3. _____According to Weber, subjective meanings are important in understanding human behavior. (13)
4. _____By applying *Verstehen*, we can better understand why there are more weddings in June and more babies born on Tuesdays. (15)
5. _____Harriet Martineau was widely recognized for her pioneering studies of social life in Great Britain and the United States. (19)
6. _____Du Bois battled racism as both a sociologist and a journalist. (18, 20)
7. _____Symbolic interactionists primarily analyze how our definitions of ourselves and others underlie our behaviors. (24-26)
8. _____According to functionalists, the family has lost all of its traditional purposes. (26-28)
9. _____All conflict theorists focus on conflict between the bourgeoisie and the proletariat. (28-29)
10. _____Globalization is likely to broaden sociological horizons, refocusing research and theory away from its concentration on U.S. society. (31)

FILL-IN-THE-BLANK QUESTIONS

1. The _____stresses the social contexts in which people are immersed and that influence their lives. (4)
2. A_____ is a statement that goes beyond the individual case and is applied to a broad group or situation. (8)
3. Using objective, systematic observations to test theories is known as the _____. (9)
4. Comte stressed that sociology would not only discover social principles, but also would apply these to social _____. (9)
5. _____ is used to uncover bias in research by repeating a study in order to compare results with original findings. (14-15)
6. If an action is intended to help some part of a system, it is a _____ function. (26)
7. Lewis Coser pointed out that _____is most likely to develop among people who are in close relationships. (29)
8. _____ is what happens when one person's actions influence someone else's. (29)
9. A tension between social reform and _____ has always run through sociology. (30-31)
10. _____ is the breaking down of national boundaries because of advances in communication, trade, and travel. (31)

ESSAY QUESTIONS

1. Explain what the sociological perspective encompasses and then, using that perspective, discuss the forces that shaped the discipline of sociology.

2. Emile Durkheim studied European society at a time when it was undergoing major social upheaval as a result of the Industrial Revolution. In this first chapter, you are introduced to some of his major contributions—his work on suicide and his conclusions about social integration and anomie. Summarize what his contributions were and then consider how they are still useful for understanding social life today.

3. The textbook notes that *Verstehen* and social facts go hand in hand; explain how this is so. Assume that you have been asked to carry out research to find out more about why growing numbers of women and children are homeless and what particular problems they face. Discuss how you could use both *Verstehen* and social facts in your study.

4. Explain why there has been a continuing tension between analyzing society and working toward reforming society since the very beginning of society.

5. Explain what Weber meant when he said that sociology should be value free. Do you think this is possible? How do values play a role in determining the purpose and use of sociology?

CHAPTER 2
CULTURE

LEARNING OBJECTIVES

After reading Chapter 2, you should be able to:

1. Define culture, discuss its effects, and differentiate between material and nonmaterial culture. (36)

2. Know what is meant by "culture shock" and provide examples of situations that may cause it. (37)

3. Define "ethnocentrism" and "cultural relativism," offer examples of both concepts, and list the positive and negative consequences of each. (37-39)

4. Define and differentiate between gestures and language. (39, 43)

5. Explain why language is the basis of culture, including why it is critical to human life and essential for cultural development. (43-44)

6. Understand the Sapir-Whorf hypothesis and provide examples of how language reflects and expresses thinking, perceptions, and experiences. (44-45)

7. Define "values," "norms," "sanctions," "folkways," "mores," and "taboos"; provide examples of each and discuss their sociological significance. (45-47)

8. Compare and contrast dominant culture, subculture, and counterculture, providing examples of each. (48)

9. Explain what the terms "value clusters" and "value contradictions" mean. Offer examples of some value clusters and value contradictions in American society. (52-53)

10. Discuss the differences between "ideal" and "real" culture. (54-55)

11. Define and identify some cultural universals and discuss how carrying out universal human activities may differ from one group to another. (55)

12. List some current new technologies and talk about how they are changing social behaviors and relationships in the United States and around the world. (56-58)

13. Define and discuss cultural lag, cultural diffusion, and cultural leveling. (57-58)

Chapter Outline

I. **What is Culture?**
   A. Culture is defined as the language, beliefs, values, norms, behaviors, and even material objects passed from one generation to the next.
      1. Material culture is things such as jewelry, art, buildings, weapons, machines, clothing, hairstyles, etc.
      2. Nonmaterial culture is a group's ways of thinking (beliefs, values, and assumptions) and common patterns of behavior (language, gestures, and other forms of interaction).
   B. Culture provides a taken-for-granted orientation to life.
      1. We assume that our own culture is normal or natural; in fact, it is not natural, but rather is learned. It penetrates our lives so deeply that it is taken for granted and provides the lens through which we perceive and evaluate things.
      2. It provides implicit instructions that tell us what we ought to do and a moral imperative that defines what we think is right and wrong.
      3. Coming into contact with a radically different culture produces "culture shock," challenging our basic assumptions.
      4. A consequence of internalizing culture is ethnocentrism, using our own culture (and assuming it to be good, right, and superior) to judge other cultures. It is functional when it creates in-group solidarity, but can be dysfunctional if it leads to discrimination against those who are different.
   C. Cultural relativism consists of trying to appreciate other groups' ways of life in the context in which they exist, without judging them as superior or inferior to our own.
      1. Because we tend to use our own culture as the standard, cultural relativism presents a challenge to ordinary thinking.
      2. At the same time, this view helps us appreciate other ways of life.
      3. Robert Edgerton suggests developing a scale for evaluating cultures on their "quality of life." He argues that those cultural practices that result in exploitation should be judged as morally inferior to those that enhance people's lives.

II. **Components of Symbolic Culture**
   A. Sociologists sometimes refer to nonmaterial culture as symbolic culture.
      1. A central component of culture is the symbol—something to which people attach meaning and use in communications.
      2. Symbols include gestures, language, values, norms, sanctions, folkways, and mores.
   B. Gestures, or using one's body to communicate with others, are shorthand means of communication.
      1. People in every culture use gestures, although the gestures and the meanings differ; confusion or offense can result because of misunderstandings over the meaning of a gesture or misuse of a gesture.
      2. There is disagreement over whether there are any universal gestures. They tend to vary considerably around the world.
      3. Because some gestures are so closely associated with emotional messages, the gestures themselves can often elicit emotions.

C. Language consists of a system of symbols that can be put together in an infinite number of ways in order to communicate abstract thought. Each word is a symbol to which a culture attaches a particular meaning. It is important because it is the primary means of communication between people.

   1. It allows human experiences to be cumulative; each generation builds on the body of significant experiences that is passed on to it by the previous generation, thus freeing people to move beyond immediate experiences.

   2. It allows for a social or shared past. We are able to discuss past events with others.

   3. It allows for a social or shared future. Language allows us to plan future activities with one another.

   4. It allows the exchange of perspectives (i.e., ideas about events and experiences).

   5. It allows people to engage in complex, shared, goal-directed behavior.

   6. The Sapir-Whorf hypothesis states that our thinking and perception not only are expressed by language, but actually are shaped by language because we are taught not only words but also a particular way of thinking and perceiving. Rather than objects and events forcing themselves onto our consciousness, our very language determines our consciousness.

D. Culture includes values, norms, and sanctions.

   1. Values are the standards by which people define good and bad, beautiful and ugly. Every group develops both values and expectations regarding the right way to reflect them.

   2. Norms are the expectations, or rules of behavior, that develop out of a group's values.

   3. Sanctions are the positive or negative reactions to the way that people follow norms. Positive sanctions (a money reward, a prize, a smile, or even a handshake) are expressions of approval; negative sanctions (a fine, a frown, or harsh words) denote disapproval for breaking a norm.

   4. To relieve the pressure of having to strictly follow the norms, some cultures have moral holidays—specified times when people are allowed to break the norms and not worry about being sanctioned. Mardi Gras is an example of a moral holiday in our society.

   5. Some societies have moral holiday places, locations where norms are expected to be broken. An example would be red light districts where prostitutes are allowed to work the street.

E. Norms vary in terms of their importance to a culture.

   1. Folkways are norms that are not strictly enforced, such as passing on the left side of the sidewalk. They may result in a person getting a dirty look.

   2. Mores are norms that are believed to be essential to core values and we insist on conformity. A person who steals, rapes, and kills has violated some of society's most important mores.

   3. Norms that one group considers to be folkways, another group may view as mores. A male walking down the street with the upper half of his body uncovered may be violating a folkway; a female doing the same thing may be violating a more.

4. Taboos are norms so strongly ingrained that even the thought of them is greeted with revulsion. Eating human flesh and having sex with one's parents are examples of such behavior.

III. Many Cultural Worlds: Subcultures and Countercultures
A. Subcultures are groups whose values and related behaviors are so distinct that they set their members off from the dominant culture.
1. Each subculture is a world within the larger world of the dominant culture, and has a distinctive way of looking at life, but remains compatible with the dominant culture.
2. U.S. society contains tens of thousands of subcultures. Some are quite broad (teenagers), while others are narrow (body builders). Some ethnic groups form subcultures, as do certain occupational groups.
B. Countercultures are groups whose values set their members in opposition to the dominant culture.
1. While usually associated with negative behavior, some countercultures are not.
2. Countercultures are often perceived as a threat by the dominant culture because they challenge the culture's values; for this reason the dominant culture will move against a particular counterculture in order to affirm its own core values. For example, the Mormons in the 1800s challenged the dominant culture's core value of monogamy.

IV. Values in U.S. Society
A. Identifying core values in U.S. society is difficult because it is a pluralistic society with many different religious, racial, ethnic, and special interest groups.
1. Sociologist Robin Williams identified ten core values: achievement and success (especially, doing better than others); individualism (success due to individual effort); hard work; efficiency and practicality; science and technology (using science to control nature); material comfort; freedom; democracy; equality (especially of opportunity); and group superiority.
2. Henslin updated Williams' list by adding education; religiosity (belief in a Supreme Being and following some set of matching precepts); and romantic love.
B. Values are not independent units; value clusters are made up of related core values that come together to form a larger whole. In the value cluster surrounding success, for example, we find hard work, education, efficiency, material comfort, and individualism all bound together.
C. Some values conflict with each other. There cannot be full expressions of democracy, equality, racism, and sexism at the same time. These are value contradictions and as society changes some values are challenged and undergo modification.
D. A cluster that is emerging in response to fundamental changes in U.S. society is made up of the values of leisure, self-fulfillment, physical fitness, and youthfulness. Another emerging value is concern for the environment.
1. Valuing leisure is reflected in the huge recreation industry that exists today.
2. Self-fulfillment is expressed through the human potential movement and on the popularity of self-help books and talk shows.

3. While physical fitness is not a new value, it is emphasized more today, as evidenced by the interest in health foods, weight and diet, and the growth in the number of health club/physical fitness centers.

4. Today, there is a new sense of urgency in being young, perhaps because of the presence of aging baby boomers who are trying to deny their biological fate.

5. Our history suggests a lack of concern for the environment; it was generally viewed as a challenge to be overcome. However, today there is a genuine concern for protecting the environment.

E. Core values do not change without meeting strong resistance.
1. Change is seen as a threat to the established way of life, something that will undermine people's present and their future.
2. Today's clash in values is often so severe that the term "culture wars" has been coined to refer to it.

F. Values and their supporting beliefs may blind people to other social circumstances. Success stories blind many people in the United States to the dire consequences of family poverty, lack of education, and dead-end jobs.

G. Ideal culture refers to the ideal values and norms of a people. What people actually do usually falls short of this ideal, and sociologists refer to the norms and values that people actually follow as real culture.

V. Cultural Universals

A. Although there are universal human activities, there is no universally accepted way of doing any of them.
1. Anthropologist George Murdock concluded that all human groups have certain cultural universals: customs about courtship, cooking, marriage, funerals, games, laws, music, myths, incest taboos, and toilet training are present in all cultures.
2. Even so, the specific customs differ from one group to another. For example: there is no universal form of the family, no universal way of disposing of the dead, and no universal method of toilet training between cultures. Even incest is defined differently from group to group.

B. Sociobiologists argue that, as a result of natural selection, the basic cause of human behavior is biology.
1. Just as physical characteristics and instinctual behavior of animals is the result of natural selection (i.e., those genetic traits that aid in survival tend to become common to a species while those that do not tend to disappear), so is human behavior.
2. Edward Wilson has argued that religion, competition and cooperation, slavery and genocide, war and peace, envy and altruism can all be explained in terms of genetic programming.
3. Most sociologists reject this claim. Unlike other species, humans are capable of reasoning and abstract thought; they can consider alternatives, reflect on outcomes, and make choices.

VI. Technology in the Global Village

A. Central to a group's material culture is its technology. In its simplest sense, technology can be equated with tools. In its broadest sense, technology also includes the skills or procedures necessary to make and use those tools.

   1. The emerging technologies of an era that make a major impact on human life are referred to as new technologies. The printing press and the computer are both examples of new technologies.

   2. The sociological significance of technology is that it sets the framework for the nonmaterial culture, influencing the way people think and how they relate to one another.

B. Not all parts of culture change at the same pace; cultural lag was William Ogburn's term for situations where the material culture changes first and the nonmaterial culture lags behind.

C. Although for most of human history, cultures have had little contact with one another, there has always been some contact with other groups, resulting in groups learning from one another.

   1. This transmission of cultural characteristics is cultural diffusion; it is more likely to produce changes in material culture than the nonmaterial culture.

   2. Cultural diffusion occurs more rapidly today, given the technology.

   3. Travel and communication unite the world to such an extent that there almost is no "other side of the world." For example, Japan, no longer a purely Eastern culture, has adapted Western economic production, forms of dress, music, and so on. This leads to cultural leveling where cultures become similar to one another.

Chapter Summary

The concept of culture is sometimes easier to grasp by description than by definition. All human groups possess culture, which consists of the language, beliefs, values, norms, and material objects that are passed from one generation to the next. Although the particulars of culture may differ from one group to another, culture itself is universal—all societies develop shared, learned ways of perceiving and participating in the world around them.

Culture can be subdivided into material culture and nonmaterial culture. Material culture consists of the tools and the technology required to use them that members of society create and utilize. This includes art, buildings, weapons, jewelry, and all other man-made objects. Nonmaterial culture includes a group's ways of thinking (beliefs, values, and other assumptions about the world) and patterns of behavior (language, gestures, and other forms of social interaction).

The effects of culture are profound and pervasive, touching almost every aspect of people's lives. However, most people are generally unaware of their own culture; culture is so engrained it is often taken for granted. People often become more aware of their own culture when their cultural assumptions are challenged by exposure to other cultures, particularly those with fundamentally different beliefs and customs.

When people come into contact with cultures that significantly differ from their own, they often experience culture shock, a condition of disorientation that requires them to question their cultural assumptions. Culture shock is influenced by ethnocentrism, the practice of viewing one's own culture as preferable and using it as a yardstick for judging other cultures.

Although all groups practice some forms of ethnocentrism, people can also employ cultural relativism, the practice of understanding a culture on its own terms without assessing its elements as any better or worse than one's own culture. Cultural relativism presents a challenge to ordinary thinking because we tend to use our own culture to judge others.

Sociologists sometimes refer to nonmaterial culture as symbolic culture because symbols are the central component of nonmaterial culture. Symbols include gestures, language, values, norms, sanctions, folkways, and mores. Gestures involve the ways that people use their bodies to communicate with one another. Although people in every culture use gestures, the gestures people use and the meanings they associate with those gestures vary greatly from one culture to another.

The primary way people communicate with each other is through language: a system of symbols that can be strung together in an infinite number of ways. Like gestures, all human groups have language. And like gestures, the meanings that people associate with different sounds and symbols can vary greatly from one culture to another.

Language is the basis of culture. It is critical to human life and essential for cultural development. Among other things, language allows human experience to be cumulative; gives people the capacity to share understandings about the past and develop common perceptions about the future; and provides for complex, shared, goal-directed behavior. According to the Sapir-Whorf hypothesis, language not only expresses our thinking and perceptions but also shapes them. The "descriptive terms" that we use can, and do, influence how we see other objects, other people, and ourselves.

All groups have values (beliefs regarding what is desirable or undesirable, good or bad, beautiful or ugly) that they channel into norms (expectations, or rules of behavior, that develop from values). Norms include folkways (norms that are not strictly enforced), mores (norms that are strictly enforced), and taboos (norms so strong that the thought of violating them is universally revolting). Norms can be enforced through both positive sanctions (rewards that range from approving looks and gestures to material compensation) and negative sanctions (punishment that range from disapproving looks and gestures to imprisonment and execution).

Cultures may contain numerous subcultures and countercultures. A subculture is a group whose values and related behaviors set it apart from the larger culture; a counterculture is a group whose values and related behaviors stand in opposition to the dominant culture.

Because the United States is a pluralistic society made up of many different groups, competing value systems are common. Some sociologists, however, have tried to identify some underlying core values in the United States. These core values (values shared by many groups that make up American society) include value clusters (a series of interrelated values that together form a larger whole) and value contradictions (values that contradict one another). Social change often occurs when a society is forced to face, and work through, its value contradictions.

Cultural universals are values, norms, or other cultural traits that are found in all cultures. Although anthropologists and sociologists have identified some universal human activities, they have also found that the ways of carrying out these activities differ from one group to another.

Technology is central to a group's material culture, while also setting the framework for its nonmaterial culture. The term "new technology" refers to any emerging technologies of an era that have a significant impact on social life. The current "new technology" includes computers, satellites, and various other forms of electronic media. Cultural lag refers to a condition in which a group's nonmaterial culture lags behind its material culture.

With the emergence of new technologies in mass transportation and mass communication, the world is becoming more interconnected. This has resulted in more cultural diffusion (the spread of characteristics from one culture to another) and culture leveling (the process by which cultures become similar to one another). Cultural leveling is occurring rapidly around the world. Mickey Mouse, Fred Flintstone, and the golden arches of McDonald's can be found in Miami, Mexico City, Moscow, and in most other major cities of the world.

KEY TERMS
After studying the chapter, review the definition for each of the following terms.

core values: the values that are central to a group, those around which it builds a common identity (49)

counterculture: a group whose values, beliefs, and related behaviors place its members in opposition to the values of the broader culture (48)

cultural diffusion: the spread of cultural characteristics from one group to another (57)

cultural lag: William Ogburn's term for human behavior lagging behind technological innovations (57)

cultural leveling: the process by which cultures become similar to one another, and especially by which Western industrial culture is imported and diffused into industrializing nations (58)

cultural relativism: not judging a culture, but trying to understand it on its own terms (38)

cultural universal: a value, norm, or other cultural trait that is found in every group (55)

culture: the language, beliefs, values, norms, behaviors, and even material objects that are passed from one generation to the next (36)

culture shock: the disorientation that people experience when they come in contact with a fundamentally different culture and can no longer depend on their taken-for-granted assumptions about life (37)

ethnocentrism: the use of one's own culture as a yardstick for judging the ways of other individuals or societies, generally leading to a negative evaluation of their values, norms, and behaviors (37)

folkways: norms that are not strictly enforced (47)

gestures: the ways in which people use their bodies to communicate with one another (39)

ideal culture: the ideal values and norms of a people, the goals held out for them (54)

language: a system of symbols that can be combined in an infinite number of ways and can represent not only objects but also abstract thought (43)

material culture: the material objects that distinguish a group of people, such as their art, buildings, weapons, utensils, machines, hairstyles, clothing, and jewelry (36)

mores: norms that are strictly enforced because they are thought essential to core values (47)

negative sanction: an expression of disapproval for breaking a norm, ranging from a mild, informal reaction such as a frown to a formal prison sentence or an execution (45)

new technology: the emerging technologies of an era that have a significant impact on social life (56)

nonmaterial culture: a group's ways of thinking (including its beliefs, values, and other assumptions about the world) and doing (its common patterns of behavior, including language and other forms of interaction) (36)

norms: the expectations, or rules of behavior, that reflect and enforce behavior (45)

pluralistic society: a society made up of many different groups (49)

positive sanction: a reward given for following norms, ranging from a smile to a prize (45)

real culture: the norms and values that people actually follow (54)

sanctions: expressions of approval or disapproval given to people for upholding or violating norms (45)

Sapir-Whorf hypothesis: Edward Sapir and Benjamin Whorf's hypothesis that language creates ways of thinking and perceiving (45)

sociobiology: a framework of thought that views human behavior as the result of natural selection and considers biological characteristics to be the fundamental cause of human behavior (55)

subculture: the values and related behaviors of a group that distinguish its members from the larger culture; a world within a world (48)

symbol: something to which people attach meaning and then use to communicate with others (39)

symbolic culture: another term for nonmaterial culture (39)

taboo: a norm so strong that it brings revulsion if it is violated (47)

technology: in its narrow sense, tools; its broader sense includes the skills or procedures necessary to make and use those tools (56)

value cluster: a series of interrelated values that together form a larger whole (52)

value contradictions: values that contradict with one another; to follow the one means to come into conflict with the other (53)

values: the standards by which people define what is desirable or undesirable, good or bad, beautiful or ugly (45)

KEY PEOPLE

Review the major theoretical contributions or findings of these people.

Charles Darwin: Darwin studied the principles on which natural selection occurred. (55)

Robert Edgerton: Edgerton attacks the concept of cultural relativism, suggesting that because some cultures endanger their people's health, happiness, or survival, there should be a scale to evaluate cultures on their "quality of life." (39, 57)

George Murdock: Murdock was an anthropologist who sought to determine which cultural values, norms, or traits, if any, were found universally across the globe. (55)

William Ogburn: Ogburn coined the term "cultural lag." (57)

Edward Sapir and Benjamin Whorf: These two anthropologists argued that language not only reflects thoughts and perceptions but that it actually shapes the way people think and perceive the world. (44-45)

William Sumner: Sumner developed the concept of ethnocentrism. (37)

Robin Williams: He identified ten core U.S. values. (49, 52)

Edward Wilson: Wilson is an insect specialist who claims that human behavior is also the result of natural selection. (56)

Eviatar Zerubavel: This sociologist offers an example of how language shapes our perceptions of the world (the *Sapir-Whorf hypothesis*). He notes that in his native Hebrew, there is no distinction made between the two forms of fruit spread—jams and jellies. It was only when he learned English that he was able to "see" the differences that were so obvious to English speakers. (45)

SELF-TEST

MULTIPLE CHOICE QUESTIONS

1. Which of the following would you use to describe a group's ways of thinking and doing, including language and other forms of interaction? (36)
    a. material culture
    b. nonmaterial culture
    c. ideological culture
    d. values

2. Which of the following is *not* part of material culture? (36)
    a. weapons and machines
    b. clothing
    c. value of individualism
    d. hairstyles

3. Which of these statements regarding culture is *not* true? (36-37)
    a. People generally are aware of the effects of their own culture.
    b. Culture touches almost every aspect of who and what a person is.
    c. At birth, people do not possess culture.
    d. Culture is the lens through which we perceive and evaluate what is going on around us.

4. In the textbook, the author describes his feeling of disorientation while in Morocco. Which of the following best describes what he was feeling? (37)
    a. cultural diffusion
    b. cultural leveling
    c. cultural relativism
    d. cultural shock

5. An American thinks citizens of another country are barbarians if they like to attend bullfights. Which of the following concepts best describes his reaction? (37)
    a. cultural shock
    b. cultural relativism
    c. ethnocentrism
    d. cultural lag

6. Which of the following statements about cultural relativism is *incorrect*? (38-39)
    a. Cultural relativism presents a challenge to our ordinary thinking.
    b. None of us can be entirely successful at practicing cultural relativism.
    c. Robert Edgerton argues that we should accept other cultures according to their customs and values.
    d. Cultural relativism is an attempt to appreciate other ways of life.

7. Which of the following statements about gestures is *correct*? (39-41)
    a. Gestures are studied by anthropologists but not sociologists.

b. Gestures are universal.

c. Gestures always facilitate communication between people.

d. Gestures can lead to misunderstandings and embarrassment.

8. Which of the following makes it possible for people to share a past, future, and common view of the world? (43)

a. language

b. cultural universals

c. gestures

d. computers

9. Sociologist Eviatar Zerubavel gives a good example when he states that his native language of Hebrew does not have separate words for jam and jelly. What is this an example of? (45)

a. sociobiology

b. the Davis-Moore theory

c. the Sapir-Whorf hypothesis

d. the Linguistic perspective

10. A monetary reward, a prize, a hug, or a pat on the back are all examples of (45)

a. norms.

b. values.

c. positive sanctions.

d. negative sanctions.

11. As you are shopping at a crowded mall, you absentmindedly forget to hold the door open for an elderly woman coming through behind you. The consequence is that the door slams in her face. Which of the following cultural components has been violated as a result of your behavior? (47)

a. taboos

b. mores

c. values

d. folkways

12. Which of the following statements about mores is *correct*? (47)

a. Mores are essential to our core values and require conformity.

b. Mores are norms that are not strictly enforced.

c. Mores state that a person should not try to pass you on the left side of the sidewalk.

d. Mores are less important in contemporary societies.

13. The author of your text cites eating human flesh as an example of (47)

a. folkways.

b. mores.

c. taboos.

d. a behavior that is universally sanctioned.

14. Subcultures (48)
    a. are a world within a world.
    b. have values and related behaviors that set their members apart from the dominant culture.
    c. include occupational groups.
    d. are all of the above.

15. The Hell's Angels are an example of a (48)
    a. motorcycle enthusiast group.
    b. perverted people.
    c. counterculture.
    d. subculture.

16. U.S. society is made up of many different groups. Which of the following terms would a sociologist use to describe this type of society? (49)
    a. a melting pot
    b. a pluralist society
    c. a conflicted society
    d. a counterculture

17. According to the author of your text, a new value cluster is emerging in the United States. Which of the following combinations of core values makes up this new value cluster? (53)
    a. achievement and success, activity and work, material comfort
    b. individualism, freedom, democracy, equality
    c. leisure, self-fulfillment, physical fitness, youthfulness
    d. youthfulness, self-fulfillment, romantic love, material comfort

18. Which of the following reflects conditions under which value contradictions can occur? (53)
    a. A value, such as the one that stresses group superiority, comes into direct conflict with other values, such as democracy and equality.
    b. Societies have very little social change.
    c. A series of interrelated values bind together to form a larger whole.
    d. Values blind people to many social circumstances.

19. Which of the following statements about ideal culture is *correct*? (54)
    a. Ideal culture is a value, norm, or other cultural trait that is found in every group.
    b. Ideal culture reflects the values and norms which people in a culture attempt to hold.
    c. Ideal culture is the norms people follow when they know they are being watched.
    d. Ideal culture is not a sociological concept.

20. Which of the following is *not* a cultural universal identified by George Murdock? (55)
    a. toilet training
    b. discipline
    c. courtship
    d. music

21. What is the perspective that views human behavior as the result of natural selection and considers biological characteristics to be the fundamental cause of human behavior? (55-56)
    a. natural science
    b. social science
    c. anthropology
    d. sociobiology

22. What would the printing press or the computer be considered? (56)
    a. inventive technologies
    b. diffused technologies
    c. examples of cultural leveling
    d. new technologies

23. There are computer tests that outperform physicians in diagnosing and prescribing treatment, yet most of us still visit doctors and rely on their judgment. What does this situation reflect? (57)
    a. resistance to new technologies
    b. cultural diffusion
    c. the social construction of technology
    d. cultural lag

24. Today bagels, woks, and hammocks are all a part of U.S. culture. The adoption of these objects illustrates which of the following processes or concepts? (57)
    a. cultural leveling
    b. nonmaterial culture
    c. cultural diffusion
    d. cultural universals

25. Coca-Cola is found in almost every country in the world. This is an example of (67)
    a. cultural sharing.
    b. cultural leveling.
    c. enrichment of local cultures through contact with U.S. material culture.
    d. culture shock.

TRUE-FALSE QUESTIONS

1. _____Culture consists primarily of nonmaterial objects that are passed from one generation to another. (36)
2. _____Culture has little to do with people's ideas of right and wrong. (36-37)
3. _____No one can be entirely successful at practicing cultural relativism. (38-39)
4. _____Without language, humans could still successfully plan future events. (43)
5. _____While folkways may change across cultures, mores are universally the same. (47)
6. _____Motorcycle enthusiasts who emphasize personal freedom and speed, while maintaining values of success, form part of a counterculture. (48)
7. _____Racism and group superiority are core values in U.S. society. (52)
8. _____Concern for the environment has always been a core value in U.S. society. (53)

9. _____Today's clash in values is so severe it is referred to as a culture war. (54)
10. _____Most sociologists do not agree with sociobiology. (55-56)

FILL-IN-THE-BLANK QUESTIONS

1. When Sue experiences disorientation from moving from the U.S. to Africa, this is known as _____. (37)
2. A _____ is something to which people attach meaning and then use to communicate with others. (39)
3. _____ are ways in which people use their body to communicate with one another. (39)
4. The Sapir-Worf hypothesis says _____ has embedded in it ways of looking at the world. (45)
5. _____ groups have values and norms that place it in opposition to the dominant culture. (48)
6. _____ are a series of interrelated values that together form a larger whole. (52)
7. Leisure time is becoming an emerging _____. (53)
8. Sociologists call the norms and values that people actually follow _____. (55)
9. Emerging technologies that have a significant impact on social life are referred to as _____. (56)
10. The process by which cultures become similar to one another is _____. (58)

ESSAY QUESTIONS

1. Explain cultural relativism and discuss both the advantages and disadvantages of practicing it.

2. As the author points out, the United States is a pluralistic society, made up of many different groups. Having read this chapter about culture, discuss some of the things that are gained by living in such a society as well as some of the problems that are created.

3. Consider the degree to which the real culture of the United States falls short of the ideal culture. Provide concrete examples to support your essay.

Thinking about William Ogburn's term cultural lag, explain why college students still attend traditional classes in the classroom when the technology is available to take classes over the Internet.

CHAPTER 3
SOCIALIZATION

LEARNING OBJECTIVES
After reading Chapter 3, you should be able to:

1. Discuss the ongoing debate over what most determines human behavior: "nature" (heredity) or "nurture" (social environment), and cite the evidence that best supports each position. (62)

2. Explain the statement, "It is society that makes people human." (62)

3. Discuss how studies of feral, isolated, and institutionalized children prove that social contact and interaction is essential for healthy human development. (62-65)

4. Understand, distinguish between, and state the respective strengths and limitations of the following theorists' insights into human development: Charles Horton Cooley, George Herbert Mead, Jean Piaget, Lawrence Kohlberg, Carol Gilligan, and Sigmund Freud. (66-70)

5. Discuss how socialization is not only critical to the internalization of cultural norms and the development of cognitive activity, but also to the development of emotions, affecting not only how people express their emotions, but also what particular emotions they may feel. (69-72)

6. Know what is meant by gender socialization and how the family, media, and other agents of socialization *teach* children to act masculine or feminine based on their sex. (73-82)

7. Describe some of the "gender messages" in the family and mass media, and discuss how these messages may contribute to social inequality between men and women. (73-76)

8. List the major agents of socialization in American society and talk about how each of these teach and influence people's attitudes, behaviors, and other orientations toward life. (77-82)

9. Define the term "resocialization" and provide examples of situations that may necessitate it. (82)

10. Understand why socialization is a lifelong process and summarize the needs, expectations, and responsibilities that typically accompany different stages of life. (83-87)

11. Discuss why human beings are not prisoners of socialization while providing examples of how people exercise a considerable degree of freedom over which agents of socialization to follow and which cultural messages to accept or reject from those agents of socialization. (87)

Chapter Outline

I. **Society Makes Us Human**

A. For centuries, people have tried to find an answer to the question of what is human about human nature. Studies of identical twins who have been reared apart help answer the question.

B. Feral (wild) children have occasionally been found: children living in the woods who may have been raised by wild animals. These stories lead one to wonder what humans would be like if left untouched by society.

C. Isolated children show what humans might be like if secluded from society at an early age. Isabelle is a case in point. Although initially believed to be retarded, a surprising thing happened when she was given intensive language training. She began to acquire language and in only two years she had reached the normal intellectual level for her age. Without language there can be no culture or shared way of living.

D. Institutionalized children show that traits such as intelligence, cooperative behavior, and friendliness are the result of early close relations with other humans. Research with children reared in orphanages and cases like Genie—the 13½-year-old who had been kept locked in a small room for years—demonstrates the importance of early interaction for human development.

E. The Harlow's studies of monkeys reared in isolation reached similar results. They concluded that if isolated for longer than six months, the adjustment becomes more difficult.

F. Babies do not "naturally" develop into human adults; although their bodies grow, human interaction is required for them to acquire the traits we consider normal for human beings. The process by which we learn the ways of our society through interaction with others is socialization.

II. **Socialization into the Self and Mind**

A. Charles H. Cooley (1864-1929) concluded that human development is socially created—that our sense of self develops from interaction with others. He coined the term "looking-glass self" to describe this process.

1. According to Cooley, this process contains three steps: (1) we imagine how we look to others; (2) we interpret others' reactions (how they evaluate us); and (3) we develop a self-concept.

2. A favorable reflection in the "social mirror" leads to a positive self-concept, while a negative reflection leads to a negative self-concept.

3. Even if we misjudge others' reactions, the misjudgments become part of our self-concept.

4. This development process is an ongoing, lifelong process.

B. George H. Mead (1863-1931) agreed with Cooley but added that play is critical to the development of a self. In play, we learn to take the role of others—to understand and anticipate how others feel and think.

1. Mead concluded that children are first able to take only the role of significant others (parents or siblings, for example); as the self develops, children internalize the expectations of other people, and eventually the entire group. Mead referred

to the norms, values, attitudes and expectations of people "in general" as the generalized other.

2. According to Mead, the development of the self goes through stages: (1) imitation (children initially can only mimic the gestures and words of others); (2) play (beginning at age three, children play the roles of specific people, such as a firefighter or the Lone Ranger); and (3) games (in the first years of school, children become involved in organized team games and must learn the role of each member of the team).

3. He distinguished the "I" from the "me" in development of the self: the "I" component is the subjective, active, spontaneous, creative part of the social self (for instance, "I shoved him"), while the "me" component is the objective part—attitudes internalized from interactions with others (for instance, "He shoved me").

4. Mead concluded that not only the self, but also the mind is a social product. We cannot think without symbols, and it is our society that gives us our symbols by giving us our language.

C. After years of research, Jean Piaget (1896-1980) concluded that there are four stages in the development of cognitive skills.

1. The sensorimotor stage (0-2 years): Understanding is limited to direct contact with the environment (touching, listening, seeing).

2. The preoperational stage (2-7 years): Children develop the ability to use symbols (especially language), which allow them to experience things without direct contact.

3. The concrete operational stage (7-12 years): Reasoning abilities become much more developed. Children now can understand numbers, causation, and speed, but have difficulty with abstract concepts such as truth.

4. The formal operational stage (12+ years): Children become capable of abstract thinking, and can use rules to solve abstract problems ("If X is true, why doesn't Y follow?").

D. Conclusions that Cooley, Mead, and Piaget came to regarding the self and reasoning appear to be universal. However, there is not consensus about the universality of Piaget's four stages of cognitive development.

1. Some adults never appear to reach the fourth stage, whether due to particular social experiences or to biology.

2. The content of what we learn varies from one culture to another; with very different experiences and the thinking processes that revolve around these experiences, we cannot assume that the developmental sequences will be the same for everyone.

III. Learning Personality, Morality, and Emotions

A. Sigmund Freud (1856-1939) believed that personality consists of three elements: the id, ego, and superego.

1. The id—inherited drives for self-gratification—demands fulfillment of basic needs such as attention, safety, food, and sex.

2. The ego balances between the needs of the id and the demands of society.

3. The superego—the social conscience we have internalized from social groups—gives us feelings of guilt or shame when we break rules, and feelings of pride and self-satisfaction when we follow them.
4. Sociologists object to Freud's view that inborn and unconscious motivations are the primary reasons for human behavior, for this view denies the central tenet of sociology—that social factors shape people's behaviors.
5. Feminist sociologists have been especially critical of Freud. According to Freud, females are inferior, castrated males.

B. Psychologist Lawrence Kohlberg concluded that humans go through a sequence of stages in the development of morality.
1. The amoral stage is when the child does not distinguish between right and wrong.
2. The preconventional stage is when the child follows the rules in order to stay out of trouble.
3. The conventional stage is when the child follows the norms and values of society.
4. The postcoventional stage is when the child reflects on abstract principles of right and wrong, using these principles to judge behavior.

C. Carol Gilligan studied differences between males and females in how they view morality.
1. Gilligan disagreed with Kohlberg's conclusions because they did not match her own experience and he had only used boys in his studies.
2. She found that females tend to evaluate morality in terms of personal relationships and how actions will affect others.
3. Males think in terms of abstract principles of right and wrong.
4. Other researchers tested Gilligan's conclusions and found no gender differences. Based on this subsequent work, Gilligan no longer supports her original position.

D. Although it appears that the looking-glass self, role taking, and the social mind are universal phenomena, emotions are not simply the result of biology; they also depend on socialization within a particular society.
1. Anthropologist Paul Ekman concluded that everyone experiences six basic emotions: anger, disgust, fear, happiness, sadness, and surprise.
2. The expression of emotions varies according to gender, social class, culture, and relationships.
3. Socialization not only leads to different ways of expressing emotions but even to expressing what we feel.

E. Most socialization is meant to turn us into conforming members of society. We do some things and not others as a result of socialization. When we contemplate an action, we know the emotion (good or bad) that would result; thus society sets up controls on our behavior.

IV. Socialization into Gender
A. By expecting different behaviors from people because they are male or female, society nudges boys and girls in separate directions from an early age, and this foundation carries over into adulthood.

B.   Parents begin the process; researchers have concluded that in our society, mothers unconsciously reward their female children for being passive and dependent and their male children for being active and independent.

C.   The mass media reinforce society's expectations of gender in many ways:
   1.   Ads perpetuate stereotypes by portraying males as dominant and rugged and females as sexy and submissive.
   2.   On television, male characters outnumber females and are more likely to be portrayed in higher-status positions.
   3.   Males are much more likely than females to play video games; we have no studies of how these games affect their players' ideas of gender.
   4.   Sociologist Melissa Milkie concluded that males use media images to discover who they are and what is expected of them as males.
   5.   We are not simply passive consumers of media images; we select those that are significant to our situation and use them to help us construct our understanding of the world.

V.   Agents of Socialization

A.   Our experiences in the family have a lifelong impact on us, laying down a basic sense of self, motivation, values, and beliefs.
   1.   Parents—often unaware of what they are doing—send subtle messages to their children about society's expectations for them as males or females.
   2.   Research by Melvin Kohn suggests that there are social class and occupational differences in child rearing. The main concern of working-class parents often is their children's outward conformity, while middle-class parents show greater concern for the motivations for their children's behavior. The type of job held by the parent is also a factor: the more closely supervised the job is, the more likely the parent is to insist on outward conformity.

B.   The neighborhood has an impact on children's development. Some neighborhoods are better places for children to grow up than other neighborhoods. For example, residents of more affluent neighborhoods watch out for children more than do residents of poorer neighborhoods.

C.   Religion plays a major role in the socialization of most Americans, even if they are not raised in a religious family. Religion especially influences morality, but also ideas about the dress, speech, and manners that are appropriate.

D.   With more mothers today working for wages, day care is now a significant agent of socialization.
   1.   One national study that followed 1,200 children from infancy through kindergarten found that the more hours per week a child spends in day care, the weaker the bonds between mother and child and the greater the child's behavior problems.
   2.   Children who spent less time in day care were more affectionate to their mothers and more cooperative.
   3.   This pattern held regardless of the quality of day care, the family's social class, or whether the child is a boy or girl.
   4.   We do not know how to explain these patterns. It could be that children who spend many hours in day care do not have their emotional needs met or that

mothers who put their children in day care for more hours are less sensitive to their children in the first place.

5. These same researchers also found that the more hours children spend in day care, the higher they score on language tests. This was especially true for children in low income or abusive homes.

E. Schools serve many manifest (intended) functions for society, including teaching skills and values thought to be appropriate. Schools also have several latent (unintended) functions.

1. At school, children are placed outside the direct control of friends/relatives and exposed to new values and ways of looking at the world. They learn *universality,* or that the same rules apply to everyone.

2. Schools also have a *hidden curriculum*—values not explicitly taught but inherent in school activities. For example, the wording of stories may carry messages about patriotism and democracy; by teaching that our economic system is just, schools may teach children to believe problems such as poverty are never caused by oppression and exploitation.

3. Schools also have a corridor curriculum—where students are taught by one another outside of the classroom. Unfortunately, these are often not positive values.

4. Conflict theorists note that schools teach children to take their place in the workforce. Children of the wealthy go to private schools, where they acquire the skills and values appropriate to their eventual higher position, while children of working class parents attend public schools, where they are rarely placed in college prep classes.

F. One of the most significant aspects of education is that it exposes children to peer groups. A peer group is a group of people of roughly the same age who share common interests. Next to the family, peer groups are the most powerful socializing force in society.

1. Research by Patricia and Peter Adler document how elementary age children separated themselves by sex and developed their own worlds and norms. They found that popular boys were athletic, cool, and tough. Popular girls depended on family background, physical appearance, and the ability to attract popular boys.

2. It is almost impossible to go against a peer group, whose cardinal rule is to conform or be rejected. As a result, the standards of peer groups tend to dominate our lives.

G. Sports are also powerful socializing agents; children are taught not only physical skills, but also values. Boys often learn that masculinity is related to success in sports—the more successful a boy is in a sport, the more masculine he is considered, and the more he is accepted.

H. The workplace is a major agent of socialization for adults; from jobs, we learn not only skills, but also matching attitudes and values. We may engage in anticipatory socialization—learning to play a role before actually entering it, and enabling us to gradually identify with the role.

VI. Resocialization
A. Resocialization refers to the process of learning new norms, values, attitudes and behaviors. Resocialization in its most common form occurs each time we learn something contrary to our previous experiences, such as going to work in a new job. It can be an intense experience, although it does not have to be.
B. Erving Goffman used the term total institution to refer to places such as boot camps, prisons, concentration camps, or some mental hospitals, religious cults, and boarding schools—places where people are cut off from the rest of society and are under almost total control of agents of the institution.
1. A person entering the institution is greeted with a degradation ceremony, which may include fingerprinting, shaving the head, banning personal items, and being forced to strip and wear a uniform. In this way, his or her current identity is stripped away and a new identity is created.
2. Total institutions are quite effective in isolating people from outside influences and information; supervising their activities; suppressing previous roles, statuses, and norms and replacing them with new rules and values; and controlling rewards and punishments.

VII. Socialization Through the Life Course
A. Socialization occurs throughout a person's entire lifetime and can be broken up into different stages.
B. Childhood (birth to 12): In earlier times, children were seen as miniature adults who served an apprenticeship. To keep them in line, they were beaten and subjected to psychological torture. Industrialization changed the way we see children. The current view is that children are tender and innocent and parents should guide the physical, emotional, and social development of their children while providing them with care, comfort, and protection.
C. Adolescence (13-17): Adolescence is a social invention. Economic changes resulting from the Industrial Revolution brought about material surpluses that allowed millions of teenagers to remain outside the labor force, while at the same time increasing the demand for education. Biologically equipped for both work and marriage but denied both, adolescents suffer inner turmoil and develop their own standards of clothing, hairstyles, language, music, and other claims to separate identities.
D. Transitional Adulthood (18-29): Adult responsibilities are postponed through extended education such as college. Even after college, many young people are returning to live with parents in order to live cheaply and establish their careers.
E. The Middle Years (30-65): This can be separated into two periods.
1. Early Middle Years (30-49): People are surer of themselves and their goals in life than before, but severe jolts such as divorce or being fired can occur. For U.S. women, it can be a trying period, as they try to "have it all"—job, family, and everything else.
2. Later Middle Years (50-65): A different view of life emerges, including trying to evaluate the past and coming to terms with what lies ahead. Individuals may feel they are not likely to get much farther in life, while health and mortality become concerns. However, for most people it is the most comfortable period in their entire lives.

F. Older years (65 and beyond): This can also be separated into two periods.
    1. The Transitional Older Years: Improvements in nutrition, public health, and medical care delay the onset of old age. For many, this period is an extension of middle years. Those who still work or are socially active are unlikely to see themselves as old.
    2. The Later Older Years: Growing frailty, illness, and eventually death mark this period.
G. The social significance of the life course is how it is shaped by social factors—the period in which the person is born and lives his or her life, as well as social location, social class, gender, and race.

VIII. Are We Prisoners of Socialization?
A. Sociologists do not think of people as little robots who simply are the result of their exposure to socializing agents. Although socialization is powerful and profoundly affects us all, we have a self, and the self is dynamic. Each of us uses our own mind to reason and make choices.
B. In this way, each of us is actively involved in the social construction of the self. Our experiences have an impact on us, but we are not doomed to keep our orientations if we do not like them. We can choose to change our experiences by exposing ourselves to other groups and ideas.

Chapter Summary

There has been and continues to be considerable debate over whether "nature" (heredity) or "nurture" (social environment) most determines human behavior. Studies of feral, isolated, and institutionalized children indicate that although heredity certainly plays a role in the "human equation," it is society that makes people "human." People *learn* what it means to be and, consequently, *become* members of the human community through language, social interaction, and other forms of human contact.

People are not born with an intrinsic knowledge of themselves or others. Rather, as the theoretical insights of Charles Horton Cooley, George Herbert Mead, Jean Piaget, Lawrence Kohlberg, and Carol Gilligan demonstrate, they develop reasoning skills, morality, personality, and a sense of self through *social* observation, contact, and interaction.

Cooley's conceptualization of the "looking-glass self" shows how a person's sense of self is inextricably linked to that person's sense of others; an individual imagines how other people see him or her, interprets their reactions to his or her behaviors, and develops a self-concept based on those interpretations. Mead's insights into "taking the role of the other"—as well as how children learn through stages of imitation, play, and games—illustrate the process by which people learn to become cooperative members of the human community and internalize the "rules" of the game of life. Furthermore, his formulation of the self as subject (the "I") and object (the "me") shows how socialization is an active process and how the human mind, as well as the self, is a social product.

Through observations of—and experiments with—young children, Piaget detailed four stages by which children typically develop the ability to reason: the sensorimotor stage (from birth to about age two), the preoperational stage (from about age two to age seven), the concrete operational stage (from about age seven to about age twelve), and the formal operational stage (after the age of about twelve). Building on Piaget's work, Kohlberg theorized that human beings develop morality through a series of stages: the amoral stage (from birth to about age seven), the preconventional stage (from about age seven to about age ten), the conventional stage (after the age of about ten), and the postconventional stage (a stage that, according to Kohlberg, most people do not reach).

Gilligan examined how gender affects the development of morality. Based on interviews with approximately 200 men and women, she concluded that women are more likely to evaluate morality in terms of personal relationships, while men tend to define right or wrong along the lines of abstract principles.

Cooley's insights into the looking-glass self and Mead's insights into role taking and the mind appear to be universally applicable. Researchers are more divided, however, on Piaget's four stages of human development. Noting cultural and individual variations in the development of reasoning skills, some researchers argue that human beings develop reasoning skills more gradually and flexibly than Piaget's model suggests. Subsequent research and testing raised questions about Gilligan's work on gender and morality, when the results found no gender differences between males and females in moral reasoning. Because of these findings, Gilligan no longer fully supports her original position.

Sigmund Freud formulated personality in terms of the id (the inborn drives for self-gratification), the ego (the balancing force between the id and the demands of society that suppress it), and the superego (the conscience, representing culture within us). Many sociologists reject Freud's contention that inborn and unconscious motivations are the primary determinants of human behavior. However, many sociologists are attracted to Freud's notion that the super ego represents the internalization of social norms. Feminists criticize Freud's theoretical assumption that "maleness" is "normal" and that females can be analyzed as inferior, castrated males suffering from "penis envy."

Socialization is not only critical to internalizing social norms, to the development of the mind, but also to the development of emotions. Although there are some basic emotions that all people experience, all people do not express these emotions the same way or to the same extent. Different socialization experiences tied to regional, gender, and class differences, for example, may not only affect how people express their emotions, but also the particular emotions they may feel. Males and females learn what it means to be boys and girls and, later, men and women through gender socialization—the ways in which society sets children onto different courses in life because they are male or female. From the time of their birth, children are constantly presented with cultural messages that teach them how to act masculine or feminine based on their sex.

Human beings learn how to think, behave, and act through agents of socialization—those people or groups that influence our self-concept, attitudes, behaviors, or other orientations toward life.

Major agents of socialization include the family, religion, daycare, school, peer groups, sports, and the workplace. When people move from one place, job, and/or life situation to another, they often have to undergo resocialization—the process of learning new norms, values, attitudes, and behaviors.

Special settings that require intense resocialization, such as boot camps, prisons, and mental institutions, are called "total institutions," a term coined by Erving Goffman to refer to a place where people are cut off from the rest of society and are almost totally controlled by the officials in charge. Socialization is not just limited to childhood; it is a lifelong process in which people are taught, learn, and/or adjust to the needs, expectations, and responsibilities that typically accompany different stages in life.

Although socialization has a tremendous influence, within the limitations of the framework laid down by our social location, on how people think and act, human beings are not prisoners of socialization. They have a considerable degree of freedom of choice, for example, to choose which agents of socialization to follow (except for family), and which cultural practices or messages to accept or reject from those agents of socialization. We can even change our sense of self. Humans are not robots, and are therefore unpredictable, which makes the job of the sociologist more difficult. Humans are not sponges that passively absorb environmental influences. They are in fact active in their own environments and receive different treatment from others around them. Even identical twins do not receive identical reactions from others.

KEY TERMS
After studying the chapter, review the definition for each of the following terms.

agents of socialization: individuals or groups that affect our self-concept, attitudes, behaviors, or other orientations toward life (77)

anticipatory socialization: the process of learning in advance an anticipated future role or status (81)

degradation ceremony: a term coined by Harold Garfinkel to refer to a ritual whose goal is to strip away someone's position (social status); in doing so, a new self-identity is stamped on the individual (82)

ego: Freud's term for a balancing force between the id and the demands of society (69)

feral children: children assumed to have been raised by animals in the wilderness isolated from other humans (62)

gender: the behaviors and attitudes that a society considers proper for its males and females; masculinity or femininity (73)

gender role: the behaviors and attitudes expected of people because they are female or male (78)

gender socialization: the ways in which society sets children onto different paths in life *because* they are male or female (73)

generalized other: the norms, values, attitudes, and expectations of people "in general"; the child's ability to take the role of the generalized other is a significant step in the development of a self (66)

id: Freud's term for our inborn basic drives (69)

latent functions: unintended beneficial consequences of people's actions (79)

life course: the stages of our life as we go from birth to death (83)

looking-glass self: a term coined by Charles Horton Cooley to refer to the process by which our self develops through internalizing others' reactions to us (66)

manifest functions: the intended beneficial consequences of people's actions (79)

mass media: forms of communication, such as radio, newspapers, television, and blogs that are directed to mass audiences (75)

peer group: a group of individuals of roughly the same age who are linked by common interests (75)

resocialization: the process of learning new norms, values, attitudes, and behaviors (82)

self: the unique human capacity of being able to see ourselves "from the outside"; the views we internalize of how others see us (66)

significant other: an individual who significantly influences someone else's life (66)

social environment: the entire human environment, including direct contact with others (62)

superego: Freud's term for the conscience; the internalized norms and values of our social groups (69)

taking the role of the other: putting oneself in someone else's shoes; understanding how someone else feels and thinks and thus anticipating how that person will act (66)

total institution: a place that is almost totally controlled by those who run it; people are cut off from the rest of society and the society is mostly cut off from them (82)

transitional adulthood: a term that refers to a period following high school when young adults have not yet taken on the responsibilities ordinarily associated with adulthood; also called adultolescence (85)

transitional older years: an emerging stage of the life course between retirement and when people are considered old; approximately age 65-75 (86)

KEY PEOPLE

Review the major theoretical contributions or findings of these people.

Patricia and Peter Adler: These sociologists have documented how peer groups socialize children into gender-appropriate behavior. (81)

Charles Horton Cooley: Cooley studied the development of the self, coining the term "the looking-glass self." (66-67)

Paul Ekman: This psychologist studied emotions in several countries and concluded that people everywhere experience six basic emotions—anger, disgust, fear, happiness, sadness, and surprise. (71-72)

Sigmund Freud: Freud developed a theory of personality development that took into consideration inborn drives (id), the internalized norms and values of one's society (superego), and the individual's ability to balance the two competing forces (ego). (69-70)

Carol Gilligan: Gilligan was uncomfortable with Kohlberg's conclusions regarding the development of morality because they did not match her own experiences and Kohlberg had used only boys in his studies. She studied gender differences in morality, concluding that men and women use different criteria in evaluating morality. (69, 70)

Erving Goffman: Goffman studied the process of resocialization in total institutions. (82)

Susan Goldberg and Michael Lewis: Two psychologists studied how parents' unconscious expectations about gender behavior are communicated to their young children. (73)

Harry and Margaret Harlow: These psychologists studied the behavior of monkeys raised in isolation and found that the length of time they were isolated affected their ability to overcome its effects. (65-66)

Lawrence Kohlberg: This psychologist studied the development of morality, concluding that individuals go through a sequence of developmental stages. (70)

Melvin Kohn: Kohn has done extensive research on the social class differences in child-rearing between working-class and middle-class parents. (78)

George Herbert Mead: Mead emphasized the importance of play in the development of the self, noting that children learn to take on the role of the other and eventually learn to perceive themselves as others do. (66-69)

Melissa Milkie: This sociologist studied how adolescent boys used media images to discover who they are as males. (75)

Jean Piaget: Piaget studied the development of reasoning skills in children and identified four stages. (68-69)

H. M. Skeels and H. B. Dye: These psychologists studied how close social interaction affected the social and intellectual development of institutionalized children. (64)

MULTIPLE CHOICE QUESTIONS

1. Which of the following statements best describes feral children? (62)
    a. After their parents supposedly abandoned them, they were reared by someone else.
    b. They supposedly were abandoned by their parents and then reared by animals.
    c. They are viewed as significant for our understanding of human nature by most social scientists.
    d. They quickly recovered from their experiences of deprivation once they were rescued.

2. From the case of Isabelle, it is possible to conclude that (62)
    a. humans have no natural language.
    b. Isabelle was retarded.
    c. a person who has been isolated cannot progress through normal learning stages.
    d. all of the above.

3. What conclusions can be made from Skeels and Dye's study of institutionalized children? (64-65)
    a. Mental retardation was biological.
    b. Early physical contact did little to change the intelligence levels of these children.
    c. The absence of stimulating social interaction was the basic cause of low intelligence among these children, not some biological incapacity.
    d. Children who are cared for by a mentally retarded adult will "learn" to be retarded, while those who are cared for by professional staff will not.

4. What do studies of isolated rhesus monkeys demonstrate? (65-66)
    a. The monkeys were able to adjust to monkey life after a time.
    b. They instinctively knew how to enter into "monkey interaction" with other monkeys.
    c. They knew how to engage in sexual intercourse.
    d. The monkeys were not able to adjust fully to monkey life and did not know instinctively how to enter into interaction with other monkeys.

5. Which of the following is *not* an element of the looking-glass self? (66)
    a. We imagine how we appear to those around us.
    b. We interpret others' reactions.
    c. We develop a self-concept.
    d. We form opinions about others based on our self-concept.

6. According to Mead's theory, at what stage do children pretend to take the roles of specific people? (67)
    a. imitation
    b. game
    c. play
    d. generalized other

7. To Mead, what is the "I"? (67-68)
    a. It is the self as subject.
    b. It is the self as object.
    c. It is the same as the id.
    d. It represents the passive robot aspect of human behavior.

8. According to Mead, which of the following is a product of society? (67-68)
    a. language
    b. the mind
    c. the self
    d. According to Mead, all three are products of society.

9. Using Piaget's theory, at which stage of cognitive development are children likely to become "young philosophers," able to talk about abstract concepts, come to conclusions based on general principles, and use rules to solve abstract problems? (68)
    a. sensorimotor
    b. preoperational
    c. concrete operational
    d. formal operational

10. What is the term Freud used to describe our inborn drives for self-gratification? (69-70)
    a. id
    b. superego
    c. ego
    d. libido

11. Larry is 8 years old. He tries very hard to be nice to his younger sister because he knows that his mother gets very upset when the two of them fight and hit each other. According to Lawrence Kohlberg, which stage of moral development is reflected in Larry's behavior? (70)
    a. amoral
    b. preconventional
    c. conventional
    d. postconventional

12. Which of the four stages of moral development are most people unlikely to ever reach, according to Kohlberg? (70)
    a. amoral
    b. preconventional
    c. conventional
    d. postconventional

13. Gilligan's early research suggests that women evaluate morality in terms of (70)
    a. abstract principles.
    b. a code of ethics.
    c. personal relationships.

    d.   concrete values.

14. Which of the following statements about emotions is *correct*? (71-72)
    a.   People around the world feel the same emotions and express them in the same way.
    b.   How we express emotions depends on our culture and our social location.
    c.   For the most part, emotions are the result of biology.
    d.   Socialization has little to do with emotions.

15. According to this chapter, what is one of the most effective ways in which society sets controls over our behavior? (72)
    a.   hiring police officers and other law enforcement officials
    b.   defining those who do not abide by the rules as "deviants"
    c.   socializing us into self and emotions
    d.   using the media effectively

16. What conclusions did psychologists Susan Goldberg and Michael Lewis reach after observing mothers with their six-month-old infants in a laboratory setting? (73)
    a.   The mothers kept their male children closer to them.
    b.   They kept their male and female children about the same distance from them.
    c.   They touched and spoke more to their sons.
    d.   They unconsciously rewarded daughters for being passive and dependent.

17. Which of the following statements reflects Melissa Milkie's research findings? (75)
    a.   Young males actively used media images to help them understand what was expected of them as males in our society.
    b.   Young males avoided talking about male images in television and movies because they wanted to avoid being labeled a "weenie."
    c.   Young females are passive consumers of media images, rather than active ones.
    d.   Young males were very similar to young females in how they used media images as role models for "cool" behavior.

18. Melvin Kohn suggests that the key to understanding social class differences in child rearing is (78)
    a.   the income level of the parents.
    b.   the type of job the parents' have.
    c.   the amount of education the parents have.
    d.   the parents' access to expert advice on how to raise children.

19. Which of the following statements is *false* regarding religion in the U.S.? (79)
    a.   Religious teaching has become a substitute for what parents teach.
    b.   Religion is a key component in teaching ideas of right or wrong.
    c.   Sixty-five percent of Americans belong to a local congregation.
    d.   During a typical week, two of five Americans attend a religious service.

20. Which of the following statements summarizes the research findings on the impact that day care has on preschool children? (79)

a. The number of hours a child spends in day care does not seem to matter in terms of their observed behavior.

b. The more hours per week a child spends in day care, the weaker the bond is between mother and child.

c. The more hours per week a child spends in day care, the more social the child.

d. The more hours per week a child spends in day care, the more prepared the child is to learn once he or she gets to primary school.

21. When students teach one another values and behaviors outside of the classroom, this is known as (79, 81)
   a. following a formal curriculum.
   b. teaching a corridor curriculum.
   c. fulfilling the hidden curriculum.
   d. satisfying a latent function of education.

22. What conclusions can be drawn about peer groups and academic achievement from Patricia and Peter Adler's research? (81)
   a. Both boys and girls avoid doing well academically.
   b. Boys want to do well academically in order to boost their standing in the peer group, but girls avoid being labeled as smart, because it will hurt their image.
   c. Both boys and girls believe that good grades will translate into greater popularity among their respective peer groups.
   d. For boys, to do well academically is to lose popularity, while for girls, getting good grades increases social standing.

23. Under which of the following conditions is resocialization likely to occur? (82)
   a. when we take a new job
   b. if we were to join a cult
   c. when we are sent to military boot camp
   d. all of the above would involve resocialization

24. Which of the following statements about total institutions is *incorrect*? (82)
   a. They suppress preexisting statuses, so that the inmates will learn that previous roles mean nothing and that the only thing that counts is their current role.
   b. They are not very effective in stripping away people's personal freedom.
   c. They are isolated, with barriers to keep inmates in and keep outsiders from interfering.
   d. They suppress the norms of the "outside world," replacing them with their own values, rules and interpretations.

25. Which stage of the life course poses a special challenge for women? (86)
   a. early middle years
   b. later middle years
   c. early older years
   d. later older years

TRUE-FALSE QUESTIONS

1. _____Studies of institutionalized children demonstrate that some of the characteristics that we take for granted as being "human" traits result from our basic instincts. (64)
2. _____Since emotions are natural human responses, socialization has very little to do with how we feel. (71)
3. _____Much of our socialization is intended to turn us into conforming members of society. (72)
4. _____Advertisements have made a concerted effort to not perpetuate gender stereotypes by portraying males as dominant and rugged and females as sexy and submissive. (75-76)
5. _____A latent function of education is transmitting the skills and values appropriate for earning a living. (79)
6. _____Work gives us the opportunity to learn anticipatory socialization, learning to play a role before entering it. (81)
7. _____Total institutions are very effective in stripping away people's personal freedom. (82)
8. _____Adolescence is a social creation in industrialized societies. (85)
9. _____Industrialization brought with it a delay in the onset of old age. (86)
10. _____Most sociologists believe that people cannot help what they do, think, or feel, for everything is simply a result of their exposure to socialization. (87)

FILL-IN-THE-BLANK QUESTIONS

1. Without _____, people have no mechanism for developing thought. (64)
2. The Harlow experiments with _____ support what we know about children raised in isolation. (65)
3. Charles H. Cooley coined the term _____to describe the process by which a sense of self develops. (66)
4. To put yourself in someone else's shoes is to learn how to _____. (66)
5. Mead used the term _____to refer to our perception of how people in general think of us. (66)
6. In the _____ stage of Piaget's model of reasoning, children develop the ability to use symbols. (68)
7. One of the main findings of the sociologist Kohn was that socialization depends on a family's _____. (78)
8. By influencing values, _____ becomes a key component in people's ideas of right and wrong. (79)
9. The stage of the life course that poses a special challenge for women in the United States is _____. (86)
10. Because individuals are not robots, their _____ is difficult to predict. (87)

ESSAY QUESTIONS

1. Explain what is necessary in order for us to develop into full human beings.

2. Why do sociologists argue that socialization is a process and not a product?

3. Having read about how the family, the media, and peers all influence our gender socialization, discuss why gender roles tend to remain unchanged from one generation to the next.

4. As the text points out, the stages of the life course are influenced by the biological clock, but they also reflect broader social factors. Identify the stages of the life course and indicate how social factors have contributed to the definition of each of these stages.

5. Are we prisoners of our socialization? Please explain.

CHAPTER 4
SOCIAL STRUCTURE AND SOCIAL INTERACTION

LEARNING OBJECTIVES
After reading Chapter 4, you should be able to:

1. Differentiate between the macrosociological and microsociological approaches to studying social life, and indicate which approach is most likely to be used by functionalists, conflict theorists, and symbolic interactionists. (92)

2. Define social structure, list its major components, and discuss how it guides people's behaviors. (93)

3. Understand the concepts of culture, social class, social status, roles, groups, and social institutions. (93-99)

4. Discuss how a person's location in the social structure underlies his or her perceptions, attitudes, beliefs, and actions. (93)

5. Identify the social institutions common to industrial and postindustrial societies and summarize their basic features. (98)

6. Discuss the disagreement between functionalists and conflict theorists regarding the purposes for, and effects of, social institutions. (99-100)

7. Know why social structure is not static and how structural changes can significantly alter the way a society organizes itself. (100)

8. Differentiate between Emile Durkheim's concepts of mechanical and organic solidarity and Ferdinand Tönnie's constructs of *Gemeinschaft* and *Gesellschaft*, and discuss why they continue to be relevant. (101-102)

9. Define stereotypes and explain their significance. (106)

10. Discuss the various ways different cultures perceive and use personal space and touching. (102, 107)

11. Know the key components of dramaturgy and discuss how people try to control other people's impressions of them through sign-vehicles, teamwork, and face-saving behaviors. (108-110)

12. Differentiate between role conflict and role strain, providing examples of each. (109)

13. Understand how and why ethnomethodologists examine different ways people use background assumptions to make sense of everyday life. (113)

14. Explain what is meant by the social construction of reality and how it is related to the "Thomas theorem." (114)

15. Know why macrosociology and microsociology are essential to understanding social life. (115, 118)

Chapter Outline

I. **Levels of Sociological Analysis**
   A. Macrosociology places the focus on large-scale features of social structure. It investigates large-scale social forces and the effects they have on entire societies and the groups within them. It is utilized by functionalist and conflict theorists.
   B. Microsociology places the emphasis on social interaction, or what people do when they come together. Symbolic interactionism uses this level of analysis.
   C. Each yields distinctive perspectives, and both are needed to gain a more complete understanding of social life.

II. **The Macrosociological Perspective: Social Structure**
   A. Social structure is defined as the patterned relationships between people that persist over time. Behaviors and attitudes are determined by our location in the social structure. Components of social structure are culture, social class, social status, roles, groups, and institutions.
   B. Culture refers to a group's language, beliefs, values, behaviors, and gestures. It includes the material objects used by a group. It determines what kind of people we will become.
   C. Social class is based on income, education, and occupational prestige. A social class is made up of large numbers of people who have similar amounts of income and education and who work at jobs that are roughly comparable in prestige.
   D. Social status refers to the positions that an individual occupies. A status may carry a great deal of prestige (judge or astronaut) or very little (gas station attendant or cook in a fast-food restaurant).
      1. Status set refers to all the statuses or positions that an individual occupies.
      2. Ascribed statuses are positions an individual either inherits at birth or receives involuntarily later in life. Examples include race, sex, and social class of parents.
      3. Achieved statuses are positions that are earned, accomplished, or involve at least some effort or activity on the individual's part. Examples include becoming a college president or a bank robber.
      4. Each status provides guidelines for how we are to act and feel.
      5. Status symbols are signs that people use because they want others to recognize that they occupy a certain status. For example, wearing wedding rings, driving fancy cars, living in expensive homes, etc.

6.   A master status—such as being male or female—cuts across the other statuses that an individual occupies. Status inconsistency is a contradiction or mismatch between statuses. A disability can become a master status for some. This condition can override other statuses and determines others' perceptions of this person.

E.   Roles are the behaviors, obligations, and privileges attached to a status. The individual occupies a status but plays a role. Roles are an essential component of culture because they lay out what is expected of people. As individuals perform their roles, those roles mesh together to form the society.

F.   A group consists of people who regularly and consciously interact with one another and typically share similar values, norms, and expectations. When we belong to a group, we give up to others at least some control over our lives.
1.   The control depends on the relationship and amount of interaction we have with that group.

III. Social Institutions
A.   Social institutions are society's standard ways of meeting its basic needs.
1.   The family, religion, law, politics, economics, education, science, medicine, and the military are all social institutions.
2.   In industrialized societies, social institutions tend to be more formal, while nonliterate societies are more informal.
3.   Each institution has its own groups, statuses, values, and norms.

B.   Social institutions are sociologically significant because they set limits and provide guidelines for our behavior.

C.   The mass media is an emerging social institution; it influences our attitudes toward social issues, other people, and even our self-concept. Of interest is who controls the mass media. Functionalists would say that the mass media represents the varied interests of the many groups that make up the nation, while conflict theorists would see that the interests of the political elite are represented.

D.   The functionalists and conflict theorists differ in how they see social institutions.
1.   Functionalists view social institutions as established ways of meeting group needs (or functional requisites), such as replacing members, socializing new members, producing and distributing goods and services, preserving order, and providing a sense of purpose.
2.   Conflict theorists look at social institutions as the primary means by which the elite maintains its privileged position.

E.   Changes in social structure occur as culture changes because of evolving values, new technologies, innovative ideas, and globalization.

F.   Many sociologists have tried to find an answer to the question of what holds society together.
1.   Emile Durkheim found the key to social cohesion—the degree to which members of a society feel united by shared values and other social bonds—in the concepts of mechanical solidarity and organic solidarity. Mechanical solidarity is a

collective consciousness that people experience as a result of performing the same or similar tasks. Organic solidarity is a collective consciousness based on the interdependence brought about by an increasingly specialized division of labor—that is, how people divide up tasks.

2. Ferdinand Tönnies analyzed how impersonal associations *(Gesellschaft)* were replacing intimate communities *(Gemeinschaft)*. *Gemeinschaft* is a society in which life is intimate; a community in which everyone knows everyone else and people share a sense of togetherness. *Gesellschaft* is a society dominated by impersonal relationships, individual accomplishments, and self-interest.

3. These concepts are still relevant today, helping us understand contemporary events such as the rise of Islamic fundamentalism.

IV. The Microsociological Perspective: Social Interaction in Everyday Life

A. The microsociological approach places emphasis on face-to-face social interaction, or what people do when they are in the presence of one another.

B. Symbolic interactionists are interested in the symbols that people use to define their worlds, how people look at things, and how that affects their behavior. Included within this perspective are studies of stereotypes, personal space, and touching.

1. Stereotypes are used in everyday life. First impressions are shaped by the assumptions one person makes about another person's sex, race, age, and physical appearance. Such assumptions affect one's ideas about the person and how one acts toward that person. Stereotypes tend to be self-fulfilling—that is, they bring out the very kinds of behavior that fit the stereotype. They even have an impact on what we accomplish. People can also resist stereotypes and change outcomes.

2. Personal space refers to the physical space that surrounds us and that we claim as our own. The amount of personal space varies from one culture to another. Anthropologist Edward Hall found that Americans use four different distance zones: (1) Intimate distance (about 18 inches from the body) for lovemaking, wrestling, comforting, and protecting; (2) Personal distance (from 18 inches to 4 feet) for friends, acquaintances, and ordinary conversations; (3) Social distance (from 4 feet to 12 feet) for impersonal or formal relationships, such as job interviews; and (4) Public distance (beyond 12 feet) for even more formal relationships, such as separating dignitaries and public speakers from the general public.

3. From our culture, we learn rules about touching. Both the frequency and the meaning of touching vary from one culture to the next. Men and women react differently to being touched.

4. We protect our personal space by controlling eye contact.

C. Dramaturgy is an analysis of how we present ourselves in everyday life.

1. Dramaturgy is the name given to an approach pioneered by Erving Goffman. Social life is analyzed in terms of drama or the stage.

2. According to Goffman, socialization prepares people for learning to perform on the stage of everyday life. *Front stage* is where performances are given (wherever lines are delivered). *Back stage* is where people rest from their performances, discuss their presentations, and plan future performances.

3. *Role performance* is the particular emphasis or interpretation that an individual gives a role, that person's "style." *Role conflict* occurs when the expectations attached to one role are incompatible with the expectations of another role—in other words, conflict between roles. *Role strain* refers to conflicts that someone feels within a role.

4. *Impression management* is the person's efforts to manage the impressions that others receive of her or him.

5. We tend to become the roles we play. Some roles become part of our self-concept. For some, when leaving a role, such as a marriage, police work, or the military, the role can become so intertwined that leaving it can threaten a person's identity.

6. Three types of *sign-vehicles* are used to communicate information about the self: (1) Social setting—where the action unfolds, which includes scenery (furnishings used to communicate messages); (2) Appearance—how a person looks when he or she plays his or her role, including props that decorate the person; and (3) Manner—the attitudes demonstrated as an individual plays her or his roles.

7. Teamwork, which is when two or more players work together to make sure a performance goes off as planned, shows that we are adept players.

8. When a performance doesn't come off, we engage in face-saving behavior, or ignoring flaws in someone's performance, which Goffman defines as tact.

9. A face-saving technique that might be used is *studied nonobservance,* in which a behavior might be completely ignored so that neither person will face embarrassment.

10. Impression management also occurs with families, businesses, colleges and even the government.

D. Ethnomethodology involves the discovery of rules concerning our views of the world and how people ought to act.

1. Ethnomethodologists try to undercover people's background assumptions, which form the basic core of one's reality and provide basic rules concerning our view of the world and how people ought to act.

2. Harold Garfinkel founded the ethnomethodological approach. He conducted experiments by asking subjects to pretend that they did not understand the basic rules of social life in order to uncover others' reactions and break background assumptions.

E. The social construction of reality refers to what people define as real because of their background assumptions and life experiences.

1. Symbolic interactionists believe that people define their own reality and then live within those definitions.

2. The Thomas theorem (by sociologists William I. Thomas and Dorothy S. Thomas) states, "If people define situations as real, they are real in their consequences."
3. Therefore, our behavior does not depend on the objective existence of something, but on our subjective interpretation or our definition of reality.
4. James Henslin and Mae Biggs conducted research to show that when physicians are performing gynecological exams, they will socially construct reality so that the vaginal exams become nonsexual.

V. The Need for Both Macrosociology and Microsociology

A. To understand human behavior, it is necessary to grasp both social structure (macrosociology) and social interaction (microsociology).
B. Both are necessary to fully understand social life because each adds to our knowledge of human experience.

Chapter Summary

People are influenced by the norms and beliefs of their cultures and society. This influence can take a more personal and intimate level or a more general and widespread level that affects large numbers of people. Sociologists who study the affect of social life on society use two approaches—macrosociology (focusing on broad features of social structure) and microsociology (concentrating on small-scale, face-to-face social interactions). Functionalists and conflict theorists tend to use the macrosociological approach, while symbolic interactionists are more likely to use the microsociological approach. Although most sociologists specialize in one approach or the other, both approaches are necessary for a complete understanding of social life.

Using the macrosociological approach, functionalists and conflict theorists examine the more expansive aspects of social structure, which refers to a society's framework and consists of the various relationships between people and groups that direct and set limits on human behavior.

The major components of social structure include culture, social class, social status, roles, groups, and social institutions. Social structure guides people's behaviors. A person's location in the social structure (his or her social class, social status, the roles he or she plays, and the culture, groups, and social institutions to which he or she belongs) underlies his or her perceptions, attitudes, and behaviors. People develop these perceptions, attitudes, and behaviors from their place in the social structure, and they act accordingly. All of the components of social structure work together to maintain social order by limiting, guiding, and organizing human behavior.

Social institutions are the organized, usual, or standard ways by which society meets its basic needs. In industrial and postindustrial societies, social institutions include the family, religion, law, politics, economics, education, science, medicine, the military, and the mass media. Functionalists and conflict theorists disagree over the purposes and effects of social institutions. According to functionalists, social institutions exist because they meet universal group needs.

Conflict theorists view social institutions as the primary means by which the elite maintains its privileged position. Social structure is not static. It responds to changes in culture, technology, economic conditions, group relationships, and societal needs and priorities.

Structural changes can sometimes fundamentally and permanently alter the way a society organizes itself. Emile Durkheim demonstrated this with the concepts of mechanical and organic solidarity; Ferdinand Tönnies used the constructs of *Gemeinschaft* and *Gesellschaft*.

While functionalist and conflict theorists tend to explore broad features of social structure from a macrosociological perspective, symbolic interactionists are more inclined to examine small-scale, face-to-face social interactions from a microsociological perspective. Symbolic interactionists are especially interested in the symbols that people use to define their worlds and how these definitions, in turn, influence human behavior. For symbolic interactionists, this may include studying stereotyping, personal space, and touching.

Stereotypes are assumptions that people make about other people based on previous associations with them or people with similar visible characteristics. Stereotypes may also be based on what they have been "told" about "such people." These assumptions may be accurate, semi-accurate, or completely inaccurate. Stereotypes affect how people define and treat other people. They influence how these "other people" define themselves and adjust their behaviors accordingly. Stereotypes based on gender, race, ethnicity, ability, and intelligence are particularly widespread and profoundly consequential in today's society.

According to symbolic interactionists, people surround themselves with a "personal bubble" that they carefully protect by controlling space, touching, and eye contact. Anthropologist Edward Hall studied how human groups have different perceptions of personal space and how much physical distance they use to keep physically apart from people in specific situations. Frequency of touching also differs across cultures. Furthermore, the meaning of touching differs not only across cultures, but also within cultures. People also protect their "personal bubble" by controlling eye contact. This includes the length of contact and whether it is direct or indirect.

Erving Goffman developed dramaturgy, an analytical approach that analyzes social life in terms of the stage. According to Goffman, everyday life consists of social actors playing assigned roles. At the core of Goffman's approach is impression management, or how people try to control other people's impressions of them through sign-vehicles (social setting, appearance, and manner), teamwork, and face-saving behavior.

Symbolic interactionists contend that reality is subjectively created by people's perceptions of "what is real." People define their own realities and then live within those definitions. The social construction of reality refers to how people construct their views of the world. Ethnomethodology is the study of how people use background assumptions (deeply embedded common understandings concerning people's views of the world and how they ought to act) to make sense of life.

Because social structure and social interaction influence human behavior, macrosociology and microsociology are essential to understanding social life.

KEY TERMS

After studying the chapter, review the definition for each of the following terms.

achieved status: a position that is earned, accomplished, or involves at least some effort or activity on the individual's part (95)

ascribed status: a position an individual either inherits at birth or receives involuntarily later in life (95)

back stage: places where people rest from their performances, discuss their presentations, and plan future performances (109)

background assumption: a deeply embedded common understanding of how the world operates and how people ought to act (113)

body language: the ways in which people use their bodies to give messages to others (108)

division of labor: the splitting of a group's or society's tasks into specialties (101)

dramaturgy: an approach, pioneered by Erving Goffman, in which social life is analyzed in terms of drama or the stage; also called *dramaturgical analysis* (108)

ethnomethodology: the study of how people use background assumptions to make sense of life (113)

face-saving behavior: techniques used to salvage a performance (interaction) that is going sour (110)

front stage: places where we give performances (108)

Gemeinschaft: a type of society in which life is intimate; a community in which everyone knows everyone else and people share a sense of togetherness (101)

Gesellschaft: a type of society dominated by impersonal relationships, individual accomplishments, and self-interest (101)

group: people who have something in common and who believe that what they have in common is significant; also called a *social group* (97)

impression management: people's efforts to control the impressions that others receive of them (108)

macrosociology: analysis of social life that focuses on broad features of society, such as social class and the relationships of groups to one another; usually used by functionalist and conflict theorists (92)

master status: a status that cuts across the other statuses that an individual occupies (95)

mechanical solidarity: Durkheim's term for the unity (a shared consciousness) that people feel as a result of performing the same or similar tasks (101)

microsociology: analysis of social life focusing on social interaction; typically used by symbolic interactionists (92)

organic solidarity: Durkheim's term for the interdependence that results from the division of labor; people depending on others to fulfill their jobs (101)

role: the behaviors, obligations, and privileges attached to a status (96)

role conflict: conflict that someone feels *between* roles because the expectations attached to one role are incompatible with the expectations of another role (109)

role performance: the ways in which someone performs a role within the limits that the role provides; showing a particular "style" or "personality" (109)

role strain: conflicts that someone feels *within* a role (109)

sign-vehicle: a term used by Goffman to refer to how people use social setting, appearance, and manner to communicate information about the self (110)

social class: according to Weber, a large group of people who rank close to one another in property, power, and prestige; according to Marx, one of two groups: capitalists who own the means of production or workers who sell their labor (94)

social construction of reality: the use of background assumptions and life experiences to define what is real (114)

social institution: the organized, usual, or standard ways that society meets its basic needs (97)

social integration: the degree to which members of a group or a society feel united by shared values and other social bonds; also known as social cohesion (101)

social interaction: what people do when they are in one another's presence (92)

social structure: the framework (or typical patterns) that surrounds us, consisting of the relationships of people and groups to one another, and giving direction to and setting limits on behavior (93)

status: the position that someone occupies in a social group (95)

status inconsistency: ranking high on some dimensions of social class and low on others; also called *status discrepancy* (96)

status set: all the statuses or positions that an individual occupies (95)

status symbols: items used to identify a status (95)

stereotype: assumptions of what people are like, whether true or false (106)

teamwork: the collaboration of two or more people to manage impressions jointly (110)

Thomas theorem: William I. and Dorothy S. Thomas' classic formulation of the definition of the situation: "If people define situations as real, they are real in their consequences." (114)

KEY PEOPLE

Review the major theoretical contributions or findings of these people.

William Chambliss: Chambliss used macro and microsociology to study high school gangs and found that social structure and interaction explained the patterns of behavior in these groups. (115, 118)

Emile Durkheim: Durkheim identified mechanical and organic solidarity as the keys to social cohesion. As societies get larger, they divide up work and this division of labor makes people depend on one another. (101-102)

Helen Ebaugh: Ebaugh interviewed people who were no longer performing a role that had once been central in their lives—people whose marriages had ended, people who had left jobs and careers as police officers, military personnel, or religious orders. Since these roles were so critical, she found that many of them struggled to define their very identit as a result of the loss of these roles. (112)

Harold Garfinkel: Garfinkel is the founder of ethnomethodology; he conducted experiments in order to uncover people's background assumptions. (113)

Erving Goffman: Goffman developed dramaturgy—the perspective within symbolic interactionism that views social life as a drama on the stage. (108-109)

Edward Hall: This anthropologist found that personal space varied from one culture to another and that North Americans use four different "distance zones." (107)

James Henslin and Mae Biggs: The author of your text, along with gynecological nurse Biggs, researched how doctors and patients constructed the social reality of vaginal examinations in order to define these exams as nonsexual. (114-115)

Elliot Liebow: This sociologist studied streetcorner men and found that their lives are not disorganized, but influenced by the same norms and beliefs of the larger society. (92)

Mark Snyder: Snyder carried out research in order to test whether stereotypes are self-fulfilling; he found that subjects were influenced to behave in a particular way based on their stereotypes. (106)

William I. Thomas and Dorothy S. Thomas: These sociologists said that, "If people define situations as real, they are real in their consequences." (114)

Ferdinand Tönnies: Tönnies analyzed different types of societies that existed before and after industrialization. He used the terms *Gemeinschaft* and *Gesellschaft* to describe the two types of societies. (101-102)

SELF-TEST

MULTIPLE CHOICE QUESTIONS

1. Which of the following statements does *not* apply to macrosociology? (92)
   a. It focuses on social interaction.
   b. It investigates large-scale social forces.
   c. It focuses on broad features of social structure.
   d. It is used by functionalists and conflict theorists.

2. Which level of analysis do sociologists use to study individuals? (92)
   a. dramaturgy
   b. ethnomethodology
   c. macrosociology
   d. microsociology

3. You want to research the perceptions that different social classes have of each other in the United States. Which would you use? (92)
   a. macrosociology
   b. microsociology
   c. functionalism
   d. conflict perspective

4. Which of the following statements about social structure is *incorrect*? (93)
   a. The sociological significance of social structure is that it guides our behavior.
   b. People learn their behaviors and attitudes because of their location in the social structure.
   c. An individual's behaviors and attitudes are due to biology (one's race or sex, for instance) as much as it is due to his/her location in the social structure.
   d. The social structure, or the framework of society, exists before we are born and will continue to exist after we die.

5. Social class is based on all the following *except* (94)
   a. income.
   b. education.
   c. occupational prestige.
   d. age.

6. Sociologists use the term status to refer to the _____ that someone occupies. (95)
   a. social class
   b. prestige
   c. role
   d. position

7. A person is simultaneously a daughter, a wife, and a mother. All together, these make up a (95)

    a.   social status.
    b.   social class.
    c.   status position.
    d.   status set.

8.   Which of the following describe an individual's race, gender, and inherited social class? (95)
    a.   ascribed statuses
    b.   achieved statuses
    c.   status inconsistencies
    d.   status incongruities

9.   Once you finish your education, you will move into some kind of occupation or profession—that is, perhaps one based on your educational training. This job or career you will eventually hold is considered a(n) (95)
    a.   voluntary membership.
    b.   involuntary membership.
    c.   ascribed status.
    d.   achieved status.

10.   Wedding rings, military uniforms, and clerical collars are all examples of (95)
    a.   social stigma.
    b.   social class.
    c.   status symbols.
    d.   achieved statuses.

11.   Which of the following statements regarding status symbols is *incorrect*? (95)
    a.   Status symbols are signs that identify a status.
    b.   Status symbols often are used to show that people have "made it."
    c.   Status symbols are always positive signs or people would not wear them.
    d.   Status symbols are used by people to announce their statuses to others.

12.   Master statuses are (95)
    a.   ascribed.
    b.   achieved.
    c.   both ascribed and achieved.
    d.   neither ascribed or achieved.

13.   Under what conditions is status inconsistency most likely to occur? (96)
    a.   when a contradiction or mismatch between statuses exists
    b.   when we know what to expect of other people
    c.   when a person wears too many status symbols at once
    d.   when a society has few clearly defined master statuses

14.   What do we call the behaviors, obligations, and privileges attached to statuses? (96)
    a.   status sets

b.　master statuses

c.　status differentiations

d.　roles

15.　Which of the following is *false* about social institutions? (97-99)

a.　education is informally structured

b.　they tend to be more formal

c.　they include economics and science

d.　they have their own statuses, values, and norms

16.　Which of the following would be found in a society characterized by organic solidarity? (101)

a.　a highly specialized division of labor

b.　members who are interdependent on one another

c.　a high degree of impersonal relationships

d.　all of the above

17.　What type of society is described as an "intimate community" where everyone knows everyone else and members conform because they are sensitive to others' opinions and want to avoid gossip? (101)

a.　*Gemeinschaft*

b.　*Gesellschaft*

c.　mechanical society

d.　organic society

18.　Which of the following statements about stereotypes is *incorrect*? (102, 106)

a.　When you first meet someone the assumptions you have about certain social characteristics have a tendency to shape your first impressions of that person.

b.　Stereotypes are unlikely to be self-fulfilling.

c.　Stereotypes can have an impact on what we are able to accomplish because they influence how others behave toward us.

d.　People are able to resist stereotypes and change outcomes.

19.　Hall observed that North Americans used different distance zones. The "zone" that marks the impersonal or formal relationship is (107)

a.　social distance zone.

b.　the intimate zone.

c.　the personal distance zone.

d.　the public distance zone.

20.　Susan is a college student who takes classes in the evening after work. One day her boss asks her to move from working days to working evenings; he wants her to work while she is supposed to be in class. In this situation, what is Susan experiencing? (109)

a.　role strain

b.　role performance

c.　role demands

d.   role conflict

21.   The professor poses a question in class. You know the answer and want to raise your hand but are afraid that if you do, you will show up the other students in the class. What are you experiencing in this situation? (109)
    a.   role strain
    b.   role conflict
    c.   role distance
    d.   role performance

22.   Which of the following statements applies to social setting, appearance, and manner? (108-110)
    a.   They are less important than role performance for impression management.
    b.   They are sign-vehicles used by individuals for managing impressions.
    c.   They are more important for females than males.
    d.   They are techniques for saving face when a performance fails.

23.   If you went to your doctor's office and he/she started cutting your hair, this would be an example of violating (113)
    a.   face-saving behavior.
    b.   impression management.
    c.   a master status.
    d.   background assumption.

24.   Within which sociological perspective would you place the Thomas theorem? (114)
    a.   functionalism
    b.   conflict theory
    c.   symbolic interactionism
    d.   exchange theory

25.   What did the research on the Saints and the Roughnecks demonstrate? (118)
    a.   Social class is unimportant when it comes to encounters with teachers, police, and the general community.
    b.   The reputations that the boys acquired as teenagers disappeared once they reached adulthood.
    c.   The Saints were significantly less delinquent than the Roughnecks because they came from more solid middle-class families.
    d.   To understand what happened to the boys in the study, William Chambliss analyzed both the social structure and the patterns of social interaction that characterized their lives.

TRUE-FALSE QUESTIONS

1.   _____Being a teenager is an example of an achieved status. (95)
2.   _____The purpose of status symbols is to tell the world that you've made it to a particular place in society. (95)

3. _____Groups that we belong to generally don't have that much control over many aspects of our behavior. (97)
4. _____The mass media is an emerging social institution. (98-99)
5. _____The Amish are an example of a *Gemeinschaft* society. (101)
6. _____We have a tendency to make assumptions about a person based on his or her visible features; these stereotypes may affect how we act toward that person. (102)
7. _____The amount of personal space we prefer in our interactions is dependent upon our culture. (102, 107)
8. _____The same setting will rarely serve as both a back and a front stage. (108-109)
9. _____Studied nonobservance is a form of face-saving behavior. (110)
10. _____Sociologists have determined that both macrosociological perspectives are sufficient for understanding human behavior. (115, 118)

FILL-IN-THE-BLANK QUESTIONS

1. _____ is what people do when they are in the presence of one another. (92)
2. The down-to-earth sociology box on football mirrors social _____. (94)
3. Income, educated, and occupational prestige indicate _____. (95)
4. A _____ is one that cuts across the other statuses you hold. (95)
5. _____ are the behaviors, obligations, and privileges attached to a status. (96)
6. _____ view social institutions as working together to meet universal needs. (97)
7. As societies get larger, their _____ becomes more specialized. (101)
8. Hall and Hall found that North Americans use _____(#) different personal distance zones. (107)
9. When two or more people collaborate to manage impressions jointly, this is referred to as _____. (110)
10. Goffman called the techniques that we use to salvage a performance that is going bad as _____. (110)

ESSAY QUESTIONS

1. Choose a research topic and discuss how you approach this topic using both macrosociological and microsociological approaches.

2. The concept of a social structure is often difficult to grasp. Yet the social structure is a central organizing feature of social life. Identify the ways in which it takes shape in our society and in our lives.

3. Today we can see many examples of people wanting to recreate a simpler way of life. Using Tönnies' framework, analyze this tendency.

4. Assume that you have been asked to give a presentation to your sociology class on Goffman's dramaturgy approach. Describe what information you would want to include in such a presentation.

5. Differentiate between role conflict, role exit, and role strain, and give examples.

CHAPTER 5
HOW SOCIOLOGISTS DO RESEARCH

LEARNING OBJECTIVES
After reading Chapter 5, you should be able to:

1. Discuss which areas of human behavior and aspects of social life are valid topics for sociological research. (122)

2. Explain why there is a need for sociological research. (122-123)

3. List and describe the eight basic steps for conducting scientific research. (123-124)

4. Know and discuss the six research methods that sociologists use, the tools that they employ, and the strengths and limitations of each. (126-127, 129-130, 132, 134)

5. Cite the four primary factors that determine which research method or methods a sociologist uses to conduct his or her research. (134)

6. Define, describe, and discuss the significance of the various elements of the research process. (123-124)

7. Define, describe, and discuss the significance of the six research methods. (126-127, 129-130, 132, 134)

8. Distinguish between quantitative and qualitative research methods. (134)

9. Discuss the role that gender can play in sociological research. (136)

10. Know the ethical guidelines that sociologists are expected to follow and talk about the ethical issues raised in Mario Brajuha's and Laud Humphrey's research. (137-138)

11. Discuss how and why research and theory need to work together in order to fully explore and understand human behavior. (138-140)

Chapter Outline

I.   What is a Valid Sociological Topic?
    A.   Sociologists research just about every area of human behavior at both the macro and micro levels.
    B.   No human behavior is ineligible for research, whether it is routine or unusual, respectable or reprehensible.

II. Common Sense and the Need for Sociological Research

A. Commonsense cannot be relied on as a source of knowledge because it is often based on limited information.

B. To move beyond common sense and understand what is really going on, it is necessary to do sociological research.

III. A Research Model

A. Selecting a topic is guided by sociological curiosity, interest in a particular topic, research funding from a governmental or private source, and pressing social issues.

B. Defining the problem involves specifying what the researcher wants to learn about the topic.

C. Reviewing the literature uncovers existing knowledge about the problem, helps narrow down the problem and identify what areas need to be researched, and provides ideas about what questions to ask.

D. Formulating a hypothesis involves stating the expected relationship between variables based on predictions from a theory. Hypotheses need operational definitions, or precise ways to measure the variables.

E. Choosing a research method is influenced by the research topic and the questions that need to be answered.

F. Collecting the data involves concerns over validity (the extent to which operational definitions measure what was intended) and reliability (the extent to which data produce consistent results). Inadequate operational definitions and sampling hurt reliability.

G. Analyzing the results involves the use of either qualitative or quantitative techniques to analyze data. Computers have become powerful tools in data analysis because they reduce large amounts of data to basic patterns, take the drudgery out of analyzing data, allow the researcher to use a variety of statistical tests, and give the researcher more time to interpret the results.

H. By writing up and publishing the results, the findings are available for replication. That is, others can repeat your study to see if they come up with similar findings.

IV. Research Methods

A. Surveys involve collecting data by having people answer a series of questions.

1. The first step is to determine a population (the target group to be studied) and select a sample (individuals from within the target population who are intended to represent the population to be studied). Random samples are those where everyone in the target population has the same chance of being included in the study. A stratified random sample is a sample of specific subgroups (e.g., freshmen, sophomores, juniors) of the target population (a college or university) in which everyone in the subgroup has an equal chance of being included in the study.

2. The respondents (people who respond to a survey) must be allowed to express their own ideas so that the findings will not be biased.

3. The questionnaires can be administered either by asking respondents to complete the survey themselves (self-administered questionnaires) or by asking respondents the questions directly (interviews). The researcher must consider the

effects that interviewers have on respondents that lead to biased answers (interviewer bias) and whether to make the questions structured (closed-ended questions in which the answers are provided) or unstructured (open-ended questions that people answer in their own words).

4. It is important to establish rapport—a feeling of trust between researchers and subjects.

B. In participant observation, the researcher participates in a research setting while observing what happens in that setting.

1. Generalizability—the extent to which the findings from one group (or sample) can be generalized or applied to other groups (or populations)—is a problem in participant observation studies.

2. Results of participant observation studies can stimulate hypotheses and theories that can be tested in other settings using other research methods.

C. Secondary analysis, which is the analysis of data already collected by other researchers, is used when resources are limited and/or existing data may provide excellent sources of information. However, because the researcher did not directly carry out the research, he or she cannot be sure that the data were systematically gathered and accurately recorded, and biases were avoided.

D. Documents—or written sources—may be obtained from many sources, including books, newspapers, police reports, and records kept by various organizations.

E. Experiments are especially useful in determining causal relationships.

1. Experiments involve independent variables (factors that cause a change in something) and dependent variables (factors that are changed).

2. Experiments require an experimental group (subjects exposed to the independent variable) and a control group (subjects not exposed to the independent variable).

F. Unobtrusive measures involve observing social behavior of people who do not know they are being studied.

G. Deciding which method to use involves four primary factors.

1. The researcher must consider resources such as time and available money.

2. Access to subjects is important. The sample may be physically inaccessible to the researcher, thereby influencing the choice of methods.

3. The researcher takes into consideration the purpose of the research, choosing the method that will be most suitable for obtaining answers to the questions posed.

4. The researcher's background or training also influences the choice of methods. Those trained in use of quantitative research methods (emphasis is placed on precise measurement and the use of statistics and numbers) are likely to choose surveys, while those trained in use of qualitative research methods (emphasis is placed on describing and interpreting people's behavior) lean toward participant observation.

V. Controversy in Sociological Research

A. Social research can be very controversial be it private, political, etc. Often the findings of social research threaten those who have a stake in the matters being studied. Peter Rossi's study of the homeless population is an example of such controversy.

VI. Gender in Sociological Research
A. Because gender can be a significant factor in social research, researchers take steps to prevent it from biasing their findings.
B. Gender can also be an obstacle to doing research, particularly when the gender of the researcher is different from that of the research subjects and the topic under investigation is a sensitive one.
C. There are also questions regarding the degree to which findings from a sample made up exclusively of one gender can be generalized to the other.

VII. Ethics in Sociological Research
A. Ethics are of fundamental concern to sociologists when it comes to doing research.
B. Ethical considerations include being open, honest, and truthful, not harming the subject in the course of conducting the research, protecting the anonymity of the research subjects, and not misrepresenting themselves to the research subjects.
C. The Brajuha research demonstrates the lengths sociologists will go to in order to protect the anonymity of research subjects, while the Humphreys research illustrates questionable research ethics.

VIII. How Research and Theory Work Together
A. Sociologists combine research and theory in different ways. Theory is used to interpret data (i.e., functionalism, symbolic interaction, and conflict theory provide frameworks for interpreting research findings) and to generate research. Research helps to generate theory.
B. Real life situations often force researchers to conduct research in ways that fall short of the ideal.

Chapter Summary

Sociologists conduct research on almost every area of human behavior. The research conducted may be at the macro level, encompassing broad matters such as social structure, or at the micro level, which addresses individualistic and small group interaction. Sociological research is necessary for a variety of reasons. Research will confirm or deny the validity and extent of what is considered to be true simply because it "makes sense." Whereas culture has a significant impact on what one believes to be true, there needs to be a more objective manner in which to discover truth. Research provides the method through which truth can be discovered. To discover this truth, scientific research is used.

Henslin identifies eight steps in the scientific research model. These are (1) Selecting a topic; (2) Defining the problem; (3) Reviewing the literature; (4) Formulating a hypothesis; (5) Choosing a research method; (6) Collecting the data; (7) Analyzing the results; and (8) Sharing the results. Other authors may identify more than or less than eight steps, but the basic model remains the same. Two key elements to research are validity and reliability. Validity addresses whether or not the research measures what it is intended to measure. Reliability is the extent to which research produces consistent or dependable results.

In conducting research, sociologists choose between six research methods: (1) Survey; (2) Participant observation; (3) Secondary analysis; (4) Documents; (5) Unobtrusive measures; and (6) Experiments. Sociologists choose their research method(s) based on four primary factors: resources, access to subjects, purpose of the research, and the researcher's background.

There are a number of factors researchers must take into consideration beyond the research method chosen. Some of these are beyond the control of the researcher, such as a change in the subject's behavior because the subject knows he or she is being studied. Gender and race are also considerations that must be controlled by the researcher, especially when the sample being studied or the subject of the research is gender or race related. Gender and race can be significant confounding factors in sociological research, and sociologists need to take careful steps to prevent gender or race differences from biasing their findings.

Ethics are of fundamental concern to sociologists when it comes to doing research. Although sociologists are expected to follow ethical guidelines that require openness, honesty, truth, and the protection of research subjects, their studies can occasionally elicit great controversies. The Brajuha research created considerable controversy and legal complications over the protection of subjects. Laud Humphreys generated a national controversy by misleading subjects when conducting sensitive research about bisexual men's personal lives. A national columnist referred to his research as the product of "sociological snoopers." A court case loomed over his actions.

Although a vital part of sociology, research cannot stand alone any more than theory can stand alone. Research and theory need to work together in order to fully explore and understand human behavior. Theories need to be tested, which requires research. And research findings need to be explained, which requires theory. In short, research produces facts and theory provides a context for those facts.

KEY TERMS
After studying the chapter, review the definition for each of the following terms.

case study: an analysis of a single event, situation, or individual (130)

closed-ended questions: questions that are followed by a list of possible answers to be selected by the respondent (129)

control group: the subjects in an experiment who are not exposed to the independent variable (132)

dependent variable: a factor in an experiment that is changed by an independent variable (132, 134)

documents: in its narrow sense, written sources that provide data; in its extended sense, archival material of any sort, including photographs, movies, CDs, DVDs, and so on (130)

experiment: the use of *control* and *experimental* groups and *dependent* and *independent variables* to test causation (132)

experimental group: the group of subjects exposed to the independent variable in a study (132)

generalizability: the extent to which the findings from one group (or sample) can be generalized or applied to other groups (or populations) (130)

hypothesis: a statement of how variables are expected to be related to one another, often according to predictions from a theory (123)

independent variable: a factor that causes a change in another variable, called the dependent variable (132, 134)

interview: direct questioning of respondents (129)

interviewer bias: effects that interviewers have on respondents that lead to biased answers (129)

open-ended questions: questions that respondents answer in their own words (129)

operational definition: the way in which a researcher measures a variable (123)

participant observation (or fieldwork): research in which the researcher participates in a research setting while observing what is happening in that setting (129)

population: the target group to be studied (126-127)

qualitative research method: research in which the emphasis is placed on observing, describing and interpreting people's behavior (134)

quantitative research method: research in which the emphasis is placed on precise measurement; the use of statistics and numbers (134)

questionnaires: a list of questions to be asked of respondents (127)

random sample: a sample in which everyone in the target population has the same chance of being included in the study (126-127)

rapport: a feeling of trust between researchers and the people they are studying (129)

reliability: the extent to which research produces consistent or dependable results (124)

replication: the repetition of a study in order to test its findings (124)

research method (or research design): one of seven procedures that sociologists use to collect data: surveys, participant observation, case studies, secondary analysis, documents, experiments, and unobtrusive measures (124)

respondents: the people who respond to a survey, either in interviews or by self-administered questionnaires (127)

sample: the individuals intended to represent the population to be studied (126-127)

secondary analysis: the analysis of data that have been collected by other researchers (130)

self-administered questionnaires: questionnaires that respondents fill out (129)

stratified random sample: a sample from select subgroups of the target population in which everyone in these subgroups has an equal chance of being included in the research (127)

structured interviews: interviews that use closed-ended questions (129)

survey: the collection of data by having people answer a series of questions (126)

unobtrusive measures: the various ways of observing people so they do not know they are being studied (134)

unstructured interviews: interviews that use open-ended questions (129)

validity: the extent to which an operational definition measures what it was intended to measure (124)

variable: a factor thought to be significant for human behavior, which can vary (or change) from one case to another (123)

KEY PEOPLE
Review the major theoretical contributions or findings of these people.

Mario Brajuha: During an investigation into a restaurant fire, officials subpoenaed notes taken by this sociologist in connection with his research on restaurant work. He was threatened with jail. (137)

Laud Humphreys: This sociologist carried out doctoral research on homosexual activity but ran into problems when he misrepresented himself to his research subjects. Although he earned his doctorate degree, he was fired from his position because of his questionable ethics. (137-138)

C. Wright Mills: Mills argued that research without theory is of little value, simply a collection of unrelated "facts," and theory that is unconnected to research is abstract and empty, unlikely to represent the way life really is. (138)

Peter Rossi: Rossi produced a controversial piece of research related to counting of the homeless, which revealed that the average number of homeless on any given night was far less than homeless advocates had been stating. (135-136)

Diana Scully and Joseph Marolla: These two sociologists interviewed convicted rapists in prison and found that rapists are not sick or overwhelmed by uncontrollable urges; rather they are men who have learned to view rape as appropriate in various circumstances. (136, 138-139)

SELF-TEST

<u>**MULTIPLE CHOICE QUESTIONS**</u>

1. A researcher doing a macro level study would choose _____ as a topic. (122)
    a. waiting in public places
    b. race relations
    c. interactions between people on street corners
    d. meat packers at work

2. Sociologists believe that research is necessary because (122)
    a. common sense ideas may or may not be true.
    b. they want to move beyond guesswork.
    c. researchers want to know what really is going on.
    d. all of the above.

3. _____ steps are involved in scientific research. (123-124)
    a. Four
    b. Six
    c. Eight
    d. Ten

4. Which of the following is *not* a reason why researchers review the literature? (123)
    a. to help them narrow down the problem by pinpointing particular areas to examine.
    b. to develop ideas about how to do their own research.
    c. to insure that their research findings will confirm their hypotheses.
    d. to determine whether the problem has been answered already.

5. A relationship between or among variables is predicted (123)
    a. by a hypothesis.
    b. by use of operational definitions.
    c. when the researcher selects the topic to be studied.
    d. when the researcher is analyzing the results.

6. Why is validity important in the research process? (124)
    a. because the researcher wants to make sure his or her research will be published.
    b. because the researcher wants to be sure that his or her operational definitions are really measuring what they are intended to measure.
    c. because the researcher is ethically bound to produce valid results.
    d. because validity is what distinguishes scientific research from common sense.

7. In analyzing data gathered by participant observation, a researcher is likely to choose (129-130, 134)
    a. computer analysis.
    b. quantitative analysis.
    c. qualitative analysis.

d.   statistical analysis.

8.   Why are computers valuable in quantitative analysis? (134)
      a.   Sociologists can analyze huge amounts of information and identify basic patterns.
      b.   Computer software programs take much of the drudgery out of data analysis.
      c.   Researchers can try various statistical tests to see which prove the most valuable for analyzing their data.
      d.   All of the above.

9.   Based on Table 5.2 in your text, all of the following are ways to measure "average" *except* (126)
      a.   medial.
      b.   mean.
      c.   median.
      d.   mode.

10.   Which of the following is *not* a method for gathering data? (126-127, 129-130, 132, 134)
      a.   ethnomethodology
      b.   surveys
      c.   unobtrusive measures
      d.   secondary analysis

11.   You have decided to compare the experiences of freshmen and seniors. You identify students in the two classes you are interested in studying, and then you select a certain number from each group, making sure that each person has an equal chance of being selected. Which of the following sampling methods have you used? (126-127)
      a.   target sampling
      b.   random sampling
      c.   stratified random sampling
      d.   random subsampling

12.   Sometimes when a researcher is asking questions of a respondent face-to-face or over the telephone, the person may feel compelled to give "socially acceptable" answers. This outcome is due to (129)
      a.   asking open-ended questions.
      b.   rapport between the respondent and researcher.
      c.   interviewer bias.
      d.   interviewee bias.

13.   Why might a researcher "load the dice" in designing a research project? (128)
      a.   The researcher doesn't know any better.
      b.   The researcher may have a vested interest in the outcome of the research.
      c.   The researcher is short on time and money but still wants to get the desired results.
      d.   All of the above.

14. You have been hired to do a survey of a community's views on a proposed anti-crime program. With only a small budget, you need to contact at least 70 percent of the residents living in the affected areas within the next month. Which method are you *most* likely to choose? (126-127, 129-130)
    a. participant observation
    b. self-administered questionnaires
    c. interviews
    d. structured interviews

15. The advantage of structured interviews is that (129)
    a. they use open-ended questions to get in-depth responses.
    b. they are faster to administer and make it easier for answers to be coded.
    c. they make it possible to test hypotheses about cause and effect relationships.
    d. none of the above.

16. Problems that must be dealt with in conducting participant observation include (129-130)
    a. the researcher's personal characteristics.
    b. developing rapport with respondents.
    c. generalizability.
    d. all of the above.

17. Sources such as newspapers, diaries, bank records, police reports, household accounts, and immigration files are all considered (130)
    a. unreliable data sources.
    b. documents that provide useful information for investigating social life.
    c. useful for doing quantitative research but not valid when doing qualitative analysis.
    d. of limited validity because it would be difficult to replicate the study.

18. To study patterns of alcohol consumption in different neighborhoods you decide to go through the recycling bins and count the beer, wine, and liquor bottles. You would be using (134)
    a. participant observation.
    b. experimental methods.
    c. unobtrusive methods.
    d. qualitative methods.

19. Which method will a researcher use if he or she is interested in determining causal relationships? (132-133)
    a. an experiment
    b. survey research
    c. participant observation
    d. none of the above.

20. In an experiment, the group *not* exposed to the independent variable in the study is (132)
    a. the guinea pig group.
    b. the control group.

c. the experimental group.

d. the maintenance group.

21. When you analyze your data you find that men who abuse women are often drunk at the time the abuse takes place. How do sociologists refer to the simultaneous presence of both alcohol and abuse? (133)
    a. simulation
    b. correlation
    c. association
    d. intervening variable

22. Surveys are more likely to be used by researchers trained in (134)
    a. social psychology.
    b. ethnomethodology.
    c. quantitative research methods.
    d. qualitative research methods.

23. Why is it important to consider gender in planning and conducting research? (136)
    a. The gender of the interviewer might produce interviewer bias.
    b. It cannot be assumed that men and women experience the social work in the same way, so both need to be studied in order to have a complete picture.
    c. Gender is a significant factor in social life.
    d. All of the above.

24. Research ethics requires (137-138)
    a. openness.
    b. that a researcher not falsify results or plagiarize someone else's work.
    c. that research subjects should not be harmed by the research.
    d. all of the above.

25. Which of the following statements best describes the relationship between theory and research? (138-140)
    a. Research is really more important than theory, since it is research that proves or disproves common sense.
    b. Research and theory are both important, since research without theory is simply facts and theory without research is abstract and empty.
    c. Theory is really more important than research, since it is theory that provides the explanations for why people do what they do.
    d. Research should always follow theory, since theory is more important to sociology than research.

TRUE-FALSE QUESTIONS

1. _____Date rape is an acceptable topic for sociological research. (122)
2. _____In general, researchers give higher priority to reliability than validity. (124)

3. _____In survey research, it is undesirable for respondents to express their own opinions. (126)
4. _____Secondary analysis and use of documents mean the same thing in terms of research methods. (130, 132)
5. _____It is always unethical to observe social behavior in people when they do not know they are being studied. (137)
6. _____The purpose of an experiment is to identify causal relationships. (132-133)
7. _____Before a researcher can conclude that a cause-effect relationship exists, it is necessary to rule out possible spurious corrections. (133)
8. _____Quantitative research methods emphasize precise measurement, or the use of statistics and numbers. (134)
9. _____Research conducted by sociologists must meet professional ethical criteria. (137-138)
10. _____The research by Scully and Marolla demonstrates that research must be done under ideal conditions in order for the findings to be valid. (138-139)

FILL-IN-THE-BLANK QUESTIONS

1. A statement about the relationship between variables according to predictions from a theory is known as a _____. (123)
2. After you gather data, it is time to _____ them. (124)
3. A survey researcher needs to make sure questions are _____. (127)
4. In order to research topics such as domestic violence, it is important that the researcher establish _____with respondents. (129)
5. A sociologist who is studying the trash left behind in garbage cans is most likely engaging in the _____ method. (134)
6. The _____ variable causes a change in another variable. (132)
7. Sociologists trained in quantitative research methods are most likely to use the _____ method. (134)
8. Sometimes in research, one's gender can lead to _____ bias. (136)
9. C. Wright Mills argued that you cannot have research without _____. (138)
10. Systematic research and the application of theory take us beyond _____. (139)

ESSAY QUESTIONS

1. Choose a topic and explain how you would go through the different steps in the research model.

2. Discuss some of the things that can go wrong in the process of doing research and provide suggestions on how to overcome such problems.

3. The author of your text discusses six different research methods. Pick a research topic of interest to you and discuss how you might try to investigate this topic using these different

methods. In your answer, consider how a particular method may or may not be suitable for the topic under consideration.

4. Explain why ethical guidelines are necessary when conducting social science research.

5. Discuss the relationship between theory and research and why commonsense is not enough.

CHAPTER 6
SOCIETIES TO SOCIAL NETWORKS

LEARNING OBJECTIVES
After reading Chapter 6, you should be able to:

1. Know the essential feature of a group and why groups are said to be the essence of life in society. (144)

2. Identify the five types of societies that have developed in the course of human history, understand how they evolved, and cite their distinct forms of social division, social labor, and social inequality. (144-150)

3. Name the four technological innovations most responsible for the social transformations of society and talk about their respective roles in those transformations. (144-148)

4. Discuss how recent advances in human genetics, such as cloning and bioengineering, may be transforming society. (148-150)

5. Distinguish between the terms "aggregate," "category," and "group." (144, 151)

6. Describe the social characteristics, relationships, and/or functions that are associated with primary groups, secondary groups, in-groups and out-groups, reference groups, and social networks. (151, 153-154)

7. Know what the term "group dynamics" means and how group dynamics are affected by group size, types of leaders, and leadership styles. (156-159)

8. Identify and compare the two types of group leaders and the three types of group leadership styles commonly found within groups. (159-161)

9. Discuss the methodology, findings, and implications of the Asch experiment and the Milgram experiment as they relate, respectively, to peer pressure and obedience to authority. (161-163)

10. Define the term "groupthink," talk about why it is dangerous, and discuss what can and should be done to prevent it. (164)

I. **Societies and Their Transformation**

    A.   Groups are the essence of life in society; the groups to which we belong help determine our goals and values, how we feel about ourselves, and even how we feel about life itself.

    B.   An essential element of a social group is that its members have something in common and they believe what they have in common makes a difference.

    C.   Society, which consists of people who share a culture and a territory, is the largest and most complex group that sociologists study. As society changes, so does the nature and types of its groups.

    D.   The first societies were hunting and gathering societies.

        1.   Their survival depended on hunting animals and gathering plants. Since an area could only support a limited number of people who obtained food this way, the groups were small in size and nomadic, moving elsewhere when the food supply ran out.

        2.   They had few social divisions beyond that based on sex. There was usually a shaman—an individual thought to be able to influence spiritual forces—but his or her status was generally not much higher than that of everyone else.

        3.   The family was the basic unit—distributing food, educating the children, nursing the sick, etc.

        4.   Since what they gathered was perishable, they did not accumulate possessions. Of all societies, they were the most egalitarian.

    E.   Hunting and gathering societies were transformed into pastoral (characterized by the pasturing of animals) and horticultural (characterized by the growing of plants) societies as a result of the domestication revolution.

        1.   The domestication of plants and animals is called the first social revolution, although the process was extremely gradual.

        2.   The resulting societies created food surpluses that allowed for increased population size and some specialized division of labor.

        3.   Increased trade and interaction between groups developed and people began to accumulate objects they considered valuable.

        4.   As families or clans acquired more goods than others, feuds and wars erupted.

        5.   Leaders began to accumulate more of these possessions than other people, and to pass these advantages along to their descendants. As a result, simple equality began to give way to inequality.

    F.   The agricultural revolution (the second social revolution) occurred with the invention of the plow about 5,000 to 6,000 years ago. Pastoral and horticultural societies were transformed into agricultural societies.

        1.   Since plows pulled by animals were used instead of hoes and digging sticks, a much larger food surplus was produced. This allowed people to engage in activities other than farming.

        2.   Sometimes referred to as the dawn of civilization, this period produced the wheel, writing, and numbers. Cities developed and groups were distinguished by their greater or lesser possessions. An elite gained control of the surplus resources.

3. Social inequalities became a fundamental feature of social life. Those with greater resources surrounded themselves with armed men to protect their possessions and growing privileges. They began to levy taxes on their "subjects." This concentration of resources and power, along with the oppression of the powerless, was the forerunner of the state.

4. Females became subjugated to males; Elise Boulding suggests that this change occurred because men were in charge of plowing and the cows.

G. The Industrial Revolution (the third social revolution) began in 1765, when the steam engine was first used to run machinery in Great Britain. Agricultural societies were transformed into industrial societies.

1. The industrial societies developed and harnessed many mechanical power sources, resulting in a dramatic shift from agriculture to manufacturing as the major sources of power, wealth, and prestige.

2. Initially, social inequality increased greatly, as did the size of the population. The individuals who first utilized the new technology accumulated great wealth, controlling the means of production and dictating the conditions under which people could work for them. A huge surplus of labor developed as masses of people were thrown off the land their ancestors had farmed.

3. Initially denied the right to unionize or strike, workers eventually won their demands for better living conditions. The consequence was that wealth spread to larger segments of society.

4. As industrialization continued, the pattern of growing inequality was reversed. Indicators of greater equality include better housing, a vast increase in consumer goods, the abolition of slavery, and more representative political systems.

H. Industrial societies are being transformed into postindustrial societies; these social changes are linked to the new technology of the microchip.

1. Postindustrial societies are moving away from production and manufacturing to service industries. The basic component of this new society is information.

2. The United States was the first country to have more than 50 percent of its workforce employed in service industries. Australia, New Zealand, Western Europe, and Japan soon followed.

3. Social analysts are suggesting that we are witnessing a fourth social revolution because our way of life has been radically transformed by the microchip.

I. Some social analysts believe that another new type of society, called biotech society, is emerging.

1. Its origins go back to either the identification of the double-helix structure of DNA or the decoding of the human genome. Its chief characteristic will be an economy that centers on the application of genetic structures.

2. Biotechnology is already replacing biology, and biochemistry is replacing chemistry.

3. It is not clear whether this is a society that will replace the postindustrial society or simply be another aspect of this information-based society. Regardless, we can look forward to revolutionary changes in health care and maybe even the human species.

J.   As society is transformed, so are we. These changes even affect the way we think about ourselves and the way we live our lives. Not all societies go through all the stages; many societies today reflect a mixture of the different types.

II.   Groups Within Society

A.   Groups are viewed as a buffer between individuals and society.
1.   Durkheim believed that small groups serve as a sort of lifeline that helps prevent anomie.
2.   Sociologists distinguish between aggregates, categories, and groups. An aggregate is made up of individuals who temporarily share the same physical space but do not have a sense of belonging together. A category is a collection of people who have similar characteristics. Unlike groups, the individuals who make up aggregates or categories do not interact with one another or take each other into account.

B.   Sociologist Charles Cooley used the term "primary group" to refer to groups characterized by cooperative, intimate, long-term, and face-to-face relationships.
1.   The group becomes part of the individual's identity and the lens through which life is viewed.
2.   It is essential to an individual's psychological well-being as humans have an intense need for associations that promote feelings of self-esteem.

C.   Secondary groups are larger, relatively temporary, more anonymous, formal, and impersonal than primary groups, and are based on some interest or activity.
1.   Members are likely to interact on the basis of specific roles, such as president, manager, worker, or student.
2.   In industrial societies, secondary groups have multiplied and become essential to our welfare.
3.   Secondary groups tend to break down into primary groups within the larger group, such as friendship cliques at school or work. The primary group serves as a buffer between the individual and the needs of the secondary group.

D.   Groups toward which individuals feel loyalty are called in-groups, while those toward which they feel antagonisms are called out-groups.
1.   The division is significant sociologically because in-groups provide a sense of identification or belonging, which often produce rivalries between groups.
2.   In-group membership leads to discrimination; given our loyalty, we favor members of our in-group. Sociologist Robert Merton identified a double standard produced by this: The behaviors by members of an in-group are seen as virtues, while the same behaviors by members of an out-group are viewed as vices.
3.   Dividing the world into "we" and "them" can sometimes lead to acts directed against the out-groups.

E.   Reference groups are the groups we use as standards to evaluate ourselves, whether or not we actually belong to those groups.
1.   They exert great influence over our behavior; people may change their clothing, hairstyle, speech, and other characteristics to match what the reference group would expect of them.
2.   Having two reference groups that clearly conflict with each other can produce intense internal conflict.

F. Social networks consist of people linked by various social ties. Clusters, or factions that form within large groups, are called cliques. Cliques, family, friends, and acquaintances can all be bases for social networks.

1. Interaction takes place within social networks that connect us to the larger society.

2. One of the ways in which people are expanding their social networks is through Facebook, an electronic way to meet "friends."

3. Stanley Milgram did an experiment that demonstrated how small our social world really is. He found that social networks are so interrelated that almost everyone in the United States is connected by just five links.

4. One reason it is so difficult to overcome social inequality is because our social networks contribute to inequality.

III. Group Dynamics

A. How individuals affect groups and groups affect individuals is known as group dynamics.

1. The study of group dynamics focuses on group size, leadership, conformity, and decision making.

2. Sociologists recognize a small group as one that is small enough for everyone in it to interact directly with all the other members.

B. As Georg Simmel noted, the size of the group is significant for its dynamics.

1. A dyad is a social group containing two members. It is the smallest and most fragile of all human groupings. Marriages and love affairs are examples: If one member loses interest, the dyad collapses.

2. A triad is a group of three persons—a married couple with a first child, for example. Triads basically are stronger than dyads but are still extremely unstable. It is not uncommon for coalitions to form in which there is alignment of some members of the group against another. Often, one member becomes an arbitrator or mediator because he or she always tries to settle disagreements between the other two members of the group.

3. As more members are added to a group, intensity decreases and stability increases because there are more linkages between more people within the group. The groups develop a more formal structure to accomplish their goals by having, for instance, a president, treasurer, and so on. This structure enables groups to survive over time.

4. Research by Darley and Latané found that as groups grow larger they tend to break into smaller groups, people are less willing to take individual responsibility (diffusion of responsibility), and they interact more formally toward one another.

C. A leader may be defined as someone who influences the behavior of others.

1. There are two types of group leaders. Instrumental (task-oriented) leaders try to keep the group moving toward its goals, reminding the members of what they are trying to accomplish. Expressive (socioemotional) leaders are less likely to be recognized as leaders but help with the group's morale. These leaders may have to minimize the friction that instrumental leaders necessarily create.

2. There are three types of leadership styles. Authoritarian leaders give orders and frequently do not explain why they praise or condemn a person's work.

Democratic leaders try to gain a consensus by explaining proposed actions, suggesting alternative approaches, and giving "facts" as the basis for their evaluation of the members' work. Laissez-faire leaders are very passive and give the group almost total freedom to do as it wishes.

3. Psychologists Ronald Lippitt and Ralph White discovered that the leadership styles produced different results when used on small groups of young boys. Under authoritarian leaders the boys became either aggressive or apathetic; under democratic leaders they were more personal and friendly; and under laissez-faire leaders they asked more questions, made fewer decisions, and were notable for their lack of achievement.

4. Different situations require different leadership styles.

5. Sociologists would disagree that people are born to be leaders. Rather they find that people with certain characteristics are more likely to become leaders. Those who represent the group's values are seen as capable of leading the group out of crisis, are more talkative, express determination and self-confidence, are taller or are judged better looking.

D. A study by Dr. Solomon Asch indicates that people are strongly influenced by peer pressure. Asch was interested in seeing whether individuals would resist the temptation to change a correct response to an incorrect response because of peer pressure.

1. Asch held cards up in front of small groups of people and asked which sets of cards matched; one at a time, they were supposed to respond aloud. All but one of the group members was a confederate, having been told in advance by the researcher how to answer the question.

2. After two trials in which everyone answered correctly, the confederates intentionally answered incorrectly, as they had previously been instructed to do.

3. Of the 50 people tested, 33 percent ended up giving the incorrect answers at least half of the time, even though they knew the answers were wrong; only 25 percent always gave the right answer despite the peer pressure.

E. Dr. Stanley Milgram sought to determine why otherwise "good people" apparently participated in the Nazis' slaughter of Jews and others.

1. He conducted experiments in which one person (the "teacher") was instructed to administer an electric shock to the other person (the "learner") for each wrong answer given to certain questions and to increase the voltage of the shock after each wrong answer.

2. In fact, the "learner" was playing a role, intentionally giving wrong answers but only pretending to be receiving an electrical shock.

3. Since a person in apparent authority (scientist, white coat, university laboratory) continually stated that the experiment had to go on, most of the "teachers" gave in to that authority and continued to administer the "shocks" even when they appeared to produce extreme pain.

4. The scientific community was disturbed not only by Milgram's findings, but also by his methods. Associations of social researchers accordingly adopted codes of ethics to require that subjects be informed of the nature and purpose of social research, and almost all deception was banned.

F.   Sociologist Irving Janis coined the word "groupthink" to refer to situations in which a group of people thinks alike and any suggestion of alternatives becomes a sign of disloyalty. Even moral judgments are put aside for the perceived welfare of the group.
1.   The Asch and Milgram experiments demonstrate how groupthink can develop.
2.   U.S. history provides examples of governmental groupthink: presidents and their inner circles have committed themselves to a single course of action (e.g., refusal to believe the Japanese might attack Pearl Harbor; continuing and expanding the war in Vietnam; and the Watergate scandal) even when objective evidence showed the course to be wrong. The leaders became cut off from information that did not coincide with their own opinions.
3.   Groupthink can be prevented only by insuring that leaders regularly are exposed to individuals who have views conflicting with those of the inner circle.

Chapter Summary

Groups are the essence of life in society. We become who we are because of our membership in human groups. The essential feature of a group is that its members have something in common and that they believe that what they have in common is significant. The largest and most complex group that sociologists study is society (people who share a culture and a territory). Because of what appears to be a "natural" need for human kind to share culture, territory, and to seek significant others, societies developed.

Anthropologists and sociologists have identified five types of societies that have developed in the course of human history. These five types of societies include hunting and gathering, pastoral and horticultural, agricultural, industrial, and postindustrial societies. Distinct forms of social division, social labor, and social inequality characterize each.

The hunting and gathering society has the fewest social divisions and is the most egalitarian. In this society, the men hunt large animals and the women usually gather edible plants, fruits, and other food found growing in the wild. The first social revolution was based on the domestication of plants and animals. This resulted in the development of the pastoral society, which concentrated on the herding of animals, and the horticultural society, which specialized in planting and harvesting crops. The horticultural society made it possible for permanent settlements to be established since it was no longer necessary for people to follow the food supply. In the third social revolution, the invention of the plow made it possible for large areas of land to be cultivated and harvested. The society that developed, known as the agricultural society, made large cities possible because it freed some members of society from being dedicated to the production of their own food. In the fourth social revolution, the invention of the steam engine introduced the industrial society, which concentrated on the manufacturing and consumption of goods. The fifth social revolution occurred with the invention of the microchip. In this postindustrial society, the emphasis is on the development and transfer of technology, information, and knowledge. A bio-economic society, believed to be emerging in the 21st century, is based on the decoding of the human genome. Some sociologists, however, believe this latest revolution is only an extension of the postindustrial society. Regardless of the change that occurs, technological innovation is critical to the development and transformation of societies.

Regardless of the technological significance of the society, all societies have a tendency to overpower the individual. This is most pronounced in the postindustrial society in which most of us now live. According to Emile Durkheim, small groups serve as a buffer between the individual and the complications and difficulty the larger society presents to the individual.

Groups can be typed in terms of their social relationships and functions. Different types of groups within society include primary groups, secondary groups, in-groups and out-groups, reference groups, and social networks.

To better understand how different groups work, sociologists study group dynamics, or the ways in which individuals affect groups and the ways in which groups influence individuals. Georg Simmel was one of the first sociologists to extensively study group size and the relationship between group members.

Group dynamics are affected by group size, types of leaders, and leadership styles. As small groups become larger, they become more stable and less intimate. Group leaders can be instrumental (task oriented) or expressive (socioemotional). Leadership styles include authoritarian (leaders who give orders), democratic (leaders who work toward and/or forge a consensus), and laissez-faire (leaders who are highly permissive).

Groups have a significant degree of influence over people's attitudes and actions. The Asch experiment demonstrated how difficult it is for individuals to resist peer pressure and how they have a need to belong. The Milgram experiment showed how difficult it is for individuals to challenge people in positions of authority.

A potentially dangerous aspect of a group's influence over its members is groupthink, a narrowing of thought by a group of people, leading to the perception that there is only one correct answer to which all members of the group are impelled, by loyalty and trust, to accept. The two space shuttle disasters (Challenger and Columbia) are examples of how NASA engineers had a limited view of their options in either launching or landing the shuttle. In each case, the decision resulted in a disaster. The key to preventing groupthink is to encourage and circulate research results that provide the greatest number of options for decision makers to consider in an atmosphere of free expression and academic freedom.

KEY TERMS
After studying the chapter, review the definition for each of the following terms.

aggregate: individuals who temporarily share the same physical space but do not see themselves as belonging together (151)

agricultural revolution: the second social revolution based on the invention of the plow, which led to agricultural societies (145-146)

agricultural society: a society based on large-scale agriculture (145-146)

authoritarian leader: an individual who leads by giving orders (160)

biotech society: a society whose economy increasingly centers on the application of genetics to produce medicine, food, and materials (148)

category: people who have similar characteristics (151)

clique: a cluster of people within a larger group who choose to interact with one another (154)

coalition: the alignment of some members of a group against others (157)

democratic leader: an individual who leads by trying to reach a consensus (160)

domestication revolution: the first social revolution, based on the domestication of plants and animals, which led to pastoral and horticultural societies (145)

dyad: the smallest possible group, consisting of two persons (156)

expressive leader: an individual who increases harmony and minimizes conflict in a group; also known as a *socioemotional leader* (159)

group: people who have something in common and believe that what they have in common is significant; also called a social group (144)

group dynamics: the ways in which individuals affect groups and the ways in which groups affect individuals (156)

groupthink: a narrowing of thought by a group of people, leading to the perception that there is only one correct answer and to even suggest alternatives becomes a sign of disloyalty (164)

horticultural society: a society based on cultivating plants by the use of hand tools (145)

hunting and gathering society: a human group that depends on hunting and gathering for its survival (144)

Industrial Revolution: the third social revolution, occurring when machines powered by fuels replaced most animal and human power (147-148)

industrial society: a society based on the use of machines powered by fuels (147-148)

in-groups: groups toward which people feel loyalty (153)

instrumental leader: an individual who tries to keep the group moving toward its goals; also known as a *task-oriented leader* (159)

laissez-faire leader: an individual who leads by being highly permissive (160)

leader: someone who influences other people (159)

leadership styles: ways in which people express their leadership (160)

out-groups: groups toward which people feel antagonism (153)

pastoral society: a society based on the pasturing of animals (145)

postindustrial (information) society: a society based on information, services, and high technology, rather than on raw materials and manufacturing (148)

primary group: a group characterized by intimate, long-term, face-to-face association and cooperation (151)

reference group: a group whose standards we refer to as we evaluate ourselves (154)

secondary group: compared with a primary group, a larger, relatively temporary, more anonymous, formal, and impersonal group based on some interest or activity (151)

shaman: the healing specialist of a tribe who attempts to control the spirits thought to cause a disease or injury; commonly called a witch doctor (144)

small group: a group small enough for everyone to interact directly with all the other members (156)

social network: the social ties radiating outward from the self that link people together (154)

society: people who share a culture and a territory (144)

triad: a group of three people (157)

KEY PEOPLE

Review the major theoretical contributions or findings of these people.

Solomon Asch: Asch is famous for his research on conformity to peer pressure. (161-162)

Herbert Blumer: He describes an industrial society as one in which goods are no longer produced by the brute force of humans or animals but by machines powered by fuels. (147)

Elise Boulding: This sociologist hypothesized that women's status in agricultural societies declined sharply once men were put in charge of plowing and the cows. (147)

Charles Cooley: It was Cooley who noted the central role of primary groups in the development of one's sense of self. (151)

John Darley and Bibb Latané: These researchers investigated how group size affects members' attitudes and behaviors. They found that as the group grew, individuals' sense of responsibility diminished, their interactions became more formal, and the larger group tends to break down into small ones. (158-159)

Emile Durkheim: Durkheim viewed the small group as a buffer between the individual and society, helping to prevent anomie. (150)

Lloyd Howells and Selwyn Becker: These social psychologists found that factors such as location within a group underlie people's choices of leaders. (159)

Irving Janis: Janis coined the term "groupthink" to refer to the tunnel vision that a group of people sometimes develops. (164)

Ronald Lippitt and Ralph White: These social psychologists carried out a classic study on leadership styles and found that the style of leadership affected the behavior of group members. (160-161)

Robert Merton: Merton observed that the traits of in-groups become viewed as virtues, while those same traits in out-groups are seen as vices. (153)

Stanley Milgram: Milgram's research has contributed greatly to sociological knowledge of group life. He did research on social networks and individual conformity to group pressure. (155-156, 160, 162-163)

Georg Simmel: This early sociologist was one of the first to note the significance of group size; he used the terms dyad and triad to describe small groups. (156-157)

SELF-TEST

MULTIPLE CHOICE QUESTIONS

1. What is the largest and most complex group that sociologists study? (144)
   a. the global community
   b. a society
   c. a nation-state
   d. a secondary group

2. Which of the following is *not* a characteristic of hunting and gathering societies? (144)
   a. They have the fewest social divisions.
   b. Usually a shaman is part of this society.
   c. They consist of 50-100 members.
   d. They accumulate few personal possessions.

3. Of all types of societies, which is the simplest? (144)
   a. hunting and gathering societies
   b. horticultural societies
   c. agricultural societies
   d. industrial societies

4. On what are pastoral societies based? (145)
   a. the cultivation of plants
   b. the pasturing of animals
   c. the invention of the plow
   d. large-scale agriculture

5. Which of the following was a consequence of the domestication revolution? (145)
   a. Human groups became larger.
   b. A food surplus was created.
   c. The division of labor became more specialized.
   d. All of the above.

6. The plow's invention ushered in a new type of society called (145-146)
   a. a pastoral society.
   b. a farming society.
   c. an agricultural society.
   d. an agrarian society.

7. In an industrial society, which of the following was an indicator of increasing equality? (147)
   a. better housing
   b. the abolition of slavery
   c. a move toward more representative political systems
   d. all of the above.

8. On what is postindustrial society based? (148)
   a. information, services, and high technology
   b. emphasis on raw materials
   c. the production of new products
   d. all of the above

9. Which was the first to have more than 50 percent of its work force in the service sector? (148)
   a. Japan
   b. the United States
   c. Australia
   d. Great Britain

10. A society in which the economy centers around the application of human genetics for medicine and plant genetics for the production of food (148)
    a. is associated with the identification of the double-helix structure of DNA.
    b. is the decoding of the human genome in 2000.
    c. may represent a new type of society or simply another aspect of postindustrial society.
    d. all of the above.

11. According to Emile Durkheim, what is the value of small groups? (150)
    a. They promote diversity.
    b. They generate change.
    c. They prevent anomie.
    d. They encourage conformity.

12. According to Cooley, which are essential to an individual's psychological well-being? (151)
    a. primary groups
    b. secondary groups
    c. therapy groups
    d. interpersonal groups

13. Secondary groups (151)
    a. have members who are likely to interact on the basis of specific roles.
    b. are characteristic of industrial societies.
    c. are essential to the functioning of contemporary societies.
    d. all of the above.

14. How do sociologists refer to groups that provide a sense of identification or belonging? (153)
    a. personal groups
    b. in-groups
    c. my-group
    d. homeboys' groups

15. What are some of the consequences of in-group membership? (153)
    a. discrimination
    b. hatred
    c. killing
    d. all of the above

16. If Sue wanted a promotion to a supervisory position, managers in her company would serve as which type of group to her? (154)
    a. primary
    b. secondary
    c. reference
    d. aggregate

17. What term describes the social ties radiating out from the self, linking people together? (154)
    a. social networks
    b. reference groups
    c. cliques
    d. inner-circles

18. In Milgram's small world study, which method of communication did he use to determine how many degrees of separation existed between two target people? (155)
    a. letters
    b. facebooking
    c. telecommuting
    d. facesaving

19. Dyads (156)
    a. are the most intense or intimate of human groups.
    b. require continuing active participation and commitment of both members.
    c. are the most unstable of social groups.
    d. all of the above.

20. Which of the following is *not* a characteristic of a triad? (157)
    a. The introduction of a third person into a dyad reduces the intensity of the interactions.
    b. A triad is inherently unstable because coalitions can form.
    c. One of the members of the group often acts as an arbitrator or mediator.
    d. The continuation of the group depends on the success of the arbitrator in settling

21. A diffusion of responsibility occurs (158)
    a. when someone does not identify with a reference group.
    b. when someone feels excluded from a coalition.
    c. when a group is larger than a dyad and each member feels that someone else will act.
    d. when the leadership is authoritarian.

22. An expressive leader (159)
    a.   tries to keep the group moving toward its goals.
    b.   is also known as a task-oriented leader.
    c.   increases harmony and minimizes conflict in a group.
    d.   is the director of the drama club.

23. According to Lippitt and White, which type of leader is *best* for most situations? (161)
    a.   authoritarian
    b.   democratic
    c.   laissez-faire
    d.   instrumental

24. According to sociologists, leaders tend to have certain characteristics that may include (159)
    a.   how they are more outgoing.
    b.   that they tend to be taller and are judged better-looking than others.
    c.   where they sit in a group.
    d.   all of the above.

25. What did the Milgram experiment demonstrate? (162-163)
    a.   that people who know they are being studied will behave differently as a result.
    b.   that peer groups have an awesome influence over their members.
    c.   that people are strongly influenced by authority.
    d.   that political leaders can become isolated.

TRUE-FALSE QUESTIONS

1. _____Society is the largest and most complex group that sociologists study. (144)
2. _____According to Elise Boulding, women's status in agricultural societies increased with the development of metals that were then attached to plows. (145-147)
3. _____Anomie is most likely to occur in the absence of ties to primary groups. (150)
4. _____Robert Merton observed that traits of our in-groups tend to be viewed as virtues, while those same traits are seen as vices when found among members of out-groups. (153)
5. _____Research by Stanley Milgram demonstrates how small our social world really is. (155-156)
6. _____As a small group grows larger, its intensity decreases and its stability increases. (158-159)
7. _____Researchers have demonstrated that group size is a factor in determining whether strangers will help one another when a problem arises. (158-159)
8. _____Sociologically speaking, a leader is one who is officially appointed or elected to be the "leader." (159)
9. _____The laissez-faire leadership style often leads to fewer results and decisions being made. (160)
10. _____The Columbia space shuttle disaster is an example of groupthink. (164)

FILL-IN-THE-BLANK QUESTIONS

1. _____ societies are based on the cultivation of plants by the use of hand tools. (144)

2. Emile Durkheim wondered what could be done to prevent _____ in society. (150)

3. The _____ gives us our basic orientation to life. (151)

4. A _____ group provides a yardstick to evaluate ourselves. (154)

5. A clique is synonymous with the term internal _____. (154)

6. A group of individuals aligned against others is referred to as a _____. (157)

7. Instrumental leaders tend to be _____ oriented. (159)

8. Milgram found that it took an average of _____ jumps for letters to reach designated individuals in his "small world phenomenon" experiment. (155-156)

9. As group size increases, stability _____ and intimacy _____. (158)

10. Irving Janis coined the term _____. (164)

ESSAY QUESTIONS

1. After summarizing the fundamental social changes that resulted from each of the different social revolutions, evaluate the degree to which the new technology of the microchip is contributing to a similar level of fundamental change.

2. Durkheim was among the first sociologists to argue that small groups stand as a buffer between the individual and the larger society. The author of your text notes that secondary groups today have become essential to our welfare, yet they fail to satisfy our deep needs for intimate association. In this essay, consider how it is possible that they are essential for our welfare if they fail to satisfy essential human needs.

3. Explain the three different leadership styles and suggest reasons why the democratic leader is the best style of leader for most situations.

4. Explore the factors that influence the emergence of groupthink and consider strategies for minimizing the development of this collective tunnel vision.

5. Discuss how the size of the group affects attitudes and behavior.

CHAPTER 7
BUREAUCRACY AND FORMAL ORGANIZATIONS

LEARNING OBJECTIVES
After reading Chapter 7, you should be able to:

1. Define the rationalization of society and discuss its ramifications. (168-169)

2. Differentiate between the views of Karl Marx and Max Weber on what led to the rationalization of society. (169-170)

3. List and discuss the characteristics of bureaucracies. (171-173)

4. Understand the difference between "ideal" and "real" bureaucracy. (174)

5. Cite and discuss examples of the dysfunctions of bureaucracies. (174-176)

6. Describe the concept of alienation. Differentiate between Marx's and Weber's perceptions of alienation, and discuss various attempts by workers to resist it. (175)

7. Know how bureaucracies perpetuate themselves. (176-177)

8. Explain the sociological significance of bureaucracies. (171-177)

9. Contrast bureaucracies with voluntary organizations. (171-178)

10. Discuss the functions of voluntary organizations and the problem of oligarchy. (178)

11. Describe and evaluate the different steps many corporations have taken to humanize their work settings and maximize the potential of their employees. (180-181)

12. Discuss the conflict perspective's critique of corporate attempts to humanize the work setting. (181)

13. Understand the hidden corporate culture and its ramifications on women and minority employees. (181-182)

14. Explain the role technology currently plays in the control of workers and how that role may soon be expanding. (183)

Chapter Outline

I.   The Rationalization of Society
   A.   Rationality—the acceptance of rules, efficiency, and practical results as the right way to approach human affairs—is a characteristic of industrial societies.

B. Historically, the traditional orientation to life is based on the idea that the past is the best guide for the present; however, this orientation stands in the way of industrialization.
   1. Capitalism requires a shift in people's thinking, away from the idea that "This is the way we've always done it" to "Let's find the most efficient way to do it."
   2. Personal relationships are replaced by impersonal, short-term contracts.
   3. The "bottom line" becomes the primary concern.
C. Marx said that the development of capitalism caused people to change their way of thinking, not the other way around. Because capitalism was more efficient—it produced the things in greater abundance and it yielded high profits—people changed their ideas.
D. Weber believed that religion held the key to understanding the development of capitalism.
   1. He noted that capitalism emerged first in predominantly Protestant countries.
   2. In *The Protestant Ethic and the Spirit of Capitalism*, Weber proposed that a set of behaviors rooted in Protestantism led to the development of capitalist activity and the rationalization of society.
   3. Weber argued that because of the Calvinistic belief in predestination, people wanted to show they were among the chosen of God. Financial success in life became a sign of God's approval; however, money was not to be spent on oneself. Rather, the investment of profits became an outlet for their excess money, while the success of those investments became a further sign of God's approval.
   4. Because capitalism demands rationalization (the careful calculation of practical results), traditional ways of doing things, if inefficient, must be replaced, for what counts are the results.
E. No one has yet been able to establish which view is correct. Consequently, the two continue to exist side by side within sociology.

II. Formal Organizations and Bureaucracies
A. Formal organizations—secondary groups designed to achieve explicit objectives— have become a central feature of contemporary life.
B. Early examples of formal organizations were guilds and the army. With industrialization, secondary groups became more common. Formal organizations, especially as they increase in size, tend to develop into bureaucracies.
C. Max Weber identified the essential characteristics of bureaucracies, which help these organizations reach their goals, as well as grow and endure. These include the following:
   1. a hierarchy where assignments flow downward and accountability flows upward.
   2. a division of labor.
   3. written rules.
   4. written communications and records.
   5. impersonality.

D. Weber's characteristics of bureaucracy describe an ideal type—a composite of characteristics based on many specific examples. The real nature of bureaucracy often differs from its ideal image.

E. Weber's model only accounts for part of the characteristics of bureaucracies. Dysfunctions can also be identified.

1. Red tape, or the strict adherence to rules, results in nothing getting accomplished.

2. A lack of communication between units means that they are sometimes working at cross purposes; sometimes one unit "undoes" what another unit has accomplished because the two fail to inform one another what each is doing.

3. Bureaucratic alienation—a feeling of powerlessness and normlessness—occurs when workers are assigned to repetitive tasks in order for the corporation to achieve efficient production, thereby cutting them off from the product of their labor.

4. To resist alienation, workers form primary groups within the larger secondary organization, relating to one another not just as workers, but also as people who value one another.

5. The alienated bureaucrat is one who feels trapped in the job, does not take initiative, will not do anything beyond what she or he is absolutely required to do, and uses rules to justify doing as little as possible.

6. Bureaucratic incompetence is reflected in the Peter principle—members of an organization are promoted for good work until they reach their level of incompetence. If this principle were generally true, then bureaucracies would be staffed by incompetents and would fail. In reality, bureaucracies are highly successful.

F. Goal displacement occurs when an organization adopts new goals after the original goals have been achieved and there is no longer any reason for it to continue.

1. The March of Dimes is an example of this.

2. It was originally formed to fight polio, but when that threat was eliminated, the professional staff found a new cause: birth defects.

3. With the possibility of birth defects some day being eliminated as our knowledge of human genes expands, the organization has adopted a new slogan—breakthroughs for babies—which is vague enough to ensure their perpetual existence.

G. To the sociologist, bureaucracies are significant because they represent a fundamental change in how people relate to one another. Prior to this rationalization, work focused on human needs, such as making sure that everyone had an opportunity to earn a living; with rationalization, the focus shifts to efficiency in performing tasks and improving the bottom line.

III. Voluntary Associations

A. Voluntary associations are groups made up of volunteers who have organized on the basis of some mutual interest.

B. All voluntary associations have one or more of the following functions:

1. to advance the particular interests they represent (e.g., youth in Scouting programs).

2. to offer people an identity and, for some, a sense of purpose in life.
3. to help govern the nation and maintain social order (e.g., Red Cross disaster aid).

C. Some voluntary associations have the following functions:
1. to mediate between the government and the individual.
2. to train people in organizational skills so they can climb the occupational ladder.
3. to help bring disadvantaged groups into the political mainstream.
4. to challenge society's definitions of what is "normal" and socially acceptable.

D. Voluntary associations represent no single interest or purpose. The idea of mutual interest is characteristic of all voluntary associations; a shared interest in some view or activity is the tie that binds members together.
1. The motivation for joining a group differs widely among its members, from the expression of strong convictions to the cultivation of personal contacts.
2. Because of this, membership turnover tends to be high.

E. Within voluntary associations is an inner core of individuals who stand firmly behind the group's goals and are committed to maintaining the organization. Robert Michels used the term "iron law of oligarchy" to refer to the tendency of this inner core to dominate the organization by becoming a small, self-perpetuating elite.
1. Some are disturbed when an oligarchy develops and many people are subsequently excluded from leadership because they don't reflect the inner circle's values or background.
2. If the oligarchy gets too far out of line with the membership, it runs the risk of rebellion by the grassroots.

IV. Working for the Corporation
A. Humanizing the Work Setting
1. Weber believed that bureaucracies would eventually dominate social life because of their efficiency and capacity to replace themselves.
2. Humanizing a work setting refers to efforts to organize the workplace in such a way that it develops rather than impedes human potential.
3. Corporate attempts to make work organizations more humane include the following:
(a) Work teams: Within these groups workers are able to establish primary relationships with other workers so that their identities are tied up with their group; the group's success becomes the individual's success.
(b) Corporate day care facilities at work: These ease the strain on parents, leading to reduced turnover, less absenteeism, and shorter maternity leaves.
(c) Conflict theorists point out that the basic relationship between workers and owners is confrontational regardless of how the work organization is structured. Their basic interests are fundamentally opposed.

B. Fads in Corporate Culture
1. Quality circles: These are small groups of workers and a manager or two who meet regularly to try and improve the quality of the work setting and the product.

2. Emotional integration: Corporations use a variety of activities, such as cook-offs or running marathons together, to help with teambuilding.

C. Self-Fulfilling Stereotypes in the "Hidden" Corporate Culture
1. Rosabeth Moss Kanter's organizational research demonstrates that the corporate culture contains hidden values that create a self-fulfilling prophecy that affects people's careers.
2. The elite have an image of who is most likely to succeed. Those whose backgrounds are similar to the elite and who look like the elite are singled out and provided with better access to information, networking, and "fast track" positions. Workers who are given opportunities to advance tend to outperform others and are more committed.
3. Those who are judged outsiders and experience few opportunities think poorly of themselves, are less committed, and work below their potential.
4. The hidden values of the corporate culture that create this self-fulfilling prophecy are largely invisible.

D. Grappling with Diversity in the Corporation
1. With more than half the U.S. workforce consisting of minorities, immigrants, and women, dealing with diversity in the workplace is becoming unavoidable.
2. Most large companies have diversity training to help employees work successfully with those of different backgrounds.
3. Data gathered by the Equal Employment Opportunity Commission indicate diversity training has little effect and, in some cases, a negative effect. It depends on the type of program. Specifically, those aimed at setting goals for increasing diversity and holding managers accountable tend to be successful.

V. Technology and the Control of Workers
A. While the computer has the capacity to improve the quality of people' lives, it also holds the potential of severe abuse.
1. Computers allow managers to increase surveillance without face-to-face supervision.
2. Computers can create the "maximum-security workplace," potentially keeping track of every movement a worker makes while on the job. Some worry that it is only a short step from this type of workplace to the "maximum-security society."

VI. Global Competition in an Age of Uncertainty
A. Today we are experiencing increased competition around the globe. In the global race to wealth and power competitors must stay nimble if they are to survive.

Chapter Summary

Society is organized "to get its job done." It does so through formal organizations and bureaucracies. The same system that can be frustrating and impersonal is also the one on which we rely for our personal welfare and to fulfill our daily needs.

The society of today, however, is not the society of yesterday, nor will it be the society of tomorrow. *The rationalization of society* refers to a transformation in people's thinking and behavior over the past 150 years, shifting the focus from personal relationships to efficiency and results. Karl Marx attributed this transformation to capitalism, while Max Weber, who disagreed with Marx, related it to Protestant ideology.

As a result of rationality, formal organizations—secondary groups designed to achieve specific objectives—have become a central feature of contemporary society. With industrialization, secondary groups have become common. Today, their existence is taken for granted. They become a part of our lives at birth and seem to get more and more complex as we move through the life course. The larger the formal organization, the more likely it will turn into a bureaucracy.

Bureaucracies are defined as formal organizations characterized by five features that help them reach their goals, grow, and endure. These five features are: (1) Clear levels, with assignments flowing downward and accountability flowing upward; (2) A division of labor; (3) Written rules; (4) Written communications with records; and (5) Impartiality.

Although bureaucracies are the most efficient form of social organization, they can also be dysfunctional. Dysfunctions of bureaucracies can include red tape, lack of communication between units, and alienation. Examples of these dysfunctions include an overly rigid interpretation of rules and the failure of members of the same organization to communicate with one another. According to Max Weber, the impersonality of bureaucracies tends to produce workers who feel detached from the organization and each other. According to Karl Marx, workers experience alienation when they lose control over their work and are cut off from the finished product of their labor.

To resist alienation, workers form primary groups and band together in informal settings during the workday to offer each other support and validation. They also personalize their workspace with family photographs and personal decorations. Not all workers, however, succeed in resisting alienation.

One reason bureaucracies endure and are so resilient is because they tend to take on a life of their own through a process called goal displacement. Once a bureaucracy has achieved its original goals, it adopts new goals in order to perpetuate its existence. A classic example of goal displacement involves the March of Dimes. Originally founded to fight polio, the organization was faced with being phased out after Jonas Salk discovered the polio vaccine. Rather than disband, it adopted a new mission, fighting birth defects, and, more recently, changed the mission again to the less explicit goal of "breakthroughs for babies."

In addition to bureaucracies, many people in the United States become involved with voluntary organizations—groups made up of volunteers who organize on the basis of some mutual interest. But even voluntary organizations are not immune from the effect of bureaucratization.

Although formal organizations provide numerous beneficial functions, they also tend to be dominated by a small, self-perpetuating elite, a phenomenon Robert Michels referred to as the *iron law of oligarchy*. The iron law of oligarchy even affects volunteer and non-profit organizations.

In an attempt to overcome the rigidity and impersonality of corporations, some are working to humanize the work setting. Fostering a corporate culture that maximizes human potential can actually be more profitable for a company as it likely increases creativity, productivity, and loyalty among employees. Examples of humanizing the work setting include worker empowerment, emotional *integration activities*, and corporate child care. On a more critical note, conflict theorists view *humanizing the work setting* as a camouflage to conceal the owners' goal of exploiting workers.

Sociologists use the term "corporate culture" to refer to an organization's traditions, values, and unwritten norms. Much of what goes on in corporate culture, however, is hidden. To ensure that the corporate culture reproduces itself at the top levels, people in positions of power groom other people they perceive to be "just like them" for similar positions of power. In the United States, personal achievement is central; workers are hired on the basis of what they can contribute to the organization that hires them.

KEY TERMS

After studying the chapter, review the definition for each of the following terms.

alienation: Marx's term for workers' lack of connection to the product of their labor; caused by their being assigned repetitive tasks on a small part of a product, which leads to a sense of powerlessness and normlessness (175)

bureaucracy: a formal organization with a hierarchy of authority and a clear division of labor; emphasis on impersonality of positions and written rules, communications, and records (171)

capitalism: an economic system characterized by the private ownership of the means of production, the pursuit of profit, and market competition (170)

formal organization: a secondary group designed to achieve explicit objectives (171)

goal displacement: an organization replacing old goals with new ones; also known as *goal replacement* (176)

hidden corporate culture: stereotypes of the traits that make for high-performing and underperforming workers (182)

humanizing a work setting: organizing a workplace in such a way that it develops rather than impedes human potential (180)

iron law of oligarchy (the): Robert Michels' term for the tendency of formal organizations to be dominated by a small, self-perpetuating elite (179)

McDonaldization of society (the): the process by which ordinary aspects of life are rationalized and efficiency comes to rule them, including such things as food preparation (173)

Peter principle: a tongue-in-cheek observation that the members of an organization are promoted for their accomplishments until they reach their level of incompetence; there they cease to be promoted, remaining at the level at which they can no longer do good work (176)

rationality: using rules, efficiency, and practical results to determine human affairs (168)

rationalization of society (the): a widespread acceptance of *rationality* and social organizations that are built largely around this idea (169)

self-fulfilling stereotype: preconceived ideas of what someone is like that lead to the person behaving in ways that match the stereotype (181)

traditional society: a society in which the past is thought to be the best guide for the present; characterizes tribal, peasant, and feudal societies (168)

voluntary association: a group made up of people who voluntarily organize on the basis of some mutual interest; also known as *voluntary memberships* and *voluntary organizations* (177)

KEY PEOPLE

Review the major theoretical contributions or findings of these people.

Elaine Fox and George Arquitt: These sociologists studied local posts of the Veterans of Foreign Wars (VFW) and found three types of members and evidence of the iron law of oligarchy. (179)

Rosabeth Moss Kanter: Kanter studied the hidden corporate culture and found that, for the most part, it continually reproduces itself by promoting those workers who fit the elite's stereotypical views. (180-183)

Karl Marx: Marx believed that the emergence of rationality was due to capitalism. Capitalism changed the way people thought about life, rather than people's orientation to life producing capitalism. (169)

Robert Michels: Michels first used the term "the iron law of oligarchy" to describe the tendency for the leaders of an organization to become entrenched. (179)

George Ritzer: Ritzer coined the term the "McDonaldization of society" to describe the increasing rationalization of modern social life. (173)

David Sills: Sills studied goal displacement in the March of Dimes and identified four additional functions that some voluntary groups perform. (176, 178)

Max Weber: Weber studied the rationalization of society by investigating the link between Protestantism and capitalism and identifying the characteristics of bureaucracy. (169-174, 180)

SELF-TEST

MULTIPLE CHOICE QUESTIONS

1. What is rationality? (168)
    a. the idea that the past is the best guide for the present
    b. making excuses for bureaucratic incompetence
    c. accepting rules, efficiency, and practical results as the way to approach human affairs
    d. none of the above

2. The idea that the past is the best guide for the present is referred to as: (169)
    a. traditional orientation.
    b. modern orientation.
    c. status quo.
    d. rationalization.

3. What was one of the major obstacles to industrialization? (169)
    a. the medieval church
    b. a traditional orientation
    c. money lenders
    d. the traditional family

4. According to Karl Marx, what was the force behind rationality replacing the traditional orientation to life? (169-170)
    a. religion
    b. technology
    c. capitalism
    d. culture

5. According to Max Weber, capitalism: (169-170)
    a. is the investment of capital in the hopes of producing profits.
    b. became an outlet for the excess money of Calvinists.
    c. produced success for many that became a sign of God's approval.
    d. all of the above.

6. In reconciling Weber's and Marx's views on rationality, sociologists feel that: (170)
    a. Weber was most correct.
    b. Marx was most correct.
    c. Weber and Marx were both incorrect.
    d. No analyst has yet reconciled the opposing views to their satisfaction.

7. A secondary group designed to achieve explicit objectives is the sociological definition of: (171)
    a. a social institution.
    b. a formal organization.
    c. a rationalized system.

    d.   none of the above.

8.   All of the following are characteristics of bureaucracy, *except*: (171-173)
    a.   a division of labor.
    b.   a hierarchy with assignments flowing upward and accountability flowing downward.
    c.   written rules, communications, and records.
    d.   impersonality.

9.   George Ritzer used the term "the McDonaldization of society" to refer to: (173)
    a.   the preference for McDonald's over Burger King.
    b.   the spread of McDonald's world-wide.
    c.   the increasing rationalization of daily living.
    d.   all of the above.

10.   What is the force behind "the McDonaldization of society"? (173)
    a.   the desire to control the marketplace with uniform products
    b.   the increased efficiency which contributes to lower prices
    c.   the security that comes from knowing the product
    d.   corporate greed

11.   As a worker in a large corporation, Linda is often unhappy. At work she feels that no one appreciates her and that the work she does is boring and repetitive. Which of the following best describes Linda's situation? (175)
    a.   bureaucratic incompetence
    b.   alienation
    c.   goal displacement
    d.   goal frustration

12.   How do workers resist alienation? (175)
    a.   by forming primary groups
    b.   by praising each other and expressing sympathy when something goes wrong
    c.   by putting pictures and personal items in their work areas
    d.   all of the above

13.   According to your text, what is the alienated bureaucrat likely to do? (175)
    a.   quit his or her job once unhappiness and dissatisfaction set in
    b.   seek counseling to overcome the problem
    c.   not do anything for the organization beyond what he or she is required to do
    d.   return to school for further training in order to move up in the organization

14.   Which of the following is true about the Peter principle: (176)
    a.   states that each employee of a bureaucracy is promoted to his or her level of competence.
    b.   states that each employee of a bureaucracy is promoted to his or her level of incompetence.
    c.   is generally true and explains why so many bureaucracies fail.

d.   was first stated by Max Weber.

15. When does goal displacement occur? (176)
     a.   when a bureaucrat has the inability to see the goals of the organization and to function as a cooperative, integrated part of the whole.
     b.   when goals conflict with one another.
     c.   when an organization adopts new goals
     d.   when members of an organization are promoted until they reach their level of incompetence.

16. The sociological significance of bureaucracy is that it: (176-177)
     a.   has always existed as a way of organizing human activity.
     b.   reflects the best way of organizing work.
     c.   is more dysfunctional than functional.
     d.   represents a fundamental change in the way people relate to one another.

17. Voluntary associations: (177)
     a.   are groups made up of volunteers who organize on the basis of some mutual interest.
     b.   include political parties, unions, professional associations, and churches.
     c.   have been an important part of American life.
     d.   all of the above

18. Why do people in the United States belong to voluntary associations? (178)
     a.   They meet people's basic needs.
     b.   People are required to belong to these organizations.
     c.   People don't have anything to do other than work.
     d.   They take the place of government agencies.

19. What are Pepsi executives a good example of? (183)
     a.   modeling diversity training in the workplace
     b.   promoting primarily within the organization
     c.   maintaining "hidden values" within the corporation
     d.   none of the above

20. What does it mean to humanize a work setting? (180)
     a.   employees bring plants, pictures, and other personal items to the office
     b.   having a period of time in which workers visit with each other, tell jokes, and get to know each other more personally
     c.   purchasing furniture that is more comfortable for employees
     d.   organizing a workplace so that human potential is developed rather than impeded

21. Research on the costs and benefits of employer-financed day care demonstrated that: (180-181)
     a.   such a benefit is costly to the employer because of strict government regulations that must be met.
     b.   such a benefit cuts into stockholders' dividends by eating up profits.

c. few employees took advantage of the benefit.

d. such a benefit can save the employer money by reducing turnover and absenteeism.

22. Business practices are subject to fads, and _____ are an excellent example. (181)
   a. quality circles
   b. cooperatives
   c. collectives
   d. corporate day care

23. Which of the following reflects the views of conflict theorists? (181)
   a. Quality circles, employee stock ownership, and small work groups are excellent ways to solve the problems encountered in bureaucracies.
   b. The interests of workers and owners both may be met by humanizing the work setting.
   c. The interests of workers and owners are fundamentally opposed and, in the final analysis, workers are always exploited.
   d. There is less conflict in the Japanese corporate model than in the U.S. model.

24. Computers in the workplace: (183)
   a. have reduced the drudgery.
   b. could lead to more surveillance of workers by managers.
   c. may be the first step towards a society in which every move a citizen makes is recorded.
   d. all of the above.

25. Which of the following statements best describes the Japanese workers' access to lifetime job security? (185)
   a. Almost all Japanese workers enjoy lifetime job security.
   b. About one half of Japanese workers, who are employed in small firms, have lifetime job security.
   c. Lifetime job security is elusive, and only about one-third of workers have it.
   d. Lifetime job security is restricted to top management only.

TRUE-FALSE QUESTIONS

1. _____Rationality involves the acceptance of rules, efficiency, and practical results as the right way to approach human affairs. (168)

2. _____Traditional orientation is based on the idea that the present is the best guide for the future. (169)

3. _____Max Weber believed that the growth of capitalism contributed to the rise of the Protestant ethic. (169-170)

4. _____Calvinists believed that thrift was a virtue and that money should not be spent on the luxuries of life. (170)

5. _____Max Weber's characteristics of bureaucracy are ideal types. (171-173)

6. _____Marx coined the term alienation to describe the reactions of workers who felt they were often treated more like objects than people. (175)

7.   _____The Peter principle has been proven to be true. (176)
8.   _____Voluntary associations may help some individuals climb the occupational ladder. (177-178)
9.   _____Corporate daycare, employee stock ownership, and small work teams are three ways companies have been attempting to humanize the workforce. (180-181)
10.   _____In real life, the Japanese corporate model works much the way that it is described. (185)

FILL-IN-THE-BLANK QUESTIONS

1.   Until recently, people were immersed in a _____ orientation to life. (168)
2.   Karl Marx was one of the first to note how tradition had given way to _____. (169)
3.   In his study of capitalism, Max Weber studied the teachings of _____. (170)
4.   In a bureaucracy, there is a _____ of labor. (172)
5.   As with culture, a bureaucracy often differs from its _____ image. (174)
6.   If _____ were generally true, then organizations would not be successful. (176)
7.   The _____ refers to how organizations come to be dominated by a small, self-perpetuating elite. (179)
8.   Rosabeth Moss Kanter stressed that corporate culture contains _____ values. (182)
9.   The conflict perspective points out that the basic relationship between workers and owners is always _____. (181)
10.   Peering beneath the surface reveals that the reality of the Japanese corporation differs from the _____. (185)

ESSAY QUESTIONS

1.   Explain what sociologists mean by the expression "rationalization of society" and discuss why this change has occurred.

2.   Explain "hidden values" within the workplace and why this continues in contemporary organizations.

3.   Define the iron law of oligarchy and discuss why this problem occurs in voluntary associations.

4.   This chapter provides discussion of strategies to humanize the workplace. After identifying some of these strategies, consider the conflict perspective on these types of initiatives.

5.   Evaluate whether the use of technology to control workers is an inevitable aspect of bureaucracy.

CHAPTER 8
DEVIANCE AND SOCIAL CONTROL

LEARNING OBJECTIVES
After reading Chapter 8, you should be able to:

1. Define "deviance" and understand why deviance is relative from a sociological perspective. (190)

2. Know why human groups need norms to exist and, consequently, develop a system of social control for enforcing norms. (190-192)

3. Describe some of the sanctions human groups use to enforce norms, including shaming and degradation ceremonies. (192, 196)

4. Differentiate between biological, psychological, and sociological explanations for why people violate norms. (192-193)

5. Discuss deviance from the symbolic interactionist perspective, describing and applying the various components of differential association theory, control theory, and labeling theory. (193-195)

6. List and discuss the five techniques of neutralization. (197)

7. From the functionalist perspective, know which functions deviance fulfills for society. (199-204)

8. Understand strain theory and discuss its social implications. (199-201)

9. Discuss the role power plays in defining and punishing deviance while discussing, from the conflict perspective, how the criminal justice system legitimates and perpetuates social inequality. (201-204)

10. Describe the different ways street crime and white-collar crime are perceived by the public and treated by the criminal justice system. (201-206)

11. Address the ramifications of the growing prison population in the United States; examine how the way society addresses crime is related to the conflict perspective. (205-208)

12. Talk about the gender, social class, and racial-ethnic biases with regard to the death penalty. (210-212)

13. Explain why crime statistics may be misleading and should be interpreted with caution. (214)

14. Know what is meant by "the medicalization of deviance" and why some sociologists view mental illness as more of a social, rather than biological, condition. (214-216)

15. Explain why the United States needs to develop a fairer and more humane approach to dealing with deviance. (216)

Chapter Outline

I. **What is Deviance?**
    A. Sociologists use the term deviance to refer to a violation of norms.
        1. According to sociologist Howard S. Becker, it is not the act itself that makes an action deviant, but rather how society reacts to it.
        2. Because different groups have different norms, what is deviant to some is not deviant to others. This is true even for criminal deviance, the violation of rules that have been written into law.
        3. Deviants are people who violate rules, whether the infraction is minor (jaywalking) or serious (murder). When sociologists study deviance, they are nonjudgmental; they are not judging whether the behavior is good or bad, just that people within the social group view it negatively. To sociologists, all people are deviants because everyone violates rules from time to time.
        4. Erving Goffman used "stigma" to refer to attributes that discredit one's claim to a "normal" identity; a stigma (e.g., blindness, mental handicaps, facial birthmarks) defines a person's master status, superceding all other statuses the person occupies.
    B. Norms make social life possible by making behavior predictable. Without norms, social chaos would exist. The reason deviance is seen as threatening is because it undermines predictability. Thus, social control (the formal and informal means of enforcing norms) is necessary for social life.
    C. When a norm is violated, sanctions are imposed.
        1. Sanctions can be either negative or positive.
        2. Negative sanctions, which reflect disapproval of a particular behavior, range from frowns and gossip for breaking a folkway to imprisonment and capital punishment for breaking a more.
        3. Positive sanctions, from smiles to formal awards, are used to reward conformity.
        4. Most sanctions are informal.
    D. Shaming is another sanction. It is particularly effective when used by members of a primary group or in a small community.
        1. Shaming can be the centerpiece of public ritual, marking the violator as deviant for the entire world to see.
        2. Harold Garfinkel used the term *degradation ceremony* to describe formal attempts to label someone as an outsider.
    E. Comparisons can be made between biological, psychological, and sociological explanations of deviance.
        1. Psychologists and sociobiologists explain deviance by looking within individuals; sociologists look outside the individual.

2. Biological explanations focus on genetic predisposition, including factors such as intelligence; the "XYY" theory (an extra Y chromosome in men leads to crime); or body type (squarish, muscular people are more likely to commit street crimes).

3. Psychological explanations focus on personality disorders (e.g., "bad toilet training," "suffocating mothers," and so on). Yet these do not necessarily result in the presence or absence of specific forms of deviance in a person.

4. Sociological explanations search outside the individual: Crime is a violation of norms written into law, and each society has its own laws against certain types of behavior. But social influences such as socialization, subcultural group memberships, or social class (people's relative standing in terms of education, occupation, income and wealth) may "recruit" some people to break norms.

II. The Symbolic Interactionist Perspective

A. Differential association is Edwin Sutherland's term to indicate that those who associate with groups oriented toward deviant activities learn an "excess of definitions" of deviance and thus are more likely to engage in deviant activities.

1. The key to differential association is the learning of ideas and attitudes favorable to following the law or breaking it. Some groups teach members to violate norms (e.g., families involved in crime may set their children on a lawbreaking path; some friends and neighborhoods tend to encourage deviant behavior; even subcultures contain particular attitudes about deviance and conformity that are learned by their members).

2. Symbolic interactionists stress that people are not mere pawns, because individuals help produce their own orientation to life and their choice of association helps shape the self.

B. According to control theory, everyone is propelled towards deviance, but a system of controls work against these motivations to deviate.

1. Walter Reckless described two complementary systems of controls. Inner controls are our capacity to withstand temptations toward deviance and include our internalized morality, integrity, fear of punishment, and desire to be good. Outer controls involve groups (e.g., family, friends, the police) that influence us not to deviate.

2. Travis Hirschi noted that strong bonds to society, based on attachments, commitments, involvements, and beliefs, lead to more effective inner controls.

C. Labeling theory is the view that the labels people are given affect their own and others' perceptions of them, thus channeling their behavior either into deviance or into conformity.

1. Gresham Sykes and David Matza use the term "techniques of neutralization" to describe the strategies deviants employ to resist society's label. These are: (1) Denial of responsibility ("I didn't do it"); (2) Denial of injury ("Who really got hurt?"); (3) Denial of a victim ("She deserved it"); (4) Condemnation of the condemners ("Who are you to talk?"); and (5) Appeal to higher loyalty ("I had to help my friends").

2. Sometimes an individual's deviant acts begin casually and he or she gradually slides into more serious deviance.

3. Most people resist being labeled deviant, but some revel in a deviant identity (e.g., motorcycle gangs who are proud of getting in trouble, laughing at death, and so on).

4. William Chambliss' study of the Saints (troubled boys from respectable middle class families) and the Roughnecks (boys from working class families who hang out on the streets) provides an excellent illustration of labeling theory, which is how labels given to people affect how others perceive them and how they perceive themselves, thus channeling their behavior into deviance or conformity. The study showed how labels open and close doors of opportunity for the individuals involved.

III. The Functionalist Perspective

A. Emile Durkheim stated that deviance, including crime, is functional, for it contributes to social order.

1. Deviance clarifies moral boundaries (a group's ideas about how people should act and think) and affirms norms.

2. Deviance promotes social unity (by reacting to deviants, group members develop a "we" feeling and collectively affirm the rightness of their own ways).

3. Deviance promotes social change (if boundary violations gain enough support, they become new, acceptable behaviors).

B. Robert Merton developed strain theory to analyze what happens when people are socialized to desire cultural goals but denied the institutionalized means to reach them.

1. Merton used "anomie" (Durkheim's term) to refer to the strain people experience when they are blocked in their attempts to achieve those goals.

2. The most common reaction to cultural goals and institutionalized means is conformity (using lawful means to seek goals society sets).

3. He identified four types of deviant responses to anomie: innovation (using illegitimate means to achieve them); ritualism (giving up on achieving cultural goals but clinging to conventional rules of conduct); retreatism (rejecting cultural goals, dropping out); and rebellion (seeking to replace society's goals).

4. According to strain theory, deviants are not pathogenic individuals but the products of society.

C. Sociologists Richard Cloward and Lloyd Ohlin developed illegitimate opportunity theory to explain why social classes have distinct styles of crime.

1. They suggest that these differences are due to differential access to institutionalized means.

2. Illegitimate opportunity structures are opportunities for crimes, such as robbery, burglary, and drug dealing, which are woven into the texture of life. These structures may result when legitimate structures fail.

3. For the urban poor, there are opportunities to make money through "hustles," such as robbery, burglary, drug dealing, prostitution, pimping, gambling, and other crimes. The "hustler" is a role model because he or she is one of the few who comes close to the cultural goals of success.

4. White-collar crime (crimes that people of respectable and high social status commit in the course of their occupations) results from an illegitimate opportunity structure among higher classes. Such crimes exist in greater numbers

than commonly perceived, and can be very costly, possibly totaling several hundred billion dollars a year. They can involve physical harm and sometimes death.

D. There have been some recent changes in the nature of crime. A major change is the growing ranks of female offenders. As women have become more involved in the professions and the corporate world, they too have been enticed by illegitimate opportunities.

IV. The Conflict Perspective

A. The state's machinery of social control represents the interests of the wealthy and powerful; this group determines the laws whose enforcement is essential for maintaining its power.

B. The criminal justice system directs its energies against violations by the working class; while it tends to overlook the harm done by the owners of corporations, flagrant violations are prosecuted. The publicity given to this level of white-collar crime helps stabilize the system by providing evidence of fairness.

C. The law is an instrument of oppression, a tool designed to maintain the powerful in privileged positions and keep the powerless from rebelling and overthrowing the social order. When members of the working class get out of line, they are arrested, tried and imprisoned in the criminal justice system.

V. Reactions to Deviance

A. Imprisonment, which follows the degradation ceremony (public trial/pronouncement that the person is unfit to live among law-abiding people), is an increasingly popular reaction to crime but fails to teach inmates to stay away from crime.

   1. The United States has the dubious distinction of having not only more prisoners than any other nation, but also a larger percentage of its population in prison.

   2. African Americans are disproportionately represented among the prison population.

   3. For about the past 20 years, the United States has followed a "get tough" policy. The "three strikes and you're out" laws have become common. Unfortunately, these laws have had some unintended consequences.

   4. The recidivism rate (the proportion of persons who are rearrested) in the United States is high. For those sentenced to prison for crimes of violence, within just three years of their release, 62 percent are rearrested, and 52 percent are back in prison.

B. The death penalty is the most extreme and controversial measure the state can take. Many argue that there are biases in the use of the death penalty. These reflect regional, gender, social class, as well as racial and ethnic biases.

C. The definition of behavior as deviant varies across societies, groups, and time periods. The emergence of hate crime legislation in the United States is an example of this.

D. Caution is needed in interpreting official crime statistics because the offender's social class influences the authorities' reactions .

   1. Crime statistics are a human creation produced within a specific social and political context for some particular purpose.

2. Police discretion—deciding whether to arrest someone or to ignore a situation—is a routine part of police work. Crime statistics reflect this and many other biases.

E. Medicalization of deviance is the view of deviance as a symptom of some underlying illness that needs to be treated by physicians.
   1. Thomas Szasz argues that mental illness is simply problem behaviors. Some forms of "mental" illnesses have organic causes (e.g., depression caused by a chemical imbalance in the brain), while others are responses to troubles with various coping devices.
   2. Szasz's analysis suggests that social experiences, and not some illness of the mind, underlie bizarre behaviors.
   3. Being mentally ill can sometimes lead to other problems such as homelessness, but being homeless can lead to unusual and unacceptable ways of thinking that are defined by the wider society as mental illness.

F. With deviance inevitable, one measure of society is how it treats its deviants.
   1. The larger issues are how to protect people from deviant behaviors that are harmful to their welfare, to tolerate those that are not, and to develop systems of fairer treatment for deviants.

Chapter Summary

Sociologists use the term *deviance* to refer to any violation of rules and norms. From a sociological perspective, deviance is relative. Definitions of "what is deviant" vary across societies and from one group to another within the same society. Howard S. Becker described the interpretation of deviance as, "… not the act itself, but the reaction to the act that makes something deviant." This coincides with the symbolic interactionist view. In some cases, an individual need not do anything to be labeled a deviant. He or she may be falsely accused or discredited because of a birth defect, race, or disease. Even crime is relative when interpreting the deviance of the actor.

Deviance is based on adherence to and violation of norms. Human groups need norms to exist. By making behavior predictable, norms make social life possible. Consequently, all human groups develop a system of social control, which involves formal and informal means of enforcing norms. Those who violate these norms face the danger of being labeled "deviant." Violators can expect to experience negative sanctions for the violation of norms. Members of society who conform to societal norms, especially those who go above and beyond what is commonly expected, receive positive sanctions. In some societies, such as the Amish, shaming is a common negative sanction that acts strongly as a means of social control, minimizing deviance.

Biologists, psychologists, and sociologists have different perspectives on why people violate norms. Biological explanations focus on genetic predispositions, psychologists concentrate on abnormalities *within* the individual (commonly known as personality disorders), and sociologists look at social factors *outside* the individual.

Symbolic interactionists interpret deviance through the following social theories: differential association theory (people learn deviance from the groups with whom they associate); control theory (people generally avoid deviance because of an effective system of inner and outer controls); and labeling theory (people are directed toward or away from deviance by the labels others pin on them).

Functionalists contend that deviance is functional for society; it contributes to the social order by clarifying moral boundaries, promoting social unity, and initiating social change. Furthermore, according to "strain theory," people are likely to experience strain, which, in turn, can lead some people to choose deviant and/or criminal behavior rather than conforming to cultural goals and/or engaging in legitimate institutional means. In addition to strain theory, functionalists stress theories addressing illegitimate opportunity structure in society.

Conflict theorists note that power plays a central role in defining and punishing deviance. The group in power imposes its definitions of deviance on other groups then uses the law and criminal justice system to maintain its power and privilege over those other groups.

Reactions to deviance in the United States include everything from mild sanctions to capital punishment. Since the 1980s, the United States has adopted a "get tough" policy on crime that has imprisoned millions of people. Prisoners are generally much younger than the average American, nearly 94 percent male, and disproportionately African-American.

Because crime statistics are produced within a specific social and political context for particular purposes, they must be interpreted with caution. Power plays a central role in determining which behaviors are defined as crimes, as well as in how actively "criminal behaviors" are prosecuted and/or punished. For example, although street crime is given the greatest attention by the media because of the violence associated with it, white-collar crime actually costs the American taxpayers more. Even cases of gross negligence that cause death are funneled into administrative hearings that, at times, result in little more than a fine for the corporation. The definition of crime is subject to change, however, and the ways various acts are treated by society changes with shifts in power and public priority.

Since the early 20th century, there has been a growing tendency toward the medicalization of deviance, in which deviance, including crime, is viewed as mental illness. Thomas Szasz offers another perspective, claiming that mental illnesses are neither mental nor illness. Rather, they are problem behaviors that are related to people's particular experiences in life. For example, disruptive and unruly behaviors that disrespect authority and deviate from social norms are now a treatable mental illness recognized as Attention Deficit Hyperactivity Disorder (ADHD).

As deviance is inevitable, the larger issues include: finding ways to protect people from those forms of deviance that harm themselves and/or others, tolerating deviant behaviors that are not harmful, and developing systems of fairer treatment for deviants.

KEY TERMS

After studying the chapter, review the definition for each of the following terms.

capital punishment: the death penalty (210, 211)

control theory: the idea that two control systems—inner and outer controls—work against our tendencies to deviate (195)

corporate crime: crimes committed by executives in order to benefit their corporation (202)

crime: the violation of norms written into law (190)

criminal justice system: the system of police, courts, and prisons set up to deal with people who are accused of having committed a crime (205)

cultural goals: the objectives held out as legitimate or desirable for the members of a society to achieve (199)

degradation ceremony: a term coined by Harold Garfinkel to refer to a ritual whose goal is to reshape someone's self by stripping away that individual's self-identity and stamping a new identity in its place (197)

deviance: the violation of norms (or rules or expectations) (190)

differential association: Edwin Sutherland's term to indicate that people who associate with some groups learn an "excess of definitions" of deviance, increasing the likelihood that they will become deviant (193)

genetic predisposition: inborn tendencies (for example, a tendency to commit deviant acts) (192)

hate crime: a crime that is punished more severely because it is motivated by hatred (dislike, hostility, animosity) of someone's race–ethnicity, religion, sexual orientation, disability, or national origin (212, 213)

illegitimate opportunity structure: opportunities for crimes that are woven into the texture of life (202)

institutionalized means: approved ways of reaching cultural goals (199)

labeling theory: the view that the labels people are given affect their own and others' perceptions of them, thus channeling their behavior into either deviance or conformity (197)

medicalize: the transformation of a human condition into a matter to be treated by physicians (214, 215)

medicalization of deviance: to make deviance a medical matter; a symptom of some underlying illness that needs to be treated by physicians (214, 215)

negative sanction: an expression of disapproval for breaking a norm, ranging from a mild, informal reaction, such as a frown to a formal reaction such as a prison sentence or an execution (192)

personality disorders: the view that a personality disturbance of some sort causes an individual to violate social norms (193)

police discretion: the practice of the police, in the normal course of their duties, to either arrest or ticket someone for an offense or to overlook the matter (214, 215)

positive sanction: a reward or positive reaction for following norms, ranging from a smile to a material award (192)

recidivism rate: the proportion of released convicts who are rearrested (210)

serial murder: the killing of several victims in three or more separate events (211)

social control: a group's formal and informal means of enforcing its norms (192)

social order: a group's usual and customary social arrangements, on which its members depend and on which they base their lives (192)

stigma: "blemishes" that discredit a person's claim to a "normal" identity (190)

strain theory: Robert Merton's term for the strain engendered when a society socializes large numbers of people to desire a cultural goal (such as success) but withholds from some the approved means of reaching that goal; one adaptation to the strain is crime, the choice of an innovative means (one outside the approved system) to attain the cultural goal (199)

street crime: crimes such as mugging, rape, and burglary (192)

techniques of neutralization: ways of thinking or rationalizing that help people deflect (or neutralize) society's norms (197)

white-collar crime: Edwin Sutherland's term for crimes committed by people of respectable and high social status in the course of their occupations; for example, bribery of public officials, securities violations, embezzlement, false advertising, and price fixing (202)

KEY PEOPLE

Review the major theoretical contributions or findings of these people.

Howard S. Becker: Becker observed that an act is not deviant in and of itself, but only when there is a reaction to it. (190)

William Chambliss: Chambliss demonstrated the power of the label in his study of two youth gangs—the Saints and the Roughnecks. (193, 198, 205)

Richard Cloward and Lloyd Ohlin: These sociologists identified the illegitimate opportunity structures that are woven into the texture of life in urban slums and provide an alternative set of opportunities for slum residents when legitimate ones are blocked. (199, 202)

Emile Durkheim: Durkheim noted that deviance is functional for society. (199, 216)

Robert Edgerton: This anthropologist's studies document how different human groups react to similar behaviors, demonstrating that what is deviant in one context is not in another. (191)

Harold Garfinkel: Garfinkel used the term degradation ceremonies to describe formal attempts to mark an individual with the status of an outsider. (196)

Erving Goffman: Goffman wrote about the role of stigma in the definition of who and what is deviant. (190)

Travis Hirschi: Hirschi studied the strength of the bonds an individual has to society in order to understand the effectiveness of inner controls. (195)

Ruth Horowitz: This sociologist conducted participant observation in a Chicano neighborhood in Chicago. She found that attitudes about honor, which were common among residents, helped to propel young men into deviance. (194)

Robert Merton: Merton developed strain theory to explain patterns of deviance within a society. (199-201, 215)

Donald Partington: This lawyer examined executions for rape and attempted rape in Virginia between 1908 and 1963 and found that only black men were executed for these crimes during those years. (212)

Walter Reckless: Reckless developed control theory, suggesting that our behavior is controlled by two different systems: one external (outer controls such as the police, family and friends) and the other internal (inner controls such as our conscience, religious principles, and ideas of right and wrong). (195)

Edwin Sutherland: Sutherland not only developed differential association theory, but was also the first to study and give a name to white collar crime—crimes that occur among the middle class in the course of their work. (193-194, 202)

Gresham Sykes and David Matza: These sociologists studied the techniques of neutralization, or the different strategies delinquent boys use to deflect society's norms. (197)

Thomas Szasz: Szasz argued that mental illness represents the medicalization of deviance. (214-215)

Mark Watson: Watson studied motorcycle gangs and found that these people actively embraced the deviant label. (198)

SELF-TEST

MULTIPLE CHOICE QUESTIONS

1. In sociology, to what does the term deviance refer? (190)
    a. behavior that sociologists believe is bad enough to warrant being punished by society
    b. all violations of social rules
    c. the violation of serious rules
    d. crime

2. Why is deviance often seen as threatening? (190-191)
    a. because it is always harmful to society
    b. because it undermines the predictability of social life
    c. because it costs society a great deal of money
    d. because it is bad

3. Frowns, gossip, and crossing people off guest lists are all examples of (192)
    a. retribution.
    b. degradation ceremonies.
    c. negative sanctions.
    d. institutionalized means to achieve goals.

4. Most negative sanctions are (192)
    a. very punitive.
    b. universally the same.
    c. generally informal.
    d. all of the above.

5. According to Erving Goffman, what is the function of stigma? (190)
    a. to punish the person because she or he violates the norms
    b. to reward society for conforming to the norms
    c. to identify the person who violates the norm as deviant
    d. to regulate behavior

6. A court martial where the guilty officer is publicly stripped of his or her rank is an example of (196)
    a. degradation ceremonies.
    b. humiliation ceremonies.
    c. stigmatization.
    d. deinstitutionalization.

7. Differential association theory is based on the (193)
    a. functionalist perspective.
    b. conflict perspective.
    c. symbolic interactionist perspective.
    d. psychological perspective.

8. According to differential association theory, why does someone become a deviant? (193-194)
    a. because of genetic predispositions
    b. because of personality disorders
    c. because of a lack of opportunities to engage in conventional activities
    d. because he learns to deviate from or conform to society's norms

9. Which of the following is *not* one of the ways of neutralizing deviance? (197)
    a. appeal to higher loyalties
    b. denial of responsibility
    c. denial of deviant labels
    d. denial of injury and of a victim

10. What does William Chambliss' study of the Saints and the Roughnecks suggest? (198)
    a. Labels are easy to cast off once a person gets away from the group doing the labeling.
    b. People often live up to the labels that a community gives them.
    c. People often rebel against the labels given them and lead a completely different life.
    d. Sociological research on labeling has produced few conclusions.

11. For Chambliss, what factors influence whether people are seen as deviant? (198)
    a. social class
    b. the visibility of offenders
    c. styles of interaction
    d. all of the above

12. Which perspective stresses that deviance promotes social unity and social change? (199)
    a. functionalist
    b. conflict
    c. symbolic interactionist
    d. differential association

13. Which of the following is/are example(s) of *institutionalized means*? (199)
    a. getting an education
    b. getting a good job
    c. working hard
    d. all of the above

14. All of the following are responses to anomie as identified by Robert Merton, *except* (200-201)
    a. ritualism.
    b. rebellion.
    c. retreatism.
    d. recidivism.

15. Steve lives in a neighborhood with high crime rates and poor schools. He believes he will never make it to college. He decides to quit school and sell drugs for a local drug dealer. He is quickly making a lot of money. He buys new clothes and a new car. Steve's behavior reflects which of Merton's deviant paths? (201)
    a. innovation
    b. ritualism
    c. retreatism
    d. rebellion

16. The illegitimate opportunity structures theory is based on (201-204)
    a. the conflict perspective.
    b. the symbolic interactionist perspective.
    c. the exchange perspective.
    d. the functionalist perspective.

17. What are crimes committed by high-status people in the course of their occupations called? (202)
    a. upper-class crime
    b. crimes of respectability
    c. white-collar crime
    d. tuxedo crime

18. Sears defrauded the poor of more than $100 million. This is an example of (202)
    a. good business practices.
    b. innovation.
    c. corporate crime.
    d. negative sanctions.

19. Corporate crime costs us several hundred _____ as a society? (203)
    a. thousand/year
    b. million/year
    c. billion/year
    d. trillion/year

20. Which country today has the largest percentage of its population in prison? (206)
    a. Cuba
    b. United States
    c. Russia
    d. China

21. Which of the following statements about the recidivism rate in the United States is *correct*? (210)
    a. As a result of the U.S. government's "get tough" policy in recent years, there has been a sharp drop in the recidivism rate.
    b. About one-half of all recidivists have been convicted of violent crimes.
    c. Approximately two-thirds of all released prisoners will be rearrested within a year.

d. It is estimated that slightly more than one-half of all prisoners have served time in the past.

22. Who is disproportionately at risk of being put to death under the death penalty? (210-213)
    a. whites
    b. African Americans
    c. Latinos
    d. Asian-Americans

23. According to statistics on hate crimes, which group is most likely to be victimized? (213-214)
    a. African Americans
    b. whites
    c. Latinos
    d. Asian-Americans

24. Hate crimes consist of (213)
    a. crime because of someone's race.
    b. crime because of someone's sexual orientation.
    c. crime because of someone's disability.
    d. all of the above.

25. With deviance inevitable, the author of your textbook suggests that one measure of a society is (216)
    a. how low the overall rates of deviance are.
    b. what types of deviance there is.
    c. what gets defined as deviance and what doesn't.
    d. how deviants are treated.

TRUE-FALSE QUESTIONS

1. _____According to your text, a college student cheating on an exam and a mugger lurking on a dark street have nothing at all in common. (190)
2. _____Symbolic interactionists stress that we are mere pawns in the hands of others. (194)
3. _____Outlaw bikers hold the conventional world in contempt and are proud of getting into trouble. (198)
4. _____In the study by Chambliss, the Saints and the Roughnecks both turned out largely as their labels would have predicted. (198)
5. _____According to strain theory, everyone has a chance to get ahead in society, but some people prefer to use illegal means to achieve their goals. (199-200)
6. _____Illegitimate opportunity structures are readily available in urban slums. (201-202)
7. _____White-collar crime is not as costly as street crime. (203)
8. _____Both functionalists and conflict theorists agree that the criminal justice system functions for the well-being of all citizens. (199-206)
9. _____Police discretion is a routine part of police work. (214)

10. _____Official statistics are accurate counts of the crimes committed in our society. (214)

FILL-IN-THE-BLANK QUESTIONS

1. Sociologists search for factors about deviance_____ of the individual. (193)
2. Researchers have found that delinquents are more likely to come from _____ that get into trouble with the law. (194)
3. Travis Hirschi noted that the stronger our bonds are with society, the more effective our _____ controls are. (195)
4. Sykes and Matza found that there are five techniques to _____ one can use to deflect society's norms. (197)
5. According to the functionalist perspective, deviance promotes social _____. (199)
6. An innovator _____ cultural goals and rejects institutionalized means. (209)
7. According to Robert Merton, people who experience strain are likely to feel _____, a sense of normlessness. (200)
8. Martha Stewart is an example of someone who committed _____ crime. (202)
9. A major change in the nature of crime is the growing number of _____ offenders. (204)
10. _____ was a well-intended law that had unintended consequences. (207)

ESSAY QUESTIONS

1. Discuss how the different sociological perspectives could be combined to provide a more complete picture of deviance.

2. Explain how forms of deviance such as street gangs can be both functional and dysfunctional at the same time.

3. Using any one of the different sociological perspectives, develop an explanation for why white-collar crime is generally treated as less serious crime in our society.

4. Discuss the "get tough" policy that the United States has followed and how successful that has been.

5. Obesity could be viewed as deviance because it is a condition that violates our cultural norms regarding appearance. Develop an explanation for how this type of deviance is increasingly subject to medicalization.

CHAPTER 9
GLOBAL STRATIFICATION

LEARNING OBJECTIVES
After reading Chapter 9, you should be able to:

1. Define social stratification and explain why it is sociologically significant. (220)

2. Describe and provide examples of the four major systems of social stratification. (220-226)

3. Discuss the relationship between gender and social stratification. (226)

4. Describe the major points of disagreement between Karl Marx and Max Weber regarding the meaning of social class in industrialized societies. (226-228)

5. As articulated by Kingsley Davis and Wilbert Moore, list the functions that social stratification provides for society. (228-229)

6. Discuss Melvin Tumin's rebuttal to Davis and Moore's functionalist view of social stratification. (229-230)

7. Explain the conflict perspective's view of social stratification as it relates to class conflict and scarce resources. (230-231)

8. Evaluate Gerhard Lenski's attempt to synthesize the functionalist and conflict perspectives' views on social stratification. (231)

9. Define ideology and understand how elite classes use it to maintain social stratification. (231-232)

10. Compare the social stratification systems in Great Britain and the former Soviet Union to the social stratification system in the United States. (233-234)

11. Identify the major characteristics associated with the Most Industrialized Nations, Industrializing Nations, and Least Industrialized Nations. (235-239)

12. Describe and evaluate the major theories pertaining to the origins and maintenance of global stratification. (239, 242-246)

Chapter Outline

I.   Systems of Social Stratification
   A.   Social stratification is a system in which large groups of people are divided into layers according to their relative power, property, and prestige.

B. Stratification exists within a society and between nations and affects our life chances and orientations to life.
C. Slavery is a form of social stratification in which some people own other people.
   1. Initially, slavery was based on debt, punishment for violation of the law, or defeat in battle.
   2. Gerda Lerner notes that women were the first people enslaved through warfare. They were valued for sexual purposes, reproduction, and labor.
   3. Slavery could be temporary or permanent and was not necessarily passed on to one's children. Typically, slaves owned no property and had no power; however, this was not universally true.
   4. The first form of slavery in the New World was bonded labor or indentured service—a contractual system in which someone voluntarily sold his or her services for a specified period of time, at the end of which time the individual was freed.
   5. Given the shortage of indentured servants, American colonists first tried to enslave Indians, and then turned to Africans who were being brought to North and South America by the British, Dutch, English, Portuguese, and Spanish.
   6. When American slave owners found it was profitable to own slaves for life, they developed beliefs to justify what they wanted and to make slavery inheritable. That is, the slaves' children could be sold, bartered, or traded. The practice of slavery was written into law.
   7. There is some debate as to whether or not slavery is still practiced in certain parts of the world today. Although denied by their governments, accusations have been made that the slave trade has been revived in Sudan and Mauritania.
D. In a caste system, status is determined by birth and is lifelong.
   1. Ascribed status is the basis of a caste system. Caste societies try to make certain that boundaries between castes remain firm by practicing endogamy (marriage within their own group) and developing rules about ritual pollution, teaching that contact with inferior castes contaminates the superior caste.
   2. Although abolished by the Indian government in 1949, the caste system remains part of everyday life in India, as it has for almost 3,000 years. This system is based on religion and is made up of four main castes that are subdivided into thousands of specialized subcastes or *jati*. Members of the lowest caste, the Dalit, are known as the "untouchables." If higher castes are contaminated by "the untouchables," then *ablutions* (washing rituals) are required.
   3. South Africa's caste system was called apartheid and based on the separation of the races. By law there were four different racial castes, and the law specified where people could live, work, and go to school. While the government dismantled this system following decades of international protest, its legacy continues to haunt South Africa. Whites still dominate and the blacks remain uneducated and poor. Political violence has been replaced by street crime.
   4. An American racial caste system developed in the United States when slavery ended. Even in the earlier parts of this century, all whites were considered higher than all African Americans and separate accommodations were maintained for the races in the South.

E. During the Middle Ages, Europe developed the estate stratification system consisting of three groups, or estates.
   1. The *first estate* was made up of the nobility, who ruled the land.
   2. The *second estate* consisted of the clergy, who not only owned vast tracts of land and collected taxes from commoners, but also set their seal of approval on rulers. Members of the nobility practiced primogeniture, allowing only firstborn sons to inherit land, so that their vast land holdings wouldn't be divided into small chunks.
   3. The *third estate* was made up of commoners, known as serfs. They were born into this estate and had few opportunities to move up.
   4. Women belonged to the their husbands' estates .
F. A class system is a form of social stratification based primarily on the possession of money or material possessions.
   1. Initial social class position is based on that of one's parents (ascribed status).
   2. With relatively fluid boundaries, a class system allows for social mobility, or movement up or down the social class ladder, based on achieved status.
G. No matter what system a society may use to divide people into different layers, gender is always an essential part of those distinctions within each layer. On the basis of gender, people are sorted into categories and given differential access to rewards. Social distinctions have always favored males. In every society, men's earnings are higher than women's, and most of the world's illiterate are women.

II. What Determines Social Class?
A. According to Karl Marx, social class is determined by one's relationship to the means of production—the tools, factories, land, and investment capital used to produce wealth.
   1. The bourgeoisie (capitalists) own the means of production; the proletariat (workers) works for those who own the means of production.
   2. While Marx recognized the existence of other groups—farmers and peasants, a lumpenproletariat, and self-employed professionals—he did not consider these groups social classes because they lacked class consciousness.
   3. As capital becomes more concentrated, the two classes will become increasingly hostile to one another.
   4. Class consciousness, or an awareness of a common identity based on position in the means of production, will develop; it is the essential basis of the unity of workers, according to Marx.
   5. Marx believed that the workers would revolt against the capitalists, take control of the means of production, and usher in a classless society. However, the workers' unity and revolution are held back by false class consciousness—workers' mistaken identification with the interests of capitalists.
B. Unlike Marx, Max Weber did not believe that property was the sole basis of a person's position in the stratification system, rather that property, prestige, and power determine social class.
   1. Property (or wealth) is an essential element; however, powerful people, like managers of corporations, control the means of production, although they do not own them.

2. Prestige may be derived from ownership of property; however, it also may be based on other factors, such as athletic skills.
3. Power is the ability to control others, even over their objections.

III. Why is Social Stratification Universal?

A. According to the functionalist view expressed by Kingsley Davis and Wilbert Moore, stratification is inevitable for the following four reasons:
   1. Society must make certain that its important positions are filled; some positions are more important than others; more important positions need to be filled by the more qualified people and these people must be offered greater rewards.
B. Melvin Tumin was the first to present a number of criticisms to the Davis and Moore thesis.
   1. He asked how the importance of a position is measured (e.g., "Is a surgeon really more important to society than a garbage collector?"). Rewards cannot be used to measure the importance of a job; there must be some independent measure of importance.
   2. He noted that if stratification worked as Davis and Moore describe it, society would be a meritocracy, a form of social stratification in which all positions are awarded on the basis of merit, but it does not work this way (e.g., the best predictor of college entrance is family income, not ability).
   3. Finally, he noted that stratification is dysfunctional to many people, thus not functional.
C. Conflict theorists stress that conflict, not function, is the basis of social stratification. Every society has limited resources to go around, and in every society, groups struggle with one another for those resources.
   1. Gaetano Mosca argued that it is inevitable that society will be stratified by power. Society cannot exist unless it is organized; thus, there must be politics to get the work of society done. Political organization results in inequalities of power because some people take leadership positions and others follow. It is human nature to be self-centered; thus, people in positions of power use their positions to bring greater rewards to themselves.
   2. Marx believed that human history is the history of class struggle; those in power use society's resources to benefit themselves and oppress others. He predicted that workers would one day revolt against their oppression.
   3. Modern conflict theorists stress that conflict between capitalists and workers is not the only important conflict in contemporary society rather, groups within the same class compete for scarce resources, resulting in conflict between many groups (e.g., young vs. old; women vs. men).
D. Gerhard Lenski offered a synthesis between functionalist and conflict theories.
   1. Functionalists are right when it comes to societies that have only basic resources and do not accumulate wealth, such as hunting and gathering societies.
   2. Conflict theorists are right when it comes to societies with a surplus. In such societies humans pursue self-interests and struggle to control those surpluses. This leads to the emergence of a small elite that then builds inequality into the society, resulting in a full-blown system of social stratification.

IV. How Do Elites Maintain Stratification?

A. Social stratification is maintained within a nation by elites who control ideas and information and use force.

    1. In Medieval Europe, the divine right of kings ideology was developed to control the commoners. This ideology says that the king's authority comes from God and, therefore, he and his representatives must be obeyed. This was more effective than coercion as it bred hostility and laid the ground for rebellion.

    2. Elites also control information in order to maintain their position of power. Fear is a common tactic among dictators.

    3. Technology, especially monitoring devices, helps the elite maintain its position. For example, the U.S. has distributed fake news reports to be broadcast to the nation.

B. Underlying the maintenance of stratification is control of social institutions, such as the legal establishment, the police, and the military.

V. Comparative Social Stratification

A. Great Britain's class system can be divided into upper, middle, and lower classes. A little over half of the population is in the lower or working class, close to half of the population is in the middle class, and only about 1 percent is in the upper class. Language and speech patterns are important class indicators. Education is the primary way the class system is perpetuated from one generation to the next.

B. The ideal of communism, a classless society, was never realized in the former Soviet Union. Before the Communist revolution, the elite was based on inherited wealth; afterward, it consisted of top party officials, a relatively small middle class, and a massive lower class of peasants and unskilled workers. How recent reforms will affect the stratification system is yet to be seen, but a class of newly rich individuals is emerging. Some of these had political connections; others had the foresight and initiative to take advantage of the changes.

VI. Global Stratification: Three Worlds

A. Until the 1980s, a simple model was used, consisting of the First World (industrialized, capitalistic nations), Second World (communist nations), and Third World (any nations that didn't fit the other categories). A more neutral way of categorizing nations is to use terms related to a nation's level of industrialization: "Most Industrialized," "Industrializing," and "Least Industrialized."

B. The Most Industrialized Nations (U.S., Canada, Great Britain, France, Germany, Switzerland, other countries of Western Europe, Japan, Australia, and New Zealand) are capitalistic, although variations exist in economic systems.

    1. These nations have only 16 percent of the world's population, but have 31 percent of the world's land.

    2. The poor in these nations live better/longer than the average citizens of the Least Industrialized Nations.

C. The Industrializing Nations include the former Soviet Union and its satellites in Eastern Europe.

    1. The dividing line between these nations and the Most Industrialized Nations is soft; consequently, it is difficult to classify some nations.

2. These nations account for 16 percent of the world's population and 20 percent of the land.

3. The people of these nations have considerably lower income and a lower standard of living than people in the Most Industrialized Nations; while their access to electricity, indoor plumbing, and other material goods is more limited than those in the Most Industrialized Nations, it is higher than those in the Least Industrialized Nations.

D. In the Least Industrialized Nations of the world, most people live on farms or in villages with low standards of living.

1. These nations account for 49 percent of the earth's land and 68 percent of the world's population.

2. High birth rates and rapidly growing populations characterize these nations (placing even greater burdens on limited facilities).

3. Most people in these nations live on less than $1,000 per year.

E. Classifying the nations of the world into these three categories creates certain problems.

1. How much industrialization does a nation need in order to be classified as Most Industrialized or Industrializing?

2. Does the fact that some nations have become "postindustrial" mean that a separate classification needs to be created?

3. While the oil-rich nations of the world are immensely wealthy, they are not industrialized. How are they classified?

VII. How Did the World's Nations Become Stratified?

A. The theory of colonialism focuses on how the nations that industrialized first got the jump on the rest of the world.

1. With profits generated by the Industrial Revolution, industrialized nations built powerful armaments and fast ships and then invaded weaker nations, making colonies of them and exploiting their labor/natural resources. European nations tended to focus on Africa, while the United States concentrated on Central and South America.

2. Powerful European nations would claim a colony and then send their representatives in to run the government, while the United States chose to plant a corporate flag, letting the corporations dominate the territory's government.

3. Colonialism shaped many of the Least Industrialized Nations. Often, the Most Industrialized Nations created states disregarding tribal or cultural considerations.

B. According to world system theory as espoused by Immanuel Wallerstein, countries are politically and economically tied together.

1. There are four groups of interconnected nations: (1) Core nations, where capitalism first developed; (2) Semi-periphery (Mediterranean area), highly dependent on trade with core nations; (3) Periphery (eastern Europe), with limited economic development, mainly limited to selling cash crops to core nations; and (4) External area (most of Africa/Asia), left out of growth of capitalism, with few economic ties to core nations.

2. A capitalist world economy (capitalist dominance) results from relentless expansion; even external area nations are drawn into commercial web.
3. Globalization (the extensive interconnections among nations resulting from the expansion of capitalism) has sped up because of new forms of communication and transportation. The consequence is that no nation is able to live in isolation.
C. John Kenneth Galbraith argued that some nations remained poor because they were crippled by a culture of poverty, a way of life based on traditional values and religious beliefs that perpetuated poverty from one generation to the next and kept some of the Least Industrialized Nations from developing.
D. Most sociologists prefer colonialism and world system theory.
1. The culture of poverty theory places the blame on the victim, focusing on the characteristics of poor nations rather than the structural arrangements that benefit some nations (the Most Industrialized Nations) at the expense of others (the Least Industrialized Nations).
2. Each theory only partially explains global stratification.

VIII. Maintaining Global Stratification
A. Neocolonialism is the economic and political dominance of the Least Industrialized Nations by the Most Industrialized Nations.
1. Michael Harrington asserts that the Most Industrialized Nations control the Least Industrialized Nations because they control markets, set prices, and so on.
2. The Most Industrialized Nations determine how much they will pay for the natural resources and raw materials they buy from the Least Industrialized Nations; they also move hazardous industries to the Least Industrialized Nations.
3. The Most Industrialized Nations sell weapons and manufactured goods to the Least Industrialized Nations on credit, turning these countries into eternal debtors. They use resources to pay off the debt, thereby preventing them from developing their own industrial capacity.
B. Multinational corporations contribute to exploitation of the Least Industrialized Nations.
1. Some exploit the Least Industrialized Nations directly by controlling national and local politics, running them as a fiefdom.
2. The Most Industrialized Nations are primary beneficiaries of profits made in the Least Industrialized Nations.
3. They often work closely with the elite of the Least Industrialized Nations, many times in informal partnerships that are mutually beneficial.
4. In some situations, multinational corporations may bring prosperity to the Least Industrialized Nations because new factories provide salaries and opportunities that otherwise would not exist for workers in those countries.
C. The new technology favors the Most Industrialized Nations, enabling them to maintain their global domination.
1. The profits of multinational corporations can be invested in developing and acquiring the latest technology, thereby generating even greater profits.
2. Many of the Least Industrialized Nations do not have the resources to invest in new technology, creating an even greater gap between the levels of industrialization globally.

3.   Global stratification has a profound impact on each person's life, including access to material possessions, education, and even the likely age at which they will die.

Chapter Summary

Social stratification is the division of large numbers of people into layers according to their relative power, property, and prestige. It applies to both nations and to people within a nation, society, or other group. Social stratification affects all of one's life chances, from access to material possessions and position in society to life expectancy. Although they may differ as to which system of social stratification they employ, all societies stratify their members. The four major systems of social stratification are slavery, caste, estate, and class.

Slavery is defined as a form of social stratification in which some people own other people. It has been common throughout world history, with references to slavery found in the Old Testament, the Koran, and Roman and Greek history. Slavery was usually based on debt, as a punishment for a crime, or a matter of conquest. Racism was not associated with slavery until southern plantation owners developed a new ideology to justify their enslavement of Africans in the 17th century. Today, slavery is known to be practiced in the Sudan, Mauritania, and the Ivory Coast.

The caste system is a form of social stratification based on ascribed status that follows an individual throughout their life. India provides the best example of a caste system. Based on Hinduism (reincarnation and karma), India's caste system has existed for almost 3,000 years. Although the Indian government formally abolished the caste system in 1949, it still remains a respected aspect of Indian tradition and is strictly followed by a significant portion of the population.

During the middle ages, Europe developed the estate stratification system. The estate system consisted of three groups, or estates: the nobility, clergy, and commoners.

In the class system, social stratification is based on the possession of money or material possessions. A major characteristic of the class system is that it allows social mobility, or movement up and down the class ladder.

Another method by which all societies stratify their members is gender. Cutting across all systems of stratification, these gender divisions universally favor males over females.

Karl Marx and Max Weber disagreed on the meaning of social class in industrialized societies. According to Marx, people's relationship to the means of production is the sole factor in determining their social class. They either belong to the bourgeoisie (those who owned the means of production) or the proletariat (those who work for the owners). According to Weber, Marx's typology is too limiting because social class, as well as people's social class standing, consists of three interrelated components: property, prestige, and power.

Although all sociologists agree that social stratification is universal, they disagree as to why it is universal. The functionalist view of social stratification, developed by Kingsley Davis and Wilbert Moore, concludes that stratification is inevitable because society must make certain that its positions are filled; ensure that the most qualified people fill the most important positions; and, finally, to motivate the most qualified individuals to fill the most important positions, society must offer them the greatest rewards.

Melvin Tumin identified three problems with the functionalist view: first, how does one determine which positions are more important than others? Second, to what degree are societies really meritocracies (promoting people on the basis of their achievements)? Third, how functional is stratification for the people on the lower ends of the stratification continuum?

Conflict theorists contend that conflict, not function, is the basis of social stratification. Italian sociologist Gaetano Mosca argued that in every society groups compete for power. The groups that gain power use it to manipulate, control, and exploit the groups "beneath them." Members of the ruling elite in every society develop ideologies that justify their society's social stratification system. By dominating their society's major social institutions and, thereby, controlling information and ideas, members of the ruling elite are able to socialize other group members into accepting their "proper places" in the social order. Marx believed the elite maintained their position at the top of the stratification system by seducing the oppressed into believing their welfare depended on keeping society stable. Gerhard Lenski suggested the key to understanding stratification is based on the accumulation of surplus.

Depending on the political climate and resources available to those in power and those who are ruled, the stratification system is maintained by various means. These means include controlling ideas, information, technology, and the use of force. The use of force is the least efficient.

Stratification is universal, although the methods for stratification vary from culture to culture. Two examples of how stratification differs are illustrated by social stratification in Great Britain and the former Soviet Union. In Britain, the most striking features of the class system are differences in speech (including accents) and education. In the former Soviet Union, communism resulted in one set of social classes being replaced by another. The nations of the world can be divided into three categories, using the extent of industrialization as a basis for stratification. This results in a triadic division of the Most Industrialized Nations, Industrializing Nations, and Least Industrialized Nations. Just as every society stratifies its members, the nations of the world are also stratified, with the Most Industrialized Nations controlling most of the world's wealth and resources. Three theories explain the origins of global stratification: colonialism, world systems theory, and the culture of poverty.

According to those who attribute stratification to colonialism, those countries that industrialized first had an advantage over other countries and, in turn, colonized them, exploiting their labor and natural resources. World systems theory, developed by conflict theorist Immanuel Wallerstein, suggests that the world is divided between core nations (most developed economies), semi-peripheral nations (developing economies), peripheral nations (least developed economies), and external areas (not included in the development of capitalism and industrialization). Economist John Kenneth Galbraith proposed that the poor, whether in the

United States or abroad, hold cultural values and beliefs that limit their own economic growth, such as fatalism (luck, fate, and destiny). There is a tendency among sociologists to reject the culture of poverty belief because it places blame on the individual and downplays the importance of capitalism.

KEY TERMS

After studying the chapter, review the definition for each of the following terms.

apartheid: the enforced separation of racial–ethnic groups as was practiced in South Africa (224)

bonded labor (indentured service): a contractual system in which someone sells his or her body (services) for a specified period of time in an arrangement very close to slavery, except that it is entered into voluntarily (221)

bourgeoisie: Marx's term for capitalists, those who own the means of production (226, 227)

caste system: a form of social stratification in which people's statuses are determined by birth and are lifelong (222)

class consciousness: Marx's term for awareness of a common identity based on one's position in the means of production (227)

class system: a form of social stratification based primarily on the possession of money or material possessions (225)

colonialism: the process by which one nation takes over another nation, usually for the purpose of exploiting its labor and natural resources (239, 242)

culture of poverty: the assumption that the values and behaviors of the poor make them fundamentally different from other people, that these factors are largely responsible for their poverty, and that parents perpetuate poverty across generations by passing these characteristics on to their children (244)

divine right of kings: the idea that the king's authority comes from God; in an interesting gender bender, also applies to queens (232)

endogamy: the practice of marrying within one's own group (222)

estate stratification system: the stratification system of medieval Europe, consisting of three groups or estates: the nobility, clergy, and commoners (225)

false class consciousness: Marx's term to refer to workers identifying with the interests of capitalists (227)

globalization of capitalism: capitalism (investing to make profits within a rational system) becoming the globe's dominant economic system (242)

ideology: beliefs about the way things ought to be that justify social arrangements (222)

means of production: the tools, factories, land, and investment capital used to produce wealth (226, 227)

meritocracy: a form of social stratification in which all positions are awarded on the basis of merit (229)

multinational corporations: companies that operate across national boundaries; also called *transnational corporations* (245)

neocolonialism: the economic and political dominance of the Least Industrialized Nations by the Most Industrialized Nations (244)

proletariat: Marx's term for the exploited class—the mass of workers who do not own the means of production (227)

slavery: a form of social stratification in which some people own other people (220)

social mobility: movement up or down the social class ladder (226)

social stratification: the division of large numbers of people into layers according to their relative power, property, and prestige; applies to both nations and to people within a nation, society, or other group (220)

world system theory: economic and political connections that tie the world's countries together (242)

KEY PEOPLE

Review the major theoretical contributions or findings of these people.

Kingsley Davis and Wilbert Moore: According to these functionalists, inequality is universal because it motivates the most qualified members of society to strive for the most important social positions. (228-229)

W. E. B. Du Bois: This sociologist wrote about slavery in the United States, noting that over time the South became committed to keeping African Americans in slavery and killing those who rebelled against this institution. (222)

John Kenneth Galbraith: This economist argued that the Least Industrialized Nations remain poor because their own culture holds them back. (243-244)

Michael Harrington: Harrington saw that colonialism has been replaced by neocolonialism. (244)

Martha Huggins: This sociologist investigated poverty in Brazil. (238)

Gerhard Lenski: Lenski offered a synthesis of functionalist and conflict views of stratification that focused on surpluses that groups accumulate. (231)

Gerda Lerner: This historian noted that women were usually the first enslaved by war and conquest. (221-222)

Oscar Lewis: This anthropologist was among the first to write about the culture of poverty. (243)

Karl Marx: Marx concluded that social class depended exclusively on the means of production; an individual's social class was determined by whether or not he owned the means of production. (226-228, 230, 233-234)

Gaetano Mosca: Mosca argued that every society is inevitably stratified by power. (230)

Melvin Tumin: Tumin was the first to offer a criticism of the functionalist view on stratification. (229)

Immanuel Wallerstein: This historian proposed a world system theory to explain global stratification. (242)

Max Weber: Weber argued that social class was based on three components: property, prestige, and power (228)

SELF-TEST

MULTIPLE CHOICE QUESTIONS

1. What is the division of large numbers of people into layers according to their relative power, property, and prestige? (220)
   a. social distinction
   b. social stratification
   c. social distance
   d. social diversification

2. What is a form of social stratification in which some people own other people? (220)
   a. a caste system
   b. slavery
   c. a class system
   d. apartheid

3. Slavery in the United States (222)
   a. started as indentured service.
   b. was based on the ideology of racism that justified importing slaves from Africa.
   c. became inheritable.
   d. all of the above.

4. Where is the best example of a caste system found? (222-223)
   a. the United States
   b. South America
   c. India
   d. South Africa

5. In which type of stratification system is endogamy most likely to be found? (222)
   a. class system
   b. caste system
   c. meritocracy
   d. socialist system

6. The South African system of social stratification known as apartheid (224)
   a. was a caste system containing four different racial categories.
   b. was enforced by law.
   c. was brought down as a result of international pressure.
   d. all of the above.

7. In the system that existed during the middle ages, who was in the *second estate*? (225)
   a. nobility
   b. military leaders
   c. the clergy
   d. commoners

8. Which of the following characterizes class systems? (226)
   a. social mobility
   b. geographic mobility
   c. distribution of social standings belonging to an extended network of relatives
   d. fixed boundaries between layers of the stratification system

9. Which of the following statements is *correct*? (226)
   a. While men generally earn more than women, there are a small but growing number of countries where women earn more than men.
   b. About 60 percent of the world's illiterate are females.
   c. Gender is no longer an important basis for stratifying people.
   d. Gender was an important basis for stratifying people in caste and estate systems, but not in slavery or class systems.

10. According to Marx, on what does social class depend? (227)
    a. wealth, power, and prestige
    b. the means of production
    c. where one is born in the social stratification system
    d. what a person achieves during his or her lifetime

11. According to Max Weber, what determines social class? (228)
    a. One's property, prestige, and power
    b. One's relationship to the means of production
    c. One's tasks and how important they are to society
    d. One's political power

12. Which of these statements is consistent with the functionalist view of stratification? (228-229)
    a. Stratification is dysfunctional for society.
    b. Stratification is the outcome of conflict between different social classes.
    c. Stratification will disappear in societies that are characterized by a meritocracy.
    d. Stratification is an inevitable feature of social organization.

13. Which of these is *not* one of Tumin's criticisms of the functionalist theory of stratification? (229)
    a. The importance of a social position cannot be measured by the rewards it carries.
    b. The functionalists ignore the impact of family background.
    c. Stratification is not functional for everyone.
    d. The functionalists focus too much on the status and power and not enough on income.

14. According to contemporary conflict theorists, the basis of social stratification is (230)
    a. functional necessity in society.
    b. conflict over limited resources.
    c. ascribed statuses.
    d. the way in which individuals perceive their social class position.

15. According to Gerhard Lenski, the key to reconciling the various explanations of stratification is (231)
    a. whether or not a social group has a surplus.
    b. the degree to which there is universal education.
    c. the type of division of labor that characterizes the society.
    d. the size of the population.

16. The key to maintaining national stratification is (231-232)
    a. having a strong police force and military to demand compliance.
    b. control of social institutions.
    c. control of information.
    d. all of the above.

17. The British perpetuate their class system from one generation to the next by (233)
    a. emphasis on material possessions such as clothes and cars.
    b. religion.
    c. education.
    d. encouraging people in all classes to marry others within their own class.

18. In the global system of stratification presented in your textbook, where would the former Soviet Union and its satellites in eastern Europe be placed? (234)
    a. the Most Industrialized Nations
    b. the Industrializing Nations
    c. the Least Industrialized Nations
    d. none of the above

19. Which of the following statement(s) is true about the Least Industrialized Nations? (238)
    a. Most people live on less than $2,000 a year
    b. These nations account for 68 percent of the Earth's land
    c. About 5 percent of their population belongs to the elite class
    d. None of the above

20. Why is it difficult to know how to classify some nations into a global system of stratification? (239)
    a. It is difficult because the lines that separate the three levels—Most Industrialized, Industrializing, and Least Industrialized—are soft.
    b. Some nations have moved beyond industrialization, becoming "postindustrial" nations.
    c. Some nations have not yet industrialized but are still extremely wealthy.
    d. All of the above reflect problems with classifying nations into a global system.

21. In what way did U.S. colonialism differ from that of European nations? (239, 242)
    a. The United States restricted its invasions to Asian nations, such as the Philippines or Hawaii.
    b. The United States usually chose to plant corporate flags rather than national flags.

    c.   Colonialism undertaken by the United States was on a much larger scale than that of other industrialized nations.

    d.   The United States was always sensitive to the cultural and religious differences of its colonies.

22.   According to world system theory, all of the following are groups of interconnected nations *except* (242)

    a.   core nations.
    b.   nations on the semiperiphery.
    c.   nations on the periphery.
    d.   nations in the internal area that have extensive connections with the core nations.

23.   Why do most sociologists reject the culture of poverty theory in trying to explain global stratification? (244)

    a.   because it was developed by an economist, not a sociologist
    b.   because it is outdated
    c.   because it focuses on culture rather than social structure
    d.   because it places the blame for poverty on the poor nations themselves, rather than focusing on the international arrangements that benefit some at the expense of others

24.   According to the neocolonialist argument, why do so many of the Least Industrialized Nations remain poor? (244-245)

    a.   The Most Industrialized Nations set the prices they will pay for these nations' raw materials and natural resources.
    b.   The Most Industrialized Nations sell these nations weapons and manufactured goods on credit.
    c.   The capital needed to develop the industrial capacity of these nations is used to pay off their debts to the Most Industrialized Nations.
    d.   All of the above.

25.   Which of the following countries have been able to enter the race for global domination because of technology and outsourced labor? (246)

    a.   Korea and India
    b.   China and India
    c.   Russia and Yugoslavia
    d.   Hungary and Hong Kong

TRUE-FALSE QUESTIONS

1.   _____ Social stratification refers only to individuals. (220)
2.   _____ Throughout history, slavery has always been based on racism. (221)
3.   _____ The first form of slavery in the New World was indentured service. (221)
4.   _____ A class system is based primarily on money or material possessions. (225-226)
5.   _____ Gender discrimination cuts across all systems of social stratification. (226)

6. _____Functionalists believe that people should be rewarded for their unique abilities and the type of position they hold in society is not important. (228)
7. _____The idea of the divine right of kings is an example of how the ruling elite use ideas to maintain stratification. (232)
8. _____Kuwait, with its wealth, is an example of the challenge of classifying nations as least, most, and industrializing (239)
9. _____The expansion of capitalism resulted in a capitalist world economy dominated by the core nations. (242)
10. _____Sociologists generally prefer the culture of poverty thesis as an explanation of global stratification. (244)

FILL-IN-THE-BLANK QUESTIONS

1. A gray area between a contract and slavery is _____ service. (221)
2. Karl Marx argued that workers suffer from _____, workers mistakenly thinking of themselves as capitalists. (227)
3. Great Britain would be classified as a _____nation. (233)
4. _____ is the primary way by which the British perpetuate their class system. (233)
5. The _____ theory focuses on how the countries that industrialized first got the jump on the rest of the world. (239)
6. Immanuel Wallerstein calls those countries that industrialized first the _____ nations. (242)
7. Assembly-for-export plants on the Mexican-United States border are known as _____. (242)
8. John Kenneth Galbraith claimed that the _____ of the Least Industrialized Nations held them back. (244)
9. Neocolonialism theory argues that keeping least industrialized countries in _____ makes them submit to trading terms dictated by the neocolonialists. (244)
10. Multinational corporations try to work closely with the _____ of Least Industrialized Nations. (245)

ESSAY QUESTIONS

1. Compare Marx's theory of stratification with Weber's theory. Discuss why Weber's is more widely accepted by sociologists.

2. Using the different theories presented in this chapter, answer the question, "Why is stratification universal?"

3. Consider why ideology is a more effective way of maintaining stratification than brute force.

Compare and contrast the three theories of global stratification.

CHAPTER 10
SOCIAL CLASS IN THE UNITED STATES

LEARNING OBJECTIVES
After reading Chapter 10, you should be able to:

1. Define social class, describe its various components, and discuss the debate between different theorists over those components. (250-256)

2. Differentiate between wealth, power, and prestige, and talk about how each is distributed in the United States. (250-255)

3. Discuss the relationship between occupations and prestige. (254)

4. Define status inconsistency and discuss its implications. (256)

5. Compare the models of social class proposed by Karl Marx, Max Weber, Erik Wright, and that proposed by Dennis Gilbert and Joseph Kahl. (256, 258-261)

6. Describe each of the six classes in Gilbert and Kahl's model of social class. (259-261)

7. Know the consequences of social class on physical health, mental health, family life, education, religion, politics, and crime. (261-264)

8. Describe the three types of social mobility. (264-265)

9. Discuss women and social mobility. (265)

10. Know how the federal government defines poverty, as well as the implications of that definition. (266-268)

11. Identify the major characteristics of the poor in the United States. (268-271)

12. Compare structural explanations of poverty to individual explanations of poverty. (272-273)

13. Discuss recent changes in welfare policy in the United States and the controversies associated with those changes. (273-274)

14. Identify the social functions of the Horatio Alger myth and discuss the myth's sociological implications. (275-276)

Chapter Outline

I. **What Is Social Class?**
   A. Sociologists do not have a clear-cut definition of social class.
   B. Most agree with Weber that social class can be defined as a large group of people who rank close to each other in wealth, power, and prestige.
   C. Wealth consists of property (what we own) and income (money we receive). Wealth and income are not always the same; a person may own much property yet have little income, or vice versa. Usually, however, wealth and income go together.
       1. Ownership of property (real estate, stocks and bonds, and so on) is not distributed evenly: 10 percent of the U.S. population owns 70 percent of the wealth, and the wealthiest 1 percent of Americans own one-third of all assets in the United States.
       2. Income is also distributed disproportionately: the top 20 percent of U.S. residents acquire 47 percent of the income; the bottom 20 percent receives 4.2 percent. Each one-fifth of the U.S. population receives approximately the same proportion of national income today as it did in 1935; those changes that have occurred reflect growing inequality.
       3. Apart from the very rich, the most affluent group in U.S. society is the executive officers of the largest corporations. Their median income (including salaries, bonuses, and stock options) is $3 million a year.
   D. Power is the ability to carry out your will despite resistance.
   E. Mills coined the term "the power elite" to refer to those who are the big decision makers in U.S. society. This group shares the same ideologies and values, belongs to the same clubs, and reinforces each other's world view.
   F. Domhoff believes that no major decision in the U.S. government is made without their approval.
   G. Prestige is the respect or regard people give to various occupations and accomplishments.
       1. Occupations are the primary source of prestige, although some people gain prestige through inventions, feats, or performing good deeds for others. Occupations with the highest prestige pay more, require more education, entail more abstract thought, and offer greater autonomy.
       2. For prestige to be valuable, people must acknowledge it. The elite traditionally have made rules to emphasize their higher status.
       3. Status symbols, which vary according to social class, are ways of displaying prestige. In the United States, they include designer-label clothing, expensive cars, prestigious addresses, and attending particular schools.
   H. Status inconsistency is the term used to describe the situation of people who have a mixture of high and low rankings in the three components of social class (wealth, power, and prestige).
       1. Most people are status consistent; they rank at the same level in all three components. People who are status inconsistent want others to act toward them

on the basis of their highest status, but others tend to judge them on the basis of their lowest status.

2. Sociologist Gerhard Lenski determined that people suffering the frustrations of status inconsistency are more likely to be radical and approve political action aimed against higher status groups.

3. Status inconsistency is common for lottery winners whose wealth is vastly greater than either their education or occupational status.

II. Sociological Models of Social Class

A. How many classes exist in industrial society is a matter of debate, but there are two main models, one that builds on Marx and the other on Weber.

B. Sociologist Erik Wright realized that not everyone falls into Marx's two broad classes (capitalists and workers, which were based on a person's relationship to the means of production). For instance, although executives, managers, and supervisors would fall into Marx's category of workers, they act more like capitalists.

    1. Wright resolved this problem by regarding some people as simultaneously members of more than one class, which he called contradictory class locations.

    2. Wright identified four classes: capitalists (owners of large enterprises); petty bourgeoisie (owners of small businesses); managers (employees who have authority over others); and workers.

C. Using the model originally developed by Weber, sociologists Dennis Gilbert and Joseph Kahl created a model to describe class structure in the United States and other capitalist countries.

    1. The capitalist class (1 percent of the population) is composed of investors, heirs, and a few executives; it is divided into "old" money and "new" money. The children of "new" money move into the old money class by attending the right schools and marrying "old" money.

    2. The upper-middle class (15 percent of the population) is composed of professionals and upper managers, almost all of whom have attended college or university and frequently have postgraduate degrees. This class is the one most shaped by education.

    3. The lower-middle class (34 percent of the population) is composed of lower managers, craftspeople and foremen. They have at least a high-school education.

    4. The working class (30 percent of the population) is composed of factory workers and low-paid white-collar workers. Most have high-school educations.

    5. The working poor (16 percent of the population) is composed of relatively unskilled blue-collar and white-collar workers and those with temporary and seasonal jobs. If they graduated from high school, they probably did not do well in school.

    6. The underclass (4 percent of the population) is concentrated in the inner cities and has little connection with the job market. Welfare is their main support.

    7. The homeless are so far down the class structure that their position must be considered even lower than the underclass. They are the "fallout" of

industrialization, especially the postindustrial developments that have led to a decline in the demand for unskilled labor.

    D.   The automobile industry illustrates the social class ladder as described by Gilbert and Kahl.

        1.   The Ford family and Ford executives represent both the upper and lower levels of the capitalist class.

        2.   Owners of Ford dealerships are members of the upper middle class, while a salesperson employed there is drawn from the lower middle class.

        3.   Mechanics who repair Ford automobiles are members of the working class. The working poor are presented by the "detail" workers.

        4.   If the agency employs day laborers to mow the lawn or clean the lot, they would come from the underclass.

III. Consequences of Social Class

    A.   The lower a person's social class, the more likely that person is to die at an earlier age than people in higher classes; this is true at all ages. Social class shapes our lifestyles, which affects our health. Also, since medical care is expensive, the higher classes receive better medical care, despite government aid to the poor; the result is a two-tiered system of medical care. Additionally, life is better for those in higher social classes. They have fewer problems and more resources to deal with the ones that those in lower classes have.

    B.   Mental health is worse for the lower classes because of stresses associated with their class position. Those higher in the class system are better able to afford vacations, psychiatrists, and counselors; their class position gives them greater control over their lives, which is a key to good mental health.

    C.   Social class also plays a role in family life.

        1.   Children of the capitalist class are under great pressure to select the right mate in order to assure the continuity of the family line. Parents in this social class play a large role in mate selection.

        2.   Marriages are more likely to fail in the lower social classes, given the challenges of inadequate income; the children of the poor are therefore more likely to live in single-parent households.

        3.   Child rearing varies by class, with each class raising its children with attitudes and behaviors suited to the kinds of occupations they will eventually hold. Lower-class families teach children to defer to authority, as is required in their jobs. Middle-class families encourage freedom, creativity, and self-expression, as is found in their jobs.

    D.   Education levels increase as one moves up the social class ladder. The change occurs not only in terms of the amount of education obtained, but also in terms of the type of education, with the capitalist class bypassing public schools in favor of exclusive private schools, where children are trained to take a commanding role in society.

    E.   All aspects of religious orientation follow class lines. Social classes tend to cluster around different denominations. Lower classes are attracted to spontaneous worship services and louder music, such as that found with Baptists, while higher classes prefer more restrained worship services, such as those found in the Methodist religion.

F. Political views and involvement are influenced by social class.
1. The rich and the poor take divergent political paths, with people in lower social classes more likely to vote Democrat, while those in higher classes vote Republican; the parties are seen as promoting different class interests.
2. People in the working class are more likely to be liberal on economic issues (more government spending) and more conservative on social issues (opposition to abortion).
3. Political participation is not equal: the higher classes are more likely to vote and get involved in politics than those in lower social classes.

G. The criminal justice system is not blind to class, either.
1. The white-collar crimes of the more privileged classes are more likely to be dealt with outside of the criminal justice system, while the street crimes of the lower classes are dealt with by the police and courts.
2. Members of lower classes are more likely to be arrested; they are more likely to be on probation, parole, or in jail; and more crimes occur in lower class neighborhoods.

IV. Social Mobility
A. There are three basic types of social mobility: intergenerational, structural, and exchange.
1. Intergenerational mobility is the change that family members make in their social class from one generation to the next. As a result of individual effort, a person can rise from one level to another; in the event of individual failure, the reverse can be true.
2. Structural mobility involves social changes that affect large numbers of people. By way of example, when computers were invented, many opportunities opened up for people to switch from blue-collar to white-collar work. While individual effort played a role, the major reason for the change in position was structural.
3. Exchange mobility is movement of people up and down the social class system, where, on balance, the system remains the same. The term refers to general, overall movement of large numbers of people that leaves the class system basically untouched.

B. Women have been largely ignored in studies of occupational mobility. Studies of social mobility among men indicate that about one-half of sons have moved beyond their fathers; about one-third have stayed at the same level; and about one-sixth have fallen down the ladder.
1. As structural changes in the U.S. economy have created opportunities for women to move up the social class ladder, studies of their mobility patterns have appeared.
2. One study indicated that women who did move up were encouraged by their parents to postpone marriage and get an education.

C. Statistics can be used either positively or negatively to explain social mobility depending on the purpose.
   1. It appears that about one-third of the poorest 10 percent and one-third of the richest 10 percent of children end up in the same social class as their parents.
D. The costs of social mobility include risking the loss of one's roots.
   1. A study of British women who had achieved middle class status through education or marriage found that these women were caught between two worlds—the one they were brought up in and their current one.
   2. An American study found that among working-class families in which the adult children had achieved upward social mobility because of parental sacrifices that enabled them to get an education, the parent-adult child relationship was marked by estrangement, lack of communication, and bitterness.

V. **Poverty**
   A. The U.S. government classifies the poverty line as families whose incomes are less than three times a low-cost food budget.
      1. This official measure is grossly inadequate since it inflates the amount of money that is spent on food. It is also the same across the country, even though the cost of living is higher in some states than others.
      2. Any modification of this measure instantly adds or subtracts millions of people and thus has significant consequences.
   B. Certain social groups are disproportionately represented among the poor population.
      1. The poor tend to be clustered in the South, a pattern that has existed for about 100 years. The poverty rate for the rural poor is higher than the national average. While they show the same racial and ethnic characteristics as the nation as a whole, they are less likely to be on welfare or to be single parents, are less skilled and educated, and find that only lower-paying jobs are available to them.
      2. Race is a major factor. Racial minorities are much more likely to be poor: 10 percent of whites, 21 percent of Latinos and 24 percent of African Americans live in poverty.
      3. The chances of being poor decrease as the amount of education increases.
      4. The gender of the person who heads a family is another major predictor of whether or not a family is poor. Most poor families are headed by women. The major causes of this occurrence, called the feminization of poverty, are divorce, births to unwed mothers, and the lower wages paid to women.
      5. Although the percentage of poor people over age 65 is practically the same as their overall percentage, elderly Hispanic Americans and African Americans are almost three times more likely to be poor than elderly white Americans.
      6. The elderly are less likely than the general population to be poor.
   C. Children are more likely to live in poverty than are adults or the elderly. This holds true regardless of race, but poverty is much greater among minority children.
   D. In the 1960s, it was suggested that the poor get trapped in a "culture of poverty" as a result of having values and behaviors that make them "fundamentally different" from other U.S. residents.

1. National statistics indicate that most poverty is short, lasting one year or less. Only 12 percent of the poor live in poverty for five or more years.
2. Since the number of people who live in poverty remains fairly constant, this means that as many people move into poverty as move out of it.

E. In trying to explain poverty, the choice is between focusing on individual explanations or on social structural explanations.
   1. Sociologists look to such factors as inequalities in education; access to learning job skills; racial, ethnic, age, and gender discrimination; and large-scale economic change to explain the patterns of poverty in society.
   2. The other explanation is individualistic, focusing on the characteristics of individuals that are assumed to contribute to their poverty.

F. In 1996, federal welfare reform was enacted. There are caps on welfare assistance, and recipients are required to look for work.
   1. In the aftermath of this, welfare rolls dropped. However, this does not mean that people are working; they may not be on welfare because they have reached their limit.
   2. Conflict theorists argue that the purpose of the welfare system is to maintain an army of reserve workers. In times of economic expansion, welfare requirements are tightened, forcing workers into the job market. When recession hits, welfare rules are relaxed.
   3. Two out of five who left welfare also moved out of poverty. Three out of five are still in poverty or back on welfare. A third that were forced off welfare have no jobs.

G. Because the poor don't see the future as different from the past, they find it difficult to defer gratification—that is, give up things now for the sake of greater gains in the future. Sociologists argue that the behaviors of the poor are not the cause of their poverty but rather a result of their poverty.

H. Because of real-life examples of people from humble origins who climbed far up the social ladder, most U.S. residents (including minorities and the working poor) believe that they have a chance of getting ahead.
   1. The Horatio Alger myth obviously is a statistical impossibility. Despite this, functionalists would stress that this belief is functional for society because it encourages people to compete for higher positions while placing the blame for failure squarely on the individual.
   2. As Marx and Weber both noted, social class affects our ideas of life and our proper place in society. At the same time, the dominant ideology often blinds us to these effects in our own lives.

Chapter Summary

"There are the poor and the rich, and then there are you and I, neither poor nor rich." This summarizes the level of consciousness most Americans have regarding social class. The fact is that sociologists have no clear-cut, agreed-upon definition of social class. However, most sociologists adopt Max Weber's components of social class, defining it as a large group of people who rank close to one another in terms of wealth, power, and prestige.

Wealth and income are not synonymous. It is possible to have great wealth and little income or little wealth but a high income. Wealth and income are unevenly distributed in the United States, with a large and growing gap separating the richest Americans from the poorest. The top 20 percent of the population receives almost half of all the income in the United States, while the bottom 20 percent receives only slightly more than 4 percent of the nation's income. An elite group of Americans, made up of the nation's wealthiest people, wields extraordinary economic, social, and political power in the United States. Conversely, the poorest Americans face tremendous hardships because they lack the means to afford even the most basic necessities of life.

Jobs that pay more, require more education, entail more abstract thought, and offer greater autonomy are ranked higher than jobs that require less education, are lower paying, involve more physical labor, and are closely supervised. A chart of occupational prestige shows that physicians, college professors, and lawyers hold the most prestigious positions, and bill collectors, factory workers, and gas station attendants are among the least prestigious positions.

Sociologists use the term "status inconsistency" to refer to people who rank higher on some dimensions of social class and lower on others. A study by Ray Gold showed that unionized apartment-house janitors made more money than many of the tenants for whom they cleaned and carried out their garbage.

Although both Karl Marx and Max Weber proposed models of social class, both of these models have been modified to be more representative of the class structure as it now exists. Modifying Karl Marx's model of social class, sociologist Erik Wright identified four classes: capitalists, petty bourgeoisie, managers, and workers. Sociologists Dennis Gilbert and Joseph Kahl developed a social class model that consists of six classes: the capitalist class, the upper middle class, the lower middle class, the working class, the working poor, and the underclass.

Among other things, social class affects and/or influences people's health, family life, education, religion, and politics. The lower one's social class, the more likely that individual will die before the expected age. People from the lower classes are also more likely to smoke, eat more fat, use drugs and alcohol excessively, become involved with violent crime, exercise less, and practice unsafe sexual behavior leading to higher rates of sexually transmitted diseases, higher rates of out-of-wedlock child births, higher infidelity rates, and higher divorce rates. Mental illness is also more closely associated with the lower class population.

Unlike other systems of stratification, class is the most fluid, offering opportunities and providing social mobility—both vertically and horizontally along the social class ladder. Sociologists have identified three basic types of social mobility: intergenerational mobility, structural mobility, and exchange mobility. The degree of mobility is significantly affected by many things, including access to technology, culture, race–ethnicity, gender, age, and, especially, marital status and where people live.

To measure the degree of poverty a family faces, the government established a standard based on family size and income. The model is based on the factor of three times what the average family of a specific size would spend on food. Families making less than the calculated amount are considered to be below the poverty line and entitled to benefits specifically available to the poor.

The poor are not evenly distributed throughout the United States. There is a clustering of poverty in the South, among African Americans and Latinos, among individuals with less education, and among women. Children are the most adversely affected by poverty and are more likely than adults to live in poverty. The number of children living in poverty is disproportionately high among single-parent families.

The reasons people are poor fall between two competing explanations: one stresses features of society that limit some people's access to opportunities; the other focuses on people's beliefs, attitudes, and behaviors. In an effort to encourage people in poverty to be more self-sufficient, the welfare system was restructured in 1996, requiring states to place a lifetime cap on welfare assistance and requiring welfare recipients to look for and take available jobs.

Portraying America as a land of limitless economic possibilities, the Horatio Alger myth equates hard work with upward social mobility. It suggests that all people who fail to achieve success in America fail because of their own shortcomings.

KEY TERMS
After studying the chapter, review the definition for each of the following terms.

anomie: Durkheim's term for a condition of society in which people become detached from the norms that usually guide their behavior (256)

contradictory class locations: Erik Wright's term for a position in the class structure that generates contradictory interests (258)

culture of poverty: the assumption that the values and behaviors of the poor make them fundamentally different from other people, that these factors are largely responsible for their poverty, and that parents perpetuate poverty across generations by passing these characteristics to their children (272)

deferred gratification: doing without something in the present in the hope of achieving greater gains in the future (275)

downward social mobility: movement down the social class ladder (265)

exchange mobility: about the same numbers of people moving up and down the social class ladder such that, on balance, the social class system shows little change (265)

feminization of poverty (the): refers to the situation that most poor families in the U.S. are headed by women (269)

Horatio Alger myth: the belief that due to limitless possibilities anyone can get ahead if he or she tries hard enough (275)

income: money received, usually from a job, business, or assets (250)

intergenerational mobility: the change that family members make in social class from one generation to the next (264)

poverty line: the official measure of poverty; calculated to include incomes that are less than three times a low-cost food budget (266)

power: the ability to get your way, even over the resistance of others (254)

power elite: C. Wright Mills' term for the top people in U.S. corporations, military, and politics who make the nation's major decisions (254)

prestige: respect or regard (254)

property: material possessions: animals, bank accounts, bonds, buildings, businesses, cars, furniture, land, and stocks (250)

social class: according to Weber, a large group of people who rank close to one another in wealth, prestige, and power; according to Marx, one of two groups: capitalists who own the means of production and workers who sell their labor (250)

status: the position that someone occupies in a social group (256)

status consistency: ranking high or low on all three dimensions of social class (256)

status inconsistency: ranking high on some dimensions of social class and low on others; also called *status discrepancy* (256)

structural mobility: movement up or down the social class ladder that is due to changes in the structure of society, not to individual efforts (265)

underclass: a group of people for whom poverty persists year after year and across generations (261)

upward social mobility: movement up the social class ladder (265)

wealth: the total value of everything someone owns, minus the debts (250)

KEY PEOPLE

Review the major theoretical contributions or findings of these people.

William Domhoff: Drawing upon the work of C. Wright Mills, Domhoff states that the power elite is so powerful that no major decision in the U.S. government is made without its approval. (254, 258)

Dennis Gilbert and Joseph Kahl: These sociologists developed a more contemporary stratification model based on Max Weber's work. (258-260, 264)

Ray Gold: In research on status inconsistency, Gold studied tenant reactions to janitors who earned more than they did. He found that the tenants acted "snooty" to the janitors, and the janitors took pleasure in knowing the intimate details of the tenants' lives. (256)

Daniel Hellinger and Dennis Judd: These sociologists identified the average citizen's belief that he/she exercises political power through the voting process as the "democratic facade" that conceals the real source of power in the United States. (254)

Elizabeth Higginbotham and Lynn Weber: These sociologists studied the mobility patterns for women. They found that those women who experienced upward mobility were most likely to have strong parental support to defer marriage and get an education. (265)

Steph Lawler: This sociologist interviewed British women who had achieved upward mobility through education or marriage. (266)

Elliot Liebow: In 1967, this sociologist studied black, street-corner men. He noted that their circumstances made it difficult for them to save for the future, since whatever funds they had were needed to survive in the present. (274)

Gerhard Lenski: Lenski noted that everyone wants to maximize his or her status, but others often judge an individual on the basis of his or her lowest status despite the individual's efforts to be judged on the basis of his or her highest status. (256)

Karl Marx: Marx believed that there were only two social classes—the capitalists and the workers. Membership is based on a person's relationship to the means of production. (250, 256, 258)

C. Wright Mills: Mills used the term "power elite" to describe the top decision makers in the nation. (254)

Richard Sennett and Jonathan Cobb: Sennett and Cobb studied the impact that a child's upward mobility had on his or her relationship with his or her parents. They found that the parents' sacrifices in order to afford the educational costs for their children were rarely appreciated; with increased education the children grew distant from the parents' world. (266)

Max Weber: Weber developed the definition of social class that is used by most sociologists. He noted that social class is made up of a large group of people who rank close to one another in terms of wealth, power, and prestige. (250, 260)

Erik Wright: Wright proposed an updated version of Marx's theory of stratification. (258)

MULTIPLE CHOICE QUESTIONS

1. According to your text, on what do most sociologists agree concerning social class? (250)
   a. It has a clear-cut, accepted definition in sociology.
   b. It is best defined by the two classes as set out by Marx.
   c. It is best defined by Weber's dimensions of social class.
   d. It has no clear-cut, accepted definition and thus is used differently by all sociologists.

2. According to Paul Samuelson, if an income pyramid were made out of a child's blocks that were 1½ in. tall, how far off the ground would the typical American be? (251)
   a. 2 ft.
   b. 6 ft.
   c. 10 ft.
   d. 12 ft.

3. Which of the following statements best describes changes in the distribution of U.S. income? (251)
   a. The income distribution has remained virtually unchanged across time.
   b. The percentage of income going to the richest 20 percent of U.S. families has declined while the percentage going to the poorest 20 percent has increased.
   c. The percentage of income going to the middle income groups has increased at the expense of groups at both the top and bottom of the income scale.
   d. The percentage of income going to the richest 20 percent of U.S. families has increased while the percentage going to the poorest 20 percent has decreased.

4. What term do Hellinger and Judd use to describe the myth that the average citizen exercises power when he or she votes for representatives to Congress or the U.S. president? (254)
   a. democratic charade
   b. popular façade
   c. democratic façade
   d. political power myth

5. Which of the statements regarding the jobs that have the most prestige is *not* true? (254)
   a. They pay more.
   b. They require more education.
   c. They require special talent or skills.
   d. They offer greater autonomy.

6. Based on his research, what did Ray Gold discover about status inconsistency? (256)
   a. College professors tend to be politically radical.
   b. Most people ignore their own inconsistent status while focusing on others.

c. Tenants related to the inconsistent status of the apartment building janitors by acting "snooty" toward them.

d. Status inconsistency is a very uncommon situation because most people try to be placed in approximately the same place in all three dimensions of stratification.

7. How did Erik Wright update Marx's class categories in response to criticisms that they were too broad? (258)
    a. He divided each of the two classes into three sub-classes, making six classes in all.
    b. He created an open scale in which people place themselves into classes.
    c. He recommended listing people's different associations and then classifying them on the basis of their most important one.
    d. He recognized that people can be members of more than one class at the same time.

8. According to Gilbert and Kahl, the members of which social class can attribute their location in the class system to having a college or postgraduate education? (258)
    a. the capitalist class
    b. the upper middle class
    c. the lower middle class
    d. the working class

9. According to Gilbert and Kahl, all of the following describe the working class *except* (258)
    a. Most are employed in relatively unskilled blue-collar and white-collar jobs.
    b. Most have attended college for one or two years.
    c. Most hope to get ahead by achieving seniority on the job.
    d. About 30 percent of the population belongs to this class.

10. Which of the following statements best describes the place of the homeless in our system today? (261)
    a. They are on the lowest rung with little or no chance of climbing anywhere.
    b. They are the "fallout" of our developing postindustrial economy.
    c. In another era, they would have had plenty of work as unskilled laborers.
    d. All of the above

11. According to your text, the typical mechanic in a Ford dealership would be in the (260)
    a. upper-middle class.
    b. lower-middle class.
    c. working class.
    d. underclass.

12. What factor or factors explain the social class difference in death rates? (262)
    a. two-tiered system of medical care
    b. lifestyle differences
    c. unequal access to medical care

d. all of the above

13. Which of the following statements about social class differences in mental health is *correct*? (262)
    a. The rich have less control over their wealth, since it is invested in the stock market, so they worry more about becoming poor.
    b. The poor have less job security and lower wages than the non-poor, which contributes to higher levels of stress.
    c. The rich experience more divorce and alcoholism, which can undermine their mental health.
    d. The middle class is squeezed by higher and higher taxes, which produces feelings of discontent and poor mental health.

14. According to Melvin Kohn, lower-class parents are concerned that their children are (263)
    a. creative.
    b. independent.
    c. conformists.
    d. all of the above

15. Which class tends to bypass public schools entirely, in favor of exclusive private schools? (263)
    a. capitalist
    b. upper-middle
    c. middle
    d. all of the above

16. Which class tends to be conservative on social issues but liberal on economic ones? (264)
    a. upper class
    b. middle class
    c. lower class
    d. working class

17. What types of criminal activities are most likely to be handled outside of the criminal justice system? (264)
    a. street crime
    b. organized crime
    c. white-collar crime
    d. petty crimes

18. A homeless person whose father was a physician has experienced (265)
    a. exchange mobility.
    b. structural mobility.
    c. upward mobility.

    d.   downward mobility.

19. Higgenbotham and Weber found that for career women from working class backgrounds (265)
    a.   intergenerational mobility was greater for sons than for daughters.
    b.   upwardly mobile women achieved higher positions despite their parent's reservations.
    c.   upwardly mobile women achieved higher class positions because of parental encouragement that began when they were just little girls.
    d.   any upward mobility was due entirely to structural changes in the economy rather than individual effort or parental influences.

20. What did sociologists Steph Lawler discover about social mobility? (266)
    a.   It was much more painful moving down the social class ladder than up.
    b.   Moving up or down the social class ladder had no effect on individuals.
    c.   It was just as painful to move up the social class ladder as down.
    d.   None of the above

21. What was the greatest challenge faced by African Americans who experienced upward social mobility? (267)
    a.   adjusting to whites as a primary reference group
    b.   adapting to new jobs and being the supervisor
    c.   moving into exclusive white neighborhoods
    d.   leaving behind one's racial/ethnic group

22. In the United States, which group has poverty rates that are lower than the national average? (271)
    a.   women
    b.   racial minorities
    c.   the elderly
    d.   children

23. In trying to explain poverty, sociologists are most likely to stress (272)
    a.   individual characteristics that are assumed to contribute to poverty.
    b.   features of the social structure that contribute to poverty.
    c.   decisions made by the poor that prevent them from ever moving out of poverty.
    d.   that poverty is intergenerational, so that most who are born poor will remain poor.

24. Why is it difficult for the poor to practice deferred gratification? (274)
    a.   because they need all their resources to survive in the present
    b.   because they lack proper values
    c.   because they care only about living in the present
    d.   because they are weak and can't save

25. The Horatio Alger myth (275-276)
    a. is beneficial for society, according to the functionalists.
    b. reduces pressures on the social system.
    c. motivates people to try harder to succeed because anything is possible.
    d. all of the above

TRUE-FALSE QUESTIONS

1. _____Within sociology, there is a clear-cut, widely accepted definition of social class. (250)
2. _____Apart from the very rich, the most affluent group in U.S. society consists of the chief executive officers of the nation's largest corporations. (254)
3. _____College professors typically are an example of status inconsistency. (256)
4. _____Lottery winners often find themselves experiencing status inconsistency. (256)
5. _____The distinctions between lower middle class and working class are more blurred than those between other classes. (260)
6. _____Marriages of the poor are more likely to fail and their children to grow up in broken homes. (263)
7. _____Members of the lower classes are more likely to be on probation, on parole, or in jail than members of the upper classes. (264)
8. _____Exchange mobility leaves the class system basically untouched. (265)
9. _____The majority of the poor live below the poverty line for more than five years. (270)
10. _____Sociological explanations of poverty tend to focus on structural features of society more than on any particular characteristics of poor individuals. (272)

FILL-IN-THE-BLANK QUESTIONS

1. _____ consists of property and income. (250)
2. Seventy percent of the total net worth of all U.S. families is owned by ___ percent of U.S. families. (251)
3. C. Wright Mills coined the term _____ to refer to those who make the big decisions in U.S. Society. (254)
4. Only about ____ percent of the U.S. population occupies the top rung of the class ladder. (259)
5. Social class is so significant it affects our chances of living and _____. (262)
6. Lower classes experience higher rates of marital friction and _____. (263)
7. _____ is the change that family members make in social class from one generation to another. (264)
8. The majority of the poor in the U.S. are clustered in the _____. (268-269)
9. _____ of poverty is the trend in the U.S. whereby most poor families are headed by women. (269)

10.	Conflict theorists believe that the purpose of welfare is to maintain a _____.
	(274)

ESSAY QUESTIONS

1.	Identify the three dimensions of social class and discuss some of the consequences of social class.

2.	Discuss why you think women have been largely ignored in studies of mobility.

3.	Describe which groups are at greater risk of poverty, and then suggest ways in which poverty can be reduced by targeting these populations.

4.	Explore why individual explanations of poverty are easier for the average American to accept than structural explanations.

5.	Discuss the Horatio Alger myth and whether or not it is functional for society.

CHAPTER 11
SEX AND GENDER

LEARNING OBJECTIVES

After reading Chapter 11, you should be able to:

1. Define gender stratification and distinguish between sex and gender. (280)

2. Understand the controversy over what most accounts for gender differences in behavior—biology or culture—and explain the dominant sociological position in the debate. (280, 282-283)

3. Describe the global nature of gender inequality and provide concrete examples of global gender discrimination. (285-289, 292)

4. Evaluate the different theories on the origins of patriarchy. (285-287)

5. Define feminism. (292)

6. Describe the three "waves" of the women's movement in the United States. (294-295)

7. Discuss the rights and gains women have achieved over the last 100 years. (292, 294-295)

8. Talk about different forms of gender inequality in everyday life, including the general devaluation of femininity. (295-305)

9. Provide examples of gender inequality in education, the workplace, and politics in the United States. (296-308)

10. Know what constitutes sexual harassment and understand how unwanted sexual advances are part of a structural problem in the United States. (305)

11. Discuss gender relations in the workplace, including the pay gap, the glass ceiling, the glass escalator, the "mommy track," and sexual harassment. (301-305)

12. Explain how and why violence against women continues to be a significant social problem in the United States. (305-307)

13. Discuss how and why women are underrepresented in American politics. (307-308)

14. Describe future scenarios of gender definitions and relations in the United States. (308)

Chapter Outline

I. **Issues of Sex and Gender**

    A. Gender stratification refers to men's and women's unequal access to power, prestige, and property.

        1. Gender is especially significant because it is a master status, cutting across all aspects of social life.

        2. No matter what we attain in our lifetime, we carry the labels male and female with us; this label guides our behavior and serves as a basis of power and privilege.

    B. Sex and gender reflect different biases.

        1. Sex is biological characteristics distinguishing males and females, including primary sex organs (organs related to reproduction) and secondary sex organs (physical distinctions not related to reproduction).

        2. Gender is a social characteristic that varies from one society to another and refers to what the group considers proper for its males and females.

        3. The sociological significance of gender is that it is the means by which society controls its members; it sorts us, on the basis of sex, into different life experiences.

    C. Some researchers argue that biological factors (two X chromosomes in females, one X and one Y in males) result in differences in conduct, with men being more aggressive and domineering and women being more comforting and nurturing.

        1. Larry Summers, the president of Harvard, made a controversial statement when he said that the reason there are fewer female engineers and scientists is due to innate differences between men and women—that is, biological (not sociological) factors account for the difference. His statement was met with anger by his colleagues at Harvard as well as by other organizations.

    D. The dominant sociological position is that social factors explain why we do what we do. People in every society determine what the physical differences separating men and women mean to them.

        1. Children learn these contrasting explanations of life and then take the positions that society assigns to them on the basis of their sex.

        2. Sociologists argue that if biology was the primary factor in human behavior, then women the world over would all behave the same way, as would men. In fact, ideas of gender vary greatly from one culture to another.

    E. The idea, however, that biological factors are involved in human behavior is being acknowledged by some sociologists. Real-life cases provide support for the argument that men's and women's behavior is influenced by biology.

        1. Alice Rossi suggested that women are better prepared biologically for "mothering" than are men; nature provides biological predispositions that are overlaid with culture.

        2. A medical accident led to a young boy being reassigned to the female sex. Reared as a female, the child behaved like a girl; however, by adolescence she was

unhappy and having a difficult time adjusting to being a female. In adolescence, the child underwent medical procedures to once again become a male.

        3.   A study of Vietnam veterans found that the men who had higher levels of testosterone tended to be more aggressive and to have more problems.

    F.   Traditional models of gender expect males to have large muscles, endurance and stamina, victory in competitive events, and achievement despite huge obstacles. They require masculinity defined as "not feminine." Females are expected to show emotion, express greater compassion, and feel and show fears and weaknesses.

    G.   New models of gender include a softer masculinity among males and stronger dominance among females.

II. Gender Inequality in Global Perspective

    A.   Around the world, gender is *the* primary division between people. Because society sets up barriers to deny women equal access, they are referred to as a minority even though they outnumber men.

    B.   The major theory of the origin of patriarchy points to social consequences of human reproduction.

        1.   Since life was short and women were tied to reproductive roles, they assumed tasks around the home.

        2.   Men took over hunting of large animals and left the home base for extended periods of time. This enabled men to make contact with other tribes, trade with those other groups, and wage war and gain prestige by returning home with prisoners of war or with large animals to feed the tribe; little prestige was given to women's more routine tasks.

    C.   A second theory focuses on the disadvantage women faced in hand-to-hand combat, which often led to the imprisonment of women for sex and labor.

    D.   After reviewing the historical record, historian and feminist Gerda Lerner has concluded that women as a group have never held decision-making power over men as a group. This was true even in the earliest known societies, in which there was much less gender discrimination.

    E.   George Murdock, who surveyed 324 premodern societies, found activities to be sex-typed in all of them; activities considered female in one society may be male in another. There is nothing about anatomy that requires this.

    F.   Universally, greater prestige is given to male activities regardless of what they are. If caring for cattle is men's work, it carries high prestige; if it is women's work, it has less prestige.

    G.   Globally, gender discrimination occurs in the areas of education, politics, paid employment, and violence against women.

III. Gender Inequality in the United States

    A.   A society's culture and institutions both justify and maintain its customary forms of gender inequality.

B. Until the twentieth century, U.S. women did not have the right to vote, hold property, make legal contracts, or serve on a jury.

1. Males did not willingly surrender their privileges; rather, greater political rights for women resulted from a prolonged and bitter struggle waged by a "first wave" of feminists in the nineteenth and early twentieth centuries.

2. This movement was divided into radical and conservative branches. The radical branch wanted to reform all social institutions, while the conservative branch concentrated only on winning the vote for women. After 1920 and the achievement of suffrage for women, the movement dissolved.

3. A "second wave" of feminism began in the 1960s. As more women gained an education and began to work outside the home, they compared their wages and working conditions to those of men. As awareness of gender inequalities grew, protest and struggle emerged. The goals of this second wave of feminism are broad, from changing work roles to changing policies on violence against women.

4. The second wave of feminism was also characterized by two branches, one conservative and the other liberal, each of which has had different goals and different tactics.

5. A "third wave" is now emerging. Three main aspects are apparent. The first is a greater focus on women in the least industrialized nations. The second is a criticism of the values that dominate work and society. The third is the removal of barriers to women's love and sexual pleasure.

6. While women enjoy more rights today, gender inequality still continues to play a central role in social life.

C. There is growing evidence of sexual discrimination in health care.

1. Studies showed that women were twice as likely to die after coronary bypass surgery than men. Physicians had not taken the complaints of chest pain as seriously in female patients as they had males. As a result, women received surgery later, after the disease had a chance to progress, thereby reducing their chance for survival.

2. Surgeons were also likely to recommend more radical surgeries to their female patients on their reproductive system than necessary.

D. There is evidence of educational gains made by women; more females than males are enrolled in U.S. colleges and universities, females earn 56 percent of all bachelor's degrees, women complete bachelor's degrees faster than men, and the proportion of professional degrees earned by women has increased sharply. Despite these gains, some old practices and patterns persist.

1. Women's sports are still underfunded because they are not considered as important as men's sports.

2. There is still the matter of gender tracking. In college, males and females are channeled into different fields; 81 percent of engineering degrees are awarded to males, while 88 percent of library science degrees are awarded to women.

3. In graduate school, the proportion of females enrolled in programs decreases with each passing year of education.

4. There is gender stratification in both the rank and pay within higher educational institutions. Women professors are less likely to be in the higher ranks of academia, are paid less than their male counterparts, and are less likely to be taken seriously.

E. Patterns of gender discrimination continue to exist in everyday life.
1. Females' capacities, interests, attitudes, and contributions are not taken as seriously as those of males. For example, the worst insult that can be thrown at a male is that he is a sissy or that he does things like a girl.
2. Patterns of conversation reflect inequalities between men and women. Men are more likely than women to interrupt a conversation and control a change in topics.

IV. Gender Inequality in the Workplace

A. One of the chief characteristics of the U.S. work force is the steady growth in the number of women who work outside the home for wages.
1. Today, nearly one in every two women is employed.
2. Men earn more than women, even when their educational achievement is the same. U.S. women who work full-time average only 68 percent of what men are paid. All industrialized nations have a pay gap.
3. Studies have found an association between height and income. Taller men (over 6 ft. tall) made more money than shorter men. Taller females also earned more than shorter women.
4. Researchers found that half of the gender pay gap is due to women choosing lower-paying careers. The other half is due to gender discrimination and the "child penalty"—women missing out on work experience while they care for their children.
5. On average, men start out with higher salaries than women after graduating from college.
6. Of the top 500 corporations, only eight are headed by women. The best chance to be CEO of the largest U.S. corporations is to have a name such as John, Robert, James, William, or Charles. One of the few women to head a Fortune 500 company had a man's name: Carleton Fiorina of Hewlett-Packard.

B. The "glass ceiling" describes an invisible barrier that women face in trying to reach the executive suites.
1. Researchers find that women are not in positions such as marketing, sales, and production, ones from which top executives are recruited. Rather, they are steered into human resources and public relations; their work is not appreciated to the same degree because it does not bring in profits.
2. Another explanation for the situation is that women lack mentors; male executives are reluctant to mentor them because they fear the gossip and sexual harassment charges if they get too close to female subordinates or because they see women as weak.

3. There are cracks in the glass ceiling as women learn to play by "men's rules" and develop a style with which men feel comfortable. In the background of about three-fourths of these women is a supportive husband who shares household duties and adapts his career to the needs of his executive wife.

4. Christine Williams found that men who go into nontraditional fields do not encounter a glass ceiling; rather, they find a "glass escalator"—they move up more quickly than female coworkers.

C. Conflict theorists examine how capitalists exploit gender divisions among workers in order to control them.

1. For example, uniform colors are based on gender with men wearing one color and women another.

2. Having women think of themselves as women workers rather than just as workers makes them easier to control. These women were less likely to file a complaint when their bosses flirted with them.

D. Until the 1970s, women did not draw a connection between unwanted sexual advances on the job and their subordinate positions at work.

1. As women began to discuss the problem, they named it *sexual harassment* and came to see such unwanted sexual advances by men in powerful positions as a structural problem. The change in perception resulted from reinterpreting women's experiences and giving them a name.

2. The meaning of the term is vague; court cases are the basis for determining what is and what is not sexual harassment.

3. Sexual harassment is an abuse of power that is structured into relationships of inequality in the workplace.

V. **Gender and Violence**

A. Most victims of violence are females.

1. Each year almost seven of every 10,000 American women age 12 and older is raped. This figure is seriously underreported, and it is more likely that the accurate total is three times this rate.

2. Most victims are between the ages of 12 and 24 years old and know their attacker.

3. An aspect of rape that is usually overlooked is the rape of men in prison; it is estimated that between 15 and 20 percent of men in prison are raped.

4. Date rape (sexual assault in which the assailant is acquainted with the victim) is not an isolated event. Most go unreported because the victim feels partially responsible, since she knows the person and was with him voluntarily.

5. Males are more likely than females to commit murder and be the victim of murder.

6. Other forms of violence against women include battering, spousal abuse, incest, and female circumcision.

7. Although women are less likely than men to kill, when they do, judges are more likely to be lenient on them. More research is required to understand why this pattern exists.

B. Feminists use symbolic interactionism to understand violence against women. They stress that U.S. culture promotes violence by males. It teaches men to associate power, dominance, strength, virility, and superiority with masculinity. Men use violence to try and maintain a higher status.

C. To solve violence, we must first break the link between violence and masculinity.

VI. The Changing Face of Politics

A. Despite the gains U.S. women have made in recent elections, they continue to be underrepresented in political office, especially in higher office.

1. Reasons for this include the fact that women have been underrepresented in law and business, the careers from which most politicians are drawn; they have not necessarily seen themselves as a voting block who need political action to overcome discrimination; they have generally found the roles of mother and politician incompatible; and men have rarely incorporated women into the centers of decision making or presented them as viable candidates.

2. There are signs that this pattern is changing. More women are going into law and business; childcare is now more likely to be seen as a mutual responsibility; and in some areas of the country, party leaders are searching for qualified candidates who can win regardless of their gender.

B. Trends in the 1990s indicate that women will participate in political life in far greater numbers than in the past.

VII. Glimpsing the Future—with Hope

A. As women play a fuller role in decision-making processes, further structural obstacles to women's participation in society will give way.

B. As gender stereotypes are abandoned, both males and females will be free to feel and express their needs and emotions, something that present arrangements deny them.

Chapter Summary

Gender stratification refers to males' and females' unequal access to power, prestige, and property on the basis of their sex. Gender is especially significant because it is a master status that cuts across all aspects of social life.

Sex refers to the biological characteristics that distinguish males from females; gender refers to the social characteristics that a society considers proper for its males and its females. Primary sex characteristics consist of organs directly related to reproduction, such as a vagina and a penis. Secondary sex characteristics are those not directly connected to reproduction but that become evident during puberty. These secondary characteristics include muscle development and the change to a lower voice in males and the development of broader hips and breasts in women. Although human beings are born male or female, they learn how to be masculine or feminine. This process of gender socialization begins at birth and continues through the life course. In short, we inherit our sex but learn our gender.

There is a significant debate over whether biology or culture is most responsible for gender differences. The dominant sociological position is that social factors, not biology, most account for gender differences in behavior, including male aggressiveness and female nurturing. A minority view within sociology, however, attributes male dominance in society to biological differences between males and females. A classic study addressing the nurture versus nature argument is the case study of an identical twin who was subjected to a sex change shortly after birth after an inept physician severed the baby's penis during circumcision. Another study of Vietnam veterans measured the relationship between testosterone level and aggressiveness.

The issue of sex typing is not an invention of the industrial society. Anthropologist George Murdock found that premodern societies sex-typed activities as male or female and that activities considered "female" in one society could be considered "male" in another society. In practically every society, however, greater prestige is given to male activities, regardless of the types of activities. Globally, females are discriminated against in areas of education and politics, average less pay than men, and are frequently subjected to acts of male violence. To some degree, this unequal treatment stems from the idea that women are considered a minority group because they are discriminated against on the basis of a physical characteristic—their sex.

A patriarchy is a society in which men dominate women and authority is vested in males. Although nobody knows the origins of patriarchy, the dominant theory contends that patriarchy was a social consequence of human reproduction. Frederick Engels, an associate of Karl Marx, proposed that patriarchy developed with the origin of private property.

In response to patriarchy, the feminist philosophy was developed. Feminism is the belief that men and women should be politically, economically, and socially equal and that gender stratification must be met with organized resistance. Feminists further believe that biology is not destiny and that stratification by gender is wrong.

In the United States, the "first wave" of the women's movement (early in the twentieth century) gained women the right to vote. The "second wave," beginning in the 1960s, contributed to women achieving more rights and gains. For example, women earn more bachelor's and master's degrees than men, have made significant breakthroughs in the political arena, have sharply increased their proportion of the labor force, and have made significant increases in their income. However, there are still many forms of gender inequality in various aspects of everyday life that continue to persist. Among these are a devaluation of things feminine, violence against women, and sexual harassment.

As females come to play a larger role in the decision-making processes of American social institutions, structural barriers and traditional stereotypes will continue to fall. This should result in less gender stratification as both males and females develop a new consciousness.

KEY TERMS

After studying the chapter, review the definition for each of the following terms.

feminism: the philosophy that men and women should be politically, economically, and socially equal; organized activities on behalf of this principle (292)

gender: the behaviors and attitudes that a society considers proper for its males and females; masculinity or femininity (280)

gender stratification: males' and females' unequal access to property, power, and prestige (280)

glass ceiling: the mostly invisible barrier that keeps women from advancing to the top levels at work (303)

matriarchy: a society in which women as a group dominate men as a group; authority is vested in females (297)

patriarchy: a society in which men as a group dominate women as a group; authority is vested in males (285)

sex: biological characteristics that distinguish females and males, consisting of primary and secondary sex characteristics (280)

sexual harassment: the abuse of one's position of authority to force unwanted sexual demands on someone (305)

KEY PEOPLE

Review the major theoretical contributions or findings of these people.

Janet Chafetz: Chafetz studied the second wave of feminism in the 1960s, noting that as large numbers of women began to work in the economy, they began to compare their working conditions with those of men. (283, 292, 294)

Donna Eder: This sociologist discovered that junior-high boys call one another "girl" when they don't hit each other hard enough during a football game. (296)

Sue Fisher: She discovered that surgeons were recommending total hysterectomies to female patients when they were not necessary. (297)

Douglas Foley: This sociologist's study of sports lends support to the view that "things feminine" are generally devalued. (296)

Marvin Harris: This anthropologist suggested that male dominance grew out of the greater strength that men had, which made them better suited for the hand-to-hand combat of tribal societies; women became the reward to entice men into battle. (287)

Alison Jaggar: She observed that as society changes, we may see a greater appreciation for sexual differences, and gender equality can become a background condition for living in society rather than a goal to strive for. (308)

Gerda Lerner: While acknowledging that in all societies women—as a group—have never had decision-making power over men, Lerner suggested that patriarchy may have had different origins in different places around the globe. (285, 287)

George Murdock: This anthropologist surveyed 324 premodern societies around the world and found that in all of them, activities were sex-typed. (287-288)

Alice Rossi: This feminist sociologist has suggested that women are better prepared biologically for "mothering" than are men. (283)

Diana Scully: She learned that surgeons "sell" unnecessary female operations to women in order to keep themselves in business. (297)

Jean Stockard and Miriam Johnson: These sociologists observed boys playing basketball and heard them exchange insults that reflect a disrespect and devaluation of women. (296)

Samuel Stouffer: In his classic study of combat soldiers during World War II, Stouffer noted the general devaluation of things associated with women. (295)

MULTIPLE CHOICE QUESTIONS

1. The term gender _____ refers to unequal access to property, power, and prestige on the basis of sex. (280)
    a. stratification
    b. socialization
    c. stereotyping
    d. roles

2. Which of the following statements about gender is *incorrect*? (280)
    a. There is not a lot of variation in gender roles around the world.
    b. Gender is a social, not a biological, characteristic.
    c. Gender consists of whatever a group considers proper for its males and females.
    d. The sociological significance of gender is that it is a device by which society controls its members.

3. If biology is the principal factor in human behavior, what would we find around the world? (282)
    a. Things would be just like they are.
    b. Men and women would be much more like each other than they currently are.
    c. Women would be one sort of person and men another.
    d. None of the above

4. The study of Vietnam veterans discussed in this chapter is an indication of how sociologists are slowly becoming open to considering _____ factors in human behavior. (283)
    a. gender
    b. testosterone
    c. biological
    d. psychological

5. Which minority group represents the largest segment of the U.S. population? (285)
    a. African Americans
    b. Latinos
    c. women
    d. children

6. Patriarchy: (285)
    a. is a society in which men dominate women.
    b. has existed throughout history.
    c. is universal.

d.   all of the above

7.   The major theory of the origin of patriarchy points to: (285)
       a.   the social consequences of human reproduction.
       b.   men's greediness.
       c.   women's willingness to give up power and control in return for protection.
       d.   men's greater strength enabling them to overpower women.

8.   In regard to the prestige of work: (288)
       a.   greater prestige is given to activities that are considered to be of great importance
              to a society, regardless of whether they are performed by females or males.
       b.   greater prestige goes to female activities that males cannot do, like pregnancy and
              lactation.
       c.   greater prestige is given to male activities.
       d.   none of the above

9.   Which statement concerning global discrimination is *incorrect*? (288-289, 292)
       a.   Of about 1 billion adults around the world who cannot read, two-thirds are
              women.
       b.   The United States leads the world in the number of women who hold public
              office.
       c.   Around the globe, women average less pay than men.
       d.   A global human rights issue has become violence against women.

10.   Which of the following is true about female circumcision? (289)
       a.   It is still practiced in some parts of the world today.
       b.   Feminists believe this is done to control female sexuality.
       c.   Fourteen African countries have banned female circumcision.
       d.   All of the above

11.   A "second wave" of protest and struggle against gender inequalities: (294)
       a.   occurred when women began to compare their working conditions with those of
              men.
       b.   began in the 1960s.
       c.   had as its goals everything from changing work roles to changing policies on
              violence against women.
       d.   all of the above

12.   A possible "third wave" of feminism is now emerging. What is the focus of this wave?
       (294)
       a.   widespread legal reforms to guarantee equality
       b.   greater compensation for victims of sexual harassment
       c.   broadening the values that underlie work and other social institutions

d.   inclusion of women's contributions to our history

13.   Gender inequality in education: (296-301)
   a.   has virtually disappeared today.
   b.   is allowed by law.
   c.   is perpetuated by the use of sex to sort students into different academic disciplines.
   d.   disappears by the time men and women enter graduate school.

14.   In which field does research show the largest gap in professional degrees obtained by men and women in 1970? (299)
   a.   dentistry
   b.   medicine
   c.   law
   d.   none of the above

15.   The pay gap between men and women: (301-303)
   a.   is found primarily among those with less than a high-school education.
   b.   is found primarily among those with college and graduate education.
   c.   is found at all educational levels.
   d.   largely has disappeared.

16.   The glass ceiling: (303-304)
   a.   keeps both men and women out of nontraditional occupations.
   b.   has largely been shattered by today's generation of businesswomen.
   c.   refers to the invisible barrier that keeps women from reaching the executive suite.
   d.   all of the above

17.   Which of the following is *not* a reason for women's absence from core corporate positions? (303-305)
   a.   The male corporate culture stereotypes potential leaders as people who look like themselves; women are seen as better at providing "support."
   b.   Women do not seek out opportunities for advancement and do not spend enough time networking with powerful executives.
   c.   Women lack mentors who take an interest in them and teach them the ropes.
   d.   Women are generally steered away from jobs that are stepping stones to top corporate office; instead they are recruited for jobs in human resources and public relations.

18.   Sexual harassment was first recognized as a problem in the _____. (305)
   a.   1950s
   b.   1960s
   c.   1970s

d.   1980s

19.   Which of the following statements about sexual harassment is *incorrect*? (305)
       a.   It is no longer exclusively a female problem.
       b.   It is rooted in the structure of the workplace rather than individual relationships.
       c.   It involves a person in authority using the position to force unwanted sex on subordinates.
       d.   Male victims of sexual harassment receive more sympathy than female victims.

20.   The pattern of date rape shows: (306)
       a.   that it is not an isolated event.
       b.   most go unreported.
       c.   it is difficult to prosecute.
       d.   all of the above

21.   While women make up 51 percent of the U.S. population ... (307)
       a.   6 out of 10 murders are committed by men.
       b.   7 out of 10 murders are committed by men.
       c.   8 out of 10 murders are committed by men.
       d.   9 out of 10 murders are committed by men.

22. Which of the following is *not* among feminist explanations for gender violence? (307)
       a.   higher testosterone levels in males
       b.   males reassert their declining power and status
       c.   the association of strength and virility with violence
       d.   cultural traditions that are patriarchal

23.   Women have been underrepresented in politics because: (308)
       a.   they are not really interested in pursuing political careers.
       b.   they are not viewed as serious candidates by the voters.
       c.   their roles as mothers and wives are incompatible with political roles.
       d.   they lack the proper educational backgrounds.

24.   What is it that keeps most males and females locked into fairly rigid gender roles? (308)
       a.   social structural obstacles
       b.   socialization
       c.   stereotypes
       d.   all of the above

25.   What is most likely to break the stereotypes locking us into traditional gender activities? (308)
       a.   stricter laws
       b.   equal pay

c. increased female participation in the decision-making processes of social institutions

d. increased male participation in nurturing activities

TRUE-FALSE QUESTIONS

1. _____The study of the medical accident with identical twins cited in the text supports the view of the role of biology in human behavior. (282)

2. _____Matriarchy, or male dominance, appears to be universal. (285)

3. _____Although female circumcision was once common in parts of Africa and Southeast Asia, it is quite rare today. (289)

4. _____In the United States, women's political rights were gained only after a prolonged and bitter struggle. (292, 294))

5. _____In the U.S. women's movement, each wave has had both a liberal and conservative wing. (294)

6. _____An alarming number of unnecessary hysterectomies in women is an example of gender discrimination in health care. (297)

7. _____Today, women and men have equal levels of achievement in higher education. (298-299)

8. _____In 2008 women were more likely than men to obtain a professional degree in dentistry. (299)

9. _____Once sexual harassment was defined as a problem, women saw some of their experiences in a different light. (305)

10. _____In the United States, males kill at about the same rate as females. (307)

FILL-IN-THE-BLANK QUESTIONS

1. Gender is a _____ status; it cuts across all aspects of social life. (280)

2. Gender consists of what behaviors and attitudes a _____ considers proper for males and females. (280)

3. _____ is a society in which men as a group dominate women as a group. (285)

4. Most sociologists take the _____ side in the nature vs. nurture debate over behaviors of males and females. (283)

5. The philosophy that men and women should be equal is known as _____. (292)

6. Research on the devaluation of things feminine shows that _____ is valued more highly, for it represents strength and success. (295)

7. Women who work full-time average only _____ percent of what men are paid. (304)

8. A female firefighter is likely to experience the glass _____. (303-304)

9. Central to sexual harassment is the abuse of _____. (305)

10. _____ women have served in the United States Senate. (307)

ESSAY QUESTIONS

1. Summarize the sociobiology argument concerning behavioral differences between men and women. Explain which position most closely reflects your own: biological, sociological, or sociobiological.

2. Compare and contrast the two waves of the feminist movement in this country by identifying the forces that contributed to both waves.

3. Discuss gender tracking and how that perpetuates inequality in education and the workforce.

4. Discuss why women are so often the victims of violence.

5. As most of the legal barriers to women's full participation in society have been eliminated, it is commonly assumed that women have gained equality. Given what you have learned in this chapter, consider whether this is the case.

CHAPTER 12
RACE AND ETHNICITY

LEARNING OBJECTIVES

After reading Chapter 12, you should be able to:

1. Explain how the concept of race is both a reality and a myth. (314, 316)

2. Distinguish between race and ethnicity and the concept of what it means to be a member of an ethnic group. (314, 316)

3. Understand the concept of multicultural identity and its importance to many Americans. (315)

4. Describe the characteristics of minority groups and dominant groups. (317-318)

5. Know what is meant by *ethnic identity* and the four factors that heighten or reduce it. (318-319)

6. Differentiate between prejudice and discrimination. (319)

7. Distinguish between individual discrimination and institutional discrimination and provide examples of both. (321)

8. Understand how prejudice is learned and how dominant group norms are internalized by members of a group. (321)

9. Understand the psychological and sociological theories of prejudice, as well as how they are similar and different. (324-327)

10. List the six patterns of intergroup relations that develop between minority and dominant groups, providing examples for each. (327-330)

11. Compare and contrast the experiences of white Europeans, Latinos, African Americans, Asian Americans, and Native Americans in the United States. (332-344)

12. Talk about the major issues and debates dominating race-ethnic relations in the United States. (344-347)

Chapter Outline

I.   Laying the Sociological Foundation
   A.   Race, a group with inherited physical characteristics that distinguishes it from another group, is both a myth and a reality.

1. It is a reality in the sense that humans come in different colors and shapes.
2. It is a myth that any race is superior to others. Throughout history, there are examples in which this myth was put into practice—for example, the Holocaust, the massacre in Rwanda, and the "ethnic cleansing" in Bosnia.
3. It is a myth because there are no pure races; what we call "races" are social classifications, not biological categories. The mapping of the human genome shows that humans are strikingly homogenous.
4. The classification of race is complex. Some scientists have classified humans into two "races" while others have found as many as two thousand.
5. The myth of race makes a difference for social life because people believe these ideas are real, and they act on their beliefs.

B. Race and ethnicity are often confused due to the cultural differences people see and the way they define race. The terms "ethnicity" and "ethnic" refer to cultural characteristics that distinguish a people.

C. Minority groups are people singled out for unequal treatment and who regard themselves as objects of collective discrimination.
1. They are not necessarily in the numerical minority. Sociologists refer to those who do the discriminating as the dominant group; they have greater power, more privileges, and higher social status. The dominant group attributes its privileged position to its superiority, not to discrimination.
2. A group becomes a minority through expansion of political boundaries by another group. Another way for a group to become a minority is by migration into a territory, either voluntarily or involuntarily.

D. Some people feel an intense sense of ethnic identity, while others feel very little.
1. An individual's sense of ethnic identity is influenced by the relative size and power of the ethnic group, its appearance, and the level of discrimination aimed at the group. If a group is relatively small, has little power, has a distinctive appearance, and is an object of discrimination, its members will have a heightened sense of ethnic identity.
2. Ethnic work refers to how ethnicity is constructed and includes enhancing and maintaining a group's distinctiveness or attempting to recover ethnic heritage. In the United States, millions of Americans are engaged in ethnic work, which has challenged the notion that our nation would be a melting pot with most groups quietly blending into a sort of ethnic stew.

II. Prejudice and Discrimination
A. Prejudice and discrimination exist in societies throughout the world.
1. Discrimination is unfair treatment directed toward someone. When based on race, it is known as racism. It also can be based on many features such as weight, age, sex, sexual preference, disability, religion, or politics.
2. Prejudice is prejudging of some sort, usually in a negative way.

175

3. Sociologists found that some people learned prejudice after association with certain groups. Racism was not the cause for joining a racist group but the result of their membership in that group.

4. It has been found that prejudice against one racial–ethnic group leads to prejudice against others.

5. People can learn to be prejudiced against their own groups by internalizing the norms of the dominant group.

6. Psychologists found through the "Implicit Association Test" that we hold biased perceptions of racial groups through the ethnic maps that we have learned in our culture.

B. Sociologists distinguish between individual discrimination (negative treatment of one person by another) and institutional discrimination (negative treatment of a minority group that is built into society's institutions).

1. Race-ethnicity is a significant factor in getting a mortgage or a car loan. Researchers found that even when two mortgage applicants were identical in terms of credit histories, African Americans and Latinos were 60 percent more likely than whites to be rejected.

2. In terms of health care, researchers compared the age, sex, race, and income of heart patients and found that whites were more likely than minorities to be given coronary bypass surgery or receive knee replacements.

III. Theories of Prejudice

A. Psychological Perspectives

1. According to John Dollard, prejudice results from frustration: people unable to strike out at the real source of their frustration find scapegoats to unfairly blame.

2. According to Theodor Adorno, highly prejudiced people are insecure, intolerant people who long for the firm boundaries established by strong authority; he called this complex of personality traits the authoritarian personality.

3. Subsequent studies have generally concluded that people who are older, less educated, less intelligent, and from a lower social class are more likely to be authoritarian.

B. Sociological Perspectives

1. To functionalists, the social environment can be deliberately arranged to generate either positive or negative feelings about people. Prejudice is functional in that it creates in-group solidarity and out-group antagonism, but dysfunctional because it destroys human relationships. Functionalists do not justify what they discover but simply identify functions and dysfunctions of human action.

2. To conflict theorists, the ruling class systematically pits group against group; by splitting workers along racial–ethnic lines, they benefit because solidarity among the workers is weakened. The higher unemployment rates of minorities create a reserve labor force from which owners can draw when they need to expand production temporarily. The existence of the reserve labor force is a constant threat to white workers, who modify their demands rather than lose their jobs to

unemployment. Racial–ethnic divisions at work are also encouraged and exploited. This weakens workers' bargaining power.

3. To symbolic interactionists, the labels we learn color our perceptions, leading to selective perception—we see certain things and are blind to others. Racial and ethnic labels are especially powerful because they are shorthand for emotionally-laden stereotypes. Symbolic interactionists stress that we learn our prejudices in interactions with others. These stereotypes not only justify prejudice and discrimination, but they also lead to a self-fulfilling prophecy—stereotypical behavior in those who are stereotyped.

IV. Global Patterns of Intergroup Relations

A. Genocide is the actual or attempted systematic annihilation of a race or ethnic group that is labeled as less than fully human. The Holocaust and the U.S. government's treatment of Native Americans are examples. Labels that dehumanize others help people compartmentalize; they can separate their acts from their sense of being good and moral people.

B. Population transfer is involuntary movement of a minority group. Indirect transfer involves making life so unbearable that members of a minority then leave; direct transfer involves forced expulsion. A combination of genocide and population transfer occurred in Bosnia, in former Yugoslavia, as Serbs engaged in the wholesale slaughter of Muslims and Croats, with survivors forced to flee the area.

C. Internal colonialism is a society's policy of exploiting a minority by using social institutions to deny it access to full benefits. Slavery is an extreme example as well as South Africa's system of apartheid.

D. Segregation is the formal separation of groups that accompanies internal colonialism. Dominant groups maintain social distance from minorities yet still exploit their labor.

E. Assimilation is the process by which a minority is absorbed into the mainstream. Forced assimilation occurs when the dominant group prohibits the minority from using its own religion, language, or customs. Permissive assimilation is when the minority adopts the dominant group's patterns in its own way and/or at its own speed.

F. Multiculturalism, also called pluralism, permits or encourages ethnic variation. Switzerland is an excellent example of multiculturalism. The French, Italians, Germans, and Romansh have kept their own languages and live in political and economic unity.

V. Race-Ethnic Relations in the United States

A. Racial and ethnic terms that are used in the United States are controversial.

1. White Americans comprise 65 percent of the U.S. population, with racial and ethnic minorities comprising the other 35 percent.

2. Minority groups tend to be clustered in areas, so the distribution of dominant and minority groups among the states rarely comes close to the national average.

B. White Anglo Saxon Protestants (WASPs) established the basic social institutions in the United States when they settled the original colonies.

1. WASPs were very ethnocentric and viewed immigrants from other European countries as inferior. Subsequent immigrants were expected to speak English and adopt other Anglo Saxon ways of life.
2. White ethnics are white immigrants to the United States whose culture differs from that of WASPs. They include the Irish, Germans, Poles, Jews, and Italians. They were initially discriminated against by WASPs, who felt that something was wrong with people with different customs.
3. The institutional and cultural dominance of Western Europeans set the stage for current ethnic relations.

C. The terms "Latino" and "Hispanic" do not refer to a race but to different ethnic groups. Latinos may be black, white, or Native American.
1. When Europeans first arrived on this continent, Latinos had already established settlements in Florida and New Mexico.
2. Today, Latinos are the largest minority group in the United States. About 32 million trace their origins to Mexico, four million to Puerto Rico, two million to Cuba, and eight million to Central and South America. While most are legal residents, large numbers have entered the United States illegally and avoid contact with public officials.
3. The migration of Mexicans across the U.S. border has become a major social issue. A group called the Minutemen, who organized through the Internet, are volunteers who offered to patrol the border.
4. Concentrated in four states (California, Texas, New York, and Florida), Latinos are causing major demographic shifts.
5. The Spanish language distinguishes them from other minorities; perhaps half are unable to speak English without difficulty. This is a major obstacle to getting well-paid jobs. Some Anglos perceive the growing use of Spanish as a threat and have initiated an "English only" movement and have succeeded in getting states to consider making English their official language.
6. Divisions of social class and country of national origin prevent political unity.
7. Compared with non-Latino whites, Latinos are worse off on all indicators of well-being. The country of origin is significant, with Cuban Americans scoring much higher on indicators of well-being and Puerto Rican Americans scoring the lowest.
8. People from South America and Cuba attain more education than those coming from elsewhere.

D. African Americans face a legacy of racism.
1. In 1955, African Americans in Montgomery, Alabama, using civil disobedience tactics advocated by Martin Luther King, Jr., protested laws believed to be unjust. This led to the civil rights movement that challenged existing patterns of racial segregation throughout the South.
2. The 1964 Civil Rights Act and 1965 Voting Rights Act heightened expectations for African Americans that better social conditions would follow these gains.

Frustration over the pace of change led to urban riots and passage of the 1968 Civil Rights Act.

3. Since then, African Americans have made political and economic progress. For example, African Americans have increased their membership in the U.S. House of Representatives in the past 30 years, and enrollment in colleges continues to increase. Forty percent of all African American families make more than $50,000 a year.

4. Despite these gains, however, African Americans continue to lag behind in politics, economics, and education. In 2008, Barack Obama became the first African American man to be elected president. Currently, African Americans average 59 percent of whites' incomes; only 11 percent of African Americans have graduated from college; and African American males are more than six times more likely to be homicide victims than whites.

5. According to William Wilson, social class (not race) is the major determinant of quality of life. The African American community today is composed of a middle-class who took advantage of the opportunities created by civil rights legislation and advanced economically, living in good housing, having well-paid jobs, and sending their children to good schools, as well as a large group of poorly educated and unskilled African Americans who were left behind as opportunities for unskilled labor declined and now find themselves living in poverty, facing violent crime and dead-end jobs, and sending their children to lesser schools.

6. Others argue that discrimination on the basis of race persists, despite gains made by some African Americans. African Americans are still paid less than white Americans for the same job.

7. Racism still continues to be a part of life. Researchers found that résumés that had white-sounding names received 50 percent more callbacks than those having more black-sounding names. Also, voices that sounded like a white voice were more likely to receive callbacks about rental apartment availability.

8. African American women are in a double bind situation. They are discriminated against because of their race–ethnicity and for being women.

E. Asian Americans have long faced discrimination in the United States.

1. Chinese immigrants were drawn here by the gold strikes in the West and the need for unskilled workers to build the railroads. In 1882, Congress passed the Chinese Exclusion Act, suspending all Chinese immigration for 10 years.

2. When the Japanese arrived, they met spillover bigotry, a stereotype that lumped all Asians together, depicting them negatively. After the attack on Pearl Harbor in World War II, hostilities toward Japanese Americans increased, with many being imprisoned in "relocation camps."

3. On the average, Asian Americans have a higher annual income and lower unemployment rates than other racial–ethnic groups. Those most likely to be in poverty, though, come from Southeast Asia.

4. The success of Asian Americans can be traced to three factors: (1) a close family life, (2) educational achievement, and (3) assimilation into the mainstream.

5. Asian American children are the most likely to grow up with two parents. They have very high rates of college graduation. The high intermarriage rate of Japanese Americans has enabled them to assimilate into mainstream culture.

6. Asian Americans are becoming more prominent in politics. Hawaii has elected several Asian American governors and sent several Asian American senators to Washington. In 1996, Gary Locke was elected governor of Washington.

F. Due to the influence of old movie westerns, many Americans tend to hold stereotypes of Native Americans as uncivilized savages, as a single group of people subdivided into separate bands.

1. In reality, however, Native Americans represent a diverse group of people with a variety of cultures and languages. Although originally numbering between five and ten million, their numbers were reduced to a low of 500,000 due to a lack of immunity to European diseases and warfare. Today there are about three million Native Americans who speak about 150 different languages.

2. At first, relations between European settlers and the Native Americans were peaceful. However, as the number of settlers increased, tension increased. Because Native Americans stood in the way of expansion, many were slaughtered. Government policy shifted to population transfer, with Native Americans confined to reservations.

3. Today, they are an invisible minority. One-third live in three states: Oklahoma, California, and Arizona; most other Americans are hardly aware of them. They have the highest rates of suicide and the lowest life expectancy of any U.S. minority. These negative conditions are the result of Anglo domination.

4. In the 1960s, Native Americans won a series of legal victories that restored their control over the land and their right to determine economic policy. Many Native Americans have opened businesses on their land, ranging from industrial parks to casinos. Today many Native Americans are interested in recovering and honoring their own traditions.

5. Pan-Indianism emphasizes elements that run through all Native American cultures in order to develop self-identification that goes beyond any particular tribe.

VI. Looking Toward the Future

A. Central to this country's history, immigration and the fear of its consequences is once again an issue facing the United States as it moves into the next century. The concern has been that "too many" immigrants will alter the character of the United States, undermining basic institutions and contributing to the breakdown of society.

1. In some states, such as California, the racial-ethnic minorities constitute a majority.

2. There is fear that Spanish speakers will threaten the primacy of the English language and that immigrants will take jobs away from native-born Americans.

B. Another central concern is the role of affirmative action. Liberals argue that this policy is the most direct way in which to level the playing field of economic opportunity, while conservatives believe that such practices result in reverse discrimination.

    1. One of the most controversial rulings was *Proposition 209*. This amendment to the California state constitution banned preferences to minorities and women in hiring, promotion, and college admission.

    2. A ruling by the court in a case about the University of Michigan admission process has continued to make this a challenging topic about the role of affirmative action.

C. In order for the United States to become a multicultural society, people must respect differences and be willing to work together without any one group dominating others, and racial categories need to be seen as an irrelevant system of categorization.

Chapter Summary

With more than six billion people on the planet, the world offers a fascinating array of human characteristics. *Race* refers to the inherited physical characteristics that distinguish one group from another. These distinguishing characteristics include a variety of complexions, colors, and shapes. Although there have been significant strides in the understanding of race and racial equality, two myths of race are still common. One is the perception that some races are superior to others; the other is that "pure" races exist. The *idea* of race remains a very real and powerful force throughout the world, shaping basic relationships between people in the United States and elsewhere.

The question of how many races inhabit the planet is a debatable topic among anthropologists and sociologists. The number of race classifications has ranged from two to two thousand. Ashley Montagu has classified humans into forty "racial" groups.

While race refers to *biological* characteristics that distinguish one group of people from another, ethnicity refers to *cultural* characteristics that distinguish one group of people from another. Derived from the Greek word "ethnos," meaning "people" or "nation," ethnicity may center on nation of origin, distinctive foods, dress, language, music, religion, or family names and relationships. It is common for people to confuse the terms "race" and "ethnic group." Jews, for example, are considered by many as being a race, but, in reality, are more accurately classified as an ethnic group. People often construct their racial and ethnic identity through a process referred to as "ethnic work." *Ethnic work* refers to activities to discover, enhance, or maintain ethnic and racial identification. This includes clothing, food, language, celebrated holidays, and religion.

Along with race and ethnicity, the concept of a minority group is often misunderstood. Louis Wirth defined a minority group as a group of people who are singled out for unequal treatment and who regard themselves as objects of collective discrimination. Four factors reduce or heighten people's ethnic identification with a group: its relative size, power, broad physical characteristics, and the degree to which it is subjected to discrimination. Although often used interchangeably, *prejudice* and *discrimination* are not the same. Prejudice refers to an *attitude*, or prejudging, usually in a negative way. Discrimination is an *act* of unfair treatment directed against an individual or group. Discrimination comes in two forms: individual discrimination, consisting of the negative treatment of one person by another on the basis of that person's perceived characteristics; and institutional discrimination, consisting of discriminatory practices embedded in and spread throughout society's social institutions.

Psychological theories of prejudice include "scapegoating" (unfairly blaming another individual or group for one's own frustrations and troubles) and authoritarian personalities (people who are more inclined to respect authority and submit to superiors).

Sociological theories of prejudice focus on the social environments that encourage or discourage prejudice. Functionalists examine the benefits and costs of discrimination; conflict theorists look at the way groups in power exploit racial and ethnic divisions; and symbolic interactionists explore how racial and ethnic stereotypes become self-fulfilling prophecies.

Sociologists have identified six global patterns of intergroup relations between dominant and minority groups. They are genocide, population transfer, internal colonialism, segregation, assimilation, and multiculturalism. Each has been practiced in the United States at one time or another, and all are presently practiced somewhere in the world.

The major ethnic groups in the United States are, from the largest to the smallest, European Americans, Latinos, African Americans, Asian Americans, and Native Americans. Each minority group faces different concerns or obstacles. For many years, white Europeans from countries other than England were not welcomed in America. Referred to as "white ethnics," these Caucasian Europeans had languages and customs different from the earliest immigrants and were considered to be inferior. Latinos are divided by country of origin. African Americans are increasingly divided into middle and lower classes. The well-being of Asian Americans varies widely by country of origin. However, the success of Asian Americans is attributed to their traditional family structures, their higher levels of education, and their assimilation into the dominant culture. For Native Americans, the primary issues are poverty, nationhood, and settling treaty obligations. All minority groups are concerned with overcoming discrimination. Every group that has immigrated to America has faced this problem, including Caucasian Europeans. It has been argued that people of color have faced greater degrees of discrimination. Current issues dominating race-ethnic relations in the United States include immigration, affirmative action, and multiculturalism.

KEY TERMS

After studying the chapter, review the definition for each of the following terms.

assimilation: the process of being absorbed into the mainstream culture (330)
authoritarian personality: Theodor Adorno's term for people who are prejudiced and rank high on scales of conformity, intolerance, insecurity, respect for authority, and submissiveness to superiors (325)
compartmentalize: to separate acts from feelings or attitudes (329)

discrimination: an act of unfair treatment directed against an individual or a group (319)

dominant group: the group with the most power, greatest privileges, and highest social status (318)

ethnic cleansing: a policy of eliminating a population; includes forcible expulsion and genocide (329)

ethnicity (and ethnic): having distinctive cultural characteristics (316)

ethnic work: activities designed to discover, enhance, or maintain ethnic and racial identity (318)

genocide: the systematic annihilation or attempted annihilation of people because of their presumed race or ethnicity (316)

individual discrimination: the negative treatment of one person by another on the basis of that person's perceived characteristics (321)

institutional discrimination: negative treatment of a minority group that is built into a society's institutions; also called *systemic discrimination* (321)

internal colonialism: the policy of exploiting minority groups for economic gain (329)

melting pot: the view that Americans of various backgrounds would blend into a sort of ethnic stew (339)

minority group: people who are singled out for unequal treatment and who regard themselves as objects of collective discrimination (317)

multiculturalism (also called *pluralism*): a philosophy or political policy that permits or encourages ethnic differences (330)

pan-Indianism: a movement that focuses on common elements in the cultures of Native Americans in order to develop a cross-tribal self-identity and to work toward the welfare of all Native Americans (344)

pluralism: the diffusion of power among many interest groups that prevents any single group from gaining control of the government (330)

population transfer: the forced movement of a minority group (329)

prejudice: an *attitude* of prejudging, usually in a negative way (319)

race: a group whose inherited physical characteristics distinguish it from other groups (319)

racism: prejudice and discrimination on the basis of race (314)

reserve labor force: the unemployed; unemployed workers are thought of as being "in reserve"—capitalists take them "out of reserve" (put them back to work) during times of high production and then put them back "in reserve" (lay them off) when they are no longer needed (326)

rising expectations: the sense that better conditions are soon to follow, which, if unfulfilled, increases frustration (338)

scapegoat: an individual or group unfairly blamed for someone else's troubles (325)

segregation: the policy of keeping racial–ethnic groups apart (330)

selective perception: seeing certain features of an object or situation, but remaining blind to others (327)

split labor market: workers are split along racial, ethnic, gender, age, or any other lines; this split is exploited by owners to weaken the bargaining power of workers (326)

WASP: a white Anglo Saxon Protestant; narrowly, an American (332)

white ethnics: white immigrants to the United States whose cultures differ from WASP culture (332)

KEY PEOPLE

Review the major theoretical contributions or findings of these people.

Theodor Adorno: Adorno identified the authoritarian personality type. (325)

Kathleen Blee: She interviewed women who were members of the KKK and Aryan Nation. She found that their racism was not the cause of their joining but the result of their membership in those groups. (321)

Ashley Doane: Doane identified four factors that affect an individual's sense of ethnic identity. (318-319)

John Dollard: This psychologist first suggested that prejudice is the result of frustration and scapegoats become the targets for their frustration. (325)

Raphael Ezekiel: This sociologist did participant observation of neo-Nazis and the Ku Klux Klan in order to examine racism from inside racist organizations. (321, 323)

Anthony Greenwald and Mahzarin Banaji: These psychologists created the "Implicit Association Test." They found that we learn the ethnic maps of our culture and a route to biased perception. (321)

Eugene Hartley: His study found that prejudice does not depend on negative experiences with others. Those who are prejudiced against racial-ethnic groups are likely to be prejudiced against others. (321)

Peggy McIntosh: Being white is a "taken-for-granted" background assumption of U.S. society. (334)

Ashley Montagu: This physical anthropologist pointed out that some scientists have classified humans into only two races while others have identified as many as two thousand. (314)

Alejandro Portes and Rueben Rumbaut: These sociologists looked at the impact that immigration has had on our country, pointing out that there has always been an anti-immigrant sentiment present. (346)

Muzafer and Carolyn Sherif: The Sherifs researched the functions of prejudice and found that it builds in-group solidarity. (326)

W.I. and D.S. Thomas: The Thomases observed that once people define a situation as real, it is real in its consequences. (316)

William Julius Wilson: Wilson is known for his work on racial discrimination, in which he argues that class is a more important factor than race in explaining patterns of inequality. (339-340)

Louis Wirth: Wirth offered a sociological definition of minority group. (317)

SELF-TEST

MULTIPLE CHOICE QUESTIONS

1. Race (314)
   a. means having distinctive cultural characteristics.
   b. means having inherited physical characteristics that distinguish one group from another.
   c. means people who are singled out for unequal treatment.
   d. is relatively easy to determine.

2. People often confuse race and ethnicity because (316)
   a. they dislike people who are different from themselves.
   b. of the cultural differences people see and the way they define race.
   c. they are unaware that race is cultural and ethnicity is biological.
   d. all of the above

3. A minority group (317)
   a. is discriminated against because of physical or cultural differences.
   b. is discriminated against because of personality factors.
   c. does not always experience discrimination.
   d. all of the above

4. To what does the dominant group in a society almost always consider its position to be due? (318)
   a. its own innate superiority
   b. its ability to oppress minority group members
   c. its ability to control political power
   d. all of the above

5. Which of the following factors affects a group's sense of ethnic identity? (318)
   a. the amount of power the group has
   b. the size of the group
   c. the degree to which the group's physical appearance differs from the mainstream
   d. all of the above

6. Many people today are tracing their family lines. This is an example of (318)
   a. ethnic identity.
   b. ethnic enclaves.
   c. ethnic work.
   d. ethnic pride.

7. Which of the following is the best description of a melting pot? (319)

a. a society in which groups quietly blend into a sort of ethnic stew
b. a society in which each ethnicity maintains its distinctiveness
c. a society where everyone adapts to the dominant group's ways
d. none of the above

8. Prejudice and discrimination (319)
   a. are less prevalent in the United States than in other societies.
   b. are more prevalent in the United States than in other societies.
   c. appear to characterize every society, regardless of size.
   d. appear to characterize only large societies.

9. Prejudice (319)
   a. is an attitude.
   b. may be positive or negative.
   c. is often the basis for discrimination.
   d. all of the above

10. From her interviews with women in the KKK and Aryan Nation, what did Kathleen Blee conclude? (321)
    a. These women are basically ignorant people who want to stir up problems.
    b. These women did extensive research on the group prior to membership.
    c. These women joined because it matched their racist beliefs.
    d. Racism was a result of membership in the group, not the cause of joining the group.

11. Discrimination that is woven into the fabric of society is referred to as (321)
    a. cultural discrimination.
    b. societal discrimination.
    c. individual discrimination.
    d. institutional discrimination.

12. What do the findings of research on patterns of mortgage lending confirm? (322)
    a. Discrimination is the result of individual bankers' decisions.
    b. Decisions to reject loans reflect sound banking practices.
    c. While African Americans and Latinos were rejected more often than whites, the rate was not significant.
    d. Discrimination is built into the country's financial institutions.

13. Why do functionalists consider prejudice functional for some groups? (326)
    a. It is a useful weapon in maintaining social divisions.
    b. It contributes to the creation of scapegoats.
    c. It helps to create solidarity within the group by fostering antagonisms directed against other groups.
    d. It affects how members of one group perceive members of other groups.

14. According to conflict theorists, prejudice (326)
    a. benefits capitalists by splitting workers along racial or ethnic lines.
    b. contributes to the exploitation of workers, thus producing a split-labor market.
    c. keeps workers from demanding higher wages and better working conditions.
    d. all of the above

15. Which sociological perspective stresses how labels create selective perception and self-fulfilling prophecies? (327)
    a. symbolic interactionism
    b. functionalism
    c. conflict perspective
    d. feminism

16. Genocide (327)
    a. occurred when Hitler attempted to destroy all Jews.
    b. is the systematic annihilation of a race or ethnic group.
    c. often requires the cooperation of ordinary citizens.
    d. all of the above

17. A society's policy of exploiting a minority group, using social institutions to deny the minority access to the society's full benefits, is referred to as (329-330)
    a. segregation.
    b. pluralism.
    c. internal colonialism.
    d. genocide.

18. Separating people on the basis of their racial and ethnic identity and then maintaining social distance is know as (330)
    a. genocide.
    b. population transfer.
    c. ethnic cleansing.
    d. segregation.

19. What is the challenge in the U.S. when trying to classify people into racial-ethnic groups? (330)
    a. Basic terms can be controversial.
    b. Racial terms might include some groups but exclude others.
    c. Racial-ethnic identity is fluid.
    d. All of the above

20. Which of the following statements about WASPs is *incorrect*? (333)
    a. They embraced whites from other European nations, helping them assimilate.
    b. They took power and determined the national agenda, controlling the destiny of the nation.

c. The term refers to white Anglo-Saxon Protestants whose ancestors came from England.

d. They were highly ethnocentric and viewed other immigrants as inferior.

21. According to your text, Latinos are distinguished from other ethnic minorities in the United States by (334)
    a. the Spanish language.
    b. the illegal entrance into the United States by virtually all Latinos.
    c. the short length of time Latinos have been in the United States.
    d. all of the above

22. Which of the following statements about African Americans who occupy higher statuses is *incorrect*? (336, 338-340)
    a. They enjoy greater opportunities.
    b. They face less discrimination.
    c. They sense discrimination hovering over them.
    d. The discrimination they experience is less painful than the discrimination received by African Americans who occupy lower statuses.

23. Which of the following statements about the experiences of Asian Americans is *incorrect*? (340-341)
    a. Much of the hostility directed toward Japanese Americans was due to Pearl Harbor.
    b. Asian Americans are becoming more prominent in politics.
    c. The view that Asian Americans have been successful in this country is basically correct.
    d. Most Asian Americans grow up in tight-knit families.

24. The overarching issue for minorities is overcoming (344)
    a. discrimination.
    b. poverty.
    c. assimilation.
    d. ethnic work.

25. What is a difference between the earlier wave of immigration at the turn of the last century and the current wave? (344-346)
    a. The current wave is much smaller.
    b. The current wave is more global in content.
    c. The current wave is experiencing a more welcoming environment.
    d. All of the above

TRUE-FALSE QUESTIONS

1. _____Prejudice is so extensive that people can show prejudice against groups that don't even exist. (314, 316)

2. _____Ethnic work depends on the degree to which an individual has an ethnic identity. (318)

3. _____Sociological theories of prejudice stress the authoritarian personality and frustration displaced toward scapegoats. (325)

4. _____Sociologists believe that individual discrimination is an adequate explanation for discrimination in the United States. (321)

5. _____According to research, even mild levels of frustration can lead to higher levels of prejudice. (325)

6. _____Adorno's research suggests that people of lower social class are more likely to be authoritarian. (325)

7. _____Symbolic interactionists stress that the labels we use encourage us to see things selectively. (327)

8. _____Genocide often relies on labeling and compartmentalization. (329)

9. _____Segregation allows the dominant group to exploit the labor of the minority while maintaining social distance. (330)

10. _____Affirmative action has worked exceptionally well in the U.S. (346)

FILL-IN-THE-BLANK QUESTIONS

1. The mapping of the human genome systems shows that humans are strikingly _____. (314)

2. _____ is both a reality and a myth. (314, 316)

3. We can use the term _____ to refer to the way people construct their ethnicity. (318)

4. Many analysts are using the term "_____" rather than "melting pot" when referring to the American ethnic experience. (319)

5. Gender and _____ also provide common bases for scapegoating. (325)

6. African Americans have _____ their membership in the U.S. House of Representatives in the past 30 years. (338)

7. _____ experienced spillover bigotry when they immigrated to the U.S. (341)

8. Native Americans can truly be called the _____. (343)

9. A highly controversial issue among Native Americans is _____. (343)

10. _____ in the state of California challenged affirmative action. (346)

ESSAY QUESTIONS

1. Explain what the author means when he says that race is both a myth and a reality.

189

2. Using the experiences of different racial and ethnic groups in the United States, identify and discuss the six patterns of intergroup relations.

3. Explore how both psychological and sociological theories can be used together to gain a deeper understanding of prejudice and discrimination.

4. Discuss the difference between individual and institutional discrimination, and give examples of both.

5. What would have to change in our society in order for us to truly be a multicultural society?

CHAPTER 13
THE ELDERLY

LEARNING OBJECTIVES
After reading Chapter 13, you should be able to:

1. Understand the "social construction of aging" and how it affects the way societies define and treat elderly members. (352)

2. Explain the effects of industrialization on life expectancy, population demographics, and the distribution of resources. (252-253)

3. Describe the "graying of America." (253-256)

4. Know the regional, gender, racial, and ethnic dimensions of aging in the United States. (253-257)

5. Describe and evaluate the various ways the symbolic interactionists, functionalists, and conflict theorists analyze aging. (256-267)

6. Provide and discuss cross-cultural examples of how people experience old age. (258-260)

7. Identify changing perceptions of old age in American society and the reasons for them. (257-258)

8. Discuss the history of and current controversies surrounding Social Security. (362-364)

9. Know the major organizations in the United States that protect and promote the political interests of the elderly. (366-367)

10. Describe and discuss some of the problems that many elderly people in the United States encounter, including social isolation, nursing homes, elder abuse, and poverty. (367-371)

11. Know how industrialization and medical advances affect the sociology of death and dying. (371-373)

12. Identify the five stages of death and dying. (372)

13. Describe some of the social factors that may affect elderly suicide rates in the United States. (273)

Chapter Outline

I. Aging in Global Perspective

   A. Every society must deal with the problem of people growing old; as the proportion of the population that is old increases, those decisions become more complex, and the tensions between the generations grow deeper.

   B. How a society views the aged and attitudes about aging are socially constructed; thus, the aging process depends on culture, not on biology.

       1. The Tiwi got rid of the old, decrepit females in their society by "covering them up." That is, they dug a hole, put the old woman in the hole, and covered her with dirt all the way with only her head showing. Returning in a day or two they found that she had died.

       2. The Abkhasians, on the other hand, pay high respect to their elderly. They may be the longest-living people in the world, with many claiming to live past 100.

       3. The main factors that appear to account for their long lives are diet, lifelong physical activity, and a highly developed sense of community.

   C. As a country industrializes, more of its people reach older ages.

       1. This reflects the higher standard of living, better public health measures, and success in fighting deadly diseases.

       2. As the proportion of elderly increases, so does the bill that younger citizens must pay in order to provide for their needs. Among industrialized nations, this bill has become a major social issue. In the Least Industrialized Nations, families are expected to take care of their own elderly, with no help from the government.

   D. In the United States, the "graying of America" refers to the proportion of older people in the U.S. population.

       1. Today, almost 13 percent of the population has achieved age 65; there are almost 7 million more elderly Americans than teenagers.

       2. Because the proportion of nonwhites in the United States is growing, the number of minority elderly is also increasing. Differences in cultural attitudes about aging, types of family relationships, work histories, and health practices will be important areas of sociological investigation in the coming years.

       3. While life expectancy (the number of years that an average person at any age, including newborns, can expect to live) has increased, the life span (maximum length of life) has not.

       4. Life expectancy is highest in the most industrialized countries and lowest in developing countries.

II. The Symbolic Interactionist Perspective

   A. There are several factors that push people to apply the label of "old."

       1. Biology changes how a person looks and feels; the person adopts the role of "old" (acts the way old people are thought to act) when experiencing these changes.

2. Personal history (an injury that limits mobility) or biography (becoming a grandmother at an early age) may affect self-concept regarding age.
3. Gender also plays a part. The relative value that culture places on men's ages is less than that of women's ages.
4. When a particular society defines a person as "old," the person is likely to feel "old." These timetables are not fixed; groups sometimes adjust expectations about the onset of old age.

B. Aging is relative; when it begins and what it means varies from culture to culture.
1. For the traditional Native American, the signal for old age is more often the inability to perform productive social roles rather than any particular birthday.
2. The Tiwi tribe is a gerontocracy (a society run by the elderly) where older men are so entrenched in power that they control all of the wealth and all of the women.
3. To grow old in traditional Eskimo society meant voluntary death. Eskimo society was so precarious that a person no longer able to pull his or her own weight was expected to simply go off and die.

C. Robert Butler coined the term "ageism" to refer to prejudice, discrimination, and hostility directed at people because of their age.
1. With the coming of industrialization, the traditional bases of respect for the elderly eroded. The distinctiveness of age was lost and new ideas of morality made the opinions of the elderly outmoded. The meaning of old age was transformed—from usefulness to uselessness, from wisdom to foolishness, from an asset to a liability.
2. The meaning of old age is being transformed with the increasing wealth of the U.S. elderly and the coming of age of the baby boom generation. The baby boom generation, given their vast numbers and economic clout, are likely to positively affect our images of the elderly.
3. The mass media communicates messages about the aged, influencing our ideas about the elderly.

III. The Functionalist Perspective
A. Functionalists examine age from the standpoint of how those people who are retiring and those who will replace them in the workforce make mutual adjustments.
B. Elaine Cumming and William Henry developed disengagement theory to explain how society prevents disruption to society when the elderly retire.
1. The elderly are rewarded in some way (pensions) for giving up positions rather than waiting until they become incompetent or die; this allows for a smooth transition of employment.
2. For many, disengagement begins during middle age, long before retirement. While not immediately disengaging, the individual begins to assign priority to certain goals and tasks.
3. This theory is criticized because it assumes that the elderly disengage and then sink into oblivion.

4. Dorothy Jerrome, a critic of disengagement theory, found in her research that the elderly exchange one set of roles for another; the new roles, centering around friendship, are no less satisfying than the earlier roles.

5. The nature of retirement has also been changing; more often, workers slow down rather than simply stop working. Many never retire but simply cut back.

C. According to activity theory, older people who maintain a high level of activity tend to be more satisfied with life than those who do not.

1. Most research findings support the hypothesis that more active people are more satisfied people.

2. Contradictory findings from a number of different studies suggest that counting the number of activities is too simplistic. Rather, researchers need to take into account what activities mean to people.

D. Continuity theory focuses on how people continue their roles in order to adjust to change. Over the course of our lives, we develop various strategies for coping with life. When confronted with old age, people continue to use these coping strategies.

1. People from higher social classes have greater resources to cope with the challenges of old age and consequently adjust better.

2. People who have multiple roles—wife, mother, worker, friend—are better equipped to handle the loss of a role than are people who do not.

3. Critics claim that this theory is too broad; it is seen as a collection of loosely connected ideas with no specific application to the elderly.

IV. The Conflict Perspective

A. Conflict theorists examine social life as a struggle between groups for scarce resources. Social Security legislation is an example of that struggle.

1. In the 1920s and 1930s, two-thirds of all citizens over 65 had no savings and could not support themselves. Francis Townsend enrolled one-third of all Americans over 65 in clubs that sought a national sales tax to finance a monthly pension for all Americans over age 65. To avoid the plan without appearing to be opposed to old-age pensions, Social Security was enacted by Congress.

2. Initially the legislation required workers to retire at 65. For decades, the elderly protested. Finally, in 1986, Congress eliminated mandatory retirement. Today, almost 90 percent of Americans retire by age 65, but they do so voluntarily.

3. Conflict theorists state that Social Security was not a result of generosity, but rather of competition among interest groups.

B. Since equilibrium is only a temporary balancing of social forces, some form of continuing conflict between the younger and the older appears inevitable.

1. The huge costs of Social Security have become a national concern. Conflict is inevitable as proportionately fewer working people are forced to pay for the benefits received by an increasing number of senior citizens.

2. The poverty rate for the elderly has decreased and is less than the national average. The success of Social Security has contributed to this. Additionally,

those 65 and older have the highest standard of living compared to any time in U.S. history.

3. Some argue that the elderly and children are on a collision course. Data indicate that as the number of elderly poor decreased, children in poverty increased. Also, the medical costs for the elderly have soared, and some fear that health care for children will be shortchanged. It has been argued that the comparison is misleading because the money that went to the elderly did not come from money intended for the children. Framing the issue in this way is an attempt to divide the working class and to force a choice between suffering children and elderly.

C. Empowering the elderly, some organizations today work to protect the gains the elderly have achieved over the years.

1. The Gray Panthers organized in the 1960s to encourage people of all ages to work for the welfare of both the elderly and the young. On the micro level, the goal is to develop positive self-concepts; on the macro level, the goal is to build a power base with which to challenge all institutions that oppress the poor, young and old alike.

2. To protect their gains, older Americans organized the American Association of Retired Persons, with 35 million members. This association monitors proposed federal and state legislation and mobilizes its members to act on issues affecting their welfare.

V. Recurring Problems

A. While the elderly are not as isolated as stereotypes would lead us to believe, there are differences between men and women. Women are especially likely to be isolated. Because of differences in mortality, most older males (71 percent) are married and live with their wives, while most older women do not (only 41 percent live with husbands).

1. What this means is that women are much more likely to take care of frail husbands than husbands are to care for frail wives.

2. Most patients in nursing homes are women.

B. About 5 percent of Americans over 65 are in nursing homes at any one time; about one-half of elderly women and one-third of elderly men will spend some time in a nursing home.

1. Nursing home residents are likely to be quite ill, over 85, widowed or never married and consequently have no family to take care of them. Over 90 percent are in wheelchairs or use walkers.

2. The quality of care varies, but even the better ones tend to strip away human dignity.

3. Researchers have found that in nursing homes that are understaffed, the patients are more likely to have bedsores and be malnourished, underweight, and dehydrated. Ninety percent of nursing homes are understaffed. Anywhere from 40 to 100 percent of nursing home staff quit each year.

4. Compared with the elderly who have similar conditions and remain in the community, those who are placed in nursing homes tend to get sicker and die sooner.

5. Continuing to be active socially, including the use of computers and the Internet to connect with family and friends, helps some elderly overcome problems of isolation, depression, and anomie.

6. A new model in which the elderly are able to be in more home-like settings, take care of themselves somewhat, and interact with staff and other residents has shown more positive results.

C. Elder abuse is a significant problem. Most abusers are members of the elderly person's family. Some researchers say the abuse occurs when an individual feels obligated to take care of a person who is highly dependent and demanding, which can be very stressful.

D. A major fear of the elderly is that their money may not last as long as their life does.
    1. Women are about sixty percent more likely than men to be poor.
    2. Elderly African Americans and Latinos are two to three times as likely as whites to be poor.
    3. As a result of governmental programs, the elderly now are less likely than the average American to be poor.

VI. The Sociology of Death and Dying

A. In preindustrial societies, the sick were cared for at home and died at home. With the coming of modern medicine, dying was transformed into an event to be managed by professionals; most people never have personally seen anyone die.
    1. The process of dying has become strange to most people; we hide from the fact of death, and we even construct a language of avoidance (e.g., a person is "gone" or "at peace now," rather than "dead").
    2. New technology has produced "technological life." This is neither life nor death; the person is brain dead, but the body lives on.

B. Elisabeth Kübler-Ross identified the stages a person passes through when told that she or he has an incurable disease: (1) denial, (2) anger, (3) negotiation, (4) depression, and (5) acceptance. Kübler-Ross noted that not everyone experiences all of these stages, and not everyone goes through them in order.

C. Elderly persons want to die with dignity in the comforting presence of friends and relatives. Due to advances in medical technology, most deaths in the U.S. occur after the age of 65.
    1. Hospitals are awkward places in which to die, surrounded by strangers in hospital garb in an organization that puts routine ahead of individual needs. Patients experience what sociologists call "institutional death."
    2. Hospices have emerged as a solution to these problems, providing greater dignity and comfort at less cost.
    3. Hospitals are dedicated to prolonging life, while hospices are dedicated to providing dignity in death and making people comfortable in the living-dying

interval—that period of time between discovering that death is imminent and death itself.

D. Suicide has a social base. The overall rate remains about the same, as does the method. Males are more likely to take their lives than females. Suicides by young people receive a lot of publicity, but such deaths are, in fact, relatively rare. The suicide rate for young people is lower than that of all other groups.
1. The highest suicide rate is for people age 85 and over.

E. When adjusting to death, family members may experience conflicting feelings. Adjusting to death can last anywhere between one and two years.
1. When death is expected, family members find it less stressful. They have been able to say their goodbyes to their loved one.
2. Unexpected deaths bring greater shock. There was no opportunity to say goodbye or bring closure to the relationship.

VII. Looking Toward the Future
A. Biomedical science is exploring ways of stretching the human life span, enabling people to live longer lives.
B. If this happens, it will raise all sorts of questions. How will these elderly contribute to society? How will society be able to support them? How will the life course be redefined to take into consideration the expansion of life? What will it mean to be elderly?

Chapter Summary

Every society must deal with the problem of people growing old. Because more of the world's population is considered "elderly" than ever before, every society is experiencing a drain on its resources. This ranges from the hunting and gathering societies of the Amazon rainforest to the most advanced nations, such as the United States. This problem of how to address the needs of the elderly is very complex because age alone does not always qualify as the measurement of being old. A society's definition and treatment of its elderly is socially constructed. Attitudes about the elderly are rooted in culture and vary from one social group to another.

When a country industrializes, its people live longer. This is the result of technological advances that include making work safer, food better, living conditions better, water cleaner, and advances in medicine more readily available. As a nation's elderly population increases, its younger citizens are increasingly expected to help pay for their needs.

People in all parts of the globe are living longer, but in the least industrialized nations the difference is measured only in weeks and months rather than in years as in the most industrialized nations. The proportion of the population that is elderly varies from country to country and within each nation by race, ethnicity, and age. The largest percentage and largest number of the elderly in the United States are white, with women outliving men.

The symbolic interactionist perspective examines the "signals," or labels and stereotypes, that people associate with aging. The signals we receive are based on biology, personal history, gender age, and timetables. Wrinkles, baldness, and the inability to do what we used to are examples of biological aging. Someone who loses his hair early in life or develops premature wrinkles is often labeled as "old." Personal history deals with events in one's life that tend to be considered as something "old" people do or become. For example, when a woman becomes a grandmother at 32, she is "old," because grandmothers are symbolized as being elderly. *Gender age* refers to a difference in the meaning the same symbols have when they are possessed by men and women. For men, many of the signs of age symbolize wisdom and maturity, but for women they simply translate as being older. *Timetables* refer to the chronological age at which someone is considered old. Everyone is on a different schedule when it comes to determining what constitutes growing old. Birthday parties at age 50 are often accompanied by dead roses. People may join the American Association of Retired People (AARP) at age 50, regardless of whether or not they are retired. For some, Social Security kicks in at age 62, which symbolizes classification as "elderly." The basic principle of symbolic interactionism is that people perceive both themselves and others according to the symbols of their culture, and these symbols change in meaning.

The functionalist perspective on aging uses disengagement theory, activity theory, and continuity theory to examine people's adjustments to aging and retirement. Disengagement theory takes the view that society prevents disruption by having the elderly vacate, or disengage, from their positions of responsibility so the younger generation can be promoted. In activity theory, satisfaction during old age is related to a person's amount and quality of activity. Continuity theory, as the term implies, refers to the tendency for people to continue into their retirement the activities they pursued previously. This could include being more involved with church activities, greater degrees of travel, or the pursuit of additional education.

The conflict perspective on aging focuses on intergenerational conflicts surrounding the allocation of limited resources. The best example of these conflicts is the management of the Social Security program through the years when the "baby boom" retires. This will tax the fund more than at any other time in history. In order to deal with their mutual needs, many elderly people have joined the Gray Panthers and the American Association of Retired Persons (AARP). The Gray Panthers has approximately 20,000 members, while the AARP is far more politically powerful with 35 million members.

Being elderly often brings with it special problems associated with dependency. Most of the elderly population in the United States is not isolated. But elderly women are more likely than elderly men to lose their spouse and, therefore, experience isolation. Although most elderly are cared for by their families, about one-half of elderly women and one-third of elderly men in the United States spend at least some time in nursing homes. Elder abuse is a significant problem in nursing homes and, even more frequently, in elderly people's own homes. Poverty among the elderly reflects the gender, racial, and ethnic patterns of general society. Elderly whites and Asian Americans are the least likely to be poor. African Americans and Latinos have the highest rates of poverty.

Industrialization has radically altered the circumstances of dying. Today, most people die in remote and clinical settings. Elisabeth Kübler-Ross identified five stages that people experience as they face their own impending death. As an alternative to hospitalization and institutional death, hospices attempt to provide a more personable, humane, and supportive environment for people who are dying.

As we enter the twenty-first century, society will need to make adjustments in determining how to best deal with the increase in its elderly population. The elderly will also be faced with meeting their own special needs, some individually and others through collective effort.

KEY TERMS

After studying the chapter, review the definition for each of the following terms.

activity theory: the view that satisfaction during old age is related to a person's amount and quality of activity (361)

age cohort: people born at roughly the same time who pass through the life course together (360)

ageism: prejudice, discrimination, and hostility directed against people because of their age; can be directed against any age group, including youth (357)

continuity theory: the focus of this theory is how people adjust to retirement by continuing aspects of their earlier lives (361)

dependency ratio: the number of workers required to support each dependent person—those 65 and older and those 15 and under (363)

disengagement theory: the view that society is stabilized by having the elderly retire (disengage from) their positions of responsibility so the younger generation can step into their shoes (360)

gender age: the relative value placed on men's and women's ages (357)

graying of America: the growing percentage of older people in the U.S. population (354)

hospice: a place (or services brought to someone's home) for the purpose of giving comfort and dignity to a dying person (372)

life expectancy: the number of years that an average person at any age, including newborns, can expect to live (354)

life span: the maximum length of life of a species; for humans, the longest that a human has lived (355)

KEY PEOPLE

Review the major theoretical contributions or findings of these people.

Robert Butler: Butler coined the term "ageism" to refer to prejudice, discrimination, and hostility directed against people because of their age. (357)

Elaine Cumming and William Henry: These two developed disengagement theory to explain how society prevents disruption when the elderly vacate their positions of responsibility. (360-361)

Charles Hart: This anthropology graduate student carried out research on the Tiwi, a gerontocracy. (351)

Dorothy Jerrome: This anthropologist is critical of disengagement theory. She pointed out that it contains implicit bias that the elderly give up productive roles in society and slip into oblivion. (361)

Elisabeth Kübler-Ross: This psychologist found that coming face-to-face with one's own death sets in motion a five-stage process. (372)

Margaret Kuhn: She founded the Gray Panthers in 1970. This organization encourages all people to work for the welfare of the young and old. (366)

Karl Pillemer and Jill Suitor: These sociologists interviewed more than 200 caregivers of Alzheimer's patients and found that the precipitating cause of elder abuse is stress from caring for a person who is dependent, demanding, and even violent. (370)

SELF-TEST

MULTIPLE CHOICE QUESTIONS

1. The Abkhasians are an interesting example regarding age because they (352)
   a. live such short lives.
   b. live such long lives.
   c. have so many words in their language for "old people."
   d. quit working when they are quite young.

2. Today, what percentage of Americans are ages 65 or older? (354)
   a. 5.5
   b. 13
   c. 18.7
   d. 22

3. The process by which older persons make up an increasing proportion of the United States population is referred to as (354)
   a. the aging process.
   b. the graying of America.
   c. the gentrification process.
   d. none of the above

4. The number of years a person is likely to live is referred to as (353-254)
   a. life span.
   b. life course.
   c. life expectancy.
   d. life history.

5. The relative value that a culture places on men's and women's ages is (357)
   a. cultural aging.
   b. ageism.
   c. gender age.
   d. relative age.

6. Factors that may push people to apply the label of "old" to themselves include (357)
   a. personal history or biography.
   b. cultural signals about when a person is old.
   c. biological factors.
   d. all of the above

7. _____ stress that old age has no inherent meaning. (358)
   a. Conflict theorists

b.   Functionalists
c.   Symbolic interactionists
d.   All of the above

8.   Which theoretical perspective claims that industrialization eroded the respect that the elderly had received? (358)
a.   symbolic interactionism
b.   functionalist
c.   conflict
d.   sapir-whorf

9.   It has been suggested that _____ will have a positive effect on U.S. social images of the elderly in the years to come, given their numbers and economic clout. (358)
a.   Congress
b.   the baby boom generation
c.   Generation X
d.   seniors living on Social Security

10. The example of the treatment of the elderly in China demonstrates that (359)
a.   there is changing sentiment about the elderly due to the effects of industrialization.
b.   increasing life span is tearing at the bonds between generations.
c.   the high status of the elderly is slowly being challenged.
d.   all of the above

11. Some researchers believe that the process of disengagement begins (360-361)
a.   when a person first starts a job.
b.   during middle age.
c.   at retirement.
d.   about one year after retirement.

12. The mass media (360)
a.   communicate messages that reflect the currently devalued status of the elderly.
b.   tell us what people over 65 should be like.
c.   often treat the elderly in discourteous and unflattering terms.
d.   all of the above

13. Which theory assumes that the more activities elderly people engage in, the more they find life satisfying? (361)
a.   disengagement theory
b.   activity theory
c.   continuity theory
d.   conflict theory

14. Continuity theory has been criticized because (361)
    a. it is too broad.
    b. it is really just a collection of loosely connected ideas.
    c. it has no specific application to the elderly.
    d. all of the above

15. Conflict theorists believe that retirement benefits are the result of (362)
    a. generous hearts in Congress.
    b. a struggle between competing interest groups.
    c. many years of hard work by elderly Americans.
    d. none of the above

16. Which aspect of the original Social Security legislation was challenged by the elderly for many years following its passage in 1934? (362)
    a. mandatory retirement at age 65
    b. survivor payments to orphaned children
    c. lack of coverage for nonworking spouses
    d. payments tied to income

17. As the population of the U.S. grays, there is concern that (363)
    a. participation in the electoral process will decline because older citizens are less likely to vote.
    b. the ratio of working people to retired people will become smaller, making it more difficult to support programs like Social Security.
    c. there will be a shortage of affordable housing for widowed individuals living on a fixed income.
    d. all of the above

18. Which of the following is *not* a problem associated with Social Security today? (363)
    a. The cash payments senior citizens receive are not tied to the money they invested in the fund.
    b. The money collected from workers for Social Security is used by the government to cover general operating expenses.
    c. The number of workers who pay into Social Security is shrinking while the number of retired who collect from Social Security is growing.
    d. Low payments have contributed to an increase in elderly poverty.

19. What is the goal of the Gray Panthers? (366-67)
    a. protect the interests of the elderly at the expense of other age groups
    b. work for the welfare of both the old and the young
    c. win special concessions for senior citizens
    d. closure of nursing homes

20. Isolation is a problem for many people over 65, especially for (367)
    a. women.
    b. minorities.
    c. the disabled.
    d. immigrants.

21. What percentage of nursing homes are understaffed? (368)
    a. 20
    b. 52
    c. 74
    d. 90

22. Researchers have found that elder abuse: (370)
    a. occurs less frequently than one might think, given the level of abuse shown in the media.
    b. is fairly extensive.
    c. is most often caused by workers in nursing homes.
    d. is easy to study because the victims are so visible.

23. Who is most likely to abuse an elderly person? (370)
    a. nursing home staff
    b. paid caretakers in the elderly person's home
    c. an elderly person's spouse
    d. an elderly person's son- or daughter-in-law

24. Who is more likely to be poor? (371)
    a. elderly men
    b. elderly women
    c. white Americans
    d. single men

25. In what way(s) did industrialization alter the circumstances of dying? (371)
    a. Death is physically less painful today than in the past because of modern medicines.
    b. Death is emotionally easier for us to accept because we know more about the diseases that can kill us.
    c. Death has been transformed into an event that is managed by professionals in hospitals.
    d. Death is no longer feared because of greater scientific knowledge and new technologies.

TRUE-FALSE QUESTIONS

1. _____When sociologists say that aging is socially constructed, what they mean is that attitudes about aging reflect cultural values rather than biological factors. (352)
2. _____According to the symbolic interactionists, a person's perceptions and definitions of "old" are influenced by stereotypes and societal definitions. (356)
3. _____In comparison to the colonial period in U.S. history, views about old age are much more positive today. (358)
4. _____In the United States today, the elderly are underrepresented on TV, in ads, and even in popular magazines. (360)
5. That older male news anchors are likely to be retained by news stations while female anchors that are the same age are more likely to be transferred to less visible positions is an example of gender age. (360)
6. _____Disengagement theory is used to explain how society prevents disruption by having the elderly vacate their positions of responsibility. (360)
7. _____The AARP is a politically powerful organization. (367)
8. _____Elderly men are more likely to experience the isolation widowhood brings. (367)
9. _____The elderly will exhibit gender roles that they learned in their younger years and carry those into old age. (367)
10. _____Elder abuse includes financial exploitation. (370)

FILL-IN-THE-BLANK QUESTIONS

1. People who are born at roughly the same time and who pass through the life course together are referred to as _____. (360)
2. Activity theory assumes that the _____ activities elderly people engage in, the more likely they find life satisfying. (361)
3. The major criticism of continuity theory is that it is too _____. (361)
4. The original Social Security legislation required people to retire at age _____. (362)
5. The _____ refers to the number of workers who are required to support each dependent person. (363)
6. The _____ is an organization that fights for the rights of all ages. (366)
7. Most elderly are cared for by _____. (367)
8. Today's elderly are _____ likely than the average American to be poor. (370)
9. The last stage in the death process is _____. (372)
10. _____ may be able to stretch the human life span. (375)

ESSAY QUESTIONS

1. Explain why sociologists say that aging is socially constructed.

2. Choose one of the three different perspectives and discuss how that perspective approaches the subject of aging. Consider both the strengths and weaknesses of the perspective you chose.

3. Discuss the impact that industrialization and technology has had on aging and dying.

4. People who come here from other parts of the world are often very critical of families who place their elderly family members in nursing homes. Assume that a friend of yours who comes from another part of the world asks you about your family's decision to move your grandparent into a nursing home. Develop an explanation that draws on the material presented in this chapter.

5. Discuss the five stages of death and what is being done to humanize the process of death and dying.

CHAPTER 14
THE ECONOMY

LEARNING OBJECTIVES

After reading Chapter 14, you should be able to:

1. Trace the transformation of economic systems through the evolutionary history of human society and, for each society, discuss the different levels of and reasons for social inequality. (380-381)

2. Know what is meant by the "medium of exchange," describe how it has evolved along with economic systems, and explain how it reflects and contributes to a country's development. (381)

3. Describe the basic components of capitalism, differentiate between laissez-faire and welfare capitalism, and understand how and why welfare capitalism developed in the United States. (385-386)

4. Identify the basic component of socialism, talk about its goals, and discuss why some countries have developed democratic socialism in response to some of its shortcomings. (386-387)

5. Describe the ideologies of capitalism and socialism, the criticisms of capitalism and socialism, and the convergence of capitalism and socialism. (385-390)

6. Know the functionalist view of the globalization of capitalism, including the functional aspects of work, corporations, and the global division of labor. (390-392)

7. Describe the inner circle of corporate capitalism and how, according to the conflict perspective, members of the inner circle consolidate their power and maximize their profits at the expense of workers. (393, 396-398)

8. Discuss how the composition of the American workforce has changed significantly over the past 100 years. (398-401)

9. Know what is meant by the term "underground economy" and recognize the extent of this underground economy in the United States. (402-404)

10. Discuss recent changes in the U.S. economy relating to the buying power of paychecks, patterns in work and leisure, and telecommuting. (404-405)

Chapter Outline

I. **The Transformation of Economic Systems**
   A. Market, or economy, is the mechanism by which values are established in order to exchange goods and services.
      1. The economy, which may be one of our most important social institutions, is the system of distribution of goods and services.
      2. The economy today, impersonal and global, is radically different from the past.
      3. The economy is essential to our welfare.
   B. As societies developed, a surplus emerged that fostered social inequality.
      1. Earliest hunting and gathering societies had subsistence economies, characterized by little trade with other groups and a high degree of social equality.
      2. In pastoral and horticultural economies, people created more dependable food supplies. As groups settled down in one location and grew in size, a specialized division of labor developed. This led to the production of a surplus and trade between groups, all of which fostered social inequality.
      3. The invention of the plow paved way for agricultural societies. As more people were freed from food production, a more specialized division of labor developed and trade expanded. This brought even more social, political, and economic inequality.
   C. The surplus (and greater inequality) grew in industrial societies. As the surplus increased, emphasis changed from production of goods to consumption. Thorstein Veblen referred to this as "conspicuous consumption."
   D. The "information explosion" and the global village are key elements of postindustrial society. According to Daniel Bell, postindustrial economies have six traits: (1) a large service sector that most work in; (2) a large surplus of goods; (3) extensive trade among nations; (4) a large variety and amount of goods available to the average person; (5) an information explosion; and (6) a global village with instantaneous, worldwide communications.
   E. We may be on the verge of yet another new type of society.
      1. This new society is being ushered in by advances in biology, especially the deciphering of the human genome system in 2001.
      2. While the specifics are still unknown, the marriage of biology and economics will yield even greater surplus and greater trade.
      3. The new society may lead to longer and healthier lives.
   F. Whenever society changes, this has implications for our lives. It impacts the type of work that those who live in the society will do.
   G. Around the globe the consequences of the information explosion are uneven. Due to political and economic arrangements, some nations and individuals will prosper while others suffer.

II. The Transformation of the Medium of Exchange

A. A medium of exchange is the means by which people value and exchange goods and services.

B. One of the earliest mediums of exchange was barter, the direct exchange of one item for another. This was common in hunting and gathering, pastoral, and horticultural societies.

C. In agricultural economies, people came to use gold and silver coins. Deposit receipts became common. Under this arrangement, the ownership of a specified amount of gold, bushels of wheat, or some other item was transferred from one person to another. Toward the end of this period, the receipts were formalized into currency (paper money). Currency represented stored value; no more could be issued than the amount of gold or silver the currency represented.

D. In industrial economies, bartering largely disappeared, and gold was replaced by paper currency. The gold standard (a dollar represents a specified amount of gold) kept the number of dollars that could be issued to a specific limit. When "fiat money" came into existence, the currency no longer could be exchanged for gold or silver.

    1. Even without a gold standard, the amount of paper money that can be issued is limited: prices increase if a government issues currency at a rate higher than the growth of its gross domestic product. Issuing more produces inflation: each unit of currency will purchase fewer goods and services.

    2. Checking accounts and credit cards have become common in industrial economies, largely replacing currency.

E. In postindustrial economies, paper money is being replaced by checks, credit cards, and debit cards. The latest phase of evolution of money is e-cash, digital money stored on the user's local computer. E-cash can be encoded in e-mail and sent over the Internet.

III. World Economic Systems

A. Capitalism has three essential features: (1) the private ownership of the means of production; (2) market competition; and (3) the pursuit of profit.

    1. Pure (laissez-faire) capitalism exists only when market forces are able to operate without interference from the government.

    2. The United States today has welfare (or state) capitalism. Private citizens own the means of production and pursue profits but do so within a vast system of laws (market restraints) that are designed to protect the public welfare. These laws include antimonopoly legislation. That is, companies must obtain federal approval before acquiring another company in the same industry.

    3. Under welfare capitalism the government supports competition but establishes its own monopoly over "common good" items; e.g., those presumed essential for the common good of the citizens.

B. Socialism also has three essential features: (1) the public ownership of the means of production; (2) central planning; and (3) the distribution of goods without a profit motive.

1. Under socialism, the government owns the means of production, and a central committee determines what the country needs, instead of allowing market forces (supply and demand) to control production and prices. Socialism is designed to eliminate competition, to produce goods for the general welfare, and to distribute them according to people's needs, not their ability to pay.

2. Socialism does not exist in pure form. Although the ideology of socialism calls for resources to be distributed according to need rather than position, socialist nations found it necessary to offer higher salaries for some jobs in order to entice people to take greater responsibility.

3. Some nations (e.g., Sweden and Denmark) have adopted democratic or welfare socialism: both the state and individuals engage in production and distribution, although the state owns certain industries (steel, mining, forestry, telephone, television stations, and airlines), while retail stores, farms, and most service industries remain in private hands.

C. Capitalism and socialism represent distinct ideologies.

1. Capitalists believe that market forces should determine both products and prices and that it is good for people to strive for profits.

2. Socialists believe that profit is immoral and represents excess value extracted from workers.

3. These two different ideologies produce contrasting pictures of how the world should be; consequently, each sees the other ideology as not only inherently evil but also as a system of exploitation.

D. The primary criticism of capitalism is that it leads to social inequality (a top layer of wealthy, powerful people, and a bottom layer of people who are unemployed or underemployed). Socialism has been criticized for not respecting individual rights and for not being capable of producing much wealth (thus the greater equality of socialism actually amounts to almost everyone having an equal chance of being poor).

E. In recent years, fundamental changes have taken place in these two economic systems. Both systems have adopted features of the other.

1. That capitalism and socialism are becoming similar is known as convergence theory.

2. In Russia and China the standard of living lagged far behind the West; both economies were plagued by the production of shoddy goods and shortages. In the 1980s and 1990s, both reinstated market forces—private ownership of property became legal, and the state auctioned off many of its industries. Making a profit was encouraged.

3. Over the years the United States has adopted many socialistic practices, such as unemployment compensation, subsidized housing, welfare, minimum wages, and Social Security.

4. While leaders in both systems accept certain elements of the other, the reality is that the two remain far from "converged," and the struggles between them continue, although they are more muted than in the past. With the pullback of socialism around the world, capitalism in its many varieties has a strong lead.

IV. The Functionalist Perspective on the Globalization of Capitalism

A. The globalization of capitalism may be the most significant economic change in the past 100 years.

B. Work is functional for society; it binds people together.

1. Work is central to Durkheim's principles of mechanical solidarity (unity from being involved in similar occupations or activities) and organic solidarity (interdependence resulting from mutual need as each individual fulfills his job).

2. Today, organic solidarity has expanded far beyond anything Durkheim envisioned, creating interdependencies that span the globe. These global interdependencies suggest a new global division of labor, although we do not yet feel a sense of unity with one another and we are increasingly dependent on one another.

C. The corporation (joint ownership of a business enterprise whose liabilities are separate from those of its owners) changed the face of capitalism.

1. Sociologists use the term "corporate capitalism" to refer to the contemporary domination of the economy by corporations.

2. One of the most significant aspects of large corporations is the separation of ownership and management, producing ownership of wealth without appreciable control, and control of wealth without appreciable ownership.

3. What makes the separation of ownership and management functional is profits. Managers are motivated to maximize profits because they will then benefit through stock options and bonuses.

4. A stockholders' revolt (stockholders of a corporation refuse to rubber-stamp management decisions) is likely to occur if the profits do not meet expectations.

D. The world is divided into three primary trading blocs: North and South America, dominated by the United States; Europe, dominated by Germany; and Asia, dominated by Japan but with China close behind.

1. Functionalists stress that this new global division benefits both the multinationals and the citizens of the world.

2. Free trade leads to greater competition, which drives the search for greater productivity. This in turn lowers prices and raises the standard of living.

3. Free trade can also be dysfunctional. When businesses move to countries where labor costs are lower, workers in the countries from which the businesses came from will lose their jobs.

V. The Conflict Perspective on the Globalization of Capitalism

A. Conflict theorists stress that the important point of global interdependence is how the wealthy benefit at the expense of workers.

B. The multinationals are headed by an inner circle. This group, in which members compete with one another, is still united by a mutual interest in preserving capitalism.

1. Oligopolies are defined as several large companies that dominate a single industry, dictate pricing, set the quality of their products, and protect the market. Often

they use their wealth and connections for political purposes (e.g., favorable legislation giving them special tax breaks or protecting their industry from imports).

2. One of the most significant developments today is the merger of giant corporations from different nations. Merging reduces competition.

3. Consolidation of power is one of the primary goals of these corporations.

4. If they find hostility, some are not above plotting murder and overthrowing governments. In 1973, ITT plotted with the CIA to unseat Salvador Allende, the democratically-elected president of Chile, because he was a socialist, which led to his assassination.

5. U.S. economic power is so integrated with politics that the inner circle can even get U.S. presidents to pitch their products.

6. The interests of the multinationals and the top political leaders have converged. Together they form a power elite.

C. Interlocking directorates occur when individuals serve as directors of several companies, concentrating power and minimizing competition.

D. As corporations have outgrown national boundaries, the result is the creation of multinational corporations, detached from the interests and values of their country of origin with no concern other than making a profit. They are becoming a primary political force in the world today.

E. Because of their detachment from national boundaries, the multinationals may be a force for global peace, or they could create a New World Order dominated by a handful of corporate leaders.

VI. Work in U.S. Society

A. In our postindustrial society, there are changes in the type of work that workers do.

1. In the 1800s, most U.S. workers were farmers; today farmers represent only 2 percent of the workforce.

2. In 1940, about half of U.S. workers worked in blue-collar jobs; today, the changing technology has reduced the market for these jobs.

3. The dominant job today is white-collar.

B. A major change in our society has been the increase in women who work outside of the home for wages. Almost one out of two workers is a woman.

1. Men and women are different in terms of how they experience work. Women seem more concerned than men with maintaining a balance between work and family life. Men seem to follow models of individualism and power, while women may stress collaboration and helping.

2. How likely a woman is to work depends on several factors such as her education and marital status; race and ethnicity have little influence.

3. The "quiet revolution" refers to the continually increasing proportions of women in the labor force. This transformation affects consumer patterns, relations at work, self-concepts, and familial relationships.

C. The underground (informal and off-the-books) economy involves the exchange of goods and services not reported to the government, including income from work done "on the side" and from illegal activities (e.g., drug dealing).
   1. The drug networks are so huge that more than 2 million Americans are arrested each year for illegal drug activities.
   2. The million or so undocumented workers who enter the United States each year are also part of the underground economy. Their employers disregard their fake Social Security cards or pay them in cash.
   3. Estimates place the underground economy at 9 percent of the regular economy, which means it may run over $1 trillion per year. As a result, the Internal Revenue Service (IRS) loses billions of dollars a year in lost taxes.
D. Since 1970, increases in workers' paychecks have not kept up with inflation; consequently, workers are falling behind.
E. Different societies have had differing amounts of leisure (time not taken up by work or required activities such as eating/sleeping).
   1. Early societies had a lot of time for leisure. Industrialization brought changes: bosses and machines controlled people's time.
   2. It is not the activity itself that makes something leisure, but rather its purpose (e.g., driving a car for pleasure or driving it to work). Patterns of leisure change with the life course, with both the young and the old enjoying the most leisure and parents with young children having the least.
   3. Compared with early industrialization, workers today have far more leisure (shorter work weeks, for example). In recent decades, the trend for more leisure has been reversed in the United States. U.S. workers now average the highest number of hours worked per year compared to any other industrialized nation.
F. New technologies are enabling millions of workers to work from home; they commute electronically. This has both positive and negative effects.
   1. Corporations are able to save office space, and workers avoid traffic jams and long commutes.
   2. Managers are concerned over the lack of control of their workers, and workers fear that their career will be hindered by being out of touch with office politics.

VII. Global Capitalism and Our Future
A. There is every indication that global trade will continue to increase beyond anything we have ever seen, as multinational corporations continue to carve up the world into major trading blocs and push for reduction or elimination of tariffs.
   1. The Most Industrialized Nations will continue to garner the lion's share of the world's wealth.
   2. A major concern is that economic inequality will increase between the richer and poorer nations.
   3. Computer-driven production will continue to reduce the number of manufacturing jobs. While technology eliminates jobs, it also creates jobs. At the same time,

those who bear the brunt of the change are low-level workers who live from paycheck to paycheck.

Chapter Summary

The economy is a system of producing and distributing goods and services. In today's postindustrial society, this process is radically different than in earlier societies.

The earliest human groups, hunting and gathering societies, had a subsistence economy. Composed of groups of 25 to 40 people, they lived off the land; produced little or no surplus; and had little, if any, social inequality. Of all societies, the hunting and gathering society was the most egalitarian. The hunting and gathering society evolved into pastoral and horticultural societies with the domestication of plants and animals. Permanent settlements began to appear, as did the development of surpluses. With the invention of the plow, the agricultural society developed, which led to the development of cities. The industrial society followed when, in 1765, the steam engine was invented. In 1973, the postindustrial society was named, placing the emphasis on service and technology. A new society, the bioeconomic society, may be developing, based on advances in biology and economics.

As societies became more complex, they consistently produced greater surpluses. With the increase in surplus, trade also increased. This, in turn, created social inequality as some people began to accumulate more than others. As societies continued to become more complex, their division of labor, surpluses, trade, and social inequality all continued to increase.

As each new type of economy evolved, so did the medium of exchange, or the means by which people value and exchange goods and services. Initially, the barter system was the primary means of exchange. As the volume of trade increased, it was necessary to develop a new medium of exchange, which was money. The postindustrial society is dominated by computers, and electronic fund transfers have become the common medium of exchange through the use of credit cards, debit cards, and e-cash.

Currently, the world's two main economic systems are capitalism and socialism. Capitalism is characterized by private ownership of the means of production, market competition, and the pursuit of profit. Socialism, in contrast, is characterized by public ownership of the means of production, central planning, and the distribution of goods without a profit motive.

There are two forms of capitalism: laissez-faire capitalism and welfare capitalism. Likewise, there are two types of socialism: socialism and democratic socialism. In recent years, there has been a convergence of capitalism and socialism with both systems adopting features of the other.

The functionalist view of the globalization of capitalism sees work as functional for society in that it binds people together. In earlier societies, people did similar work and had a greater sense of unity. With industrialization, labor became more divided. As a result, people felt less social solidarity with one another, even as they became more economically sound.

As the division of labor has become global in recent years, workers—and nations—around the globe have become more economically interdependent. Although they continue to be socially divided by class, there is a greater reliance among nations to share raw materials, labor, financial aid, and markets on a global scale. The globalization of capitalism is leading to a new world structure based on three primary trading blocs: North and South America, Europe, and Asia.

The functionalist perspective on the globalization of capitalism is that it unites the world in a state of interdependence and creates solidarity. One of the most surprising but functional aspects of the globalization of capitalism is the separation of ownership and management; as a result, managers run the corporation instead of the owners. Free trade worldwide also promotes greater competition, which creates greater productivity, lower prices, and a higher standard of living.

The conflict theory's view of the globalization of capitalism focuses on power and exploitation. According to conflict theorists, multinational corporations are headed by an inner circle of leaders who use political connections in their own countries and economic interventions in others to consolidate their power and maximize their profits. As multinational corporations do business around the globe, conflict theorists point out that they become increasingly detached from the interests and values of their country of origin. Their primary allegiance is to profits and market share, rather than to any nation or workers.

As the industrial society in America has evolved into the postindustrial society over the past 100 years, the composition of the American workforce has changed significantly. The percentage of farmers has drastically declined. The number of blue-collar workers has dropped from nearly 50 percent in 1940 to less than half this amount. White-collar workers, on the other hand, have doubled during the same period of time. From a gender perspective, the percentage of women in the American labor force has steadily increased so that women currently make up just under half of all U.S. workers.

The underground economy consists of the exchange of goods and services not reported to the government. An estimated 18 million Americans use illegal drugs, contributing billions of dollars to the underground economy. However, this economy goes well beyond drugs and includes money earned for services as innocent as babysitting by teenage girls or less-innocent pursuits like prostitution and organized crime. Drug dealing is the single greatest source of illegal income in the underground economy. Illegal immigration also significantly contributes to the underground economy.

Although workers in the United States are among the most productive in the world, they are earning less money today, controlling for inflation, than they were in 1970. Although the average rate of pay has jumped from $3 an hour in 1970 to almost $19 an hour today, workers can buy about as much today as they did in 1970.

Compared with workers in earlier industrialized societies, today's workers in industrialized countries have more leisure. In the United States, however, the trend toward more leisure has been reversed, with American workers currently averaging more hours of work a year than any industrialized nation.

Global trade and the new technology will continue to affect the worldwide economy in ways that are likely to increase the economic inequality between richer and poorer nations. New technologies are inevitable and, just as inevitably, destroy old jobs and create new jobs. The basic question is whether they will destroy old jobs faster than they create new jobs and how societies can and/or should react to these transformations.

KEY TERMS

After studying the chapter, review the definition for each of the following terms.

barter: the direct exchange of one item for another (381)

capitalism: an economic system characterized by the private ownership of the means of production, the pursuit of profit, and market competition (385)

conspicuous consumption: Thorstein Veblen's term for a change from the Protestant ethic to an eagerness to show off wealth by the elaborate consumption of goods (380)

convergence theory: the view that as capitalist and socialist economic systems each adopt features of the other, a hybrid (or mixed) economic system will emerge (388)

corporate capitalism: the domination of the economic system by giant corporations (392)

corporation: a business enterprise, often jointly owned, whose assets, liabilities, and obligations are separate from those of its owners; as a legal entity, it can enter into contracts, assume debt, and sue and be sued (392)

credit card: a device that allows its owner to purchase goods and to be billed later (384)

currency: paper money (383)

debit card: a device that allows its owner to charge purchases against his or her bank account (384)

democratic socialism: a hybrid economic system in which the individual ownership of businesses is mixed with the state ownership of industries thought essential to the public welfare, such as the postal service and the delivery of medicine and utilities (387)

deposit receipt: a receipt stating that a certain amount of goods is on deposit in a warehouse or bank; the receipt is used as a form of money (383)

e-cash: digital money that is stored on computers; it is of two types, e-currency and e-gold (384)

economy: a system of producing and distributing goods and services (380)

fiat money: currency issued by a government that is not backed by stored value (383)

global superclass: a small group of highly interconnected individuals in which wealth and power are so concentrated that they make the world's major decisions (396)

gold standard: paper money backed by gold (383)

gross domestic product (GDP): the amount of goods and services produced by a nation (483)

inflation: an increase in prices (383)

interlocking directorates: the same people serving on the board of directors of several companies (396)

laissez-faire capitalism: unrestrained manufacture and trade (literally, "hands off" capitalism) (403)

laissez-faire leader: an individual who leads by being highly permissive (385)

leisure: time not taken up by work or necessary activities (323)

market forces: the laws of supply and demand (386)

mechanical solidarity: Durkheim's term for the unity (a shared consciousness) that people feel as a result of performing the same or similar tasks (390)

medium of exchange: the means by which people place a value on goods and services in order to make an exchange—for example, currency, gold, and silver (381)

money: any item (from sea shells to gold) that serves as a medium of exchange; today, currency is the most common form (382)

monopoly: the control of an entire industry by a single company (386)

multinational corporations: companies that operate across national boundaries; also called *transnational corporations* (393)

organic solidarity: Durkheim's term for the interdependence that results from the division of labor; people depending on others to fulfill their jobs (390)

quiet revolution: the fundamental changes in society that follow when vast numbers of women enter the workforce (401)

socialism: an economic system characterized by the public ownership of the means of production, central planning, and the distribution of goods without a profit motive (486)

stockholders' revolt: the refusal of a corporation's stockholders to authorize decisions made by its managers (392)

stored value: the goods that are stored and held in reserve that back up (or provide the value for) a currency (383)

subsistence economy: a type of economy in which human groups live off the land and have little or no surplus (380)

underground economy: exchanges of goods and services that are not reported to the government and thereby escape taxation (402)

KEY PEOPLE

Review the major theoretical contributions or findings of these people.

Daniel Bell: Bell identified six characteristics of the postindustrial society. (380)

Emile Durkheim: Durkheim contributed the concepts of mechanical and organic solidarity to our understanding of social cohesion. (390)

Louis Gallambos: This historian of business has predicted that the new global business system will change the way everyone lives and works. (390)

Karl Marx: Marx was an outspoken critic of capitalism who wrote about the basis for profits under capitalism. (387)

Michael Useem: Using a conflict perspective, Useem studied the activities of the "inner circle" of corporate executives. (392, 396)

Thorstein Veblen: Veblen created the term "conspicuous consumption" to refer to the eagerness to show off one's wealth through the elaborate consumption of material goods. (380)

MULTIPLE CHOICE QUESTIONS

1. What is an economy? (380)
    a. It is a system of buying and selling.
    b. It is a system of producing and distributing goods and services.
    c. It means the movement of vast amounts of goods across international borders.
    d. All of the above

2. Which of the following characterizes hunting and gathering societies? (380)
    a. market economy
    b. surplus economy
    c. subsistence economy
    d. maintenance economy

3. Which of the following took place in pastoral and horticultural economies? (380)
    a. A subsistence economy existed.
    b. A more dependable food supply led to the development of a surplus.
    c. The plow was used extensively.
    d. Extensive trade developed.

4. Which of the following is *not* a feature of industrial economies? (380)
    a. Machines are powered by fuels.
    b. A surplus unlike anything the world has seen is created.
    c. The steam engine was invented and became the basis for the economy.
    d. A service sector developed and employed the majority of workers.

5. What did Veblen label the lavishly wasteful spending of goods designed to enhance social prestige? (380)
    a. prestigious consumption
    b. wasteful consumption
    c. conspicuous prestige
    d. conspicuous consumption

6. Which of the following is *not* a defining characteristic of postindustrial economies? (380)
    a. a large surplus of goods
    b. extensive trade among nations
    c. machines powered by fuels
    d. a "global village"

7. The author of your text suggests that a new type of society may be emerging. What two forces have combined to produce this new society? (381)

a. biology and politics
b. politics and economics
c. biology and economics
d. biology and religion

8. In what society was bartering a common medium of exchange? (381)
   a. postindustrial
   b. agricultural
   c. industrial
   d. pastoral and horticultural

9. In which type of society was money first used extensively? (382)
   a. agricultural
   b. industrial
   c. postindustrial
   d. pastoral and horticultural

10. In the past, the U.S. government maintained a policy whereby it would issue only as many paper dollars as it had gold stored in the vaults at Fort Knox. This policy was called (383)
    a. the gold reserves.
    b. the cash standard.
    c. the gold standard.
    d. the Fort Knox standard.

11. What term is used to describe the total goods and services that a nation produces? (383)
    a. the gross domestic product
    b. the net national product
    c. the national debt
    d. the medium of exchange

12. The debit card came into existence in the (384)
    a. agricultural economy.
    b. industrial economy.
    c. postindustrial economy.
    d. none of the above

13. Private ownership of the means of production is an essential feature of (385)
    a. communism.
    b. socialism.
    c. democracy.
    d. capitalism.

14. The ownership of machines and factories by individuals who decide what to produce is (385)
    a. state socialism.
    b. personal capitalism.
    c. private ownership of the means of production.
    d. public ownership of the means of production.

15. Which system has public ownership, central planning, and no profit motive? (386)
    a. democratic socialism
    b. socialism
    c. capitalism
    d. communism

16. For Marx, what is the amount of value created by workers' labor but withheld from them? (387)
    a. market prices
    b. profits
    c. labor costs
    d. overhead

17. Which of the following is not an essential feature of Capitalism? (387)
    a. protect welfare of the population
    b. private ownership of means of production
    c. market competition
    d. pursuit of profit

18. The theory that capitalism and socialism will grow more alike as they develop is called (388)
    a. unity theory.
    b. convergence theory.
    c. amalgamation theory.
    d. merger theory.

19. Which perspective views work as the tie that binds us together? (390)
    a. functionalist
    b. conflict
    c. symbolic interactionist
    d. ethnomethodological

20. As societies industrialize, they become based on (390)
    a. mechanical solidarity.
    b. organic solidarity.
    c. social solidarity.

d.   none of the above

21.   Jointly owning an enterprise, with liabilities and obligations independent of its owners is (392)
    a.   an oligopoly.
    b.   a monopoly.
    c.   a corporation.
    d.   an interlocking directorate.

22.   A stockholders' revolt occurs when (392)
    a.   major stockholders dump their holdings in the open market.
    b.   stockholders lead workers in a protest against company policies.
    c.   stockholders refuse to rubber-stamp the recommendations made by management.
    d.   people boycott the stocks of certain companies that are socially irresponsible.

23.   Which of the following statements about Michael Useem's inner circle is *incorrect*? (396-397)
    a.   Members of the inner circle are united by a mutual interest in preserving capitalism.
    b.   Relationships among members of the inner circle are always cooperative rather than competitive.
    c.   Within their own country, they have close ties with political leaders who stand firmly for the private ownership of property.
    d.   Globally, they promote the ideology of capitalism.

24.   What is corporate capitalism? (392)
    a.   the control of an entire industry by several large companies
    b.   the control of an entire industry by a single company
    c.   illegal in the United States
    d.   the domination of an economic system by giant corporations

25.   Which of the following statements about wages is *correct*? (404)
    a.   The buying power of today's wages is greater than any time in the last 30 years.
    b.   In current dollars, workers today are paid less than they were 30 years ago.
    c.   The buying power of today's wages is actually less than it was 30 years ago.
    d.   Both the buying power and current value of wages are greater today than they were 30 years ago.

TRUE-FALSE QUESTIONS

1.   _____Hunting and gathering societies were the first economies to have a surplus. (380)
2.   _____In pastoral and horticultural economies, some individuals were able for the first time in human history to devote their energies to tasks other than food production. (380)

3. _____In postindustrial societies people bartering for goods and services is a common practice. (380)
4. _____Industrial economies are based on information processing and providing services. (380)
5. _____The earliest medium of exchange was barter. (381)
6. _____The gold standard was a medium of exchange in industrial economies. (383)
7. _____Credit cards and debit cards are the same thing. (384)
8. _____The "quiet revolution" refers to the continually increasing proportions of women who have joined the ranks of paid labor. (401)
9. _____Industrialization increased the amount of leisure time workers had. (404-405)
10. _____The current technological revolution is making it possible for millions of workers to work from their homes; this trend is called *telecommuting*. (405)

FILL-IN-THE-BLANK QUESTIONS

1. Sweden and Denmark developed democratic _____. (387)
2. That capitalism and socialism are becoming similar is known as _____. (388)
3. A _____ is a business that is treated legally as person. (392)
4. The top members of the capitalist class who make the major decisions that affect the world are called the _____. (396)
5. _____ theorists stress how the elite consolidate their power through interlocking directorates. (396)
6. Today, almost one in _____ workers are women. (399)
7. The illegal immigrants who enter the U.S. to work are known as _____. (403)
8. Patterns of leisure change with the life course, following the _____. (405)
9. _____ allows workers to work from home while they communicate electronically with their company. (405)
10. In comparing work hours, _____ is the country that puts in the least amount of hours. (405)

ESSAY QUESTIONS

1. Discuss the advantages and disadvantages of both capitalism and socialism as ideologies and as economic systems.

2. Explain why functionalists believe that work is functional for society.

3. Take the perspective of a conflict theorist and explain the goals of corporate leaders and the strategies they use to achieve these goals.

4. Discuss what is meant by the underground economy and the extent to which it exists.

5.   The chapter discusses several different economic trends that have been occurring in the second half of this century. Discuss the impact of each of the following: the movement of women into the economy, the underground economy, shrinking paychecks, changing patterns of work and leisure, and the emergence of the alternative office.

CHAPTER 15
POLITICS

LEARNING OBJECTIVES
After reading Chapter 15, you should be able to:

1. Understand the relationship between power and politics, and power and the state. (412-413)

2. Know the difference between authority and coercion, and explain why and how the state is able to claim a monopoly on the legitimate use of violence. (412-413)

3. Describe the three ideal types of authority identified by Max Weber and, for each type, explain how authority is transferred from one leader to another. (413-415)

4. Distinguish between monarchies, democracies, dictatorships, and oligarchies. (416-419)

5. Discuss how the two major political parties in the United States are different from and similar to one another. (419-420)

6. Describe the differences between the democratic systems of the United States and Europe, and explain how these differences affect the role of minor political parties in each system. (421)

7. Identify the major voting patterns in the United States and discuss the reasons for voter alienation and voter apathy. (421-424)

8. Discuss the role that money plays in American politics and how lobbyists and special-interest groups influence the political process. (425)

9. Compare and evaluate the competing views of functionalists and conflict theorists on the distribution of power in American politics. (426-427)

10. Discuss the causes, costs, and ramifications of war throughout human history, as well as the current threats involving nuclear, chemical, and biological weapons. (427-435)

11. Evaluate the possibilities for and the potential implications of a new world order characterized by global political and economic unity. (435-437)

Chapter Outline

I. **Micropolitics and Macropolitics**
    A. Politics refers to power relations wherever they exist.
    B. Power is the ability to carry out one's will despite resistance.

C. Symbolic interactionists use micropolitics to refer to exercise of power in everyday life.

D. Macropolitics is the exercise of large-scale power over a large group. Governments are examples of macropolitics.

II. Power, Authority, and Violence

A. Authority is legitimate power that people accept as right, while coercion is power that people do not accept as just.

B. The state claims a monopoly on legitimate force or violence in society; violence is the ultimate foundation of political order.

1. Revolution (armed resistance to overthrow a government) is a rejection by the people of a government's claim to rule and of its monopoly on violence.

2. What some see as coercion, others see as authority.

3. A government that is viewed as legitimate is more stable than one that is not.

C. Traditional authority (based on custom) is prevalent in preliterate groups, where custom determines relationships. When society industrializes, traditional authority is undermined but does not die out. For example, parental authority is traditional authority.

D. Rational–legal authority (based on written rules, also called *bureaucratic authority*) derives from the position an individual holds, not from the person. Everyone (no matter how high the office) is subject to the rules.

E. Charismatic authority (based on an individual's personal following) may pose a threat. Because this type of leader works outside the established political system and may threaten the established order, the authorities are often quick to oppose this type of leader.

F. Weber's three bases of authority—traditional, rational-legal, and charismatic—are ideal types representing composite characteristics found in real-life examples. In rare instances, traditional and rational-legal leaders possess charismatic traits, but most authority is one type or another.

G. Orderly transfer of authority upon death, resignation, or incapacity of a leader is critical for stability. Succession is more of a problem with charismatic authority than with traditional or rational-legal authority because there are no rules for orderly succession.

H. To deal with succession, some charismatic leaders will appoint a successor who may or may not be received favorably by the followers. Another strategy is to build an organization. This routinization of charisma refers to the transfer of authority from a charismatic leader to either traditional or rational–legal authority.

III. Types of Government

A. A monarchy is a government headed by a king or queen.

1. As cities developed, each city-state (an independent city whose power radiated outward, bringing adjacent areas under its rule) had its own monarchy.

2. As city-states warred with one another, the victors would extend their rule, eventually over an entire region. As the size of these regions grew, people began to identify with the region; over time this gave rise to the state.

B. A democracy is a government whose authority derives from the people.

1. The original American colonies were small and independent; after the American Revolution the colonies united and formed a democratic government.

2. This was not the first democracy. It existed about 2,000 years ago in Athens. Members of some Native American tribes were able to elect chiefs; in some, women also voted and even held the position of chief.

3. Because of their small size, these groups were able to practice direct democracy (eligible voters meet to discuss issues and make decisions). Initially, the colonies and then the states practiced direct democracy because they were small. Representative democracy (voters elect representatives to govern and make decisions on their behalf) emerged as the U.S. population grew in size and spread out across the country, making direct democracy impossible.

4. It is possible that some form of direct democracy may re-emerge, given the new interactive communications technologies that make "electronic town meetings" possible.

5. Today, citizenship (people having basic rights by virtue of birth or residence) is taken for granted in the United States; this idea is quite new to the human scene. Universal citizenship (everyone having the same basic rights) came into practice very slowly and only through fierce struggle.

C. Dictatorship is government where power is seized and held by an individual; oligarchy results when a small group of individuals seizes power. Dictators and oligarchies can be totalitarian; this is when the government exercises almost total control of a people.

IV. The U.S. Political System

A. The Democratic and Republican parties emerged by the time of the Civil War.

1. The Democrats are often associated with the poor and working class and the Republicans with people who are financially better off.

2. Since each appeal to a broad membership, it is difficult to distinguish conservative Democrats from liberal Republicans; however, it is easy to discern the extremes. Those elected to Congress may cross party lines because although officeholders support their party's philosophy, they do not necessarily support all of its specific proposals.

3. Despite their differences, however, both parties support the fundamentals of U.S. society, such as freedom of religion, free public education, a strong military, and capitalism.

4. Third parties do play a role in U.S. politics, although generally they receive little public support. Ross Perot's "United We Stand" party is one exception.

B. Not all democracies around the world are like ours.

1. U.S. elections are based on a winner-takes-all electoral system; most European countries use proportional representation (legislative seats divided according to the proportion of votes each political party received).

2. The U.S. system discourages minority parties; the proportional representation system encourages them. The United States has centrist parties, representing the center of political opinion. Noncentrist parties (representing marginal ideas) develop in European systems with proportional representation.

3. Three main results follow from proportional representation: (1) minority parties can gain access to the media, which keeps their issues alive; (2) minority parties can gain power beyond their numbers; and (3) the government may be unstable due to the breakdown of coalitions (a coalition occurs when a country's largest party aligns itself with one or more smaller parties to get required votes to make national decisions).

C. Voting Patterns

1. U.S. voting patterns are consistent: the percentage of people who vote increases with age; non-Hispanic whites are more likely to vote than African Americans, while Latinos are considerably less likely to vote than either; those with higher levels of education are more likely to vote, as are people with higher levels of income; women are slightly more likely than men to vote.

2. The more that people feel they have a stake in the system, the more likely they are to vote. Those who have been rewarded by the system feel more socially integrated and perceive that elections directly affect their lives and the society in which they live.

3. People who gain less from the system in terms of education, income, and jobs are more likely to be alienated. Those who are alienated from the system don't vote because they feel their vote won't count. Voter apathy is indifference/inaction to the political process. As a result of apathy, nearly half of eligible American voters do not vote for president, and even more do not vote for members of Congress.

4. Today, we recognize a gender gap in voting. Men are split between Democratic and Republican candidates, while women are more likely to vote for Democratic candidates.

5. There is an even larger racial-ethnic gap in politics; few African Americans vote for a Republican presidential candidate.

D. Special-interest groups are people who think alike on a particular issue and can be mobilized for political action.

1. Lobbyists (paid to influence legislation on behalf of their clients) are employed by special interest groups and have become a major force in politics.

2. Political action committees (PACs) solicit and spend funds to influence legislation and bypass laws intended to limit the amount any individual, corporation, or group can give a candidate. PACs have become a powerful influence, bankrolling lobbyists and legislators, and PACs with the most clout gain the ear of Congress.

227

3. A few PACs represent broad social interests. Most stand for the financial interest of groups such as the dairy, oil, banking, and construction industries.

E. The cost of elections contributes to the importance of lobbyists and PACs in Washington and state capitols.

    1. An average candidate for the Senate will spend $5 million on the campaign. Once a candidate is elected, she or he owes people who helped with financing the campaign and wants to get reelected.

    2. To finance a reelection campaign the average senator needs to raise more than $2,000 every day of the six-year term.

    3. The major criticism against lobbyists and PACs is that their money buys votes. Rather than representing the people who elected them, legislators support the special interests of groups able to help them stay in power.

V. Who Rules the United States?

A. According to the functionalists, the state was created because it fulfilled a basic social need.

    1. People must find a balance between having no government (anarchy) and having a government that may be too repressive, turning against its own citizens.

    2. The functionalists say that pluralism, the diffusion of power among interest groups, prevents anyone from gaining control of the government. Functionalists believe it helps keep the government from turning against its citizens.

    3. To balance the interests of competing groups, the founders of the U.S. system of government created a system of checks and balances in which separation of powers among the three branches of government ensures that each is able to nullify the actions of the other two, thus preventing the domination by any single branch.

    4. Our society is made up of many different groups representing special interests, such as ethnic groups, women, farmers, factory workers, bankers, bosses, and the retired, to name a few. Since these groups need to negotiate and compromise with one another to meet their goals, conflict is minimized.

    5. In this system, power is widely dispersed; as each group pursues its interests, it is balanced by others pursuing theirs.

B. According to the conflict perspective, lobbyists and even Congress are not at the center of decision making; rather, the power elite make the decisions that direct the country and shake the world.

    1. As stated by C. Wright Mills, the power elite (heads of leading corporations, powerful generals and admirals in the armed forces, and certain elite politicians) rule the United States. The corporate heads are the most powerful, as all three view capitalism as essential to the welfare of the country; thus, business interests come first.

    2. According to William Domhoff, the ruling class (the wealthiest and most powerful individuals in the country) runs the United States. Its members control the United States' top corporations and foundations; presidential cabinet

members and top ambassadors to the most powerful countries are chosen from this group.

    3.   The power elite is not a secret group. Their unity comes from the similarity of their backgrounds. Most have attended prestigious schools, belong to exclusive clubs, and are extremely wealthy.

C.   While the functionalist and conflict views of power in U.S. society cannot be reconciled, it is possible to employ both. The middle level of C. Wright Mills' model best reflects the functionalist view of competing interests holding each other at bay. At the top is an elite that follows its special interests, as conflict theorists suggest.

VI. War and Terrorism: Implementing Political Objectives

A.   The state uses violence to protect citizens from individuals and groups, occasionally turning violence against other nations. War (armed conflict between nations or politically distinct groups) is often part of national policy.

B.   War is not characteristic of all human groups, but simply one option for settling disputes.

C.   At the same time, war is a fairly common occurrence. Pitirim Sorokin counted 967 wars between 500 B.C. and A.D. 1925, for an average of one war every two to three years. Since 1850, the United States has intervened militarily around the world more than 150 times, for an average of more than once a year.

D.   Nicholas Timasheff identified three essential conditions of war:

    1.   An antagonistic situation exists, with two or more states confronting incompatible objectives.

    2.   There is a cultural tradition of war; because they have fought wars in the past, leaders see war as an option.

    3.   A "fuel" heats the antagonistic situation to the boiling point, so that people move from thinking about war to engaging in it. Timasheff identified seven fuels: revenge, power, prestige, unity, position, ethnicity, and beliefs.

E.   Despite the fact that war is costly to society, it continues to be a common technique for pursuing political objectives.

    1.   The cost in human life grows with industrialization and technological advances.

    2.   War is costly in terms of the money spent. The United States has spent $6 trillion on ten major wars.

F.   The Most Industrialized Nations lament regional conflicts that can quickly expand into larger wars; at the same time, they relentlessly pursue profits by selling powerful weapons to the Least Industrialized Nations; the United States is the chief merchant of death to the Least Industrialized Nations.

    1.   Seeds of future wars are sown through arms deals involving conventional and nuclear weapons. Nations such as India, China, and North Korea possess nuclear weapons.

    2.   The U.S. formed an organization called the G7. It consists of Canada, France, Germany, Great Britain, Italy, Japan, and the U.S. The purpose of the group was to perpetuate their global dominance, divide up the world's markets, and regulate

global economic activity. In 2002, Russia was invited to become a member of this group. China has potential to also participate and move this group to be known as the G9.

    3.   Conflict continues to erupt with Iraq and Iran as the U.S. seeks to protect its interests in this oil-rich region.

G.   Today, terrorism has become a reality for Americans.

    1.   Terrorism is the use of violence to create fear so that a group can meet its political objectives.

    2.   Hatred between ethnic groups can serve as an impetus for terrorist activities.

    3.   Suicide terrorism is one of the few options available to a weaker group that wants to retaliate against a powerful country, for example, the attacks on the World Trade Center and the Pentagon.

    4.   The real danger is from nuclear, chemical, and biological weapons that could be unleashed against civilian populations.

H.   War has an effect on morality.

    1.   Exposure to brutality and killing often causes dehumanization (reducing people to objects that do not deserve to be treated as humans).

    2.   Characteristics of dehumanization include (1) increased emotional distance from others; (2) an emphasis on following procedures; (3) inability to resist pressures; and (4) a diminished sense of personal responsibility.

    3.   War exalts cruelty and killing, and medals are given to glorify actions that otherwise would be condemned in other contexts of life. The prisoner abuse at Abu Ghraib prison provides an excellent example of this.

    4.   Dehumanization does not always insulate the self from guilt; after the war ends, returning soldiers often find themselves disturbed by what they did during the war. Although most eventually adjust, some live with the guilt forever.

VII. A New World Order?

A.   Today the embrace of capitalism and worldwide flow of information, capital, and goods has made national boundaries less meaningful. There are many examples of nations working together to solve mutual problems, such as the North American Free Trade Agreement (NAFTA), the European Union (EU), and the United Nations (UN).

B.   The United Nations is striving to be the legislative body of the world. It operates a World Court and has a rudimentary army.

C.   The resurgence of fierce nationalism represents a challenge to a new world order.

D.   If global political and economic unity does come about, it is still not clear what type of government will emerge. Under a benevolent government, there is tremendous potential for human welfare, but if a totalitarian government arises, the future could be bleak.

Chapter Summary

Although most people associate the term *politics* with government and governmental processes, the term is actually much broader. Politics refers to power relations wherever they exist, including those in one's own life. Every group is political, for in every group there is a power struggle of some sort. Weber defined power as "the ability to get your own way even over the resistance of others." *Micropolitics* refers to the exercise of power in everyday life; *macropolitics* refers to the exercise of power over a large group.

For society to exist there must be a system of leadership and power. Authority is the legitimate use of power that people accept as right. In contrast, coercion is the illegitimate use of power that people do not accept as just. The government, also called the *state*, is a political entity that claims a monopoly on the legitimate use of force or violence in a particular territory. It also claims an exclusive right to punish people for violating its laws. The more that its power is seen as legitimate, the more stable a government is. When people reject a government's claim of rule over them, it may result in revolution—armed resistance with the intent to overthrow and replace a government.

Max Weber identified three ideal types of authority: traditional authority, rational-legal authority, and charismatic authority. Traditional authority is based on custom. Rational-legal authority is based on laws or written rules and regulations. Charismatic authority is based on an individual's outstanding personal traits.

For all societies, the orderly transfer of authority from one leader to another is crucial for social stability. Under traditional authority, customs dictate who is next in line; under rational-legal authority, procedures define rules of succession. The transfer of authority in societies headed by charismatic leaders is the most unstable. It can result in the breakup of the society or a bitter struggle for succession.

Major types of government include monarchies, democracies, dictatorships, and oligarchies. A monarchy is headed by a king or queen, while a democracy is headed by an elected official. Dictatorships are usually headed by a single individual who seizes power; oligarchies are based on small groups seizing power.

Since the time of the Civil War, politics in the United States has been dominated by two major political parties, the Democrats and the Republicans. Although these two parties represent different philosophical principles, each party appeals to a broad membership, strives to be seen as centrist in its positions, and firmly supports core American policies.

Democratic systems are not always the same, however. The democratic systems of the United States and Europe differ in their election policies. The United States has a "winner-take-all" system, while most European countries have a proportional representation system.

Voting patterns in the United States consistently demonstrate that the more people are integrated into society and have a stake in the political system, the more likely they are to vote. The percentage of people who vote increases with age. Women are more likely than men to vote;

other groups likely to vote are whites, college graduates, and married people. Income is also a factor in voting, with a steady increase in the likelihood someone will vote as their income increases.

Voter alienation and voter apathy are feelings of indifference over the importance of one's vote. Because of voter apathy, half of all eligible voters in the United States do not vote in presidential elections, and two-thirds do not vote in Congressional races.

Because the costs of running for political office are so high in the United States, money is a significant factor in American politics. As such, lobbyists and special interest groups play an influential role in helping political candidates get elected to office.

Functionalists and conflict theorists have different views on the distribution of power in American politics. Functionalists contend that the many competing interest groups tend to balance one another out and that our system of checks and balances provides a pluralistic form of government. Conflict theorists argue that the nation's top corporate, political, and military leaders make up a power elite that runs the country.

Periodically, governments direct the violence they monopolize against other nations. This armed conflict between nations is referred to as *war*. War is not a characteristic of all human groups. Some groups handle conflicts with other groups without resorting to violence. Even so, war has been a common and costly occurrence in human history. In fact, war is so common that it has been referred to as a normal state of society. With the proliferation of nuclear, biological, and chemical weapons, war has become a greater threat to the survival of mankind than ever before. Although the cold war between the major super powers ended in the late 1980s, many of the most industrialized nations continue to sell large amounts of arms and advanced weapons technology to the Least Industrialized Nations. This, in conjunction with a traditional hatred and misunderstanding between certain groups, has sown the seeds for terrorism and regional wars.

The globalization of capitalism, however, may someday lead to one state or empire ruling over the entire planet. This new world order is unlikely to occur within the immediate future, but the basis for such a creation has been laid with milestone pacts such as the North Atlantic Treaty Organization and the development of the European Union.

KEY TERMS
After studying the chapter, review the definition for each of the following terms.

anarchy: a condition of lawlessness or political disorder caused by the abuse or collapse of governmental authority (426)

authority: power that people consider legitimate, as rightly exercised over them; also called *legitimate power* (412)

centrist party: a political party that represents the center of political opinion (421)

charismatic authority: authority based on an individual's outstanding traits, which attract followers (414)

checks and balances: the separation of powers among the three branches of U.S. government—legislative, executive, and judicial—so that each is able to nullify the actions of the other two, thus preventing any single branch from dominating the government (426)

citizenship: the concept that birth (and residence or naturalization) in a country imparts basic rights (417)

city-state: an independent city whose power radiates outward, bringing the adjacent area under its rule (416)

coalition government: a government formed by two or more political parties working together to obtain a ruling majority (421)

coercion: power that people do not accept as rightly exercised over them; also called *illegitimate power* (412)

dehumanization: the act or process of reducing people to objects that do not deserve the treatment accorded humans (428)

democracy: a government whose authority comes from the people; the term, based on two Greek words, translates literally as "power to the people" (416)

dictatorship: a form of government in which an individual has seized power (419)

direct democracy: a form of democracy in which the eligible voters meet together to discuss issues and make their decisions (417)

lobbyists: people who influence legislation on behalf of their clients (425)

macropolitics: the exercise of large-scale power, the government being the most common example (412)

micropolitics: the exercise of power in everyday life, such as deciding who is going to do the housework or use the remote control (412)

monarchy: a form of government headed by a king or queen (416)

nationalism: a strong identification with a nation, accompanied by the desire for that nation to be dominant (437)

noncentrist party: a political party that represents less popular ideas (421)

oligarchy: a form of government in which a small group of individuals holds power; the rule of the many by the few (419)

pluralism: the diffusion of power among many interest groups that prevents any single group from gaining control of the government (426)

political action committee (PAC): an organization formed by one or more special-interest groups to solicit and spend funds for the purpose of influencing legislation (425)

politics: the exercise of power and attempts to maintain or to change power relations (412)

power: the ability to carry out your will, even over the resistance of others (412)

power elite: C. Wright Mills' term for the top people in U.S. corporations, military, and politics who make the nation's major decisions (426)

proportional representation: an electoral system in which seats in a legislature are divided according to the proportion of votes each political party receives (421)

rational–legal authority: authority based on law or written rules and regulations; also called *bureaucratic authority* (414)

representative democracy: a form of democracy in which voters elect representatives to meet together to discuss issues and make decisions on their behalf (417)

revolution: armed resistance designed to overthrow and replace a government (413)

routinization of charisma: the transfer of authority from a charismatic figure to either a traditional or a rational–legal form of authority (415)

ruling class: another term for the power elite (427)

special-interest group: a group of people who support a particular issue and who can be mobilized for political action (425)

state: a political entity that claims a monopoly on the use of violence in some particular territory; commonly known as a country (413)

terrorism: the use of violence or the threat of violence to produce fear in order to attain political objectives (431)

totalitarianism: a form of government that exerts almost total control over people (419)

traditional authority: authority based on custom (413)

universal citizenship: the idea that everyone has the same basic rights by virtue of being born in a country (or by immigrating and becoming a naturalized citizen) (418)

voter apathy: indifference and inaction on the part of individuals or groups with respect to the political process (424)

war: armed conflict between nations or politically distinct groups (427)

KEY PEOPLE
Review the major theoretical contributions or findings of these people.

Peter Berger: Berger argued that violence is the ultimate foundation of any political order. (413)

William Domhoff: Like Mills, Domhoff saw that power resides in the hands of an elite, which he referred to as the "ruling class." He focused on the top 1 percent of Americans who belong to the super rich. (427)

C. Wright Mills: Mills suggested that power resides in the hands of an elite made up of the top leaders of the largest corporations, the most powerful generals of the armed forces, and certain elite politicians. (426-427)

Alejandro Portes and Ruben Rumbaut: These sociologists studied the process of assimilation of immigrants into American society, observing that the first step in the process is the group's political organization to protect their ethnic interests. (423)

Pitirim Sorokin: Sorokin studied wars from 500 B.C. to A.D. 1925 and found that war was a fairly common experience. There had been 967 wars during this time span, for an average of a war every two or three years. (428)

Nicholas S. Timasheff: Timasheff identified three essential conditions of societies going to war—a cultural tradition of war, an antagonistic situation in which two or more countries have incompatible objectives, and a "fuel" that heats the situation to a boiling point so the line is crossed from thinking about war to actually waging it. (428)

Max Weber: Weber identified three different types of authority: traditional, rational–legal, and charismatic. (412-413, 415)

MULTIPLE CHOICE QUESTIONS

1. Which of the following relates to power? (412)
    a. The concept was defined by Max Weber.
    b. It is the ability to carry out one's will in spite of resistance from others.
    c. It is an inevitable part of everyday life.
    d. All of the above

2. Governments, whether dictatorships or the elected forms, are examples of (412)
    a. coercion.
    b. macropolitics.
    c. micropolitics.
    d. none of the above

3. What is coercion? (412)
    a. legitimate authority
    b. power people do not accept as just
    c. micropolitics
    d. macropolitics

4. What did Peter Berger consider to be the ultimate foundation of any political order? (413)
    a. laws
    b. elections
    c. violence
    d. leaders

5. Revolutions (413)
    a. are most likely to occur on the death of a charismatic leader.
    b. are a people's rejection of the government's claim to rule over them.
    c. occur only when economic conditions are bleak.
    d. all of the above

6. Traditional authority (413)
    a. is the hallmark of tribal groups.
    b. is based on custom.
    c. declines with industrialization.
    d. all of the above

7. In which type of authority is power based on law and written procedures? (414)
    a. traditional
    b. rational-legal

    c.   charismatic
    d.   coercion

8.   In the Middle Ages, soldiers followed Joan of Arc into battle because they saw her as a messenger of God, fighting on the side of justice. They accepted her leadership because of these appealing qualities. Her authority to lead would be considered (414)
    a.   traditional.
    b.   rational-legal.
    c.   charismatic.
    d.   feminine.

9.   John F. Kennedy (415)
    a.   was a rational-legal leader.
    b.   was a charismatic leader.
    c.   is an example of a leader who is difficult to classify in terms of ideal types.
    d.   all of the above

10.   Which of the following is considered the least stable type of authority? (415)
    a.   traditional
    b.   rational-legal
    c.   charismatic
    d.   monarchy

11.   Representative democracy (417)
    a.   is a form of democracy in which elected officials represent citizens' interests.
    b.   is perhaps the greatest gift the United States has given the world.
    c.   was considered revolutionary when it was first conceived.
    d.   all of the above

12.   The idea that everyone has the same rights by virtue of being born in a country is (418)
    a.   direct democracy.
    b.   universal citizenship.
    c.   state citizenship.
    d.   an ideal that has rarely been realized.

13.   An individual who seizes power and imposes his will onto the people is known as a (419)
    a.   charismatic leader.
    b.   dictator.
    c.   totalitarian leader.
    d.   monarch.

14.   Which form of government exerts almost total control over the people? (419)
    a.   monarchy
    b.   dictatorship

c. totalitarian regime

d. oligarchy

15. The United States has (419-421)

    a. centrist parties.

    b. noncentrist parties.

    c. proportional representation.

    d. none of the above

16. Which of the following statements about political parties in the U.S. is *incorrect*? (419-421)

    a. Because both parties appeal to a broad membership, it is often difficult to distinguish one from the other, except at the extremes of both parties.

    b. Members of Congress maintain strict party allegiances and will never cross party lines to vote for legislation proposed by a member of the other party.

    c. Democrats and Republicans represent different slices of the center, firmly supporting fundamental principles of U.S. political philosophy.

    d. Because most Americans think a vote for a third party is a waste, third parties do very poorly in elections.

17. Which electoral system is most likely to encourage formation of minority political parties? (421)

    a. a winner-take-all system

    b. a proportional representation system

    c. direct democracy

    d. representative democracy

18. What do studies of voting patterns in the United States show? (421)

    a. Voting patterns are too inconsistent to draw meaningful conclusions.

    b. Voting varies by age, race/ethnicity, education, employment, income, and gender.

    c. Younger people are more likely to vote than older individuals.

    d. All of the above

19. According to Portes and Rumbaut, on what basis do immigrants initially organize politically? (423)

    a. gender

    b. age

    c. social class

    d. race–ethnicity

20. Which of the following statements regarding participation in presidential elections today is *correct*? (422)

    a. Only about one-third of eligible voters actually vote.

    b. About one-half of eligible voters cast a ballot.

c. About three-fourths of eligible voters participate in presidential elections today.

d. Slightly less than two-thirds of eligible voters vote.

21. Lobbyists are (425)

    a. people paid to influence legislation on behalf of their clients.

    b. bankrolled by political action committees.

    c. a major force in American politics.

    d. all of the above

22. Functionalists see that _____ prevents groups from having total government control. (426)

    a. the existence of a powerful elite

    b. the presence of checks and balances

    c. the presence of many PACs, to which politicians owe allegiance,

    d. all of the above

23. Which perspective suggests that conflict is minimized as special-interest groups negotiate with one another and reach compromises? (426)

    a. functionalists

    b. conflict theorists

    c. symbolic interactionists

    d. political sociologists

24. Members of the power elite are drawn from (426)

    a. the largest corporations.

    b. the armed forces.

    c. top political offices.

    d. all of the above

25. According to conflict theorists, the ruling class is (427)

    a. a group that meets and agrees on specific matters.

    b. a group that tends to have complete unity on issues.

    c. made up of people whose backgrounds and orientations to life are so similar that they automatically share the same goals.

    d. a myth.

TRUE-FALSE QUESTIONS

1. _____ In every group, large or small, some individuals have power over others. (412)

2. _____ Coercion refers to legitimate power. (412)

3. _____ The state claims a monopoly on violence within some designated territory. (413)

4. _____ Even with industrialization, some forms of traditional authority go unchallenged. (414)

5. _____Most political action committees represent broad social interests, such as environmental protection. (425)
6. _____Functionalists believe that pluralism prevents any one group from gaining control of the government and using it to oppress the people. (426)
7. _____Conflict theorists claim that no one group holds power in America; that the country's many competing interest groups balance each other. (427)
8. _____There were 967 documented wars in Europe from 500 B.C. to A.D. 1925. (48)
9. _____Because of technological advances in killing, the cost of war in terms of money spent and human lives lost has decreased. (429)
10. _____The globalization of capitalism and the trend toward regional economic and political unions may indicate that a world political system is developing. (435)

FILL-IN-THE-BLANK QUESTIONS

1. The _____ holds the potential for transforming the way we vote and pass laws. (418)
2. _____ is almost total control of a people by the government. (419)
3. Most European countries base their elections on a system of _____. (421)
4. Many people do not vote because of voter _____. (424)
5. The dairy industry is an example of a _____ group. (425)
6. The major criticism leveled against lobbyists and political action groups is that their _____ in effect buys votes. (425)
7. The system of _____ was designed to ensure that no one branch of government dominates. (426)
8. C. Wright Mills coined the phrase the _____. (426)
9. Sociologist William Domhoff uses the term _____ to refer to the power elite. (427)
10. _____ is the use of violence to create fear in an effort to bring about political objectives. (431)

ESSAY QUESTIONS

1. Distinguish between macropolitics and micropolitics, explaining what each is and which perspectives are associated with each, and provide your own examples to illustrate each.

2. Compare and contrast the systems of democracy found in the United States and Europe, and discuss how some of the problems associated with our system, such as voter apathy, the power of political action committees, and the concentration of power, are related to our system.

3. Discuss the two major political parties in the United States. Explain differences and similarities.

4. Discuss why wars happen.

CHAPTER 16
MARRIAGE AND FAMILY

LEARNING OBJECTIVES
After reading Chapter 16, you should be able to:

1. Explain why it is difficult to precisely define the term "family," and discuss some of the different ways that family systems can be organized and classified. (442)

2. Identify the common cultural themes that run through marriage and the family. (443-445)

3. Explain why the family is universal, and list the basic societal needs it fulfills. (445)

4. Contrast the functionalist, conflict, and symbolic interactionist perspectives regarding marriage and family. Provide examples that illustrate each of the perspectives. (445-447)

5. Identify the major elements of the family life cycle, and discuss how each of these elements may be affected by age, education, social class, race-ethnicity, sex, and/or religion. (447-454)

6. Describe the distinctive characteristics of family life in African American, Latino, Asian American, and Native American families, and discuss the role that social class and culture play in affecting these distinctions. (454-456)

7. Discuss the characteristics and concerns of one-parent, childless, blended, and gay and lesbian families in the United States. (457-459)

8. Identify the general patterns and trends in marriage and family life in the United States, and discuss how these are reflected in postponement of marriage, cohabitation, the sandwich generation, divorce, and remarriage. (459-463)

9. Discuss the different measures of divorce rates, the adverse effects of divorce on children, and the factors that most help children adjust to divorce in the United States. (463-467)

10. Explain how divorce affects men and women differently. (467)

11. Describe the "dark side" of family life as it relates to battering, child abuse, marital rape, and incest. (467-470)

12. Identify the "bright side" that makes marriages happy. (470-471)

13. Discuss future patterns and trends in marriage and family life in the United States. (471-472)

Chapter Outline

I. **Marriage and Family in Global Perspective**
A. The term "family" is difficult to define because there are many types.
1. In some societies men have more than one wife (polygyny) or women have more than one husband (polyandry).
2. Many groups have various customs regarding marriage or family. For example, in the 1980s and 1990s several European countries legalized same-sex marriages. In 2003, so did Canada, and the state of Massachusetts did in 2004.
3. In other societies, sexual relationships or discipline of a child do not characterize a family. As such, a broad definition of family is needed.
4. A family is a group of people who consider themselves related by blood, marriage, or adoption.
5. In contrast, a household consists of people who occupy the same housing unit.
6. A family is classified as a nuclear family (husband, wife, and children) or an extended family (a nuclear family plus other relatives, such as grandparents, aunts, uncles, and cousins).
7. The family of orientation is the family in which a person grows up, while the family of procreation is the family formed when a couple's first child is born. A person who is married but has not had a child is part of a couple, not a family.
8. Marriage is a group's approved mating arrangements, usually marked by a ritual to show the couple's new public status.
B. Common cultural themes run through marriage and family.
1. Patterns of mate selection are established to govern whom one can and cannot marry. Endogamy is the practice of marrying within one's own group, while exogamy is the practice of marrying outside of one's own group. The best example of exogamy is the incest taboo, which prohibits sex and marriage among designated relatives. Some norms of mate selection are written into law; others are informal.
2. Three major patterns of descent (tracing kinship over generations) are (a) bilateral (descent traced on both the mother's and the father's side); (b) patrilineal (descent traced only on the father's side); and (c) matrilineal (descent traced only on the mother's side).
3. Mate selection and descent are regulated in all societies in order to provide an orderly way of passing property and other things to the next generation. In a bilateral system, property passes to males and females; in a patrilineal system, property passes only to males; in a matrilineal system, property passes only to females.
4. Patriarchy is a social system in which men dominate women, and it runs through all societies. No historical records exist of a true matriarchy, a system in which women-as-a-group dominate over men-as-a-group. In an egalitarian social system, authority is more or less equally divided between men and women.

II. Marriage and Family in Theoretical Perspective

A. The functionalist perspective stresses how the family is related to other parts of society and how it contributes to the well-being of society.

   1. The family is universal because it serves functions essential to the well-being of society: economic production, socialization of children, care of the sick and aged, recreation, sexual control, and reproduction.

   2. The incest taboo (rules specifying which people are too closely related to have sex or marry) helps the family avoid role confusion and forces people to look outside the family for marriage partners, creating a network of support.

   3. Unlike the extended family, the nuclear family has fewer people that it can depend on for material and emotional support; thus, the members of a nuclear family are vulnerable to "emotional overload." The relative isolation of the nuclear family makes it easier for the "dark side" of families (incest and other types of abuse) to emerge.

B. Central to the conflict perspective is the struggle over power; who has it and who resents not having it?

   1. Throughout history men have had more power than women in marriage. In the United States, wives have gained more and more power in marriage.

   2. According to Figure 16.1, wives make more of the families decisions concerning weekend activities, household purchases, to managing the family finances.

C. Using the symbolic interactionist perspective, we can explore the different meaning that housework has for men and women and how each sex experiences marriage differently.

   1. In the United States, both husbands and wives are spending more time taking care of the children. Parents are able to spend more hours with their children by spending less time on other activities such as housework. Technological advances like dishwashers and microwaves might be responsible for the ability to accomplish more household tasks in less time.

   2. Husbands and wives spend their time differently. Gendered division of labor shows that husbands still have the primary responsibility of income for the family and wives have the responsibility of child care and household. But there are changes in that wives are spending more time earning incomes and husbands are spending more time on housework and child care than in the past.

III. The Family Life Cycle

A. Romantic love is the idea of people being sexually attracted to one another and idealizing the other.

   1. Research by Jankowiak and Fischer on 166 societies around the world found that the idea of romantic love existed in 88 percent, although its role was different.

   2. It provides the ideological context in which Americans seek mates and form families.

   3. Romantic love has two components: (1) emotional, a feeling of sexual attraction; and (2) cognitive, the feeling we describe as being "in love."

B. The social channels of love and marriage in the United States include age, education, social class, race, and religion.
   1. Homogamy is the tendency of people with similar characteristics to marry one another, usually resulting from propinquity (spatial nearness).
   2. Interracial marriage, which has increased sharply, is an exception to these social patterns. About 7 percent marry someone of another race, which totals about 4 million couples.
   3. One of the most dramatic changes is marriages between African Americans and whites.
C. As more mothers today are employed outside the home, child care has become an issue.
   1. In comparing married couples and single mothers, child care arrangements appear to be quite similar. The main difference is the role played by the child's father while the mother is at work. For married couples, almost one of four children is cared for by the father, while for single mothers this arrangement occurs for about only one of fourteen children. Grandparents often help fill the child care gap left by absent fathers in single-mother homes.
   2. About one in six children is cared for in day care centers. Only a minority of U.S. day care centers offer high-quality care. The very low wages paid to day care workers seems to account for this. Two factors that seem to be associated with higher quality of care are (1) fewer children per staff worker, and (2) staff training in early childhood development.
   3. Nannies have become popular among upper-middle-class parents. A recurring problem is tensions between parents and the nanny.
   4. According to Melvin Kohn, parents socialize children into the norms of their respective work worlds. Working-class parents want their children to conform to societal expectations. Middle-class parents are more concerned that their children develop curiosity, self-expression, and self-control.
D. Later stages of family life bring both pleasures and problems.
   1. The "empty nest" is a married couple's domestic situation after the last child has left home. The empty nest is not so empty anymore.
   2. With prolonged education and a growing cost of establishing households, U.S. children are leaving home much later or are returning after having left.
   3. Eighteen percent of all 25-29 year olds are living with their parents. These "adultolescents" face issues with their parents between being independent and dependent.
   4. Women are more likely than men to face the problem of adjusting to widowhood, for not only does the average woman live longer than a man, but she has also married a man older than herself.
   5. The survivor is faced with identity issues of who he or she is. The adjustment is even more difficult when death is unexpected.

IV. Diversity in U.S. Families

    A.   As with other groups, the family life of African Americans differs by social class.

        1.   The upper class is concerned with maintaining family lineage and preserving their privilege and wealth; the middle class focuses on achievement and respectability; poor African American families face the problems that poverty brings.

        2.   Poor men are likely to have few job skills and to be unemployed. As such, it is difficult to fulfill the cultural roles of husband and father. Poor families tend to be headed by females and to have a high rate of birth to single mothers. Divorce and desertion are also more common among the poor.

        3.   Compared to other groups, African American families are the least likely to be headed by married couples and the most likely to be headed by women. The women are also more likely to marry men who are less educated than themselves.

    B.   The effects of social class on families also apply to Latinos. In addition, families differ by country of origin.

        1.   What really distinguishes Latino families is culture—especially the Spanish language, the Roman Catholic religion, and a strong family orientation, coupled with a disapproval of divorce.

        2.   Machismo, the emphasis on male strength and dominance, used to be a characteristic of Latino families. Currently, machismo characterizes a small proportion of Latino husband–fathers.

    C.   The structure of Asian American families is almost identical to that of white families.

        1.   Because Asian Americans come from 20 different countries, family life varies considerably, reflecting these different cultures. The more recent the immigration, the closer the family life is to that of the country of origin.

        2.   Bob Suzuki points out that while Chinese American and Japanese American families have adopted the nuclear family pattern of the United States, they have retained Confucian values that provide a distinct framework to family life: humanism, collectivity, self-discipline, hierarchy, respect for the elderly, moderation, and obligation.

        3.   Asian Americans tend to be more permissive than Anglos in child rearing and more likely to use shame and guilt than physical punishment to control their children's behavior.

    D.   For Native American families, the issue is whether to follow traditional values or to assimilate. The structure of Native American families is almost identical to that of Latinos; like others, these families differ by social class.

        1.   Native American families are permissive with their children and avoid physical punishment.

        2.   Elders play a much more active role in their children's families than they do in most U.S. families; they provide child care and teach and discipline children.

    E.   There has been an increase in one-parent families.

        1.   This is due to the high divorce rate and the sharp increase in births to unmarried women.

2. The concern about one-parent families has more to with their poverty than that they are headed by a single parent. The reason for the poverty is that most are headed by women who earn less than men.

3. Children from one-parent families are more likely to drop out of school, become delinquent, be poor as adults, divorce, and have children outside of marriage.

F. Overall, about 20 percent of U.S. married couples never have children. Although somewhat influenced by race and ethnicity, in general, the more education a woman has, the more likely she is to expect to bear no children.

1. The main reason couples choose not to have children is they want to be free to be able to change jobs or do spontaneous things; they want to avoid the expenses of raising a child or the stresses associated with having children. Some do not like children, are in an unstable marriage, or feel they will be bored.

2. The proportion of couples who remain childless is likely to increase due to more education and career choice available to women, legal abortion, advances in contraception, the high cost of child rearing, and the emphasis on owning material things.

3. For many families, choice is not the reason they have no children; they are infertile. Some adopt, while a few turn to new reproductive technologies.

G. A blended family is one whose members were once part of other families (two divorced persons marry, bringing children into a new family unit). Blended families are increasing in number and often experience complicated family relationships.

H. Many homosexual couples live in monogamous relationships that resemble heterosexual marriages in many respects.

1. In 1989, Denmark became the first country to legalize marriage between people of the same sex. Holland, Norway, and Sweden have since made same-sex marriages legal.

2. In 2004, Massachusetts became the first state to legalize same-sex marriages.

3. Twenty-two percent of lesbian couples and 5 percent of gay couples have children from their heterosexual marriage.

4. Gay and lesbian couples also have the usual problems of heterosexual marriages: housework, money, careers, problems with relatives, and sexual adjustment. However, same-sex couples are more likely to break up.

V. **Trends in U.S. Families**

A. The average age of American brides is the oldest it has been since records first were kept.

1. As a result, the age at which U.S. women have their first child is also the highest in U.S. history.

2. While many young people postpone marriage, they have not postponed the age at which they set up housekeeping with someone of the opposite sex.

B. Cohabitation, living together as an unmarried couple, has increased 12 times since the 1970s.

1. Forty percent of children will spend some time in a cohabiting family.

2. Commitment is the essential difference between cohabitation and marriage: marriage assumes permanence; cohabiting assumes remaining together "as long as it works out."
3. Couples who cohabit before marriage are more likely to divorce than couples who did not live together before marriage. Many who live together feel pressure to marry and end up marrying a partner that they may not have chosen.

C. The "sandwich generation" refers to people who find themselves sandwiched between two generations, responsible for the care of their children and for their own aging parents. These people are typically between the ages of 40 and 55. Corporations have begun to offer some kind of elder-care assistance to their employees, including seminars, referral services, and flexible work schedules.

VI. Divorce and Remarriage

A. There are problems when it comes to measuring the extent of divorce in U.S. society.
1. Although the divorce rate is reported at 50 percent, this statistic is misleading because, with rare exceptions, those who divorce do not come from the group who married that year.
2. An alternative is to compare the number of divorces in a given year to the entire group of married couples. The divorce rate for any given year is less than 2 percent of all married couples.
3. A third way is to calculate the percentage of all adult Americans who are divorced. People's race and ethnicity makes a difference in the likelihood of divorce.
4. Research has found that people who go to college, belong to a religion, and wait to get married and have children have a much better chance of their marriage lasting.
5. Working with coworkers of the opposite sex and working with people who are recently divorced increase one's risk for divorce.

B. Each year, more than 1 million children are in families affected by divorce. Divorce profoundly threatens a child's world.
1. Compared with children whose parents are not divorced, children from divorced families are more likely to experience emotional problems, more likely to be juvenile delinquents, less likely to complete high school, and more likely to divorce.
2. There is a debate between two psychological studies conducted by Judith Wallerstein and Mavis Hetherington. Wallerstein claims that divorce scars children, making them depressed and leaving them with insecurities that follow them into childhood. Hetherington's study found that 75 to 80 percent of children of divorce function as well as children who are reared by both of their parents.
3. Several factors help children adjust to divorce. Children adjust well if they experience little conflict, they feel loved, they live with the parent making a good adjustment, have consistent family routines, and the family has adequate money

for its needs. Children also adjust better if a second adult can be counted on for support.

   4.   Adult children who come from a divorced family have a chance of a successful marriage if they marry someone whose parent did not divorce. Those marriages where both husband and wife come from a divorced family are more likely to be marked by high distrust and conflict, leading to higher chance of divorce.

C.   Sociologists have found that the effects of divorce continue across generations. Sociologists found that the grandchildren of divorce have weaker ties to their parents, they don't go as far in school, and they have more marital discord with their spouses.

D.   Fathers who were married to the mothers of their children, are older and more educated, and have higher incomes are more likely to continue to have contact with their children following divorce.

E.   Women are more likely than men to feel that divorce gives them a new chance at life. The spouse who initiates the divorce usually gets over it sooner and usually remarries sooner. Many divorced couples maintain contact with ex-spouses because of their children. Divorce likely spells economic hardship for women, especially mothers of small children; the former husband's standard of living is likely to increase. The more education a woman has, the better prepared she is to survive financially after divorce.

F.   Most divorced people eventually remarry, although the length of time between divorce and remarriage is longer today than in the past.

   1.   Most divorced people remarry other divorced people. Men are more likely to remarry than women; women who are most likely to remarry are mothers with small children and women who have not graduated from high school.

   2.   The divorce rate of remarried people without children is about the same as that of first marriages; remarriages in which children are present are more likely to end in divorce.

VII. Two Sides of Family Life

A.   Spousal battering, child abuse, marital rape, and incest represent the dark side of family life.

   1.   Although wives are about as likely to attack their husbands as husbands are to attack their wives, it is generally the husband who lands the last and most damaging blow. Violence against women is related to the sexist structure of society and our socialization.

   2.   Each year about 2 million U.S. children are reported to the authorities as victims of abuse or neglect; about 800,000 of these cases are substantiated.

   3.   Marital rape is more common than previously thought. Victims of marital rape are less likely to report the rape.

   4.   Rape victims include those in cohabiting and lesbian relationships.

   5.   Incest is sexual relations between relatives, such as brothers and sisters or parents and children. It is most likely to occur in families that are socially isolated, and it is more common than previously thought. Uncles are the most common offenders; brother-sister incest is more common than father-child incest.

B. A study of couples who had been married fifteen years or longer reported these factors in making a relationship successful: thinking of their spouses as their best friend, liking their spouse as a person, having a commitment to the marriage and seeing it as sacred, agreeing with their spouse on aims and goals, believing that their spouse has grown more interesting, wanting the relationship to succeed, and laughing together.

    1. Sociologists have also found that marriages are happier when couples get along with their in-laws and when they do leisure activities that they both enjoy.

C. While the statistics are important in order to gain a deeper understanding of the state of marriages and families in U.S. society, it is also important to remember that these are describing an overall pattern and not an individual case.

    1. Our own chances of having a successful marriage depend on our own situation, especially the way we, *as individuals*, approach marriage.

    2. From a symbolic interactionist perspective, we create our own worlds; we interpret our experiences and act accordingly. If we think our marriage will fail, we increase the likelihood that it will. We tend to act according to our ideas, creating a sort of self-fulfilling prophecy.

VIII. The Future of Marriage and Family

A. In spite of problems, marriage will continue because it is functional. The vast proportion of Americans will continue to marry; many of those who divorce will remarry and "try again."

B. It is likely that cohabitation, births to single mothers, age at first marriage, and parenting by grandparents will increase. More married women will join the work force and continue to gain marital power. Finally, more families will struggle with the twin demands of raising children and caring for aging parents.

C. We will continue to deal with the conflict between the bleak picture of marriage and family painted by the media and the rosy one painted by cultural myths. Sociologists can help correct the distortions through research.

Chapter Summary

The practices of marriage and family differ around the world. Although every human group organizes its members in families, how families are organized varies greatly from culture to culture. Broadly defined, a family consists of two or more people who consider themselves related by blood, marriage, or adoption. A household, in contrast, consists of people who occupy the same housing unit.

Every human group establishes norms to govern who can marry whom. Although these norms vary from culture to culture, all societies use family and marriage to establish patterns of mate selection, descent, inheritance, and authority. Most societies demand endogamy, the practice of marrying someone within one's own group. In contrast, norms of exogamy specify that people may marry outside their group. Western culture norms are based on exogamy and use a bilateral system of descent, which means children are considered as related to both their mother's side and the father's side of the family. In a patrilineal system, descent is traced only on the father's side; in a matrilineal system, descent is traced only on the mother's side. In a society that practices these patterns of descent, the pattern of inheritance would be similar. A social system in which men dominate women-as-a-group is referred to as *patriarchy*. Although a *matriarchy* would be a society dominated by women, there is no historical record of a true matriarchy existing. Family patterns in America are becoming more egalitarian, or equal, although many of today's customs still reflect a patriarchal origin.

According to the functionalist perspective, the family is universal because it serves six essential functions: economic production, socialization of children, care of the sick and aged, recreation, sexual control, and reproduction. Conflict theorists focus on the inequalities within the institution of the family and marriage, particularly as they relate to the subservience of women. Symbolic interactionists examine how the contrasting experiences and perspectives of men and women are played out in marriage.

The major elements of the family life cycle are love and courtship, marriage, childbirth, child rearing, and the family in later life. Romantic love, people being sexually attracted to one another and idealizing the other, plays a significant role in courtship in Western culture. In Western culture, love is mostly regarded as the basis for marriage. Many Eastern cultures still practice arranged marriages, usually negotiated by the parents of the bride and groom. Choices of who marries whom in the United States follow highly predictable social channels of age, education, social class, race, and religion. In either case, a group's marriage practices match its values and patterns of social stratification. Compared to the 1970s and 1980s, both mothers and fathers are spending more time with their children because they are spending less time on housework (cooking & cleaning) and are less fussy about how their home looks. Some young adults are either not leaving or are returning home, leading to a not-so-empty nest.

Although there are some variations in family life between white, African American, Latino, Asian American, and Native American families, the primary distinctions in families result from cultural differences and social class.

The decline of the traditional family and the changing definitions of family are evident in the significant increase in one-parent, childless, blended, and gay and lesbian families. The percentage of U.S. children living with two parents has dropped from 85 percent in 1970 to 70 percent in 2010. The number of married women not giving birth has doubled over the past twenty years to an average of 20 percent today. Most childless married couples have made a choice to not have children. Referred to as DINKs (dual income, no kids), these couples prefer the personal comforts and convenience of not having children. With advances in contraception, the legalization of abortion, the high cost of raising a child, and the emphasis on materialism, this trend will likely continue. Blended families—those that have members who were previously parts of other families—are also on the rise. Although gay marriages are not allowed in most of the states, gay unions are becoming more public.

Several trends since the 1960s are very apparent in U.S. families. Significant changes in the characteristics of the family include: postponement of first marriages and childbirth, the cultural acceptance and increase in cohabitation, and the rise in births to unwed mothers. Moreover, with more people living longer, many middle-aged couples find themselves "sandwiched" between providing for their children's needs and caring for their aging parents.

Divorce often has adverse effects on children that can carry over into adulthood. Children of divorced parents who are not made to choose sides, feel loved, live with a parent who is making a good adjustment, have consistent routines, and grow up in households with adequate finances to meet the family's needs adjust best to the effects of divorce.

Men and women experience divorce differently. For men, divorce often results in weakened relationships with their children. For women, it typically means a decline in their standard of living.

Although the institutions of marriage and the family fulfill universal needs, some marriages and families are characterized by a "dark side" that includes spouse battering, child abuse, marital rape, and incest. On the brighter side, a survey showed that out of 351 couples who had been married fifteen years or longer, 300 considered themselves to be happily married. They thought of their spouse as their best friend, considered marriage a lifelong commitment, and believed marriage to be sacred. They strongly wanted their marriages to succeed and often laughed together.

Patterns of marriage and family life in the United States are undergoing a fundamental shift, with trends pointing to further increases in cohabitation, more births to single women, a higher age at first marriage, and an increased presence of married women in the workforce. Since we are living longer, more couples will find themselves sandwiched between caring for their parents and caring for their children.

KEY TERMS

After studying the chapter, review the definition for each of the following terms.

bilineal (system of descent): a system of reckoning descent that counts both the mother's and the father's side (444)

blended family: a family whose members were once part of other families (458-459)

cohabitation: unmarried couples living together in a sexual relationship (459)

egalitarian: authority more or less equally divided between people or groups (in marriage, for example, between husband and wife) (445)

endogamy: the practice of marrying within one's own group (443)

exogamy: the practice of marrying outside one's group (443)

extended family: a nuclear family plus other relatives, such as grandparents, uncles and aunts (462)

family: two or more people who consider themselves related by blood, marriage, or adoption (442)

family of orientation: the family in which a person grows up (443)

family of procreation: the family formed when a couple's first child is born (443)

homogamy: the tendency of people with similar characteristics to marry one another (448)

household: people who occupy the same housing unit (442)

incest: sexual relations between specified relatives, such as brothers and sisters or parents and children (470)

incest taboo: the rule that prohibits sex and marriage among designated relatives (443)

machismo: an emphasis on male strength, high sexuality, and dominance (456)

marriage: a group's approved mating arrangements, usually marked by a ritual of some sort (443)

matriarchy: a society in which women-as-a-group dominate men-as-a-group (445)

matrilineal (system of descent): a system of reckoning descent that counts only the mother's side (445)

nuclear family: a family consisting of a husband, wife, and child(ren) (442)

patriarchy: a group in which men-as-a-group dominate women-as-a-group; authority is vested in males (445)

patrilineal (system of descent): a system of reckoning descent that counts only the father's side (444)

polyandry: a form of marriage in which women have more than one husband (442)

polygyny: a form of marriage in which men have more than one wife (442)

romantic love: feelings of sexual attraction accompanied by an idealization of the other (448)

system of descent: how kinship is traced over the generations (443)

KEY PEOPLE

Review the major theoretical contributions or findings of these people.

Paul Amato and Jacob Cheadle: These sociologists were the first to study the grandchildren of divorced parents. They found that the effects of divorce continue across generations. (457, 463, 466-467)

Philip Blumstein and Pepper Schwartz: These sociologists interviewed same sex couples and found that they face the same problems as heterosexual couples. (459)

Urie Bronfenbrenner: This sociologist studied the impact of divorce on children and found that children adjust better if there is a second adult who can be counted on for support. (466)

Andrew Cherlin: Cherlin notes that our society has not yet developed adequate norms for remarriage. (467)

Donald Dutton and Arthur Aron: These researchers compared the sexual arousal levels of men who were in dangerous situations with men in safe situations. They found that the former were more sexually aroused than the latter. (448)

David Finkelhor and Kersti Yllo: These sociologists interviewed 10 percent of a representative sample of women from Boston who reported that their husbands used physical force to compel them to have sex. (470)

Lori Girshick: She interviewed lesbians who had been sexually assaulted by their partners. (470)

Mavis Hetherington: A psychologist whose research shows that 75 to 80 percent of children of divorce function as well as children who are reared by both parents. (466)

William Jankowiak and Edward Fischer: These anthropologists surveyed data on 166 societies and found that the majority of them contained the ideal of romantic love. (448)

Melvin Kohn: Kohn found that the type of work that parents do has an impact on how they rear their children. (453)

Jeanette and Robert Lauer: These sociologists interviewed 351 couples who had been married fifteen years or longer in order to find out what makes a marriage successful. (470-471)

Diana Russell: Russell found that incest victims who experience the most difficulty are those who have been victimized the most often over longer periods of time and whose incest was "more intrusive." (470)

Nicholas Stinnett: Stinnett studied 660 families from all regions of the United States and parts of South America in order to find out what the characteristics of happy families are. (471)

Murray Straus: This sociologist has studied domestic violence and found that, while husbands and wives are equally likely to attack one another, men inflict more damage on women than the reverse. (468)

Bob Suzuki: This sociologist studied Chinese American and Japanese American families and identified several distinctive characteristics of Asian American families. (456)

Judith Wallerstein: This psychologist claims that divorce has detrimental, long-term effects on children. (463, 466)

SELF-TEST

MULTIPLE CHOICE QUESTIONS

1. Polyandry is (442)
    a.   a marriage in which a woman has more than one husband.
    b.   a marriage in which a man has more than one wife.
    c.   male control of a society or group.
    d.   female control of a society or group.

2. A household differs from a family in which of the following ways? (442)
    a.   It includes only those people who are related by blood.
    b.   It is a broader definition because it includes people who support the family, such as housekeepers and nannies.
    c.   It is only used by government agencies for statistical purposes.
    d.   It pertains only to people who occupy the same housing unit or living quarters.

3. The family of orientation is (442)
    a.   the family formed when a couple's first child is born.
    b.   the same thing as an extended family.
    c.   the same as the family of procreation.
    d.   a family in which a person grows up.

4. Endogamy is (443)
    a.   the practice of marrying outside one's group.
    b.   the practice of marrying within one's own group.
    c.   the practice of marrying someone within one's own family.
    d.   none of the above

5. In a matrilineal system (444)
    a.   descent is figured only on the mother's side.
    b.   children are not considered related to their mother's relatives.
    c.   descent is traced on both the mother's and the father's side.
    d.   descent is figured only on the father's side.

6. In terms of authority within the family, an increasing number of U.S. families are (445)
    a.   matriarchal.
    b.   patriarchal.
    c.   egalitarian.
    d.   without authority.

7. The incest taboo (445)
    a.   are rules specifying the degrees of kinship that prohibit sex or marriage.

b. helps families avoid role confusion.
c. facilitates the socialization of children.
d. all of the above

8. Which theoretical perspective looks at how weakened family functions increase divorce? (445)
   a. symbolic interactionism
   b. functionalism
   c. conflict theory
   d. feminism

9. Conflict theorists focus on inequality in marriages, especially unequal power between _____ and _____. (446)
   a. parents, children
   b. mothers, daughters
   c. fathers, sons
   d. husbands, wives

10. According to Morin and Cohn, most of the decisions at home are made by (446)
    a. husbands
    b. wives
    c. couples divided equally
    d. none of the above

11. According to research findings, significant changes have taken place in responsibilities in U.S. families. There has been an increase in time spent caring for children by (447)
    a. husbands
    b. wives
    c. husbands and wives
    d. siblings

12. According to research by Dutton and Aron, what does love usually start with? (448)
    a. sexual attraction
    b. a commitment
    c. a cognitive awareness of our feelings
    d. a chance meeting

13. The tendency of people with similar characteristics to marry one another is (448)
    a. propinquity.
    b. erotic selection.
    c. homogamy.
    d. heterogamy.

14. Families of the same _____ are likely to be similar, regardless of their race–ethnicity. (448)
    a. age
    b. social class
    c. region
    d. religion

15. In what ways do child care arrangements of married couples and single mothers differ? (452)
    a. Single mothers are more likely to leave their children home alone.
    b. Single mothers are much less likely to rely on the child's father for help.
    c. Single mothers are much more likely to rely on the child's father for help.
    d. Single mothers are more likely to enroll their children in poor-quality child care.

16. In comparing child rearing styles of middle- and working-class parents, Kohn concluded that (452-453)
    a. parents of all social classes socialize their children similarly.
    b. middle-class parents are more likely to use physical punishment.
    c. working-class parents are more likely to withdraw privileges or affection.
    d. none of the above

17. What percentage of 25- to 29-year-olds are living with their parents? (453)
    a. 18%
    b. 32%
    c. 40%
    d. 42%

18. A major concern of upper-class African American families is (454)
    a. achievement and respectability.
    b. problems of poverty.
    c. family background of those whom their children marry.
    d. all of the above

19. Machismo (456)
    a. distinguishes Latino families from other groups.
    b. is an emphasis on male strength and dominance.
    c. is seen in some Chicano families where the man has a strong role in his family.
    d. all of the above

20. In what ways do Native American families differ from most U.S. families? (456)
    a. There are more single-parent families.
    b. There is less nonmarital childbirth.
    c. Elders play a more active role in their children's families.
    d. They have higher rates of divorce and marital instability.

21. Since 1970, the number of children in the United States who live with both parents has (458)
    a. remained stable.
    b. dropped.
    c. increased.
    d. has gone down and is now up again.

22. Children from one-parent families are more likely to (457)
    a. drop out of school.
    b. become delinquent.
    c. be poor as adults.
    d. all of the above

23. The three major changes that characterize U.S. families today include all of the following except (459-461)
    a. postponement of first marriage
    b. increase in cohabitation
    c. increase in caring for both children and aging parents at the same time
    d. increase in interracial marriages

24. _____ states do not allow same-sex marriages? (458)
    a. 30
    b. 36
    c. 41
    d. 44

25. Cohabitation (459)
    a. is the condition of living together as an unmarried couple.
    b. has increased ten times in the past 30 years.
    c. has occurred before about half of all couples marry.
    d. all of the above

TRUE-FALSE QUESTIONS

1. _____Marriage and cohabitation are mechanisms for governing mate selection, reckoning descent, and establishing inheritance and authority. (442)
2. _____The family of procreation is the family formed when the couple has their own child. (442)
3. _____Laws of endogamy in the United States prohibit interracial marriages. (443)
4. _____Today, family authority patterns in the United States are becoming more egalitarian. (445)

5. _____The structure of Asian American families is almost identical to that of white families. (456)

6. _____Depending on what numbers you choose to compare, you can produce almost any divorce rate you wish, from 50 percent to less than 2 percent. (463)

7. _____Today's average first-time bride and groom are older than at any time in U.S. history. (459)

8. _____While cohabitation has seen a drastic increase since 1970, the age at which people marry has remained fairly stable. (460)

9. _____Most divorced fathers do not maintain ongoing relationships with their children. (467)

10. _____According to research by Finkelhor and Yllo, one in ten women who were part of a representative sample reported that their husbands used physical force to compel them to have sex. (470)

FILL-IN-THE-BLANK QUESTIONS

1. The Roman Catholic religion and strong family orientation distinguish _____ families from others. (455)

2. Sociologists use the term _____ kin to refer to the stretching of kinship. (454)

3. The concern expressed over one-parent families may have more to do with _____ than with children being reared by one parent. (457)

4. _____ are families whose members were once part of other families. (458)

5. Postponing _____ is today's norm. (459)

6. _____ is the essential difference between cohabitation and marriage. (461)

7. It is becoming increasingly common for children to take care of their own _____. (461)

8. The main reason for the surge of cohabitation in the U.S. is changed ideas of _____. (462)

9. Women are more likely than men to feel divorce is giving them a _____ in life. (467)

10. _____ is more likely to occur in families that are socially isolated. (470)

ESSAY QUESTIONS

1. Discuss whether the family still provides a useful function.

2. Discuss what factors contribute to successful marriages and to happy families.

3. Identify the stages in the family life cycle, discussing what tasks are accomplished in each stage and what event marks the transition from one stage to the next.

4. Identify the trends among U.S. families today, and explain the social forces that have contributed to each of them.

5. Discuss the impact that divorce has on family members—men, women and children.

CHAPTER 17
EDUCATION

LEARNING OBJECTIVES

After reading Chapter 17, you should be able to:

1. Summarize the development of modern education and discuss the links between democracy, industrialization, and universal education. (476-477)

2. Compare education in earlier societies; understand how and why the concept of education changes as society becomes more industrialized. (477)

3. Compare the educational systems of Japan, Russia, and Egypt, and talk about how they represent the differences in education between Most Industrialized, Industrializing, and Least Industrialized Nations. (477-481)

4. From the functionalist perspective, identify and evaluate the manifest and latent functions of education. (481-485)

5. From the functionalist perspective, identify how education has replaced certain family functions, the reasons for this transition, and the controversy this situation has created. (483)

6. From the conflict perspective, explain and discuss the different ways the education system reinforces basic social inequalities. (485-488)

7. Understand and specify what is meant by the "hidden curriculum" and the purposes it serves in the educational system. (485)

8. From the symbolic interactionist perspective, cite the research into and discuss the effects of teachers' expectations on students' performances. (488-491)

9. Identify the major problems that exist within the U.S. educational system, and evaluate some of the potential solutions. (491-497)

Chapter Outline

I. The Development of Modern Education
   A. In earlier societies, education was synonymous with acculturation (transmission of culture from one generation to the next), not a separate institution.
      1. In societies where a sufficient surplus developed, a separate institution arose. Some individuals devoted themselves to teaching, while those who had leisure became their students. Education gradually came to refer to a group's *formal* system of teaching knowledge, values, and skills.

2. During the Dark Ages, only the monks and a handful of the wealthy nobility could read and write.

3. Industrialization created a need for the average citizen to be able to read, write, and work with figures because of the new machinery and new types of jobs.

B. In the years following the American Revolution, the founders of the Republic believed formal education should be the principal means for creating a uniform national culture.

1. In the early 1800s, there was a jumble of schools administered by separate localities with no coordination. Children of the wealthy attended private schools; children of the lower classes (and slaves) received no formal education.

2. Horace Mann, a Massachusetts educator, proposed that "common schools," supported through taxes be established throughout his state; the idea spread throughout the country.

3. Industrialization and universal education occurred at the same time. Since the economy was undergoing fundamental change, political and civic leaders recognized the need for an educated work force. They also feared the influx of "foreign" values and looked on public education as a way to Americanize immigrants.

4. Mandatory education laws requiring children to attend school to a specified age or a particular grade level were enacted in all U.S. states by 1918.

5. As industrialization progressed, education came to be seen as essential to the well-being of society; Industrialized Nations developed into credential societies.

6. Today, a larger proportion of the population attends colleges and universities in the United States than in any other industrialized country in the world; 60 percent of all high-school graduates now enter college. One in seven Americans has not made it through high school. This leads to economic problems for most of them for the rest of their life.

II. Education in Global Perspective

A. A central principle of education is that a nations' education reflects its culture. Education in the Most Industrialized Nations: Japan

1. Japanese education reflects a group-centered ethic. Children in grade school work as a group, mastering the same skills/materials; cooperation and respect for elders (and positions of authority) are stressed.

2. College admission procedures are based on test scores; only the top scorers are admitted, regardless of social class. However, the children from richer families are more likely to be admitted to college. It is likely that these families have spent more money on tutors to help their children prepare for the college entrance exams.

B. Education in the Industrializing Nations: Russia

1. After the Revolution of 1917, the new Soviet government insisted that socialist values dominate education, seeing education as a means to build support for the new political system.

2. Universal education, including college, was free, and math and natural sciences were stressed. Education was centralized, with schools across the nation following the same curriculum.

3. Today, Russians are in the midst of "reinventing" education. Private, religious, and even foreign-run schools are operating; teachers are allowed to develop their own curriculum; and students are encouraged to think for themselves.

4. The primary difficulty facing the post-Soviet educational system is the rapidly changing values and worldviews currently under way.

C. Education in the Least Industrialized Nations: Egypt

1. In the Least Industrialized Nations, most children do not get an education beyond a few years, either because their families see no reason for it or because they cannot afford it. Generally, it is the wealthy who have the time and money to receive an education.

2. Several centuries before the birth of Christ, Egypt was a world-renowned center of learning. Primary areas of study during this period were physics, astronomy, geometry, geography, mathematics, philosophy, and medicine. After defeat in war, education declined, never to rise to its former prominence.

3. Today, the Egyptian constitution makes five years of grade school free and compulsory for all children; however, qualified teachers are few, classrooms are crowded, and education is highly limited. As a result, one-third of Egyptian men and more than half of Egyptian women are illiterate. Those individuals that do receive a formal education attend grade school for five years, preparatory school for three years, and high school for three years.

III. The Functionalist Perspective: Providing Social Benefits

A. Functionalists use the term *manifest function* to refer to the positive outcomes that are intended by human actions and *latent functions* to refer to positive outcomes that were not intended.

B. Education's most obvious manifest function is to teach knowledge and skills.

1. Increasingly, what often counts is not the learning but the certification of learning.

2. A credential society is one in which employers use diplomas and degrees to determine job eligibility. The sheer size, urbanization and consequent anonymity of U.S. society is a major reason why credentials are required. Diplomas/degrees often serve as sorting devices for employers; because they do not know the individual personally, they depend on schools to weed out the capable from the incapable.

C. Another manifest function is cultural transmission of values. There are numerous ways in which cultural values like individualism, competition, and patriotism are transmitted—through the curriculum, the architecture of the schools, and the structure of the school day. Each country teaches its students that they live in the best country.

D. Schools facilitate social integration by molding students into a more cohesive unit and helping socialize them into mainstream culture. This forging of a national identity is to stabilize the political system. Today, children with disabilities are increasingly being integrated in regular social activities through the policy of inclusion or mainstreaming.

E.   Gatekeeping, determining which people will enter which occupations, is another function of education. Tracking students into particular educational curricula supports gatekeeping. Schools facilitate social placement—that is, they funnel people into a society's various positions and hold out higher rewards for those who are willing to put up with years of rigorous education.

F.   Over the years schools have expanded and have assumed some of the functions of the family, like child care, sex education, and offering birth control advice.

G.   Other functions include (1) matchmaking (people finding a future spouse in school); (2) social networking; (3) reducing the unemployment rate (keeping unskilled individuals out of the labor market); and (4) stabilizing society (keeping people off the streets so that they aren't marching and protesting).

IV.   The Conflict Perspective: Perpetuating Social Inequality

A.   Conflict theorists see that the educational system is a tool used by those in the controlling sector of society to maintain their dominance.

B.   The "hidden curriculum" refers to the unwritten rules of behavior and attitude (e.g., obedience to authority, conformity to cultural norms) taught in school in addition to the formal curriculum. Such values and work habits teach the middle and lower classes to support the status quo.

C.   Conflict theorists criticize IQ (intelligence quotient) testing because it measures not only intelligence but also culturally-acquired knowledge. By focusing on these factors, IQ tests reflect a cultural bias that favors the middle class and discriminates against minority and lower-class students.

D.   Because public schools are largely financed by local property taxes, there are rich and poor school districts. Unequal funding stacks the deck against minorities and the poor.

E.   The correspondence principle is how schools correspond to (or reflect) the social structure of society. The U.S. educational system is designed to turn students into dependable workers who will not question their bosses. It is also intended to produce innovators in thought and action, but who will still be loyal to the social system.

F.   Based on research, family background affects the educational system. Those students, regardless of personal abilities, who come from more well-to-do families are not only more likely to go to college but also to attend the nation's most elite schools.

G.   Schools reproduce not only social class inequalities, but also those based on race and ethnicity. Whites are more likely to complete high school, go to college, and get a degree than are African Americans and Latinos. The education system helps pass privilege (or lack thereof) across generations.

V.   The Symbolic Interaction Perspective: Teacher Expectations

A.   Symbolic interactionists study face-to-face interaction inside the classroom. They have found that expectations of teachers are especially significant in determining what students learn.

B. The Rist research (participant observation in an African American grade school with an African American faculty) found tracking begins with teachers' perceptions.
1. After eight days, and without testing for ability, teachers divided the class into fast, average, and slow learners.
2. Rist found that social class was the underlying basis for assigning children to different groups.
3. Students from whom more was expected did the best; students in the slow group were ridiculed and disengaged themselves from classroom activities.
4. The labels applied in kindergarten tended to follow the child through school. What occurred was a self-fulfilling prophecy (Robert Merton's term for an originally false assertion that becomes true simply because it was predicted).
C. The Rosenthal-Jacobson experiment showed that teacher expectations were based on what they had been told about their students.
1. After testing children's abilities using standard IQ tests, researchers randomly classified 20 percent of the students as "spurters." This was the basis for their report to teachers concerning which students would probably experience a learning spurt during the school year.
2. Those who had been labeled as "spurters" made more progress than other students simply because teachers expected them to and encouraged them more, another example of a self-fulfilling prophecy.
D. Teachers shaped the experiences the students had within the classroom.
1. George Farkas found students scoring the same on course material may receive different grades: females get higher grades, as do Asian Americans.
2. Farkas used symbolic interactionism to understand this pattern. He noticed that some students signal that they are interested in what the teacher is teaching; teachers pick up these signals and reward those students with better grades.

VI. **Problems in U.S. Education—and Their Solutions**
A. A variety of factors have been identified as the major problems facing the U.S. educational system today. These problems include mediocrity, violence, cheating, and grade inflation and they it relate to social promotion and functional illiteracy, the influence of peer groups, and violence in schools.
B. Student achievement on the SAT sharply declined from the 1960s to 1980. Educators and Congress expressed concern. Schools raised their standards, and the recovery in math has been excellent; but that has not been the case with the verbal scores. The SAT is now shorter, and students are given more time to answer questions. The analogies and antonyms sections were dropped to make the verbal part easier.
C. It appears that grade inflation has become a widespread issue from high schools to the Ivy League. A result is functional illiteracy; high school students have difficulty with reading and writing.
D. Sociologists have found that peer groups are an incredibly important factor in how teens do in school. Teens who hang out with good students tend to do well; those who hang out with friends who do poorly do poorly themselves.

E. School violence and shootings are an issue for some schools. However, there is no trend toward greater school violence.

F. The way we learn and what we learn are being transformed by technology.

Chapter Summary

Education is a formal agent of socialization and a formal system for teaching knowledge, values, and skills. In earlier societies, education consisted of informal learning and was synonymous with *acculturation*, or the transmission of culture from one generation to the next. As societies developed a more efficient method of agriculture that produced surpluses, a separate institution developed devoted to teaching. With industrialization, the approach to learning shifted from acculturation to a more formal system to meet the needs of the industrializing society. The emerging industrial age created jobs that required workers to read, write, and work accurately with figures—the classic "three Rs" of the nineteenth century: reading, writing, and arithmetic.

In general, formal education reflects a nation's culture and economy. Formal education is extensive in the Most Industrialized Nations, such as Japan and the United States. The public school system can trace its origin to the "common schools" proposed by Horace Mann in 1837. Public education became the way to "Americanize" immigrants. By 1918, all states had passed mandatory education laws requiring children to attend school. As fewer and fewer people were required for farming, education became essential to one's economic well-being. In the Least Industrialized Nations, education is emphasized much less. In the Least Industrialized Nations, where most people work the land or take care of families, most children do not go to school beyond the first couple of grades. Even though many of the Least Industrialized Nations have mandatory school attendance laws, they are not enforced.

According to functionalists, the benefits of education include the teaching of knowledge and skills, providing credentials, cultural transmission of values, social integration, gatekeeping, and mainstreaming. Many industrial nations, such as the United States, have become credential societies in which diplomas and degrees are used to determine job eligibility. Education also provides a means to forge a national identity and stabilize the political system. Over the years, the functions of U.S. schools have expanded to include family functions such as child care and sex education, which has led to controversy since some families resent schools replacing parents in these roles.

Unlike functionalists who look at the benefits of education, conflict theorists examine how education helps the elite to maintain their dominance. Conflict theorists contend that education reproduces the social class structure. As such, they argue that the education system reinforces society's basic social inequalities. It does so through a hidden curriculum of unwritten goals, such as the cultural transmission of obedience to authority, unequal funding of schools, and the use of culturally-biased IQ tests.

Symbolic interactionists focus on face-to-face interactions inside the classroom, examining, for example, how the expectations of teachers profoundly affect students' performances. Observations made by sociologist Ray Rist demonstrated that placing students in "fast," "average," and "slow" learning groups without the benefit of appropriate testing had a profound effect on the students' success in learning how to read. In another study, sociologist George Farkas discovered that some students are successful at "signaling" their teachers that they are better students. Students who perfect the signaling process were found to receive better grades than other students who were less successful at signaling, even though both groups scored identically on exams.

Major problems in the United States education system include mediocrity, low achievement, cheating, grade inflation, social promotion, functional illiteracy, and violence in schools. Potential solutions to these problems include providing basic security for students and restoring high educational standards. As we move forward, technology is changing the way we teach and what we teach.

KEY TERMS

After studying the chapter, review the definition for each of the following terms.

correspondence principle: the sociological principle that schools correspond to (or reflect) the social structure of their society (486)

credential society: the use of diplomas and degrees to determine who is eligible for jobs, even though the diploma or degree may be irrelevant to the actual work (481)

cultural transmission of values: the process of transmitting values from one group to another; often refers to how cultural traits are transmitted across generations and, in education, the ways in which schools transmit a group's culture, especially its core values (482)

education: a formal system of teaching knowledge, values, and skills (476)

functional illiterate: a high school graduate who has difficulty with basic reading and math (492)

gatekeeping: the process by which education opens and closes doors of opportunity; another term for the *social placement* function of education (483)

grade inflation: higher grades given for the same work; a general rise in student grades without a corresponding increase in learning (492)

hidden curriculum: the unwritten goals of schools, such as obedience to authority and conformity to cultural norms (485)

inclusion: helping people to become part of the mainstream of society; also called *mainstreaming* (482)

latent functions: unintended beneficial consequences of people's actions (481)

mandatory education laws: laws that require all children to attend school until a specified age or until they complete a minimum grade in school (477)

manifest functions: the intended beneficial consequences of people's actions (481)

self-fulfilling prophecy: Robert Merton's term for an originally false assertion that becomes true simply because it was predicted (490)

social capital: privileges accompanying a social location that help someone in life (480)

social placement: a function of education—funneling people into a society's various positions (483)

social promotion: passing students to the next level even though they have not mastered basic materials (492)

tracking: in education, the sorting of students into different educational programs on the basis of perceived abilities (483)

KEY PEOPLE

Review the major theoretical contributions or findings of these people.

Samuel Bowles and Herbert Gintis: Bowles and Gintis used the term "correspondence principle" to refer to the ways in which schools reflect the social structure of society. Bowles also compared college attendance among the brightest and weakest students. Of the intellectually weakest students, 26 percent from affluent homes went to college, compared to 6 percent from poorer homes. (485-487)

Anthony Carnevale and Stephen Rose: They confirmed the research conducted by Bowles. They found that regardless of personal abilities, children from more well-to-do families are more likely not only to go to college, but to attend the more elite schools. (487)

James Coleman and Thomas Hoffer: A study of students in Catholic and public high schools by these two sociologists demonstrated that higher performance was based on setting higher standards for students rather than on individual ability. (492-493)

Randall Collins: Collins studied the credential society. (481)

Kingsley Davis and Wilbert Moore: They pioneered a view known as social placement. People are funneled into a society's various positions. Rewards of high income and prestige are offered to motivate capable people to postpone gratification and to put up with years of rigorous education. (483)

Adrian Dove: A social worker in Watts, he believes that the IQ test has bias so that children from certain social backgrounds will perform better than others. (486)

George Farkas: Farkas and a team of researchers investigated how teacher expectations affect student grades. They found that students signal teachers that they are good students by being eager and cooperative and working hard. (490)

Horace Mann: An educator from Massachusetts, he proposed that "common schools," supported through taxes, be established throughout his state. (477)

Robert Merton: He coined the term "self-fulfilling prophecy." This is a false assumption of something that is going to happen, which then comes true simply because it was predicted. (490)

Talcott Parsons: He was another functionalist who suggested that a function of schools is to funnel people into social positions. (483)

Ray Rist: This sociologist's classic study of an African American grade school uncovered some of the dynamics of educational tracking. (488-490)

Robert Rosenthal and Lenore Jacobson: These social psychologists conducted a study of teacher expectations and student performance and found that a self-fulfilling prophecy had taken place—when teachers were led to believe certain students were smart, they came to expect more of them, and the students gave more in return. (490)

SELF-TEST

MULTIPLE CHOICE QUESTIONS

1. In Japan, college admission is based on (480)
    a. the ability of parents to pay the tuition.
    b. making a high score on a national test.
    c. being known by teachers as a "hard worker."
    d. the same procedures that prevail in the United States.

2. Since the collapse of the Soviet Union, which of the following has occurred? (480)
    a. There is a renewed interest in the humanities.
    b. Tens of thousands of teachers have lost their jobs.
    c. Teachers are allowed to encourage students to question and think for themselves.
    d. They have committed more money to education.

3. Which of the following statements about education in Egypt is *incorrect*? (481)
    a. Because education is free at all levels, the most talented children attend, regardless of parents' economic resources.
    b. The Egyptian constitution guarantees five years of free grade school for all children.
    c. The educational system consists of five years of grade school, three years of preparatory school, and three years of high school.
    d. Only 39 percent of women and 64 percent of men are literate.

4. Using diplomas to hire employees, even when the diplomas are irrelevant to the work, is (481)
    a. a credential society.
    b. a certification mill.
    c. employer discretion in hiring.
    d. none of the above

5. According to functionalists, all of the following are functions of education, *except* (481-483)
    a. maintaining social inequality.
    b. transmitting cultural values.
    c. helping mold students into a more or less cohesive unit.
    d. teaching patriotism.

6. Which of the following is *not* one of the cultural values transmitted through the U.S. educational system? (482)
    a. individualism
    b. competition

  c. cooperation

  d. patriotism

7. _____ refers to educators incorporating students with disabilities into regular school activities. (482)

  a. Mainstreaming

  b. Disability rights

  c. Enabling

  d. Incorporation

8. _____ and _____ are two examples of gatekeeping. (483)

  a. Credentialing, tracking

  b. Mainstreaming, social placement

  c. Cultural transmission of values, tracking

  d. Social integration, mainstreaming

9. The "hidden curriculum" refers to (485)

  a. the extra curriculum costs that are buried in school budgets.

  b. the lessons that teachers hide from the eyes of prying school boards.

  c. the unwritten rules of behavior and attitudes that are taught in school.

  d. all of the above

10. IQ tests have been criticized because (486)

  a. they are difficult to score.

  b. they are expensive to administer.

  c. they are often administered at the wrong point in a child's intellectual development.

  d. they are culturally biased.

11. Public schools are largely supported by (486)

  a. state funding.

  b. federal funding.

  c. local property taxes.

  d. none of the above

12. The ways in which schools correspond to, or reflect, the social structure of society is (486)

  a. the reproduction of social class.

  b. the correspondence principle.

  c. the status quo quotient.

  d. the status maintenance process.

13. Research by Samuel Bowles on the connection between social class and college attendance showed that (487)

a. regardless of ability, students from affluent homes were more likely to go to college than students from poor homes.
b. regardless of the family's social class, students with ability went on to college.
c. among the brightest students, family background made no difference in terms of the student's decision to attend college.
d. there were no social class differences among the weakest students in terms of their decision to go on to college.

14. All of the following examples are ways in which schools correspond to the needs of society *except* for which one? (485-491)
a. encourage cooperation
b. unequal funding of schools
c. enforce punctuality in attendance and homework
d. promote patriotism

15. Which sociologists view education as reproducing the social structure? (487)
a. symbolic interactionists
b. functionalists
c. conflict theorists
d. feminists

16. Which of the following is true regarding race–ethnicity and education? (489)
a. Whites and Latinos are the most likely to attend college.
b. Whites and African Americans are the most likely to attend private colleges.
c. Native Americans are the most likely to attend two-year colleges.
d. Asian Americans are the most likely to attend four-year colleges.

17. What did Rist's research demonstrate? (490)
a. the ability of teachers to sort children accurately into ability groups
b. the power of labels
c. the importance of individual effort
d. the cultural biases of the school system

18. The Rosenthal-Jacobson experiment tended to confirm which of these concepts? (490)
a. cooling out
b. cultural transmission
c. acculturation
d. self-fulfilling prophecy

19. Research by George Farkas focused on (490)
a. education of elite children.
b. how teacher expectations affect a kindergarten class.
c. how teacher expectations are influenced by students' alleged IQ scores.

d.   how teacher expectations affect students' grades.

20. When compared to scores of twenty to thirty years ago, today's student scores on tests such as the SAT (491-492)
    a.   are higher.
    b.   are lower.
    c.   have remained about the same.
    d.   none of the above

21. The practice of passing students from one grade to the next even though they have not mastered the basic materials is called (492)
    a.   age-based promotion.
    b.   social promotion.
    c.   expedient promotion.
    d.   functional promotion.

22. High-school graduates who have difficulty with basic reading and math are known as (492)
    a.   "boneheads."
    b.   functional literates.
    c.   functional illiterates.
    d.   underachievers.

23. Research by James Coleman and Thomas Hoffer, comparing student performance at Roman Catholic and public schools, found that: (492-493)
    a.   Students at public schools performed better because they had more resources available to them.
    b.   Students at public schools performed better because they were taught by better qualified teachers.
    c.   Students at Roman Catholic schools performed better because the teachers set higher standards for them to meet.
    d.   Students at Roman Catholic schools performed better because they had higher levels of faith.

24. Which of the following private industry job areas made higher salaries than public school teachers? (493)
    a.   Physics
    b.   Accounting
    c.   Engineering
    d.   All of the above

25. Based on the statistics of shooting deaths that have occurred in U.S. schools, which of the following statements is *correct*? (495)

a. There has been a dramatic increase in the number of shooting deaths over the last decade.
b. The number of shooting deaths at the end of the 1990s was half what it was at the beginning of the decade.
c. Girls are more likely than boys to be the targets of school shootings.
d. Other types of homicides committed at school (stabbings, beatings, etc.) are just as common as shooting homicides.

TRUE-FALSE QUESTIONS

1. _____In earlier societies, there was a separate social institution called education. (476)
2. _____By 1918, all American states had mandatory education laws. (477)
3. _____College graduation in the United States today is still less common than high school graduation was in 1910. (479)
4. _____Japanese schools teach the value of competition to their students. (480)
5. _____Since the breakup of the Soviet Union, Russia has allowed the establishment of private, religious, and even foreign-run schools. (480)
6. _____Because Egyptian education is free at all levels, including college, children of the wealthy are no more likely than children of the poor to get a college education. (481)
7. _____The United States is a credential society. (481)
8. _____Education's most obvious manifest function is to teach knowledge and skills. (481)
9. _____American schools discourage individualism and encourage teamwork. (482)
10. _____Students everywhere are taught that their country is the best country in the world. (482)

FILL-IN-THE-BLANK QUESTIONS

1. In early societies, education was synonymous with _____. (476)
2. Horace Mann proposed the concept of _____ schools supported through taxes. (477)
3. Today, almost _____ of all undergraduates in the United States are enrolled in community colleges. (478)
4. A central sociological principal of education is that a nation's education reflects its _____. (477)
5. One result of Egypt's educational system is that _____ of Egyptian men are illiterate. (481)
6. _____ refers to the attitudes and unwritten rules of behavior that schools teach in addition to the formal curriculum. (485)
7. _____ is higher grades given for the same work. (492)
8. Students perform better when they are expected to meet _____ standards. (493)

9. One of the main problems in education pointed out by the author is cheating by
   _____. (494)
10. _____ is transforming education, changing what we learn and the way we learn
    it. (496-497)

ESSAY QUESTIONS

1. Explain the link between democracy, industrialization, and universal education.

2. Compare the educational systems of Japan, Russia, and Egypt, and discuss what is meant
   by the statement that education reflects culture.

3. Select one of the three perspectives and design a research project to test the claims of that
   perspective about the nature of education.

4. In discussing solutions to educational problems, the author suggests that one direction in
   which schools should go is toward setting higher educational standards. Both the research
   by James Coleman and Thomas Hoffer and the success of Jaime Escalante support this.
   Discuss social factors that might explain why such a proposal has not been widely adopted
   by public schools across the country.

CHAPTER 18
RELIGION

LEARNING OBJECTIVES

After reading Chapter 18, you should be able to:

1. Define religion and explain its essential elements. (502)

2. Describe the functions and dysfunctions of religion from the functionalist perspective. (503-506)

3. Know what is meant by and provide examples of functional equivalents of religion. (505-506)

4. Apply the symbolic interactionist perspective to religious symbols, rituals, and beliefs. Discuss how each of these help to establish and/or maintain communities of like-minded people. (506-509)

5. From the conflict perspective, discuss how religion supports the status quo, as well as reflects, reinforces, and legitimizes social inequality. (509)

6. Summarize Max Weber's analysis of religion and the spirit of capitalism, explaining its significance. (512-513)

7. Identify the characteristics of the world's major religions. (513-518)

8. Define the terms *cult*, *sect*, *church*, and *ecclesia*, and describe the process by which some groups move from one category to another. (518-521)

9. Describe the three major patterns of adaptation that occur when religion and culture conflict with one another. (521)

10. Know how religious membership varies by region, social class, age, and race-ethnicity. (522-523)

11. Describe and discuss the major features of religious groups in the United States. (523-524)

12. Define *secularization* and distinguish between the secularization of religion and the secularization of culture. (526-528)

13. Discuss what accounts for the fundamental significance of religion in people's lives and why, in all likelihood, religion will remain a permanent fixture in human society. (528-529)

Chapter Outline

I. What Is Religion?

A. Sociologists who do research on religion analyze the relationship between society and religion and study the role that religion plays in people's lives.

B. According to Durkheim, religion is the beliefs/practices separating the profane from the sacred, uniting adherents into a moral community.

   1. "Sacred" refers to aspects of life having to do with the supernatural that inspire awe, reverence, deep respect, or deep fear.

   2. "Profane" refers to the ordinary aspects of everyday life.

C. Durkheim defined religion by three elements: (1) beliefs that some things are sacred (forbidden, set off from the profane); (2) practices (rituals) concerning things considered sacred; and (3) a moral community (a church) resulting from a group's beliefs and practices.

II. The Functionalist Perspective

A. Religion performs certain functions: (1) answering questions about ultimate meaning (the purpose of life, why people suffer); (2) providing emotional comfort; (3) uniting believers into a community that shares values and perspectives; (4) providing guidelines for life; (5) controlling behavior; (6) helping people adapt to new environments; (7) providing support for the government; and (8) spearheading social change on occasion (as in the case of the civil rights movement in the 1960s).

B. A functional equivalent of religion is a substitute that serves the same functions; some are difficult to distinguish from a religion. Although the substitute may perform similar functions, its activities are not directed toward God, gods, or the supernatural. Examples include psychotherapy, humanism, transcendental meditation, or belonging to a political party.

C. War and terrorism, as well as religious persecution, are dysfunctions of religion.

III. The Symbolic Interactions Perspective

A. All religions use symbols to provide identity and social solidarity for members. For members, these are not ordinary symbols, but sacred symbols evoking awe and reverence, which become a condensed way of communicating with others.

B. Rituals are ceremonies or repetitive practices helping unite people into a moral community by creating a feeling of closeness with God and unity with one another.

C. Symbols, including rituals, develop from beliefs. A belief may be vague ("God is") or specific ("God wants us to prostrate ourselves and face Mecca five times each day"). Religious beliefs include not only values (what is considered good and desirable) but also a cosmology (unified picture of the world).

D. Religious experience is a sudden awareness of the supernatural or a feeling of coming in contact with God. Some Protestants use the term "born again" to describe people who have undergone a religious experience.

E. Shared meanings that come through symbols, rituals, and beliefs unite people into a moral community, which is powerful. It provides the basis for mutual identity and establishes norms that govern the behavior of members. Not only are members bound together by shared beliefs and rituals, but they are also separated from those who do not share their symbolic world. Removal from the community is a serious concern for those whose identity is tied to that community.

IV. The Conflict Perspective

A. Conflict theorists are highly critical of religion. Karl Marx called religion the "opium of the people" because he believed that the workers escape into religion. He argued that religion diverts the energies of the oppressed from changing their circumstances because believers focus on the happiness they will have in the coming world rather than on their suffering in this world.

B. Religious teachings and practices reflect a society's inequalities. Gender inequalities are an example: when males completely dominated U.S. society, women's roles in churches and synagogues were limited to "feminine" activities, a condition which is beginning to change.

C. Religion legitimizes social inequality; it reflects the interests of those in power by teaching that the existing social arrangements of a society represent what God desires.

V. Religion and the Spirit of Capitalism

A. Weber saw religion as a force for social change, observing that European countries industrialized under capitalism. Thus religion held the key to modernization (transformation of traditional societies into industrial societies).

B. To explain this connection, Weber wrote *The Protestant Ethic and the Spirit of Capitalism*. In it he concluded that:
   1. the spirit of capitalism (desire to accumulate capital as a duty, as an end in itself) was a radical departure from the past.
   2. religion (including a Calvinistic belief in predestination and the need for reassurance as to one's fate) is the key to why the spirit of capitalism developed in Europe.
   3. a change in religion (from Catholicism to Protestantism) led to a change in thought and behavior (the Protestant ethic), which resulted in the "spirit of capitalism."

C. Critics of Weber noted that he overlooked the lack of capitalism in Scotland (a Calvinist country) and that the Industrial Revolution originated in England, a non-Calvinist country.

D. Today the spirit of capitalism and the Protestant ethic are by no means limited to Protestants; they have become cultural traits that have spread throughout the world.

VI. The World's Major Religions

A. The origin of Judaism is traced to Abraham, who lived about 4,000 years ago in Mesopotamia.

1. It was the first religion based on monotheism, the belief in only one God. Prior to this, religions were based on polytheism, the belief that there are many gods.
2. Contemporary Judaism in the United States has three main branches: Orthodox (adheres to the laws espoused by Moses); Reform (more liberal, uses the vernacular in religious ceremonies and has reduced much of the ritual); and Conservative (falling somewhere between).
3. The history of Judaism is marked by conflict and persecution (anti-Semitism).
4. Central to Jewish teaching is the requirement to love God and do good deeds.

B. Christianity developed out of Judaism and is based on the belief that Christ is the Messiah God promised the Jews.
   1. During the first 1,000 years of Christianity, there was only one church organization, directed from Rome; during the eleventh century, Greek Orthodoxy was established.
   2. In the Middle Ages, the Roman Catholic Church, aligned with the political establishment, grew corrupt. The Reformation of the sixteenth century, led by Martin Luther, was a reaction to the Church's corruption.
   3. The Reformation marked the beginning of a splintering of Christianity; today, there are about two billion Christians, divided into hundreds of groups.

C. Islam (whose followers are known as Muslims) began in the same part of the world as Judaism and Christianity; like the Jews, Muslims trace their ancestry to Abraham.
   1. The founder, Muhammad, established a theocracy; a government based on God being the ruler, his laws the statutes of the land, and priests his earthly administrators.
   2. After Muhammad's death, a struggle for control split Islam into two branches that remain today: the Shi'ites, who are more conservative and inclined to fundamentalism (the belief that true religion is threatened by modernism and that faith as it was originally practiced should be restored), and the Sunni, who are generally more liberal.
   3. It is the duty of each Muslim to make a pilgrimage to Mecca during his or her lifetime. The Muslims practice polygyny and can have up to four wives.

D. Hinduism, the chief religion of India, goes back about 4,000 years but has no specific founder or canonical scripture (texts thought to be inspired by God). Instead several books expound on the moral qualities people should strive to attain.
   1. Hindus are polytheists (believe there are many gods). A central belief is karma, spiritual progress. They believe that there is no final judgment, but reincarnation, a cycle of life, death, and rebirth.
   2. Some Hindu practices, such as child marriage and suttee (cremating a widow along with her deceased husband) have been modified as a result of protest.
   3. Every twelve years, the purifying washing in the Ganges River takes place. Millions of people participate.

E. About 600 B.C., Siddhartha Gautama founded Buddhism, which emphasizes self-denial and compassion.

      1.   During meditation he discovered the "four noble truths," which emphasize self-denial and compassion.

      2.   Buddhism is similar to Hinduism in that the final goal is to escape from reincarnation into nonexistence of blissful peace.

      3.   Buddhism spread rapidly into many parts of Asia.

F.   Confucius (China 551-479 B.C.) urged social reform and developed a system of morality based on peace, justice, and universal order.

      1.   The basic moral principle of Confucianism is to maintain *jen* (sympathy or concern for other humans). The basic principle was to treat those who are subordinate to you as you would like to be treated by those superior to you.

      2.   Originally, Confucianism was atheistic; however, as the centuries passed, local gods were added to the teachings, and Confucius himself was declared a god.

VII. Types of Religious Groups

A.   A cult is a new religion with few followers that maintains teachings and practices that put it at odds with the dominant culture and religion.

      1.   All religions began as cults. Cults often begin with the appearance of a charismatic leader (exerting extraordinary appeal to a group of followers).

      2.   Christianity, the most popular religion in the world, began as a cult, as did Islam.

      3.   Each cult meets with rejection from society. The message given by the cult is seen as a threat to the dominant culture.

      4.   The cult demands intense commitment, and its followers confront a hostile world.

      5.   Although most cults ultimately fail because they are unable to attract a large enough following, some succeed and make history.

B.   A sect is larger than a cult but still feels substantial hostility from and toward society.

      1.   At the very least, members remain uncomfortable with many of the emphases of the dominant culture; nonmembers feel uncomfortable with sect members.

      2.   Sects usually are loosely organized; emphasize personal salvation (an emotional expression of one's relationship with God); and work toward recruitment of new members (evangelism).

      3.   If a sect grows, its members tend to become respectable in society, and the sect is changed into a church.

C.   A church is a large, highly organized religious group with formal, sedate services and less emphasis on personal conversion. The religious group is highly bureaucratized (including national and international offices that give directions to local congregations). Most new members come from within the church, from children born to existing members rather than from outside recruitment.

D.   An ecclesia is a religious group so integrated into the dominant culture that it is difficult to tell where one begins and the other leaves off.

      1.   Ecclesia are also called state religions. The government and religion work together to try to shape the society.

      2.   There is no recruitment of members, for citizenship makes everyone a member. The majority of the society belongs to the religion in name only.

3. The Church of England, the Lutheran church in Sweden and Denmark, and Islam in Iran and Iraq are ecclesiae.

E. Not all religions go through all stages. Although all religions began as cults, not all varieties of a religion have done so.

1. Some die out because they fail to attract members; some remain sects. Few become ecclesias.

2. A denomination is a "brand name" within a major religion (e.g., Methodism within Christianity).

F. Three major patterns of adaptation occur when religion and the culture in which it is embedded find themselves in conflict.

1. Members of a religion may reject the dominant culture and withdraw from it socially, although they continue to live in the same geographic area.

2. A cult or sect rejects only specific elements of the prevailing culture.

3. The society rejects the religious group entirely and may even try to destroy it. The destruction of the Branch Davidians by the U.S. government is an example of this third pattern.

VIII. Religion in the United States

A. About 65 percent of Americans belong to a church or synagogue.

1. Each religious group draws members from all social classes, although some are more likely to draw members from the top of the social class system and others from the bottom. The most top-heavy are Episcopalians and Jews, the most bottom-heavy the Baptists and Evangelicals. People who change social class are also likely to change their denomination.

2. All major religious groups in the United States draw from various racial and ethnic groups; however, people of Hispanic or Irish descent are likely to be Roman Catholics, those of Greek origin belong to the Greek Orthodox Church, and African Americans are likely to be Protestants.

3. Although many churches are integrated, there is still much segregation along racial lines. This is based on custom, not law.

B. Characteristics of religious groups in the United States:

1. Diversity—with 300,000 congregations, there is no dominant religion in the U.S.

2. Pluralism and freedom—no government interference with religion. However, if officials feel threatened by a religious group, then they violate their hands-off policy.

3. Competition for believers from many religions.

4. Commitment—reflected in the high proportion of believers in God. About 44 percent report that they attend religious services each week. This commitment is backed up with generous financial support for religion and its charities.

5. Toleration for religious beliefs other than one's own are reflected in the attitudes that religions have a right to exist as long as they do not brainwash or bother anyone and no one says which religion is the true religion. While each believer

may be convinced about the truth of his or her religion, trying to convert others is considered obnoxious.

      6.   Fundamentalist revival occurs because mainstream churches fail to meet basic religious needs of large numbers of people. As a result, mainstream churches are losing members while fundamentalists are gaining.

      7.   The electronic church—televangelists reach millions of viewers and raise millions of dollars.

      8.   Religious groups now maintain home pages on the Internet and discussion groups have formed around religion.

   C.   Secularization is the process by which worldly affairs replace spiritual interests.

      1.   Secularization of religion is the replacement of a religion's other-worldly concerns with concerns about this world. It occurs when religion's influence is lessened (both on a society's institutions and on individuals). The secularization of religion explains why Christian churches have splintered into so many groups: changes in social class of the members may create different needs, thereby failing to meet the needs of those whose life situation has not changed.

      2.   Secularization of culture is the process whereby religion has less influence in society. Secularization is due to the spread of scientific thinking, industrialization, urbanization, and mass education that reflects modernization. Even though the culture has secularized, religious participation remains strong.

IX. The Future of Religion

   A.   Prominent intellectuals once believed that science would replace religion. However, religion continues to thrive in the most advanced scientific nations.

   B.   Religion has fundamental significance in people's lives.

   C.   Science cannot answer questions about four concerns many people have: the existence of God, the purpose of life, morality, and the existence of an afterlife.

Chapter Summary

Religion is a unified system of beliefs and practices relative to sacred things. Sociologists who do research on religion analyze the relationship between society and religion and study the role that religion plays in people's lives. They do not seek to prove that one religion is better than another.

Durkheim said religion is defined by three elements: beliefs, practices, and a moral community. He also discovered that all religions separate the profane (common elements of everyday life) from the sacred (things set apart or forbidden that inspire fear, awe, reverence, or deep respect).

According to functionalists, religion meets basic human needs by providing answers to questions about ultimate meaning, emotional comfort, social solidarity, guidelines to everyday life, social control, adaptation to a new environment, support for government, and, occasionally, an impetus for social change. Many of the functions that religion provides can also be fulfilled by functional equivalents (other components of society that serve the same functions as religion). Communism had its prophets, sacred writings, sacred symbols, and rituals. Other examples of the functional equivalent of religion include Alcoholics Anonymous and transcendental meditation. But in addition to being functional for society, religion can also bring harmful results. Referred to as dysfunctions, religion has been used to justify war, terrorism, and religious persecution.

Symbolic interactionists focus on the meanings that people give their experiences, especially how they use symbols. Through the use of religious symbols, rituals, and beliefs, people build and maintain a community of similarly-minded people. All religions use symbols to provide identity and social solidarity for their members.

Conflict theorists examine how religion reflects and reinforces a society's social inequalities. In general, conflict theorists are highly critical of religion. Karl Marx was an atheist and believed that the existence of God was impossible. Other conflict theorists concentrate on religious ideologies such as the "divine right of kings" to support social inequality.

Weber disagreed with the conflict perspective's position that religion impedes social change. He viewed religion as a source of social change. Weber believed a change in people's thinking based on Calvinism produced capitalism. To explain his conclusions, Weber wrote *The Protestant Ethic and the Spirit of Capitalism*. In this work, Weber emphasized how Calvin's interpretation of the Bible, which emphasized working from sunup to sundown six days a week, predestination, delayed gratification, and asceticism, influenced savings and the investment of capital and resulted in a surge in production.

The world's major religions and the number of followers are Christianity (2 billion), Islam (1.2 billion), and Hinduism (820 million). Buddhism ranks as the fifth largest religion based on the number of followers (360 million) and Judaism ranks seventh (14 million).

Sociologists have identified four types of religious groups: cults, sects, churches, and ecclesiae. Although the word "cult" often conjures up bizarre images, cults are not necessarily odd in practice or belief. In fact, all religions began as cults. As cults become larger and more organized, they become *sects*. Although a sect still feels tension between its views and the views of the broader society, it has a greater potential to grow and become integrated into society. A highly bureaucratic religious group with national and international headquarters is known as a church. Unlike cults and sects, the church is likely to have less emphasis on personal salvation and emotional expression. An ecclesia is a religion well integrated into a culture and strongly aligned with the government. Also called state religion, in an ecclesia the government and religion work together to try to shape society.

In the United States, religious membership varies by region, social class, age, race, and ethnicity. Although most religious groups draw members from all social classes, some are "top heavy" and others "bottom heavy" in representation. Many religions are associated with race and ethnicity. Although many American churches are integrated, Sunday morning between 10 a.m. and 11 a.m. has been called "the most segregated hour in the United States."

The major features of religious groups in the United States include diversity, pluralism and freedom, competition and recruitment, commitment, toleration, fundamentalist revival, the electronic church, and, more recently, use of the Internet.

The term "secularization" refers to the process by which worldly affairs (e.g., science and technology) replace spiritual interests. Some religions and religious denominations, as well as members of some cultures, and industrialized societies, have experienced the influence of secularization. Sociologists use the term "secularization of culture" to refer to a culture that, once heavily influenced by religion, loses much of its religious influence.

A group of prominent intellectuals once foresaw an end to religion. As science advanced, they said, it would explain everything. But these theorists were wrong. Because science cannot answer people's "spiritual" questions about the existence of God, the purpose of life, the possibility of an afterlife, and morality, religions are likely to be a permanent fixture in human life.

KEY TERMS

After studying the chapter, review the definition for each of the following terms.

animism: the belief that all objects in the world have spirits, some of which are dangerous and must be outwitted (514)

anti-Semitism: prejudice, discrimination, and persecution directed against Jews (514)

born again: a term describing Christians who have undergone a religious experience so life-transforming that they feel they have become new persons (508)

charisma: literally, an extraordinary gift from God; more commonly, an outstanding, "magnetic" personality (518)

charismatic leader: literally, someone to whom God has given a gift; in its extended sense, someone who exerts extraordinary appeal to a group of followers (518)

church: according to Durkheim, one of the three essential elements of religion—a moral community of believers; also refers to a large, highly organized religious group that has formal, sedate worship services with little emphasis on evangelism, intense religious experience, or personal conversion (502)

civil religion: Robert Bellah's term for religion that is such an established feature of a country's life that its history and social institutions become sanctified by being associated with God (505)

cosmology: teachings or ideas that provide a unified picture of the world (508)

cult: a new religion with few followers whose teachings and practices put it at odds with the dominant culture and religion (518)

denomination: a "brand name" within a major religion, for example, Methodist or Baptist (520)

ecclesia: a religious group so integrated into the dominant culture that it is difficult to tell where the one begins and the other leaves off; also called a *state religion* (520)

evangelism: an attempt to win converts (520)

functional equivalent: a substitute that serves the same functions (or meets the same needs) as religion; for example, psychotherapy (505)

modernization: the transformation of traditional societies into industrial societies (512)

monotheism: the belief that there is only one God (514)

polytheism: the belief that there are many gods (514)

profane: Durkheim's term for common elements of everyday life (502)

Protestant ethic: Weber's term to describe a self-denying, highly moral life accompanied by hard work and frugality (512)

reincarnation: in Hinduism and Buddhism, the return of the soul (or self) in a different form after death (516)

religion: according to Durkheim, beliefs and practices that separate the profane from the sacred and unite its adherents into a moral community (502)

religious experience: a sudden awareness of the supernatural or a feeling of coming in contact with God (527)

rituals: ceremonies or repetitive practices; in religion, observances or rites, often intended to evoke a sense of awe of the sacred (508)

sacred: Durkheim's term for things set apart or forbidden that inspire fear, awe, reverence, or deep respect (502)

sect: a group larger than a cult that still feels substantial hostility from and toward society (520)

secular: belonging to the world and its affairs (526)

secularization of culture: the process by which a culture becomes less influenced by religion (527)

secularization of religion: the replacement of a religion's "other-worldly" concerns with concerns about "this world" (527)

spirit of capitalism: Weber's term for the desire to accumulate capital—not to spend it, but as an end in itself—and to constantly reinvest it (512)

state religions: government-sponsored religion; also called ecclesia (505)

KEY PEOPLE

Review the major theoretical contributions or findings of these people.

Emile Durkheim: Durkheim investigated world religions and identified elements that are common to all religions, such as separation of sacred from profane, beliefs about what is sacred, practices surrounding the sacred, and a moral community. (502, 525, 530)

John Hostetler: Hostetler is known for his research and writings on the Amish. (509)

Benton Johnson: Johnson analyzed types of religious groups, such as cults, sects, churches, and ecclesia. (518)

William Kephart and William Zellner: These sociologists also investigated the Amish religion and way of life. (509)

Karl Marx: Marx was critical of religion, calling it the opium of the masses. (505, 509)

Liston Pope: This sociologist studied types of religious groups. (518)

Lynda Powell: She was an epidemiologist who evaluated the research done on the effects of religion on health. (504)

Stanley Presser and Linda Stinson: They examined written reports of how people spent their Sundays. They concluded that about 30 percent or so attend church weekly. (524)

Ian Robertson: Robertson noted that there is a fundamental distinction between a religion and its functional equivalent; unlike the latter, the activities of a religion are directed toward God, gods, or some supernatural. (524)

Ernst Troeltsch: He is another sociologist who is associated with types of religious groups from cults to ecclesia. (518)

Max Weber: Weber studied the link between Protestantism and the rise of capitalism and found that the ethic associated with Protestant denominations was compatible with the early needs of capitalism. (512-513)

SELF-TEST

MULTIPLE CHOICE QUESTIONS

1. What was Durkheim's purpose in writing *The Elementary Forms of the Religious Life*? (502)
    a. He wanted to explain the development of Protestantism.
    b. He set to chart the history of world religions.
    c. He wanted to study the development of religion from sect to church.
    d. He wanted to identify elements common to all religions.

2. What did Durkheim mean by the word *profane*? (502)
    a. aspects of life having to do with the supernatural
    b. aspects of religion that are mysterious
    c. aspects of life that are part of everyday life
    d. aspects of religious worship

3. According to Durkheim, a church (502)
    a. is a large, highly organized religious group.
    b. has little emphasis on personal conversion.
    c. is a group of believers with a set of beliefs and practices regarding the sacred.
    d. all of the above

4. All of the following are functions of religion, *except* (503-505)
    a. encouraging wars for holy causes.
    b. support for the government.
    c. social change.
    d. social control.

5. 5. What did researchers discover about the effects of religion on health? (504)
    a. They discovered that there was little relationship.
    b. Prayer (or meditation) changes people's brain activity and improves their immune response.
    c. People who were hospitalized were more religious than the doctors realized.
    d. Regular prayer can cure many diseases.

6. War and religious persecution are (506)
    a. manifest functions of religion.
    b. latent functions of religion.
    c. dysfunctions of religion.
    d. functional equivalents of religion.

7. A unified picture of the world, such as the belief in one God, who is the creator of the universe, is called (508)
    a. an ideology.
    b. a cosmology.
    c. a dogma.
    d. a religious creed.

8. What are Protestants referring to when they use the term *born again*? (508)
    a. reincarnation
    b. Christ's rebirth after his crucifixion
    c. a personal, life-transforming religious experience
    d. finding salvation in the afterlife

9. Which of the following statements about the practice of shunning is *incorrect*? (509)
    a. Persons who are shunned are treated as if they do not exist.
    b. Family members are exempt from having to follow the practice when it involves one of their own.
    c. It is a serious matter for those whose identity is bound up in the community.
    d. The shunning occurs in all situations and at all times.

10. Religion is the opium of the people according to (509)
    a. Max Weber.
    b. Emile Durkheim.
    c. Karl Marx.
    d. Charles Cooley.

11. An example of the use of religion to legitimize social inequalities is (509)
    a. the divine right of kings.
    b. a declaration that the Pharaoh or Emperor is god or divine.
    c. the defense of slavery as being God's will.
    d. all of the above

12. Weber believed that religion held the key to (512)
    a. modernization.
    b. bureaucratization.
    c. institutionalization.
    d. socialization.

13. Weber analyzed how Protestantism gave rise to the Protestant ethic, which stimulated what he called the (512)
    a. spirit of capitalism.
    b. secularization of religion.
    c. secularization of culture.

d.   ecclesia.

14. Which major religion was the first to practice monotheism? (514)
     a.   Judaism
     b.   Christianity
     c.   Islam
     d.   Hinduism

15. The belief that all objects in the world have spirits is (514)
     a.   a central belief of Islam.
     b.   referred to as animism.
     c.   no longer accepted by people around the world.
     d.   the same as monotheism.

16. What was an unanticipated outcome of the Reformation? (515)
     a.   the splintering of Christianity
     b.   the reunification of the Catholic Church
     c.   the elimination of corruption in the Church
     d.   the downgrading of women's status in the Church hierarchy

17. Which branch of Islam is more conservative and inclined to fundamentalism? (516)
     a.   orthodox
     b.   Sunni
     c.   Shi'ite
     d.   black Muslim

18. Polytheism is the belief that (516)
     a.   God is a woman.
     b.   there is only one God.
     c.   there are many gods.
     d.   God does not exist.

19. The religion with no specific founder is (516)
     a.   Islam.
     b.   Hinduism.
     c.   Buddhism.
     d.   Confucianism.

20. Reincarnation (516)
     a.   is found only in Buddhism.
     b.   is the return of the soul after death in the same form.
     c.   is the return of the soul after death in a different form.
     d.   none of the above

21. All religions began as (518)
    a. cults.
    b. sects.
    c. churches.
    d. ecclesiae.

22. Although larger than a cult, a _____ still feels tension from society. (520)
    a. commune
    b. ecclesia
    c. sect
    d. church

23. Which of the following is *not* a feature of religious groups in the U.S.? (522-523)
    a. diversity of beliefs
    b. competition for members
    c. intolerance of differences
    d. commitment to beliefs

24. Secularization of religion occurs as a result of (527)
    a. industrialization.
    b. urbanization.
    c. mass education.
    d. all of the above

25. That religion has less impact on public affairs in the United States today is an example of (527-528)
    a. secularization of religion.
    b. secularization of culture.
    c. a civil religion.
    d. an ecclesia.

TRUE-FALSE QUESTIONS

1. _____Fundamentalism is the belief that modernism threatens religion and that the faith as it was originally practiced should be restored. (516)
2. _____Some Hindu practices were modified as a consequence of social protest. (517)
3. _____The basic moral principle of Confucianism is to maintain sympathy or concern for other humans. (517)
4. _____Judaism, Christianity, and Islam are all polytheistic religions. (513-516)
5. _____Unlike cults, sects do not stress evangelism. (518-520)
6. _____Islam in Iran and Iraq is an example of ecclesia. (520)
7. _____Reform Judaism is a denomination. (521)

8. _____Many religions around the world are associated with race and ethnicity. (523)
9. _____Many local ministers are very supportive of the electronic church because they are happy to see people who do not attend church hearing religious messages. (524)
10. _____Secularization of religion leads to a splintering of religious groups because some see it as a desertion of the group's fundamental beliefs. (527)

FILL-IN-THE-BLANK QUESTIONS

1. Sociologists do not seek to prove that one religion is _____ than another. (502)
2. According to Durkheim, church and _____ community were synonymous terms. (502)
3. Alcoholics Anonymous is a _____ equivalent of religion. (505)
4. A bar mitzvah is an example of a _____ practiced by Jews. (508)
5. A sudden awareness of the supernatural is known as a _____. (508)
6. When an offender is being ignored in all situations, they are being _____. (509)
7. Weber concluded that religion held the key to _____. (512)
8. The origin of Judaism is traced to _____. (513)
9. Today, _____ is the most popular religion in the world. (515)
10. The followers of Islam are known as _____. (516)

ESSAY QUESTIONS

1. Assume that you have been asked to make a presentation about religion to a group of people who have absolutely no idea what religion is. Prepare a speech in which you define religion and explain why it exists.

2. The functionalists point out the many functions of religion but also note how it has certain dysfunctions. Discuss both the functions and dysfunctions, and then consider whether it is possible for religion to fulfill its functions without producing dysfunctions.

3. Discuss the process by which a religion matures from a cult into a church.

4. Consider why fundamentalist Christian churches in the United States are currently undergoing a revival.

5. Discuss the major patterns of adaptation that occur when religion and culture conflict with one another.

CHAPTER 19
MEDICINE AND HEALTH

LEARNING OBJECTIVES

After reading Chapter 19, you should be able to:

1. Understand the role of sociology in studying medicine. (534)

2. Use the symbolic interactionist perspective to explain how culture affects health and illness. (534)

3. Identify the components of health. (534-535)

4. Know what is meant by the "sick role" and describe the social factors that can affect and/or influence people's claim to it. (535-536)

5. Explain how global stratification adversely affects the quality of medical care in the Least Industrialized Nations. (536-537)

6. Describe the process by which medicine was professionalized and monopolized in the United States, and discuss the consequences. (537-539)

7. Talk about the changes in health patterns in the United States over the past 100 years and the consequences of those changes. (539-541)

8. Identify the social inequalities in the American health care system. (541-543)

9. Describe the current problems in the American health care system, and discuss some of the attempts to deal with these problems. (541-551)

10. Identify the factors that contribute to the soaring costs of health care in the United States, and evaluate the job that HMOs and diagnosis-related groups are doing to help reduce those costs. (549-551)

11. Discuss the pros and cons of rationing medical care. (551-552)

12. Describe the major health threats in the United States and those that are worldwide issues. (551-560)

13. Discuss what can be done on the individual and group level to improve the quality of people's health and the health care system in the United States. (560-562)

Chapter Outline

I. **Sociology and the Study of Medicine and Health**
   A. Medicine is a society's standard way of dealing with illness and injury. U.S. medicine is a profession, a bureaucracy, and a big business.
   B. Sociologists study how medicine is influenced by ideals of professional self-regulation, the bureaucratic structure, and the profit motive; they also are interested in how illness and health are related to cultural beliefs, lifestyle, and social class.

II. **The Symbolic Interactionist Perspective**
   A. Health is affected by cultural beliefs.
      1. In Western culture a person who hears voices and sees visions might be locked up; in a tribal society, such an individual might be a shaman, the healing specialist who attempts to control the spirits thought to cause a disease or injury.
      2. "Sickness" and "health" are not absolutes but a matter of definition. We are provided with guidelines to determine whether we are healthy or sick.
   B. Expanding on the views of international health experts, the author of your text argues that health is a human condition measured by four components: physical, mental, social, and spiritual. What makes someone healthy varies from culture to culture. Sociologists analyze the effects that people's ideas of health and illness have on their lives and even how people determine that they are sick.

III. **The Functionalist Perspective**
   A. Functionalists point out that societies must set up ways to control sickness. They develop a system of medical care and make rules to keep too many people from "being sick."
   B. The "sick role" is a social role that you are forced to play when you are not well.
      1. It has four elements: (1) you are not held responsible for being sick; (2) you are exempt from normal responsibilities; (3) you don't like the role; and (4) you will get help so you can return to your usual routines. People who do not seek competent help are considered responsible for being sick and cannot claim sympathy from others.
      2. Often there is ambiguity between the well role and the sick role because most situations are not as clear-cut as having a heart attack. A decision to claim the sick role typically is more of a social than a physical matter.
      3. Parents and physicians are the primary gatekeepers, mediating between children's feelings of illness and the right to be released from responsibilities.
      4. Gender is a significant factor in the sick role. Women are more willing than men to claim the sick role when they don't feel well. They go to doctors more frequently than men, and they are hospitalized more often than men.

IV. The Conflict Perspective

A. The primary focus of conflict theorists is the struggle over scarce resources, including medical treatment.

B. One consequence of global domination by the Most Industrialized Nations is the international stratification of medical care.

1. The Least Industrialized Nations cannot afford the same lifesaving technology available in highly industrialized nations. Differences in life expectancy and infant mortality rates illustrate the consequences of global stratification.

2. Global stratification even changes the face of diseases. People living in the Least Industrialized Nations located in the tropics face illness and death from four major sources: malaria, internal parasites, diarrhea, and malnutrition. People in the Most Industrialized Nations live longer, with the consequence that they face "luxury" diseases such as heart disease and cancer.

3. Many diseases that ravage populations of poor countries are controllable; the problem is having the funds to spend on public health. Generally, the money is spent by members of the elite on themselves.

C. In order to understand how medicine grew into the largest business in the United States, it is necessary to understand how medicine became professionalized.

1. In the 1700s, a person learned to be a physician by becoming an apprentice or simply hanging out a shingle to proclaim that he was a physician. During the 1800s, a few medical schools opened and there was some licensing.

2. By 1906, the United States had 160 medical schools. The Carnegie Foundation funded Abraham Flexner to visit every medical school and make recommendations for change.

3. The Flexner Report resulted in the professionalization of medicine—the development of medicine into a field in which physicians undergo a rigorous education, claim an understanding of illness, regulate themselves, assert that they are performing a service for society, and take authority over clients.

4. Laws restricted medical licenses to graduates of approved schools; only graduates of these schools were eligible to be faculty members who trained the next generation of physicians. This select group of physicians gained control over U.S. medicine and set itself up as the medical establishment, taking control of medicine and either refusing to admit women and minorities to medical schools or placing severe enrollment limits on them. It wasn't until 1915 that the American Medical Association (AMA) allowed women members.

5. U.S. medicine always had a fee-for-service approach, but now it came under the physicians' control, who set their own fees and had no competition. Although the poor received services from some physicians and hospitals, many remained without medical care.

6. Until the 1960s, the medical establishment fought all proposals for government-funded medical treatment, including Medicare (government-sponsored medical insurance for the elderly) and Medicaid (government-paid medical care for the

poor). Following the creation of these programs, physicians discovered how lucrative they were.

7. The medical establishment consists not only of physicians, but also of nurses, hospital personnel, pharmaceutical companies, pharmacists, manufacturers of medical technology, and corporations that own hospitals.

V. Historical Patterns of Health

A. Epidemiology is the study of the distribution of medical disorders throughout a population; it provides answers about patterns of health and illness over time.

B. There are different ways of determining the current state of physical health in the United States.

    1. One way is to compare leading causes of death in 1900 to the present period. Four of the top ten causes of death in 1900 aren't even on the list today. Today's top two killers, heart disease and cancer, ranked fourth and eighth in 1900. Diabetes and Alzheimer's disease didn't make the top ten in 1900, but currently they do.

    2. Are Americans healthier today? If being healthier is measured by life expectancy, then Americans are healthier than their ancestors.

C. When it comes to mental health, no rational basis for comparisons exists. Perhaps there were fewer mental health problems in the past; however, it is also possible that there is greater mental health today than in the past.

VI. Issues in Health Care

A. A primary controversy in the United States is whether medical care is a right or a privilege. If it is a right, then all should have good access to it; if it is a privilege, then the rich will have access to one type of care and the poor another.

    1. Today, the average person living in the United States spends $8,000 a year on health care, as compared to spending $150 a year in 1960.

    2. Factors contributing to the increase in medical costs are the growing elderly population; the new expensive technology; and more expensive malpractice insurance.

B. Social class affects the incidence of illnesses and the quality of treatment.

    1. The lower the social class is, the higher is the proportion of serious mental problems. As compared with middle- and upper-class Americans, the poor have less job security, lower wages, more unpaid bills and insistent bill collectors, more divorce, greater vulnerability to crime, more alcoholism, and so on. Such conditions deal severe blows to their emotional well-being.

    2. In general, few poor people have a personal physician and often wait in crowded public health clinics to receive care. When hospitalized, the poor are often in understaffed/underfunded public hospitals, treated by rotation interns who do not know them and cannot follow up on their progress.

    3. The U.S. has a two-tiered system of medical care in which the wealthy receive superior medical care and the poor inferior medical care.

C. Prior to this century, doctors had four main treatments (purging, bleeding, blistering, and vomiting); today, science and technology have made advances, diagnoses are more accurate, and treatments are more effective.
   1. At the same time, the number of malpractice suits has risen; patients hold doctors to a higher standard and are quick to sue if there is a mistake.
   2. Physicians practice defensive medicine—that is, seeking consultations with colleagues and ordering additional lab tests—simply because a patient may sue. Defensive medicine greatly increases the cost of medicine.
D. While medical mistakes are not everyday occurrences, they do happen.
   1. Doctors correctly diagnose their patients' illnesses only 55 percent of the time.
   2. If death from medical errors were an official classification, it would rank as the sixth leading cause of death in the U.S.
   3. There are various suggestions for reducing the number of needless deaths. One recommendation is establish a Federal Center for Patient Safety to investigate medical injuries and deaths. Another suggestion is to implement a safety checklist for healthcare professionals to help avoid simple errors.
E. Depersonalization is the practice of dealing with people as though they were cases and diseases, not individuals.
   1. Many patients get the impression that they are trapped by a cash machine with physicians watching the clock and calculating dollars while talking to the patient.
   2. Although students begin medical school wanting to "treat the whole person," as they progress through school, their feelings for patients are overpowered by the need to be efficient.
F. Physicians may encounter conflicts of interest in prescribing medications, or referring patients to hospitals, pharmacies, or medical supply companies when they have a financial stake in the prescribed course of treatment.
G. Because of the high volume of health insurance claims that are filed on a daily basis (2 million Medicare claims daily), a large number of physicians, billing companies, and medical providers and suppliers are able to make fraudulent claims, engaging in medical fraud.
H. Medicine is not immune to sexism and racism; there is evidence that women and men and different racial–ethnic groups are treated differently by the medical establishment.
   1. Physicians do not take women's health complaints as seriously as they do men's.
I. Medicalization is the transformation of something into a matter to be treated by physicians. Examples include balding, weight, wrinkles, small breasts, and insomnia; yet there is nothing inherently medical in such conditions.
   1. Symbolic interactionists stress that medicalization is based on arbitrary definitions, part of a view of life that is bound to a specific historical period.
   2. Functionalists would stress how the medicalization of such issues is functional for the medical establishment since they can broaden their customer base. It also benefits patients who have someone to listen to their problems and who are sometimes helped.

3. Conflict sociologists assert that this process is another indication of the growing power of the medical establishment, and that as physicians medicalize more aspects of life, their power and profits increase.

J. With modern technology, machines can perform most bodily functions even when the person's mind no longer works; this has created the question, "Who has the right to pull the plug?"

1. Proponents of medically assisted suicides say that it allows people to die with dignity. Opponents say that it legalizes murder.

2. Some people believe that physicians should practice euthanasia (mercy killing) and help patients die if they request death to relieve insufferable pain or to escape from an incurable disease ("assisted suicide"). Others believe that this should never occur or that euthanasia should be allowed only in specific circumstances.

3. In Holland, in about 1,000 cases, physicians kill their patients without the patients' express consent.

4. Jack Kevorkian assisted 120 people in committing suicide. Eventually, he was convicted of second-degree murder and sentenced to 10 to 25 years in prison.

K. Medical costs in the United States have soared because of expensive technology, a growing elderly population, defensive medicine, and health care that operates as a commodity. There are attempts today to curb costs.

1. Health maintenance organizations (HMOs) represent a recent attempt to contain medical costs. HMOs are based on paying a predetermined fee to physicians to take care of the medical needs of employees. Although this arrangement may eliminate unnecessary procedures, it also creates pressure to reduce necessary medical treatment.

2. The federal government has classified all illnesses into 468 diagnostic-related groups and set the reimbursement amount for each. Hospitals make a profit only if they move patients through the system quickly. Although the average hospital stay has dropped, some patients are discharged before being fully ready to go home, and others are refused admittance because they might cost the hospital money instead of making it a profit.

3. One consequence of the desire to turn a profit on patient care is the practice of dumping, or sending unprofitable patients to public hospitals. With 44 million primarily poor Americans uninsured, pressure has grown for a national health insurance plan. Those in favor of national health care cite the social inequalities of medicine and the inadequacy of health care for the poor. Those opposed to national health insurance point to administrative concerns, such as the vast amount of red tape that would be required.

4. One maverick solution that has been implemented is to replace individual consultation with group care. For example, eight or ten pregnant women may go in for their obstetrics check-up together. Other doctors refuse to treat patients who want to pay by insurance. They have a pay-as-you-go system in which patients pay by cash, credit card, or check.

5. The most controversial suggestion is to ration medical care.

VII. Threats to Health
A. Acquired immune deficiency syndrome (AIDS) is probably the most pressing health issue in the world today.
1. In the United States, AIDS has been transformed from a death sentence to a chronic disease that can be managed with expensive drugs. Globally, it is still out of control, with Africa the hardest hit region in the world.
2. Its exact origin is unknown, although it is suspected that hunters who killed chimpanzees infected with a similar virus became infected through contact with the animals' blood.
3. It is transmitted through sexual contact and transfusions of contaminated blood. Patterns of transmission vary from one society to another.
4. AIDS hits men the hardest. However, in the United States, each year women account for a larger percentage of new cases. The risks vary by race and ethnicity; this is due to factors such as rates of intravenous drug use and the use of condoms, not to any genetic factors.
5. One of the most significant sociological aspects of AIDS is the stigma, which contributes to its spreading because people are afraid to be tested and stigmatized.
6. Drugs have been found to slow the progress of AIDS, but there is no cure.
B. As of 1998, two-thirds of Americans are overweight. We are the fattest nation on earth. People who are obese are more likely to have strokes, suffer heart attacks, diabetes, and cancer. The Centers for Disease Control recently found that being a little overweight is good. It may reduce bad cholesterol.
C. Alcohol and tobacco are the most frequently-used drugs in the United States.
1. Alcohol is the standard recreational drug in the United States. The average drinker in the United States consumes about 26 gallons of alcoholic beverages per year. Underage drinking is common.
2. Of all drugs, nicotine is the most harmful to health. Smoking increases a person's risk of heart attack and causes progressive emphysema and several types of cancer. People continue to smoke despite harmful health effects for two major reasons: addiction and advertising.
D. A disabling environment is one that is harmful to health.
1. Some occupations have high health risks that are evident (e.g., mining, riding bulls in a rodeo, and so on). In others, the risk becomes evident only after people have worked for years in what they thought was a safe occupation (e.g., laborers who worked with asbestos).
2. Industrialization not only increased the world's standard of living, but it has also led to the greenhouse effect, a warming of the Earth that may change the globe's climate, melt its polar ice caps, and flood its coastal shores. Use of fluorocarbon gases is threatening the ozone shield (the protective layer of the Earth's upper

stratosphere that screens out a high proportion of the sun's ultraviolet rays). In humans, this high-intensity ultraviolet radiation causes skin cancer.

E. At times, physicians and government officials have carried out research that has jeopardized the health and welfare of the individuals they are sworn to protect.

1. One example of such research is the Tuskegee Syphilis Experiment. In this experiment, 399 African American men suffering from syphilis were left untreated for 40 years so that the U.S. Public Health Service could observe what happened.

2. During the Cold War, the U.S. government conducted radiation experiments in which soldiers were ordered to march through an area just after an atomic bomb had been detonated. The purpose of this research was to determine if individuals could withstand fallout without any radiation equipment.

3. Those in official positions, in some instances, believe that they can play God and determine who shall live and who shall die. The most expendable citizens, and therefore the ones who serve as subjects in such research, are the poor and the powerless. In order to protect ourselves against such gross abuse of professional positions, such research must be publicized, and those who direct and carry out such experiments must be vigorously prosecuted.

F. Global travel has increased the number of diseases that are appearing worldwide. Antibiotics appear to be ineffective against many of them. So far, containment efforts have been successful.

VIII. Treatment or Prevention?

A. Values and lifestyles have a major impact on health.

1. Within the same society, subcultural patterns and lifestyles produce specific patterns of health and illness. For example, although Nevada and Utah are adjacent states with similar levels of income, education, medical care, and other assets, the death rate is much higher in Nevada. This is because Utah is inhabited mostly by Mormons, who encourage conservative living and disapprove of the consumption of tobacco, alcohol, and caffeine.

2. Many of the threats to health are preventable. Individuals can exercise regularly, eat nutritious food, maintain sexual monogamy, and avoid smoking and alcohol abuse in order to prevent disease.

3. Instead of treatment, the U.S. medical establishment should have "wellness" as its goal. To achieve such a goal the medical establishment must make a fundamental change in its philosophy and see profitability in keeping patients well.

4. On a broader scale, there needs to be a systematic attempt to eliminate disabling environments and the use of harmful drugs.

IX. The Future of Medicine

1. Alternative medicine refers to nontraditional medicine typically imported from Asian cultures. Most Western doctors have regarded alternative medicine as a superstitious practice. However, many U.S. patients have begun to demand alternative medicine, and the U.S. medical establishment has started to accommodate those demands.

2. Technology is bound to change medicine as it does every aspect of our society. Medicine in the United States is moving into the digital age as, for instance, patients can now visit their doctors online.

Chapter Summary

"Medicine" refers to a society's standard ways of dealing with illness and injury. The sociology of medicine is one of the applied fields of sociology, and it is one of the social institutions that sociologists study. As practiced in the United States, medicine is a profession, a bureaucracy, and a business.

For symbolic interactionists, definitions of health and illness are influenced by culture. As such, what is defined as "healthy" or "sick" varies from culture to culture and, in a pluralistic society, from group to group. Hence, sickness and health are not absolute terms but matters of definition. Each culture provides guidelines that its people use to determine whether they are "healthy" or "sick."

Functionalists examine how societies set up ways to control sickness and make up rules to keep too many people from "being sick." They do this so their members can continue to perform their functional roles and activities. The primary method functionalists use to restrict too many people in society from "being sick" is the sick role. The sick role excuses those who are ill from completing their normal responsibilities. In exchange, the sick individuals make a sincere effort to seek competent help so they can return to their routine.

For conflict theorists, health care is a scarce resource for which groups compete. On a global level, the people in the world's industrialized nations have better access to quality health care and, consequently, enjoy better physical health than the people in the world's poorer nations. Global stratification also has a major bearing on what diseases people contract and on their life expectancy.

The medical profession has not always enjoyed the high prestige that it does today. Prior to 1800, someone could become a physician through apprenticeship or even be self-trained. In 1906, the 160 medical schools that existed in the United States were evaluated by the Carnegie Foundation. This led to external funding and the raising of standards in the most promising schools. In turn, medicine was professionalized and monopolized in the United States by a "medical establishment" that turned medicine into the largest business in the country.

With advances in medicine, health patterns changed dramatically in the United States. Compared to Americans 100 years ago, we now live longer and healthier lives. Mental health, on the other hand, is not as easy to evaluate. Although there are indicators that Americans were happier in the past, some of these indicators are no more than myths. In reality, it is difficult to judge how extensive mental illness is today or to make comparisons between the past and present.

Because medical care is a commodity, not a right, in the United States, America has developed a two-tiered system of medical care. This includes quality medical care for those who can afford it or have adequate public or private health care insurance and inferior medical care for those who cannot afford it.

Current problems in the American health care system include the practice of defensive medicine, medical incompetence, depersonalization of care, a conflict of interest created as insurance carriers place profit over the health of the insured, medical fraud, sexism in medicine, the medicalization of society, and medically-assisted suicide.

A significant problem in the American health care system is the soaring cost of preventing, diagnosing, and treating medical problems. Attempts to curb these costs include the establishment of health maintenance organizations (HMOs) and diagnosis-related groups. Although such programs have been effective in reducing costs, they have often done so at the expense of denying needed care to patients. Two controversial proposals for dealing with the problem of spiraling health care costs include the establishment of a national health insurance plan and rationing medical care.

As we enter the twenty-first century, major threats to health loom both in the United States and worldwide. These threats include AIDS, obesity, drugs, disabling environments, misguided medical experiments, and the globalization of disease. Although AIDS has been brought under control in the United States, it is the leading cause of death in sub-Saharan Africa. Other issues that are more threatening to Americans than AIDS include obesity, alcohol abuse, the use of nicotine, and the health risks associated with working in unsafe environments.

Improving the quality of people's health in the United States requires, on the individual level, getting people to adopt healthier lifestyles and, on the group level, practicing preventive medicine.

KEY TERMS

After studying the chapter, review the definition for each of the following terms.

alternative medicine: medical treatment other than that of standard Western medicine (also called *nontraditional medicine*); often refers to practices that originate in Asia, but may also refer to taking vitamins not prescribed by a doctor (561)

defensive medicine: medical practices done not for the patient's benefit but in order to protect a physician from malpractice suits (544)

depersonalization: dealing with people as though they were objects; in the case of medical care, as though patients were merely cases and diseases, not people (545)

disabling environment: an environment that is harmful to health (558)

dumping: the practice of sending unprofitable patients to public hospitals (551)

epidemiology: the study of disease and disability patterns in a population (539)

euthanasia: mercy killing (548)

fee-for-service: payment to a physician to diagnose and treat the patient's medical problems (539)

health: a human condition measured by four components: physical, mental, social, and spiritual (534)

medicalization: the transformation of a human condition into a matter to be treated by physicians (547)

medicine: one of the major social institutions that sociologists study; a society's organized ways of dealing with sickness and injury (534)

professionalization of medicine: the development of medicine into a specialty in which education becomes rigorous and physicians claim a theoretical understanding of illness, regulate themselves, claim to be doing a service to society (rather than just following self-interest), and take authority over clients (539)

shaman: the healing specialist of a tribe who attempts to control the spirits thought to cause a disease or injury; commonly called a witch doctor (534)

sick role: a social role that excuses people from normal obligations because they are sick or injured, while at the same time expecting them to seek competent help and cooperate in getting well (559)

two-tier system of medical care: a system in which the wealthy receive superior medical care and the poor inferior medical care (543)

KEY PEOPLE

Review the major theoretical contributions or findings of these people.

Jack Haas and William Shaffir: These sociologists did a participant observation of medical students and discovered that over the course of medical school their attitudes change from wanting to "treat the whole person" to needing to be efficient in treating the specific ailment. (546)

Talcott Parsons: Parsons was the first sociologist to analyze the sick role, pointing out that it has four elements: (1) not being responsible for your sickness; (2) being exempt from normal responsibilities; (3) not liking the role; and (4) seeking competent help in order to return to daily routines. (535)

SELF-TEST

MULTIPLE CHOICE QUESTIONS

1. Sociologists focus on medicine as (534)
    a.   a profession.
    b.   a bureaucracy.
    c.   a business.
    d.   all of the above

2. A _____ is the healing specialist of a preliterate tribe who tries to control the spirits thought to cause a disease or injury. (534)
    a.   soothsayer
    b.   high priest
    c.   shaman
    d.   medicine man

3. As practiced in the U.S., the primary characteristics of the social institution of medicine include all of the following except (536-539)
    a.   personalization.
    b.   professionalization.
    c.   bureaucracy.
    d.   profit motive.

4. How would a sick or injured person who can't fulfill normal role obligations be described? (535-536)
    a.   a hypochondriac
    b.   in the sick role
    c.   deviant
    d.   all of the above

5. The individual's claim to the sick role is legitimized primarily by (535-536)
    a.   demonstrating to others that he or she is ill.
    b.   a doctor's excuse.
    c.   employers, teachers, and sometimes parents.
    d.   other workers or students who vouch for the individual that is ill.

6. Why are women more likely than men to claim the sick role when they feel poorly? (536)
    a.   They are generally not as healthy as men.
    b.   They have more reasons to see a doctor than men because of reproductive problems.
    c.   They are socialized for greater dependency and self-disclosure.
    d.   All of the above

7. Which sociological perspective views health care as one of the scarce resources over which groups compete? (536)
   a. symbolic interactionism
   b. functionalism
   c. conflict theory
   d. feminism

8. Professionalization of medicine includes (537)
   a. rigorous education.
   b. a theoretical understanding of illness.
   c. self-regulation.
   d. all of the above

9. Which of the following statements about the medical monopoly is *incorrect*? (537-539)
   a. While doctors were able to control women's access to medical schools, they were never very effective in keeping other minorities out.
   b. The medical establishment was able to get laws passed to restrict medical licensing to graduates of approved schools.
   c. Because they operated as a monopoly, they were able to set themselves up as the most lucrative profession in the country, setting their own fees and controlling competition.
   d. The medical establishment was so powerful it was able to take childbirth away from the control of midwives.

10. The inverse correlation between mental problems and social class is apparent in that (542)
    a. the lower the social class, the less mental problems there are.
    b. the lower the social class, the more mental problems there are.
    c. the higher the social class, the more mental problems there are.
    d. none of the above

11. What is the study of disease and disability patterns in a population? (539)
    a. epidemiology
    b. anatomy
    c. biology
    d. demography

12. Today, the average American spends _____ a year on health care. (542)
    a. $150
    b. $1,100
    c. $4,500
    d. $8,000

13. In the United States, medical care is (541)
    a. a right.

b. a commodity.
c. socialized.
d. none of the above

14. According to the author of your text, why has the practice of defensive medicine grown in recent decades? (544)
    a. Doctors have found that they can provide the best care when they order a whole set of tests.
    b. The federal government requires such tests in order to protect patient interests.
    c. The insurance companies are willing to cover the costs of extensive tests.
    d. Doctors want to establish a paper trail to protect themselves in the event they are sued by a disgruntled patient.

15. Which of the following statements about depersonalization is *incorrect*? (545)
    a. It is less common today because of all the reforms brought about by HMOs.
    b. It is the practice of dealing with people as though they were objects.
    c. It means treating patients as though they were merely cases and diseases.
    d. It occurs when an individual is treated as if he or she was not a person.

16. What underlies the sexism that continues to exist within medicine? (547)
    a. ignorance
    b. male doctors are not sensitive to women's needs
    c. continuing male dominance of medicine
    d. women's willingness to accept the status quo

17. _____ is the transformation of something into a matter to be treated by physicians. (547)
    a. Sexism in medicine
    b. Medicalization of society
    c. Monopolization of medicine
    d. Holistic medicine

18. The state of _____ passed a law allowing for medically assisted suicide. (549)
    a. Oregon
    b. California
    c. Florida
    d. Ohio

19. Which of these is *not* a reason why U.S. medical costs have risen dramatically? (549-551)
    a. Tests are performed for defensive rather than medical reasons.
    b. The size of the elderly population has increased.
    c. People want doctors to do unnecessary tests to assure themselves they are healthy.
    d. Health care is seen as a commodity.

20. AIDS is known to be transmitted by (553)
    a. casual contact between a carrier and a noncarrier in which bodily fluids are exchanged.
    b. exchange of blood and/or semen.
    c. airborne passage of the virus from carrier to non-carrier through coughing or sneezing.
    d. all of the above

21. Which racial and/or ethnic group is at greater risk of contracting AIDS? (553)
    a. Whites
    b. African Americans
    c. Latinos
    d. Asian Americans

22. _____ is more life threatening to Americans than AIDS or alcohol abuse. (557)
    a. Smoking
    b. Obesity
    c. Accidents
    d. SARS

23. Which of the following statements about smoking is *incorrect*? (557)
    a. Nicotine may be as addictive as heroin.
    b. The rate of cigarette smoking continues to climb, despite warnings about the dangers.
    c. The tobacco industry has a huge advertising budget to encourage people to smoke.
    d. When compared with nonsmokers, smokers are three times as likely to die before age 65.

24. An example of physicians' and the government's callous disregard of people's health is (558)
    a. the delay in providing open heart surgery for women patients.
    b. the Tuskegee Syphilis Experiment.
    c. the failure to curb advertising of tobacco products.
    d. all of the above

25. To implement a national policy of "prevention, not intervention" would require (561)
    a. a fundamental change in the philosophy of the medical establishment.
    b. a change in the public's attitudes toward medicine and health care.
    c. eliminating disabling environments and reducing the use of harmful drugs.
    d. all of the above

TRUE-FALSE QUESTIONS

1. _____ Health is not only a biological matter, but it is also intimately related to society. (534)

2. _____People who don't seek competent help when they are sick are just behaving as expected, according to the social definition of the sick role. (535)
3. _____There is little ambiguity between the well role and the sick role. (535)
4. _____Professionalization of medicine includes self-regulation of physicians. (539)
5. _____An international black market exists for selling human body parts. (538)
6. _____Women were allowed to be members of the American Medical Association in 1915. (539)
7. _____People receive equal medical treatment regardless of social class. (541)
8. _____Today in the United States, AIDS is viewed as a chronic disease that can be controlled with medications. (551)
9. _____In general, people are very aware when they are working in a disabling environment, one that is harmful to their health. (558)
10. _____Acupuncture is a form of alternative medicine that has become accepted in U.S. medical practice. (561)

FILL-IN-THE-BLANK QUESTIONS

1. When medicine became a profession, it also became a _____. (539)
2. According to the conflict perspective, the struggle between doctors and midwives was really a _____ struggle. (540)
3. Diabetes and _____ now make the top ten list of causes of death in the U.S. (541)
4. A primary controversy in the United States is whether or not medical care is a _____ or a privilege. (541)
5. To protect themselves from malpractice suits, physicians practice _____ medicine. (544)
6. If the number of Americans killed by medical _____ were an official classification of death, it would rank as one of the top ten leading causes of death. (544)
7. To curb spiraling costs, the federal government has classified all illnesses into _____. (550)
8. The most controversial suggestion for how to reduce medical costs is to _____ medical care. (551-552)
9. In sub-Saharan Africa, _____ is the leading cause of death. (553)
10. From the perspective of Western medical theory, _____ medicine does not make sense. (561)

ESSAY QUESTIONS

1. Describe the elements of the sick role, and identify variations in the pattern of claiming this role.

2. Discuss why medicine developed into a monopoly in this country and what the consequences of this development have been for the delivery of medical treatment.

3. Explain the pattern of the worldwide AIDS epidemic, and suggest reasons why this threat to the health of the world's population has not been addressed more aggressively.

4. Define depersonalization and present evidence from the chapter as to its presence within medicine. Consider why it is present in a system that is supposed to care about an individual who is sick or injured.

5. Discuss a couple of threats to health either in the United States or worldwide.

CHAPTER 20
POPULATION AND URBANIZATION

LEARNING OBJECTIVES

After reading Chapter 20, you should be able to:

1. Know what is meant by "the Malthus theorem" and state the major points and counterpoints in the debate between the New Malthusians and the Anti-Malthusians. (568-571)

2. Identify the primary causes of famines and starvation. (571-573)

3. Understand why people in the Least Industrialized Nations have so many children, and discuss the implications of different rates of population growth. (573-576)

4. Describe the three demographic variables used to estimate population growth, and explain why it is difficult to forecast population growth. (577-580)

5. Define urbanization and trace the development of cities from ancient times through industrialization. (583)

6. Know the trends contributing to the emergence of metropolises and megalopolises. (583, 586)

7. Identify urban patterns in the United States. (586-590)

8. Describe and evaluate the four models of urban growth. (590-592)

9. Discuss how some people find a sense of community in cities, while others become alienated. (592, 594)

10. Describe the five types of urban dwellers identified by sociologist Herbert Gans. (595)

11. Explain why many urban dwellers follow a norm of noninvolvement and how this norm, in turn, may contribute to a dysfunctional diffusion of responsibility. (595-596)

12. Identify the primary problems of urban life today, and discuss how suburbanization, disinvestment, and deindustrialization contribute to these problems. (596, 598)

13. Know why large numbers of Americans have begun moving from cities and suburbs to rural areas. (596, 598)

14. Evaluate current attempts to address urban problems in the United States, and discuss the three guiding principles for developing future policies to deal with these problems. (599-600)

<u>**Chapter Outline**</u>

I. Population in Global Perspective

A. Demography is the study of size, composition, growth, and distribution of populations.

II. A Planet with No Space for Enjoying Life?

A. Thomas Malthus wrote *An Essay on the Principle of Population* (1798) stating the Malthus theorem: population grows geometrically while food supply increases arithmetically; thus if births go unchecked, population will outstrip food supplies.

B. New Malthusians believe Malthus was correct. The world population is following an exponential growth curve (where numbers increase in extraordinary proportions): 1800, one billion; 1930, two billion; 1960, three billion; 1975, four billion; 1987, five billion; 1999, six billion; And in 2011, seven billion.

C. Anti-Malthusians believe that the three-stage process of population growth, known as the demographic transition, provides a model for the future.

    1. They cite the historical experiences of European countries over the last two centuries as an example.

    2. Stage 1 is characterized by a fairly stable population (high birth rates offset by high death rates); stage 2, by a "population explosion" (high birth rates and low death rates); and stage 3, by population stability (low birth rates and low death rates).

    3. They assert this transition will happen in the Least Industrialized Nations, which currently are in the second stage.

D. Who is correct? Only the future will prove the accuracy of the projections of either the New Malthusians or the Anti-Malthusians.

    1. The Least Industrialized Nations are currently in stage 2 of the demographic transition—their birth rates remain high, while the death rates have dropped.

    2. There are signs that birth rates in the Least Industrialized Nations are dropping, but the two sides greet this news differently. The New Malthusians say that the populations in the Least Industrialized Nations will continue to climb, only at a slower rate, while the Anti-Malthusians say that the slow rate is a sign that these nations are beginning to move into stage 3.

    3. Population shrinkage (a country's population is smaller because birth rate and immigration cannot replace those who die and emigrate) is now occurring in 65 nations, suggesting a fourth stage to the demographic transition.

    4. Some Anti-Malthusians predict a "demographic free fall." Eventually, the world's population will peak at 8 or 9 billion and then begin to grow smaller.

E. Why are people starving?

1. Anti-Malthusians note that the amount of food produced for each person in the world has increased: famines are not the result of too little food production but of maldistribution of existing food.
2. The New Malthusians counter that the world's population continues to grow, and the Earth may not be able to continue to produce sufficient food.
3. Recently, famines have been concentrated in Africa. However, these famines are not due to too many people living on too little land. Rather, these famines are due to drought, outmoded farming techniques, and ongoing political instability that disrupt harvests and food distribution.
4. Starvation in Africa is a result of the maldistribution of food rather than overpopulation.

III. Population Growth

A. Three reasons poor nations have so many children are (1) the status that parenthood provides; (2) the community supports this view; and (3) children are considered to be economic assets (the parents rely on the children to take care of them in their old age).
   1. The symbolic interactionist perspective stresses that we need to understand these patterns within the framework of the culture and society in which the behavior occurs.
   2. The conflict perspective stresses that in the Least Industrialized Nations, men dominate women in all spheres of life, including that of reproduction. There is an emphasis on male virility and dominance, including the fathering of many children, as a means of achieving status in the community.
B. Demographers use population pyramids (graphic representations of a population, divided into age and sex) to illustrate a country's population dynamics.
   1. Different population growth rates have different implications. Countries with rapid growth rates have to cope with increased numbers of people among whom to share resources; this can result in a declining standard of living.
   2. A declining standard of living may result in political instability followed by severe repression by the government.
C. Estimated population growth is based on three demographic variables:
   1. Fertility, measured by the fertility rate (number of children an average woman bears), is sometimes confused with fecundity (number of children a woman theoretically can bear). To compute a country's fertility rate, demographers use crude birth rate (annual number of births per 1,000 people).
   2. Middle Africa has the highest fertility rate and Macao and Hong Kong have the lowest fertility rates.
   3. Mortality, measured by the crude death rate (number of deaths per 1,000 people). The highest death rates occur in Afghanistan in Asia and the lowest, in Qatar, another Asian country.
   4. Migration, measured by the net migration rate (difference between the number of immigrants moving in and emigrants moving out per 1,000 population).

(a) There are two types: movement between regions within a country and movement between countries. "Push" factors make people want to leave where they are living (e.g., persecution, lack of economic opportunity); "pull" factors attract people (e.g., opportunities in the new locale).

(b) Around the world, the flow of migration is from the Least Industrialized Nations to the Industrialized Nations. The U.S. admits more immigrants each year than all the other nations of the world combined.

(c) There is a debate as to whether immigrants are a net contributor or a drain on our economy.

D. The growth rate equals births minus deaths plus net migration.

1. Economic changes, wars, famines, and plagues all make it difficult to forecast population growth. The primary unknown factor that influences a country's growth rate is its rate of industrialization—in every country that industrializes, the growth rate declines. Industrialization creates new opportunities for work, but it also makes it more expensive to have children.

2. Some countries are concerned about underpopulation. Other countries, like China, are concerned about overpopulation and have instituted policies to limit childbearing.

3. Because of the difficulties in forecasting population growth, demographers formulate several predictions simultaneously, each depending on different assumptions.

IV. Urbanization

An introduction to what was once a garbage dump, now the district of El Tiro in Medellin, Colombia, provides a context for understanding urban life.

V. The Development of Cities

A. A city is a place in which a large number of people are permanently based and do not produce their own food. Small cities with massive defensive walls existed as far back as 10,000 years ago; cities on a larger scale originated about 3500 B.C. as a result of the development of more efficient agriculture and a food surplus. The key to the origin of cities is the development of more efficient agriculture.

B. The Industrial Revolution drew people to cities to work. Today, urbanization means not only that more people live in cities, but also that today's cities are larger; today well over 300 of the world's cities contain at least 1 million people.

C. Urbanization is the process by which an increasing proportion of a population lives in cities. There are specific characteristics of cities, such as size and anonymity, that give them their unique urban flavor.

1. A "metropolis" refers to a city that grows so large that it exerts influence over a region; the central city and surrounding smaller cities and suburbs are connected economically, politically, and socially.

2. A "megalopolis" refers to an overlapping area consisting of at least two metropolises and their many suburbs.

3. A "megacity" is a city of 10 million or more residents. Today there are 19 megacities, and most are located in the Least Industrialized Nations.

D. In 1790, only about 5 percent of Americans lived in cities; by 1920, 50 percent of the U.S. population lived in urban areas; today, 79 percent of Americans live in urban areas.

1. The U.S. Census Bureau divided the country into 274 metropolitan statistical areas (MSAs), which consist of a central city of at least 50,000 people and the urbanized areas that are linked to it. About 60 percent of the entire U.S. population lives in just fifty or so MSAs.

2. As Americans migrate in search of work and better lifestyles, a two-way pattern of migration between regions appears. Today, five of the ten fastest-growing U.S. cities are in the West and five are in the South. Of the ten shrinking cities, most are in the Northeast.

3. As Americans migrate and businesses move to serve them, edge cities have developed (a clustering of service facilities and residential areas near highway intersections).

4. Gentrification, the movement of middle-class people into rundown areas of a city, is another major U.S. urban pattern. As a consequence of gentrification, the poor are often displaced from their neighborhoods. A common pattern is for the gentrifiers to be white and the displaced to be minorities.

5. Suburbanization is the movement from the city to the suburbs. The automobile served as the major impetus for suburbanization. Also, after racial integration occurred, many whites fled the cities.

6. The most recent trend is the development of micropolitan areas. A micropolis is a city of 10,000 to 50,000 residents that is not a suburb.

7. Some Americans are retreating to rural areas. Fears of urban crime and violence are "push" factors. The "pull" factors to these rural areas are safety, lower cost of living, and more living space.

VI. Models of Urban Growth

A. Robert Park coined the term "human ecology" to describe how people adapt to their environment (known as "urban ecology"); human ecologists have constructed four models that attempt to explain urban growth patterns.

B. Ernest W. Burgess proposed the concentric zone model.

1. The city consists of a series of zones emanating from its center, with each characterized by a different group of people and activity: zone 1 is the central business district; zone 2 is in transition, with deteriorating housing and rooming houses; zone 3 is an area to which thrifty workers have moved to escape the zone in transition while maintaining access to work; zone 4 is more expensive apartments, single-family dwellings, and exclusive areas where the wealthy live; and zone 5 is a commuter zone consisting of suburban areas or satellite cities that have developed around rapid transit routes.

2. Burgess intended this model to represent the tendency for towns and cities to expand outward from the central business district.

C. Homer Hoyt proposed the sector model, which sees urban zones as wedge-shaped sectors radiating out from the center.
   1. A zone might contain a sector of working-class housing, another sector of expensive housing, a third of businesses, and so on, all competing with one another for the same land.
   2. In an invasion-succession cycle, poor immigrants move into a city, settling in the lowest-rent area available to them; as their numbers grow, they begin to encroach upon adjacent areas. As the poor move closer to the middle class, the middle class leave, expanding the sector of lower-cost housing.

D. The multiple-nuclei model, developed by Chauncey Harris and Edward Ullman, views the city as composed of multiple centers, or nuclei, each of which focuses on a specialized activity (e.g., retail districts, automobile dealers, and others).

E. Chauncey Harris later developed the peripheral model of urban development to account for more recent changes in the use of urban space. In this model, people and services move away from the central city into the periphery; highways radiating out from the center encourage this development along the edges of metropolitan areas.

F. These models tell only a partial story of how cities are constructed. They reflect both the time frame and geographical region of the cities that were studied. They cannot explain medieval cities or cities in other Most Industrialized or Least Industrialized Nations.

VII. City Life

A. Cities provide opportunities but also create problems. Humans have a need for community, which some people have a hard time finding in cities, leading them to experience alienation.

B. Louis Wirth argued that the city undermines kinship and neighborhood, which are the traditional bases of social control and social solidarity.
   1. Urban dwellers live in anonymity; their lives marked by segmented and superficial encounters that make them grow aloof from one another and indifferent to other people's problems.

C. The city can also be viewed as containing a series of smaller worlds, within which people find a sense of community or belonging.

D. Herbert Gans identified five types of people who live in the city.
   1. Cosmopolites—intellectuals, professionals, students, writers, and artists who live in the inner city to be near its conveniences and cultural benefits.
   2. Singles—young, unmarried people who come seeking jobs and entertainment.
   3. Ethnic villagers—live in tightly knit neighborhoods that resemble villages and small towns; they are united by ethnicity and social class.
   4. The deprived—the very poor or emotionally disturbed individuals who live in neighborhoods more like urban jungles than urban villages.

5. The trapped—(1) those who could not afford to move when their neighborhood was invaded by another ethnic group; (2) downwardly mobile persons who have fallen from a higher social class; (3) elderly people who have drifted into the slums because they are not wanted elsewhere and are powerless to prevent their downward slide; and (4) alcoholics and drug addicts.

E. The city is divided into worlds that people come to know down to the smallest detail.
   1. City people create a sense of intimacy for themselves by personalizing their shopping (by frequenting the same stores and restaurants, people become recognized as "regulars").
   2. Spectator sports also engender community identification. People maintain emotional allegiances to the team of the city in which they grew up even if they have moved to other parts of the country.

F. Urban dwellers are careful to protect themselves from the unwanted intrusions of strangers.
   1. They follow a norm of noninvolvement, such as using a newspaper or a Walkman to indicate inaccessibility for interaction, to avoid encounters with people they do not know.
   2. The more bystanders there are to an incident, the less likely people are to help because people's sense of responsibility becomes diffused.
   3. The norm of noninvolvement and the diffusion of responsibility may help urban dwellers get through everyday city life, but they are dysfunctional because people do not provide assistance to others.

VIII. Urban Problems and Social Policy

A. U.S. cities have declined due to suburbanization and disinvestment and deindustrialization.
   1. As people have moved out of the city, so have the businesses and jobs.
   2. This shift has left behind people who had no choice but to live in the city. William Wilson notes that this transformed the inner city into a ghetto. Those left behind were trapped by poverty, unemployment, and welfare dependency and became the victims of street crime.
   3. The automobile has been a major fuel for suburbanization. This trend accelerated after the racial integration of schools in the 1950s and 1960s, as whites fled the cities.
   4. Suburbanites, preferring that the city keep its problems to itself, fight movements to share suburbia's revenues with the city. However, the time may come when suburbanites may have to pay for their attitudes toward the city.
   5. As suburbs age, they are becoming mirror images of the city, leading to a spiraling sense of insecurity, more middle-class flight, and a further reduction of property values.

B. As the cities' tax base shrank and services declined, neighborhoods deteriorated.

1. Banks began redlining. That is, they drew a line on a map around problem areas and refused to make loans for housing and businesses located in these areas. This disinvestment pushed these areas into further decline.
2. The development of a global market has led to deindustrialization. Manufacturing firms have relocated from the inner city to areas where production costs are lower. As millions of urban manufacturing jobs were eliminated, inner-city economies were unable to provide alternative employment for poor residents, thereby locking them out of the economy.

C. Social policy usually takes one of two forms.
1. Urban renewal involves tearing down and rebuilding the buildings in an area. As a result of urban renewal, residents can no longer afford to live in the area and are displaced to adjacent areas.
2. Enterprise zones are economic incentives to encourage businesses to move into the area. Most businesses, however, refuse to move into high-crime areas.

D. If U.S. cities are to change, they must become top-agenda items of the U.S. government, with adequate resources in terms of money and human talents focused on overcoming urban woes.
1. William Flanagan suggests three guiding principles for working out specific solutions to urban problems: (1) regional and national planning is necessary; (2) growth needs to be channeled in such a way that makes city living attractive; and (3) social policy must be evaluated in terms of its effects on people.
2. Finally, unless the root causes of urban problems, such as poverty, poor schools, and lack of jobs, are addressed, solutions will serve only as Band-Aids that cover the real problems.

Chapter Summary

The study of the size, composition, growth, and distribution of human populations is called *demography*. Among its objectives, demography makes an effort to predict world population growth and whether or not the planet will be able to support its future population.

Over 200 years ago, Thomas Malthus observed that populations grow geometrically, while food supplies increase arithmetically. In his classic book, *An Essay on the Principle of Population* (1798), Malthus warned that at the current rate of growth (based on statistics available in the eighteenth century) the population of the world would outstrip its food supply. Referred to as the "Malthus theorem," demographers continue to debate the accuracy of Malthus' original prediction. The "New Malthusians" agree with Malthus' original grim calculations. Another group, the "Anti-Malthusians," contends that world population growth is slowing, and the problem in the future will be too few babies being born, not too many. It is too early to tell who is right, the New Malthusians or Anti-Malthusians.

The New Malthusians point out that millions of people are starving worldwide, which supports their argument. Even though some parts of the world are decimated by famines, the amount of food currently produced worldwide is higher than ever. These famines are primarily caused by drought, inefficient farming, and wars that disrupt harvests and food distributions, *not* by overpopulation.

The population of the Least Industrialized Nations is growing about sixteen times faster than that of the Most Industrialized Nations. At these rates it will take 800 years for the Most Industrialized Nations to double in population, but only 42 years for the Least Industrialized Nations to do so. People in the Least Industrialized Nations continue to have large families because parenthood elevates their status and large numbers of children are economic assets. The implication of these different growth rates can be illustrated using population pyramids—graphic representations of a population divided into age and sex.

To project population trends, demographers use three demographic variables: fertility, mortality, and migration. Fertility refers to the number of children the average woman bears, while mortality is measured by the crude death rate (the annual number of deaths per 1,000 population). Known as the basic demographic equation, the growth rate equals births minus deaths, plus net migration. The growth rate is affected by anticipated variables, such as the percentage of women who are in their childbearing years, and unanticipated variables, such as wars, famines, and changing economic and political conditions.

Industrialization is the primary factor that influences a country's growth rate. In every country that industrializes, the growth rate declines and the standard of living improves, including life expectancy. The invention of the plow, which predates the Industrial Revolution, led to the development of cities. For most of human history, cities were small. After the Industrial Revolution, the number and size of cities in the world grew rapidly. As cities grew, so did their influence. Urbanization is so extensive today that many cities have become metropolises, and some metropolises have expanded into megalopolises.

Of special interest to sociologists is people adapt to their environment. Known as human ecology or urban ecology, there are four major models of urban growth. These include the concentric zone model, the sector model, the multiple-nuclei model, and the peripheral model. Another important aspect of urban sociology includes an analysis of who lives in cities and why. Herbert Gans identified five types of urban dwellers: cosmopolites, singles, ethnic villagers, the deprived, and the trapped.

Some people find a sense of community in cities; others find alienation. To create a sense of intimacy, many people who live in cities personalize their shopping, identify with sports teams, and develop sentimental attachments to their city. A common characteristic of city dwellers is that they follow a norm of noninvolvement. This norm, in turn, contributes to a diffusion of responsibility that can be dysfunctional in emergency situations.

The primary problems of urban life today are poverty, decay, and a general decline of quality of life exacerbated by suburbanization, disinvestment, and deindustrialization. Reversing past trends, large numbers of Americans are now moving from cities and suburbs to rural areas. The potential for urban revitalization is based on several factors. A combination of urban renewal and the development of enterprise zones have traditionally been used in an effort to improve cities. Although successful to some degree, each of these is accompanied by other problems they create, such as the displacement of people who once lived in the areas of the city targeted for improvement. Replacing old buildings with new ones is not necessarily the answer. To be truly successful, efforts to improve cities and city life need to follow three guiding principles. These include scale (regional and national planning), livability (appeal to human need), and social justice (how it affects people).

KEY TERMS

After studying the chapter, review the definition for each of the following terms.

alienation: Marx's term for workers' lack of connection to the product of their labor; caused by workers being assigned repetitive tasks on a small part of a product, which leads to a sense of powerlessness and normlessness. Others use the term in the general sense of not feeling a part of something (592)

basic demographic equation: the growth rate equals births minus deaths plus net migration (579)

city: a place in which a large number of people are permanently based and do not produce their own food (583)

crude birth rate: the annual number of live births per 1,000 population (577)

crude death rate: the annual number of deaths per 1,000 population (577)

deindustrialization: The process of industries moving out of a country or region (598)

demographic transition: a three-stage historical process of population growth: first, high birth rates and high death rates; second, high birth rates and low death rates; and third, low birth rates and low death rates; a fourth stage in which deaths outnumber births has made its appearance in the Most Industrialized Nations (570)

demographic variables: the three factors that influence population growth: fertility, mortality, and net migration (577)

demography: the study of the size, composition, growth, and distribution of human populations (568)

disinvestment: the withdrawal of investments by financial institutions, which seals the fate of an urban area (598)

enterprise zone: the use of economic incentives in a designated area to encourage investment (599)

edge city: a large clustering of service facilities and residential areas near highway intersections that provides a sense of place to people who live, shop, and work there (588)

exponential growth curve: a pattern of growth in which numbers double during approximately equal intervals, showing a steep acceleration in the later stages (568)

fecundity: the number of children that women are capable of bearing (577)

fertility rate: the number of children that the average woman bears (577)

gentrification: middle-class people moving into a rundown area of a city, displacing the poor as they buy and restore homes (588)

growth rate: the net change in a population after adding births, subtracting deaths, and either adding or subtracting net migration (579)

human ecology: Robert Park's term for the relationship between people and their environment (such as land and structures); also known as *urban ecology* (590)

invasion-succession cycle: the process of one group of people displacing a group whose racial–ethnic or social class characteristics differ from their own (591)

Malthus theorem: an observation by Thomas Malthus that although the food supply increases arithmetically (from 1 to 2 to 3 to 4 and so on), population grows geometrically (from 2 to 4 to 8 to 16 and so forth) (568)

megacity: a city of 10 million or more residents (586)

megalopolis: an urban area consisting of at least two metropolises and their many suburbs (586)

metropolis: a central city surrounded by smaller cities and their suburbs (583)

metropolitan statistical area (MSA): a central city and the urbanized counties adjacent to it (586)

net migration rate: the difference between the number of immigrants and emigrants per 1,000 population (578)

population pyramid: a graph that represents the age and sex of a population (576)

population shrinkage: the process by which a country's population becomes smaller because its birth rate and immigration are too low to replace those who die and emigrate (595)

redlining: a decision by the officers of a financial institution not to make loans in a particular area (598)

suburb: a community adjacent to a city (588)

suburbanization: the migration of people from the city to the suburbs (588)

urban renewal: the rehabilitation of a rundown area, which usually results in the displacement of the poor who are living in that area (599)

urbanization: the process by which an increasing proportion of a population lives in cities and has a growing influence on the culture (583)

zero population growth: women bearing only enough children to reproduce the population (580)

KEY PEOPLE

State the major theoretical contributions or findings of these people.

Ernest Burgess: Burgess developed the concentric zone model of urban development. (590-591)

John Darley and Bibb Latané: These social psychologists found that people tend to remain uninvolved when they perceive there are others around who might become involved; they referred to this as the *diffusion of responsibility.* (596)

William Faunce: Writing about the far-reaching implications of exponential growth, this sociologist's views are consistent with the New Malthusians. (569)

William Flanagan: Flanagan has suggested three guiding principles for finding solutions to pressing urban problems: (1) use of regional planning, (2) awareness of human needs, and (3) equalizing the benefits as well as the impact of urban change. (583, 599)

Herbert Gans: Gans studied urban neighborhoods, with the result that he documented the existence of community within cities and identified the several different types of urban dwellers that live there. (594-595)

Chauncey Harris and Edward Ullman: These two geographers developed the multiple-nuclei model of urban growth. Harris later introduced the peripheral model of urban growth to account for more recent developments. (591-592)

Homer Hoyt: Hoyt modified Burgess' model of urban growth with the development of the sector model. (591)

Thomas Malthus: Malthus was an economist who made dire predictions about the future of population growth. (568)

Steven Mosher: This anthropologist did field work in China and wrote about the ruthlessness with which the "one couple, one child" policy is enforced. (579-580)

Robert Park: Park coined the term "human ecology" to describe how people adapt to their environment. (590)

William Julius Wilson: Wilson observed that the net result of shifting population and resources from central cities to suburbs was the transformation of the cities into ghettos. (596)

Louis Wirth: Wirth wrote a classic essay, "Urbanism as a Way of Life," in which he argued that city life undermines kinship and neighborhood. (592, 594)

MULTIPLE CHOICE QUESTIONS

1. Studying the size, composition, growth, and distribution of human population is known as (568)
    a. population growth theory.
    b. growth specialists.
    c. demography.
    d. social development theory.

2. The proposition that the population grows geometrically while food supply increases arithmetically is known as the (568)
    a. food surplus equation.
    b. Malthus theorem.
    c. exponential growth curve.
    d. demographic transition.

3. Which of the following statements is consistent with beliefs of the Anti-Malthusians? (570)
    a. People will blindly reproduce until there is no room left on earth.
    b. It is possible to project the world's current population growth into the indefinite future.
    c. Most people do not use intelligence and rational planning when it comes to having children.
    d. The demographic transition provides an accurate picture of what the future looks like.

4. The three-stage historical process of population growth is known as the (570)
    a. demographic equation.
    b. demographic transition.
    c. exponential growth curve.
    d. implosion growth curve.

5. The process by which a country's population becomes smaller because its birth rate and immigration are too low to replace those who die and emigrate is (571)
    a. population transfer.
    b. population annihilation.
    c. population shrinkage.
    d. population depletion.

6. Starvation occurs because (571-573)
    a. there is not enough fertile land worldwide on which to grow food.
    b. some parts of the world lack food while other parts of the world produce more than they can consume.

c.   population is growing at a faster rate than the world's ability to produce food.

d.   people do not eat a well-balanced diet.

7.   Why do people in the Least Industrialized Nations have so many children? (573-575)

a.   Parenthood provides status.

b.   Children are considered to be an economic asset.

c.   The community encourages people to have children.

d.   All of the above

8.   For conflict theorists, the explanation for why women in poor nations have so many children is that (575)

a.   women derive special meaning from children.

b.   children's labor can be exploited by their parents.

c.   men control women's reproductive choices.

d.   women use sex as a means of control over men.

9.   According to the author, Mexico's current population will continue to (576)

a.   grow slowly.

b.   grow rapidly.

c.   decline slowly.

d.   decline rapidly.

10.   To illustrate population dynamics, demographers use (576)

a.   population growth charts.

b.   population pyramids.

c.   fertility rates.

d.   demographic models.

11.   What are the factors that influence population growth called? (577)

a.   demographic variables

b.   demographic transitions

c.   demographic equations

d.   demographic constants

12.   _____ refers to the number of children the average woman bears. (577)

a.   Fertility rate

b.   Fecundity

c.   Crude birth rate

d.   Real birth rate

13.   The annual number of deaths per 1,000 population is the (577)

a.   crude death rate.

b.   crude mortality rate.

320

    c.   crude life expectancy rate.

    d.   net death rate.

14. What factors might push someone to migrate? (578)

    a.   poverty

    b.   lack of religious and political freedom

    c.   political persecution

    d.   all of the above

15. Around the globe, the flow of migration is generally from (578)

    a.   Most Industrialized Nations to Least Industrialized Nations.

    b.   one of the Least Industrialized Nation to another one.

    c.   Least Industrialized Nations to Industrializing Nations.

    d.   Least Industrialized Nations to Most Industrialized Nations.

16. According to your text, why is it difficult to forecast population growth? (579-580)

    a.   Government programs may encourage or discourage women from having children.

    b.   Government bureaus may be dishonest in reporting data.

    c.   There is a lack of computer programs to deal with data adequately.

    d.   Births, deaths, and migration are human behaviors and thus impossible to predict.

17. China's practice of female infanticide is rooted in (581)

    a.   sexism.

    b.   economics.

    c.   traditions that go back centuries.

    d.   all of the above

18. The process by which an increasing proportion of a population lives in cities is (583)

    a.   suburbanization.

    b.   gentrification.

    c.   megalopolitanism.

    d.   urbanization.

19. What does today's rapid urbanization mean? (583)

    a.   More people live in cities.

    b.   Today's cities are larger.

    c.   City life will have a growing influence on U.S. culture.

    d.   All of the above

20. All of the following are true about metropolitan statistical areas (MSAs) *except* (586)

    a.   there are 280 metropolitan statistical areas.

    b.   MSAs consist of a central city of at least 50,000 people.

    c.   about three of five Americans live in just fifty or so MSAs.

d.　an MSA consists of the urbanized counties adjacent to it.

21.　What is a megacity? (586)
   a.　a city of 10 million or more residents
   b.　a city that is at the center of a megalopolis
   c.　a city with a multitude of problems
   d.　a central city of at least 50,000 people and the urbanized areas linked to it

22.　Edge cities (588)
   a.　consist of a clustering of shopping malls, hotels, office parks, and residential areas near the intersections of major highways.
   b.　overlap political boundaries and include parts of several cities or towns.
   c.　provide a sense of place to those who live there.
   d.　all of the above

23.　When a new group of immigrants enters a city, they tend to settle in low-rent areas. As their numbers increase, those already living in the area begin to move out; their departure creates more low-cost housing for the immigrants. Sociologists refer to this process as (591)
   a.　progressive population replacement.
   b.　reverse gentrification.
   c.　cycle of assimilation.
   d.　invasion-succession cycle.

24.　The model that suggests that land use in cities is based on several centers, such as a clustering of restaurants or automobile dealerships, is the (592)
   a.　sector model.
   b.　concentric zone model.
   c.　multiple-nuclei model.
   d.　commerce model.

25.　Darley and Latane found that the more bystanders there are, the less likely people are to help. They referred to this as (596)
   a.　ethnic villagers.
   b.　cosmopolites.
   c.　diffusion of responsibility.
   d.　community.

TRUE-FALSE QUESTIONS
1.　_____Thomas Malthus was a sociologist at the University of Chicago in the 1920s. (568)
2.　_____The exponential growth curve is based on the idea that if growth doubles during approximately equal intervals of time, it accelerates in the later stages. (568)
3.　_____The Anti-Malthusians believe that people breed like germs in a bucket. (570)
4.　_____There are two stages in the process of demographic transition. (570)

5. _____The main reason why there is starvation is because there are too many people in the world today and too little food to feed them all. (572)
6. _____The major reason why people in the Least Industrialized Nations have so many children is because they do not know how to prevent conception. (573)
7. _____Migration rates do not affect the global population. (577)
8. _____The concentric zone model is based on the idea that cities expand from their central business district outward. (590)
9. _____The multiple-nuclei model is the most accurate model of urban growth. (592)
10. _____Urban renewal involves tearing down deteriorated buildings and replacing them with decent, affordable housing units. (599)

FILL-IN-THE-BLANK QUESTIONS

1. To reduce the number of children, China has a _____ national policy. (579)
2. A demographic condition in which women bear only enough children to reproduce the population is _____. (580)
3. _____ refers to masses of people moving to cities and to these cities having a growing influence in society. (583)
4. An overlapping area consisting of at least two metropolises and their many suburbs is a _____. (586)
5. _____ is a city of 10,000 to 50,000 residents that is not a suburb. (590)
6. Harris and Ullman noted that some cities have several centers or _____. (592)
7. The urban growth model that portrays the impact of radial highways on the movement of people and services away from the central city to its outskirts is the _____ model. (592)
8. _____ is a sense of not belonging; a feeling that no one cares about to you. (592)
9. _____ are a city's students, intellectuals, professionals, musicians, artists, and entertainers. (595)
10. Darley and Latane uncovered in their research that the more bystanders there are in a situation the _____ likely people are to offer help. (596)

ESSAY QUESTIONS

1. State the positions of the New Malthusians and the Anti-Malthusians, and discuss which view you think is more accurate based on the information provided about each position.

2. Identify some of the population challenges that affect the Most Industrialized and the Least Industrialized Nations, and provide explanations for these problems.

3. Identify the problems that are associated with forecasting population growth.

4. Discuss the five types of urban dwellers that Gans describes and how life in the city is different for each of these groups.

5. Discuss the factors that fueled suburbanization, and consider the impact that this population shift had on cities.

CHAPTER 21
COLLECTIVE BEHAVIOR AND SOCIAL MOVEMENTS

LEARNING OBJECTIVES
After reading Chapter 21, you should be able to:

1. Discuss early explanations of collective behavior, focusing on the transformation of the individual. (604-605)

2. Know the five stages, as identified by Herbert Blumer, that crowds go through before they become an acting crowd, as well as the five kinds of crowd participants as identified by Ralph Turner and Lewis Killian. (605-606)

3. Evaluate contemporary views of collective behavior, including the minimax strategy and emergent norms, emphasizing the rationality of the crowd. (606-607)

4. Provide examples of and discuss lynchings, riots, panics, moral panics, mass hysteria, rumors, fads, fashions, and urban legends. (607-615)

5. Differentiate between proactive and reactive social movements. (616)

6. Identify and contrast the different types of social movements. (616-617)

7. Discuss the tactics that social movements employ, and how and why these tactics are chosen. (617-618)

8. Describe the role that propaganda and the mass media play in helping to determine the effectiveness of social movements. (618-619)

9. Evaluate the different theories that explain why people are attracted to social movements and the conditions that underlie their attraction. (619, 621-622)

10. Discuss the special role of the agent provocateur in some social movements. (622)

11. Identify the five stages of social movements, talk about what social movements need to do in order to succeed, and explain why most social movements are unsuccessful. (622-626)

Chapter Outline

I.   Collective Behavior

    A.   Collective behavior is characterized by a group of people who bypass the usual norms governing their behavior and do something unusual. It is a broad term and covers a wide range of acts.

II. Early Explanations: The Transformation of the Individual

A. In 1852, Charles Mackay concluded that when people were in crowds, they sometimes "went mad" and did "disgraceful and violent things"; just as a herd of cows will stampede, so can people come under the control of a "herd mentality."

B. Based on Mackay's idea, Gustave LeBon stressed that the individual is transformed by the crowd.

    1. In a crowd, people feel anonymous, not accountable for what they do; they develop feelings of invincibility, believing that together they can accomplish anything. A collective mind develops.

    2. They become highly suggestible; this paves the way for contagion, a kind of collective hypnosis, which releases the destructive instincts that society has so carefully repressed.

C. To LeBon's analysis, Robert Park added the ideas of social unrest, which is transmitted from one individual to another, and circular reaction, the back-and-forth communication between the members of a crowd whereby a "collective impulse" is transmitted.

D. Synthesizing both LeBon's and Park's ideas, Herbert Blumer identified five stages that precede what he called an "acting crowd."

    1. A background condition of social unrest exists when people's routine activities are thwarted or when they develop new needs that go unsatisfied.

    2. An exciting event occurs—one so startling that people are preoccupied with it.

    3. People engage in milling—the act of standing or walking around as they talk about the exciting event and circular reaction sets in.

    4. A common object of attention emerges—people's attention becomes riveted on some aspect of the event.

    5. Stimulation of the common impulses occurs—people collectively agree about what they should do. Social contagion, described as a collective excitement passed from one person to another, becomes the mechanism that stimulates these common impulses. The end result is an acting crowd. Not all acting crowds are negative or destructive; nor are they all serious.

III. The Contemporary View: The Rationality of the Crowd

A. Sociologists argue that beneath the surface, crowds are actually quite rational, taking deliberate steps to reach some goal and often acting in a cooperative manner.

B. Richard Berk pointed out that people use a minimax strategy (trying to minimize their costs and maximize their rewards) whether in small groups or in crowds; the fewer the costs and the greater the rewards that people anticipate, the more likely they are to carry out a particular act.

C. Ralph Turner and Lewis Killian noted that human behavior is regulated by the normative order—socially approved ways of doing things that make up our everyday life. However, when an extraordinary event occurs and existing norms do not cover the new situation, people develop new norms to deal with the problem (emergent norms).

1. There are five kinds of crowd participants: (1) the ego-involved, who feel a high personal stake in the event; (2) the concerned, who have a personal interest in the event but less than the ego-involved; (3) the insecure, who have little concern about the issue but have sought out the crowd because it gives them a sense of power and security; (4) the curious spectators, who are inquisitive and may cheer the crowd on even though they do not care about the issue; and (5) the exploiters, who do not care about the issue but use it for their own purposes (e.g., hawking food or T-shirts).

2. These participants have different points of view. Their contrasting attitudes, emotion, and motives help to set the crowd on a particular course of action. As a common mood for new norms emerges, activities that are "not OK" in everyday life may now seem "OK."

3. The concept of emerging norms is important because it points to a rational process as the essential component of collective behavior.

IV. Forms of Collective Behavior

A. Sociologists view collective behavior as they do other forms of behavior. They seek to understand the roles that age, gender, race–ethnicity, and social class may play.

B. Riots are defined as violent crowd behavior aimed against people and property.

1. Frustration and anger at deprivation are usually at the root of a riot; the riot that broke out in Los Angeles after the verdict in the Rodney King trial is an example of this.

2. Beginning with a perception of being kept out of the mainstream society (limited to a meager education and denied jobs and justice), people's frustration builds to such a boiling point that it takes only a precipitating event to erupt in collective behavior.

3. It is not only the deprived who participate in the riots; others who are not deprived but who still feel frustration at the underlying social conditions that place them at a disadvantage also get involved.

4. For some, riots are a handy event. It allows them to loot and participate in an event apart from their humdrum life.

5. The event that precipitates a riot is important, but so is the riot's general context.

C. Rumors thrive in conditions of ambiguity, functioning to fill in missing information.

1. Rumors are unverified information about some topic or interest. Most rumors are short-lived and arise in a situation of ambiguity, only to dissipate when they are replaced either by another rumor or by factual information. A few rumors have a long life because they hit a responsive chord (e.g., rumors of mass poisoning of soft drink products that spread to many countries).

2. Three main factors why people believe rumors are that they (1) deal with a subject that is important to an individual, (2) replace ambiguity with some form of certainty, and (3) are attributed to a creditable source.

3. Rumors usually pass from one person to another, though they can originate from the mass media.

D. Panic, like the one that occurred following the broadcast of H. G. Wells' "War of the Worlds," is behavior that results when people become so fearful that they cannot function normally.
   1. One explanation as to why people panic is because they are anxious about some social condition.
   2. It is against the law to shout "Fire!" in a public building when no such danger exists. If people fear immediate death, they will lunge toward the nearest exit in a frantic effort to escape (e.g., the Beverly Hills Supper Club fire in Kentucky in 1977, in which 165 people died trying to get out of the two exits).
   3. Sociologists who studied this panic found what others have discovered—that not everyone panics. Only 29 percent of the employees of the Beverly Hills Supper Club left when they learned of the fire. They extended their role to help customers, fought the fire, or searched for friends and relatives.
   4. In some life-threatening situations, a sense of order prevails. During the World Trade Center attack, many people helped injured friends and strangers.

E. Moral panics occur when large numbers of people become intensely concerned, even fearful, about some behavior that is perceived as a threat to morality; the threat is seen as enormous, and hostility builds toward those thought responsible. They are often fueled by the mass media.
   1. The most famous moral panic was the fear of witches in Europe between the years 1400 and 1650.
   2. Moral panics are often fueled by the mass media and center around a sense of danger.
   3. Moral panics are often fed by rumor, information for which there is no discernible source and that is usually unfounded.
   4. Moral panics also thrive on uncertainty and anxiety.

F. A fad is a temporary pattern of behavior that catches people's attention, while fashion is a more enduring version of the same.
   1. Very short, intense fads are called crazes. They appear suddenly and are gone quickly.
   2. Fads come in many forms, and no one is immune to getting caught up in one. Some fads involve millions of people, die out quickly, and then make a comeback.
   3. Fashion is a behavior pattern that catches people's attention, lasting longer than a fad. Most often thought of in terms of clothing fashions, it can also refer to hairstyles, home decorating, design and colors of buildings, and language.

G. Urban legends are stories with an ironic twist that sound realistic but are false. Jan Brunvand, who studied the transmission of urban legends, concluded that urban legends are passed on by people who think that the event really happened to someone such as a "friend of a friend"; the stories have strong appeal and gain credibility from naming specific people or local places. Urban legends are "modern morality stories," with each teaching a moral lesson about life; they are related to social change; and they are calculated to instill guilt and fear.

V. Social Movements

A. Social movements consist of large numbers of people who organize either to promote or resist social change.

B. At the heart of social movements lie grievances and dissatisfactions. Proactive social movements promote social change because a current condition of society is intolerable. In contrast, reactive social movements resist changing conditions in society that they perceive as threatening.

C. To further their goals, people develop social movement organizations like the National Organization of Women or the Stop ERA. They use attention-grabbing devices to recruit members and publicize grievances.

D. Mayer Zald suggests that a cultural crisis can give birth to a wave of social movements. According to Zald, when a society's institutions fail to keep up with social changes, many people's needs go unfulfilled, massive unrest follows, and social movements come into being to bridge the gap.

VI. Types and Tactics of Social Movements

A. Social movements can be classified into four broad categories according to the type and amount of social change they seek.

   1. Two types seek to change people but differ in terms of the amount of change desired: alterative social movements seek to alter only particular aspects of people (e.g., the Woman's Christian Temperance Union), while redemptive social movements seek to change people totally (e.g., a religious social movement such as fundamental Christianity that stresses conversion).

   2. Two types seek to change society but also differ in terms of the amount of change desired: reformative social movements seek to reform only one part of society (e.g., animal rights or the environment); transformative social movements seek to change the social order itself and replace it with their own version of the ideal society (e.g., revolutions in the American colonies, France, and Russia).

   3. One of the more interesting types of transformative social movements is the millenarian movement, which is based on prophecies of a coming calamity. Cargo cults, a social movement in which South Pacific islanders destroyed their possessions in the anticipation that their ancestors would send items by ship, are an interesting example of millenarian movements.

   4. Today, some social movements have a global orientation, committed to changing a specific condition throughout the world. They are called transnational (or new) social movements. The women's, environmental, and animal rights movements are examples.

   5. A rare type of social movement, metaformative social movements, exists, whose goal is to change the social order itself of an entire civilization or entire world. We are witnessing another metaformative social movement, that of Islamic fundamentalism.

B. Tactics of social movements are best understood by examining levels of membership, publics they address, and their relationship to authorities.

1. Three levels of membership are (1) the inner core (the leadership that sets goals, timetables, and so on); (2) people committed to the goals of the movement, but not to the same degree as members of the inner core; and (3) people who are neither as committed nor as dependable. The chosen tactics depend on the predispositions and backgrounds of the inner core.

2. Publics are made up of a dispersed group of people who may have an interest in an issue. They can be described as sympathetic (sympathize with goals of movement but have no commitment to movement); hostile (keenly aware of group's goals and want the movement stopped); and people who are unaware of or indifferent toward the movement. In selecting tactics, the leadership considers these different types of publics.

3. The movement's relationship to the authorities is important in determining tactics: if authorities are hostile to a social movement, aggressive or even violent tactics are likely; if authorities are sympathetic, violence is not likely. If a social movement is institutionalized, accepted by the authorities, and given access to resources they control, the likelihood of violence is very low.

4. Other factors that can influence the choice of tactics include the nature of friendships, race, and even the size of towns.

C. In selecting tactics, leaders of social movements are aware of their effects on the mass media. Their goal is to influence public opinion about some issue.

1. Propaganda is a key to understanding social movements. Propaganda simply means the presentation of information in an attempt to influence people.

2. Propaganda, in the sense of organized attempts to influence public opinion, is a regular part of everyday life.

3. The mass media play a critical role in social movements. They have become, in effect, the gatekeepers to social movements. If those who control and work in the mass media are sympathetic to a "cause," it will receive sympathetic treatment. If the social movement goes against their own biases, it will either be ignored or receive unfavorable treatment.

VII. Why People Join Social Movements

A. According to deprivation theory, people who are deprived of things deemed valuable in society, whether money, justice, status, or privilege, join social movements with the hope of redressing their grievances.

1. Absolute deprivation is people's actual negative condition; relative deprivation is what people think they should have relative to what others have or even compared with their own past or perceived future.

2. While the notion of absolute deprivation provides a beginning point for looking at why people join social movements, it is even more important to look at relative deprivation in trying to understand why people join social movements.

3. Improved conditions fuel human desires for even better conditions and thus can spark revolutions.

B. Declining privilege theory focuses on those who have enjoyed relatively good circumstances in life and have experienced a decline in their status and power.

C. James Jasper notes that people join a particular social movement because of moral issues and an ideological commitment to the movement. It is the moral component that is a primary reason for some people's involvement in social movements.

D. An agent provocateur is a special type of social movement participant.

1. As an agent of the government or of a rival social movement, the agent provocateur's job is to spy on the leadership and sabotage their activities. Some are recruited from the membership itself, while others go underground and join the movement.

2. On occasion a police agent is converted to the social movement on which he or she is spying. Sociologist Gary Marx noted that this occurs because the agent, to be credible, must share at least some of the class, age, ethnic, racial, religious, or sexual characteristics of the group. This makes the agent more likely to sympathize with the movement's goals and to become disenchanted with the means being used to destroy the group.

3. Sometimes the agent provocateur will go to great lengths, even breaking the law, to push the social movement into illegal activities.

VIII. On the Success and Failure of Social Movements

A. Social movements have a life course—that is, they go through five stages as they grow and mature.

1. Initial unrest and agitation because people are upset about some social condition; leaders who verbalize people's feelings emerge at this point.

2. Resource mobilization by leaders of a relatively large number of people who demand that something be done about the problem; charismatic leaders emerge during this stage.

3. Emergence of an organization with a division of labor, a leadership who makes policy decisions, and a rank and file that actively supports the movement.

4. Institutionalization as the movement becomes bureaucratized; leadership passes to career officials who may care more about their position in the organization than about the movement itself.

5. Decline of the organization; but there may be a possibility of resurgence. Some movements cease to exist; others become reinvigorated with new leadership from within or by coming into conflict with other social movements fighting for the opposite side of the issue (e.g., social movements relating to abortion).

B. Seldom do social movements actually solve problems. In order to mobilize sufficient resources to survive, they find it necessary to appeal to a broad constituency, and to do so, they must focus on large-scale issues that are deeply embedded in society. Such broad problems do not lend themselves to easy or quick solutions.

C. Many social movements do vitally affect society. Some make valuable contributions to solving problems, for they highlight areas of society to be changed. Others become powerful forces for resisting the social change that its members consider undesirable.

D.   Decline is not inevitable. New, more idealistic and committed leaders may emerge and reinvigorate the movement, or conflict between groups on opposing sides of an issue may continually invigorate each side and prevent the movement's decline.

Chapter Summary

Collective behavior refers to extraordinary activities carried out by groups of people. Early theorists of collective behavior argued that crowds transformed people, causing them to participate in activities as part of a group in which, individually, they would not ordinarily engage. This includes participating in less-controversial activities such as rumors, fads, fashions, and urban legends, as well as in more serious and even criminal behavior including lynchings, riots, moral panics, and mass hysteria. Conditions of discontent and uncertainty provide fertile ground for collective behavior, and each form provides a way of dealing with these conditions.

Explanations of collective behavior emphasize the rationality of the crowd. A common explanation for collective behavior was offered by Charles Mackay in 1852 when he compared collective human behavior to a "herd mentality." Approximately fifty years later, Gustave LeBon suggested that a collective mind develops and people can be swept up by almost any suggestion when feeling anonymous in a crowd, forming the basis of contagion theory. Robert Park theorized that collective behavior was the result of back-and-forth communication between members of a group in a process he referred to as circular reaction.

To explain crowd behavior, Herbert Blumer synthesized the ideas of LeBon and Park to describe a five-stage process that precedes what he called an *acting crowd*. The process includes: (1) tension or unrest, (2) an exciting event, (3) milling, (4) a common object of attention, and (5) common impulses. The contemporary view of crowd behavior is that beneath a chaotic surface, crowds are actually quite rational. Included in the contemporary theories are the minimax strategy and emergent norm theory.

Related to collective behavior are social movements. Social movements consist of large numbers of people who organize to promote or resist social change. Those that promote social change are classified as proactive social movements. Those that resist change are classified as reactive social movements. To further their goals, whether it be to advance or resist change, people develop social movement organizations.

Social movements are classified according to their target and the amount of change they seek. Alternative and redemptive social movements target individuals. Reformative and transformative social movements target society. To achieve their goals, the leaders of social movements choose between a variety of tactics, which can include the effective use of membership in the organization, and violent or nonviolent behaviors. The leaders of social movements try to manipulate the mass media in order to influence public opinion. The mass media play a crucial role in determining the potential success or failure of any given social movement.

Although many people may share in the discontent a certain social situation creates, not everyone joins a social movement. A major reason that people join social movements is because they know others in the movement. This includes family members, friends, and acquaintances who may channel them into the movement. Other theories as to why people join social movements include relative deprivation theory, declining privilege theory, and ideological commitment theory.

Social movements go through several stages. They begin with initial unrest and agitation and then proceed through mobilization, organization, institutionalization, and decline. To succeed, a social movement has to appeal to broad constituencies by focusing on widespread concerns, which, generally, are deeply embedded in society and resist change. Because of the complexity and difficulty involved in developing a successful social movement, most social movements fail in the first stage of initial unrest and agitation.

KEY TERMS

After studying the chapter, review the definition for each of the following terms.

acting crowd: an excited group of people who move toward a goal (605)

agent provocateur: someone who joins a group in order to spy on it or to sabotage it by provoking its members to commit extreme acts (622)

alterative social movement: a social movement that seeks to alter only some specific aspects of people and institutions (616)

cargo cult: a social movement in which South Pacific islanders destroyed their possessions in the anticipation that their ancestors would ship them new goods (617)

circular reaction: Robert Park's term for a back-and-forth communication among the members of a crowd whereby a "collective impulse" is transmitted (604)

collective behavior: extraordinary activities carried out by groups of people; includes lynchings, rumors, panics, urban legends, and fads and fashions (604)

collective mind: Gustave LeBon's term for the tendency of people in a crowd to feel, think, and act in extraordinary ways (604)

emergent norms: Ralph Turner and Lewis Killian's term for the idea that people develop new norms to cope with a new situation; used to explain crowd behavior (606)

fad: a temporary pattern of behavior that catches people's attention (614)

fashion: a pattern of behavior that catches people's attention and lasts longer than a fad (614)

mass hysteria: an imagined threat that causes physical symptoms among a large number of people (611)

metaformative social movement: a social movement that has the goal to change the social order not just of a country or two, but of a civilization, or even the entire world (617)

millenarian social movement: a social movement based on the prophecy of coming social upheaval (617)

milling: a crowd standing or walking around as they talk excitedly about some event (605)

minimax strategy: Richard Berk's term for the efforts people make to minimize their costs and maximize their rewards (606)

moral panic: a fear that grips a large number of people over the possibility that some evil threatens the well-being of society; followed by hostility, sometimes violence, toward those thought responsible (613)

panic: the condition of being so fearful that one cannot function normally, and may even flee (609)

proactive social movement: a social movement that promotes some social change (616)

propaganda: in its broad sense, the presentation of information in the attempt to influence people; in its narrow sense, one-sided information used to try to influence people (618)

public: in this context, a dispersed group of people relevant to a social movement; the sympathetic and hostile publics have an interest in the issues on which a social movement focuses; there are also unaware or indifferent publics (618)

public opinion: how people think about some issue (618)

reactive social movement: a social movement that resists some social change (616)

redemptive social movement: a social movement that seeks to change people and institutions totally, to redeem them (616)

reformative social movement: a social movement that seeks to reform some specific aspects of society (616)

relative deprivation theory: in this context, the idea that people join social movements based on what they think they should have compared with what others have (621)

resource mobilization: a theory that social movements succeed or fail based on their ability to mobilize resources such as time, money, and people's skills (624)

riot: violent crowd behavior directed at people and property (607)

role extension: the incorporation of additional activities into a role (611)

rumor: unfounded information spread among people (608)

social movement: a large group of people who are organized to promote or resist some social change (615)

social movement organization: an organization whose purpose is to promote the goals of a social movement (616)

transformative social movement: a social movement that seeks to change society totally, to transform it (617)

transnational social movement: a social movement whose emphasis is on some condition around the world, instead of on a condition in a specific country; also known as a *new social movement* (617)

urban legend: a story with an ironic twist that sounds realistic but is false (614)

KEY PEOPLE

Review the major theoretical contributions or findings of these people.

William Bainbridge: This sociologist found that some people did become frightened after the broadcast of "War of the Worlds," and a few even got into their cars and drove like maniacs, but most of the panic was an invention of the news media. (610)

Richard Berk: Berk developed the minimax strategy to explain collective behavior; that people are more likely to act when costs are low and anticipated rewards are high. (606)

Herbert Blumer: Blumer identified five stages that precede the emergence of an active crowd (an excited group that moves towards a goal). These are tension or unrest, an exciting event, milling, a common object of attention, and common impulses. (605-606)

Jan Brunvand: This folklorist studied urban legends and suggests that they are modern morality stories. (615)

Hadley Cantril: This psychologist suggests that people panicked after hearing the famous "War of the Worlds" because of widespread anxiety about world conditions. (609)

James Jasper: This sociologist argued that many become involved in social movements because of moral issues and an ideological commitment. (622-623)

Drue Johnston and Norris Johnson: These sociologists studied the behavior of employees during the Beverly Hills Supper Club fire and found that most continued to carry out their roles. (611)

Gustave LeBon: LeBon argued that a collective mind develops within a crowd, and people are swept away by any suggestion that is made. (604-606)

Alfred and Elizabeth Lee: These sociologists found that propaganda relies on seven basic techniques, which they labeled "tricks of the trade." (620)

Charles Mackay: Mackay was the first to study collective behavior; he suggested that a "herd mentality" takes over and explains the disgraceful things people do when in crowds. (604)

Gary Marx: This sociologist investigated the agent provocateur and found that some are converted to the movement because they share some of the same social characteristics as the movement's members. (622)

Clark McPhail: This sociologist studied the behavior of crowds, noting that the behavior of crowd participants is cooperative. (626-628, 630)

Robert Park: Park suggested that social unrest is the result of the circular reaction of people in crowds. (604-606, 608)

Victor Rodriguez: This sociologist suggests that minorities in the middle class might participate in riots when they feel frustrated with being treated as second-class citizens even when they are employed and living stable lives. (608)

Alexis de Tocqueville: This nineteenth-century observer of social life noted that people organize collectively to improve their conditions when they are experiencing relative deprivation rather than absolute deprivation. Having experienced some improvement and being able to see better conditions ahead, they are motivated to work for change. (621)

Ralph Turner and Lewis Killian: These sociologists use the term "emergent norm" to explain the rules that emerge in collective behavior. They note that crowds have at least five kinds of participants: the ego-involved, the concerned, the insecure, the curious spectators, and the exploiters. (604, 606)

Mayer Zald: This sociologist explained that social movements are like a rolling sea; during one period of time, a few may appear, but shortly afterward, a whole wave of them role in. He suggested that cultural crises give rise to social movements. (616, 624)

MULTIPLE CHOICE QUESTIONS

1. Which of the following statements about Charles MacKay is *incorrect*? (604)
    a. He noticed that ordinary people did disgraceful things when in a crowd.
    b. He suggested that people have a "herd mentality" when in a crowd.
    c. He proposed that a collective mind develops once a group of people congregate.
    d. His work marked the beginnings of the field of collective behavior.

2. LeBon's term for the tendency of people in a crowd to feel, think, and act in extraordinary ways is (604)
    a. social unrest.
    b. the "herd mentality."
    c. collective behavior.
    d. collective mind.

3. According to Park, which is most conducive to the emergence of collective behavior? (604)
    a. social alienation
    b. social apathy
    c. social unrest
    d. social cohesion

4. A crowd's back-and-forth communication whereby a collective impulse is transmitted is (604)
    a. a circular reaction.
    b. milling.
    c. an acting crowd.
    d. a collective mind.

5. An "acting crowd" is (605)
    a. a term coined by Herbert Blumer.
    b. an excited group that collectively moves toward a goal.
    c. the end result of the five stages of collective behavior.
    d. all of the above

6. Richard Berk used the term "minimax strategy" to describe the tendency for (606)
    a. crowds to operate with a minimum of strategy.
    b. for humans to minimize costs and maximize rewards.
    c. those in authority to maximize the costs of an action in order to minimize rewards.
    d. society to respond to even the most minimum of social movements.

7. The development of new norms to cope with a new situation is called (606)

a. emergent norms.
b. developmental norms.
c. surfacing norms.
d. none of the above

8. According to Turner and Killian, which crowd participant's role is most important? (607)
   a. the ego-involved
   b. the concerned
   c. the curious spectators
   d. the exploiters

9. Which of the following are kinds of participants in crowds? (607)
   a. the ego-involved
   b. the insecure
   c. the exploiters
   d. all of the above

10. Sociologists refer to unfounded information spread among people as (608)
    a. hearsay.
    b. scuttlebutt.
    c. rumor.
    d. gossip.

11. Which of the following is true about rumors? (609)
    a. Most last at least six months.
    b. They persist even when there is factual information.
    c. Rumors can lead to the destruction of entire communities.
    d. Most riots occur after a rumor has been spread.

12. Sociologists have found that when a disaster such as a fire occurs, (611)
    a. everyone panics.
    b. some people continue to perform their roles.
    c. people leave it to the police and firefighters to solve the problem.
    d. no one panics.

13. Which statement about moral panics is *incorrect*? (613)
    a. Moral panics occur when people are concerned about something viewed as immoral.
    b. Moral panics are generally based on an event that has been verified as true.
    c. Moral panics thrive on uncertainty and anxiety.
    d. Moral panics are fueled by the mass media.

14. Which of the following would be an example of a fashion? (614)
    a. the bungalow house

b. mini skirts

c. the use of the word "cool"

d. all of the above

15. The Woman's Christian Temperance Union is an example of which type of social movement? (616)

a. alternative social movement

b. redemptive social movement

c. reformative social movement

d. transformative social movement

16. A millenarian movement is a social movement (617)

a. in which South Pacific islanders destroyed all their possessions.

b. that seeks to alter only particular aspects of people.

c. based on the prophecy of coming social upheaval.

d. that seeks to change individuals totally.

17. Today some social movements have a global orientation because many important issues cross national boundaries. This new type of social movement is called a (617)

a. global social movement.

b. multinational social movement.

c. transnational social movement.

d. worldwide social movement.

18. The public that social movements face can really be divided into (618)

a. supporters and opponents.

b. informed supportive public, informed oppositional public, and uninformed mass.

c. receptive audience, hostile audience, and disinterested mass.

d. sympathetic public, hostile public, and disinterested people.

19. What factors influence a social movement's choice of tactics? (618)

a. the predispositions and background of the inner core

b. the movement's relationship to authorities

c. the size of the town in which the movement is operating

d. all of the above

20. How people think about some issue is (618)

a. irrelevant to most social scientists.

b. public opinion.

c. propaganda.

d. mass-society theory.

21. Which statement about propaganda is *incorrect*? (619)

a.   Propaganda plays a key role in social movements.

b.   Propaganda generally involves negative images.

c.   Propaganda has become a regular and routine part of modern life.

d.   Propaganda is the presentation of information in an attempt to influence people.

22. The mass media (619)

a.   are the gatekeepers to social movements.

b.   engage in biased reporting, controlled by people who have an agenda to get across.

c.   are sympathetic to some social movements, while ignoring others; it all depends on their individual biases.

d.   all of the above

23. Sociology sensitizes us to _____ in that it helps us recognize that, on any topic, there are competing points of view that represent different realities based on different people's experiences. (619)

a.   a set of rules or guidelines to govern our behavior

b.   propaganda

c.   multiple realities

d.   answers to basic questions concerning morality

24. Which of the following is an explanation for why people participate in a social movement with the hope of solving their grievances? (619, 621)

a.   mass society theory

b.   deprivation theory

c.   differential association theory

d.   propaganda

25. In order to turn a group of people who are upset about a social condition into a social movement, there must be (624)

a.   agitation.

b.   resource mobilization.

c.   organization.

d.   institutionalization.

TRUE-FALSE QUESTIONS

1.   _____Collective behavior is characterized by a group of people becoming emotionally aroused and engaging in extraordinary behavior. (604)

2.   _____ Gustave LeBon's central idea was that the individual is transformed by the crowd. (604)

3.   _____People believe rumors because they replace ambiguity with some form of certainty. (608-609)

4.   _____The fears that produce moral panics are generally out of proportion to any supposed danger. (613)

5.   _____Urban legends are just another kind of rumor. (614-615)

6.   _____A social movement that promotes some social change is known as a reactive social movement. (616)

7.   _____A social movement based on the prophecy of coming social upheaval is known as a millenarian social movement. (617)

8.   _____A social movement's relationship to authorities is significant in determining whether the tactics to be used are peaceful or violent. (618)

9.   _____Propaganda and advertising are defined quite differently from one another. (619)

10. _____Deprivation theory and relative deprivation theory are identical perspectives. (619, 621)

FILL-IN-THE-BLANK QUESTIONS

1. For about ten years, quality circles were _____. (614)
2. To further goals to make social change, people develop _____ organizations. (615)
3. Millenarian social movements are based on the _____ of coming calamity. (617)
4. The goal of _____ social movements is to change the entire world. (617)
5. If a social movement is _____, violence will not be directed toward the authorities. (618)
6. _____ relies on seven basic techniques known as "tricks of the trade." (618)
7. Jasper argued that people feel an _____ and thus they join social movements. (622)
8. Some people join social movements because of _____ issues. (622)
9. _____ are agents of the government who join a group in order to spy on it. (622)
10. The fifth and final stage of a social movement is _____. (624)

ESSAY QUESTIONS

1. Compare and contrast the early explanations of collective behavior, as advanced by Charles Mackay, Gustave LeBon, Robert Park, and Herbert Blumer, with more contemporary explanations developed by Richard Berk, Ralph Turner, and Lewis Killian.

2. Develop an explanation as to why panics, rumors, and urban legends thrive in society.

3. Discuss the different theories about why people join social movements, and consider how they could all be accurate.

4. Explain what propaganda is and why it is so important in the development of social movements.

5. Discuss the difference between fads and fashion and provide examples.

CHAPTER 22
SOCIAL CHANGE AND THE ENVIRONMENT

LEARNING OBJECTIVES

After reading Chapter 22, you should be able:

1. Describe the social transformation of society in terms of the four major social revolutions; the shift from *Gemeinschaft* to *Gesellschaft* societies; and the development of capitalism, industrialization, and modernization. (630-631)

2. Compare the general characteristics, material relations, social relationships, and norms of traditional and modern societies. (631)

3. Discuss conflict, power, and global practices in post-World War II, including geopolitics and current ethnic conflicts. (632-634)

4. Identify and evaluate the different theories of social change, including cultural evolution, cycles, conflict theory, and William Ogburn's processes of invention, discovery, and diffusion. (634-637)

5. Define cultural lag and provide examples. (636)

6. Talk about the different ways that technological innovations are able to change society, including changes in social organizations, changes in ideology, changes in values, and changes in social relationships. (637-639)

7. Identify the most significant elements of social change, including the role of computers in education, the workplace, and finance and business. (638-643)

8. Recognize changes in war and terrorism and how advances in technology have changed armed conflict around the world. (643-645)

9. Describe how the globalization of capitalism contributes to environmental decay. (646)

10. Identify and compare the environmental problems of the Most Industrialized Nations, the Industrializing Nations, and the Least Industrialized Nations. (646-650)

11. Talk about the goals and activities of the environmental movement and the main assumptions of environmental sociology. (650-653)

12. Suggest different ways to achieve harmony between technology and the environment. (653)

Chapter Outline

I. How Social Change Transforms Society

A. Social change is a shift in the characteristics of culture and societies over time.

B. There have been four social revolutions: the domestication of plants and animals, from which pastoral and horticultural societies arose; the invention of the plow, leading to agricultural societies; the industrial revolution, which produced industrial societies; and now the information revolution, resulting in postindustrial societies. Another type of society is emerging based on biotechnology.

C. The shift from agricultural to industrial economic activity was accompanied by a change from *Gemeinschaft* (daily life centers on intimate and personal relationships) to *Gesellschaft* (people have fleeting, impersonal relationships) societies.

D. Different sociologists have focused on different forces in order to explain the changes that took place in society at the time of the Industrial Revolution.

    1. Karl Marx identified capitalism as the basic reason behind the breakup of feudal (agricultural) societies. He focused his analysis on the means of production (factories, machinery, and tools): those who owned them dictated the conditions under which workers would work and live. This development set in motion antagonistic relationships between capitalists and workers that remain today.

    2. Max Weber saw religion as the core reason for the development of capitalism: as a result of the Reformation, Protestants no longer felt assured that they were saved by virtue of church membership and concluded that God would show visible favor to the elect. This belief encouraged Protestants to work hard and be thrifty. An economic surplus resulted, stimulating industrialization.

    3. Modernization (the change from agricultural to industrial societies) refers to the sweeping changes in societies brought about by the Industrial Revolution.

    4. When technology changes, societies change. An example today would be how technology from the industrialized world is transforming traditional societies.

E. Social movements highlight the cutting edges of change in a society. Large numbers of people organize to demand or resist changes. With globalization, these issues increasingly cut across international boundaries.

F. Global divisions of power began to emerge in the sixteenth century; in the eighteenth and nineteenth centuries, capitalism and industrialization extended the economic and political ties among the world's nations.

    1. Dependency theory asserts that because those nations that were not industrialized became dependent on those that had industrialized, they were unable to develop their own resources.

    2. Today's information revolution, including the new bioeconomics, will have far-reaching consequences for global stratification. Those who make the fastest advances in these areas are destined to dominate in the coming generations.

    3. The world's industrial giants (the United States, Canada, Great Britain, France, Germany, Italy, and Japan—the G7) have decided how they will share the world's markets; by regulating global economic and industrial policy, they

guarantee their own dominance, including continued access to cheap raw materials from the Least Industrialized Nations.

4. Russia joined the G7, and it is now known as the G8.

5. The recent resurgence of ethnic conflicts threatens the global map drawn by the G8.

6. If China follows the rules set forth by the G8, it may be incorporated into this exclusive group.

II. Theories and Processes of Social Change

A. Theories that focus on cultural evolution are either unilinear or multilinear.

1. Unilinear theories assume that all societies follow the same path, evolving from simple to complex through uniform sequences; however, these theories have been discredited, and seeing one's own society as the top of the evolutionary ladder is now considered unacceptably ethnocentric.

2. Multilinear theories assume that different routes can lead to a similar stage of development; thus societies need not pass through the same sequence of stages to become industrialized.

3. Both unilinear and multilinear theories assume the idea that societies progress toward a higher state. However, because of the crises in Western culture today, this assumption has been cast aside and evolutionary theories have been rejected.

B. Theories of natural cycles examine great civilizations, not a particular society; they presume that societies are like organisms: they are born, reach adolescence, grow old, and die.

1. Toynbee proposed that civilization is initially able to meet challenges, yet when it becomes an empire, the ruling elite loses its capacity to keep the masses in line "by charm rather than by force," and the fabric of society is then ripped apart.

2. Oswald Spengler proposed that Western civilization was on the wane; some analysts think the crisis in Western civilization may indicate he was right.

C. Marx's conflict theory viewed social change as a dialectical process in which the following occurs:

1. A thesis (a current arrangement of power) contains its own antithesis (a contradiction or opposition), and the resulting struggle between the thesis and its antithesis leads to a synthesis (a new arrangement of power).

2. Thus, the history of a society is a series of confrontations in which each ruling group creates the seeds of its own destruction (e.g., capitalism sets workers and capitalists on a collision course).

D. William Ogburn identified three processes of social change.

1. *Inventions* can be either material (computers) or social (capitalism); *discovery* is a new way of seeing things; and *diffusion* is the spread of an invention, discovery, or idea from one area to another.

2. Ogburn coined the term "cultural lag" to describe the situation in which some elements of a culture adapt to an invention or discovery more rapidly than others.

344

We are constantly trying to catch up with technology by adapting our customs and ways of life to meet its needs.

     3.   Ogburn has been criticized because of his view that technology controls almost all social change. People also take control over technology, developing the technology they need and selectively using existing technology. Both can happen; technology leads to social change, and social change leads to technology. In general, Ogburn stressed that the usual direction of change is for material culture (technology) to change first and the symbolic culture (people's ideas and ways of life) to follow.

III. How Technology Changes Society

    A.   Technology refers to both the tools used to accomplish tasks and to the skills or procedures to make and use those tools.

        1.   Technology is an artificial means of extending human abilities.

        2.   Although all human groups use technology, it is the chief characteristic of postindustrial societies because it greatly extends our abilities to analyze information, communicate, and travel.

    B.   New technologies can reshape an entire society. Four ways in which technology can shape an entire society are as follows:

        1.   Changes in social organization (For example, the introduction of factories changed the nature of work: people gathered in one place to do their work, were given specialized tasks, and became responsible for only part of an item, not the entire item.)

        2.   Changes in ideology (For example, the new technology that led to the factory stimulated new ideologies such as maximizing profits.)

        3.   Changes in ostentatious consumption (For example, if technology is limited to clubbing animals, then animal skins are valued; with technological change, Americans make sure that their trendy clothing labels are displayed. The emphasis on materialism depends on the state of technology.)

        4.   Changes in social relationships (For example, as men went to work in the factories, family relationships changed; as more women work outside the home, family relationships again are changing. However, new technology is now allowing many to work at home. This may strengthen families.)

    C.   The automobile was one of the greatest inventions that shaped U.S. society.

        1.   The Model T was mass produced in 1908. As cars decreased in price, Americans found this more convenient than public transportation.

        2.   Commercial and home architecture changed as people needed a place to park their automobiles.

        3.   By the 1920s, the automobile was used extensively for dating, and children were no longer under the watchful eyes of their parents.

        4.   Women were able to drive as well as men, and this removed them from the confines of the home. It allowed them to participate in areas of social life not connected to the home.

D. The computer is an example of how technology shapes our lives. Some people have reservations about our computerized society, fearing that government will be able to exert complete control over us.

1. Within the field of education, computers are transforming the way children from kindergarten through college learn. There is concern today about a digital divide in education, with wealthier school districts able to provide the latest technology to their students, while poor school districts are left behind.

2. Computers are altering the way we work, the types of social relationships we establish with co-workers, and even the location of work.

3. In the world of business and finance, computers have made national borders meaningless, as vast amounts of money are instantly transferred from one country to another.

4. The way wars are fought has also changed because of computers.

E. Computers shrink the world in terms of both time and space. With the information superhighway, homes and businesses are connected by a rapid flow of information.

1. Several million workers now work out of their home. This could be the beginning of a historical shift in which families are brought closer together.

2. The negative side of the technology is the increased surveillance of workers and depersonalization that occurs.

3. National borders have become meaningless as information can be transferred from one country to another.

4. On a national level, we may end up with information have-nots among inner-city and rural residents, thus perpetuating existing inequalities.

5. On a global level, the Most Industrialized Nations will control the information superhighway, thereby destining the Least Industrialized Nations to a perpetual pauper status.

IV. The Growth Machine versus the Earth

A. The globalization of capitalism underlies today's environmental decay.

1. The Most Industrialized Nations continue to push for economic growth; the Industrialized Nations strive to achieve faster economic growth; and the Least Industrialized Nations, anxious to enter the race, push for even faster growth.

2. If our goal is a sustainable environment, we must stop trashing the Earth.

B. Industrialization led to a major assault on the environment. While it has been viewed as good for the nation's welfare, it has also contributed to today's environmental problems.

1. The major polluters of the Earth are the Most Industrialized Nations.

2. Many of our problems today, including depletion of the ozone layer, acid rain, the greenhouse effect, and global warming, are associated with our dependence on fossil fuels.

3. There is an abundant source of natural energy that would provide low-cost power and therefore help raise the living standards of humans across the globe. Better technology is needed to harness this energy supply. From a conflict perspective,

such abundant sources of energy present a threat to the multinationals' energy monopoly. We cannot expect the practical development and widespread use of alternative sources of power until the multinationals have cornered the market on the technology that will harness them.

4. Racial minorities and the poor are disproportionately exposed to air pollution, hazardous waste, pesticides, and the like. To deal with this issue, environmental justice groups have formed that fight to close polluting plants and block construction of polluting industries.

C. Environmental degradation is also a problem in the Industrializing and the Least Industrialized Nations, as these countries rushed into global industrial competition without the funds to purchase expensive pollution controls and have few antipollution laws.

1. Pollution was treated as a state secret in the former Soviet Union. With protests stifled, no environmental protection laws to inhibit pollution, and production quotas to be met, environmental pollution was rampant. Almost half of Russia's arable land is unsuitable for farming; air pollution in cities is ten times higher than that permitted in the United States; and half the tap water is unfit to drink. Pollution may be partially responsible for the drop in life expectancy.

2. The combined pressures of population growth and almost nonexistent environmental regulations destined the Least Industrialized Nations to become the Earth's major source of pollution. Some companies in the Most Industrialized Nations use the Least Industrialized Nations as a garbage dump for hazardous wastes and for producing chemicals no longer tolerated in their own countries.

3. As tropical rain forests are cleared for lumber, farms, and pastures, the consequence may be the extinction of numerous plant and animal species. As the rain forest is destroyed, thousands of animal and plant species are extinguished.

D. Concern about the world's severe environmental problems has produced a worldwide social movement. Political parties whose concern is the environment, such as the green parties, are formed. Activists in the environmental movement seek solutions in education, legislation, and political activism.

E. Environmental sociology examines the relationship between human societies and the environment. Its basic assumptions include: (1) the physical environment is a significant variable in sociological investigation; (2) humans are but one species among many that are dependent on the environment; (3) because of intricate feedbacks to nature, human actions have many unintended consequences; (4) the world is finite, so there are potential physical limits to economic growth; (5) economic expansion requires increased extraction of resources from the environment; (6) increased extraction of resources leads to ecological problems; (7) these ecological problems place restrictions on economic expansion; and (8) the state creates environmental problems by trying to create conditions for the profitable accumulation of capital. The goal is not to stop environmental problems but rather to study how humans affect the physical environment and how that environment affects human activities.

F. If we are to have a world that is worth passing on to the coming generations, we must seek harmony between technology and the natural environment. As a parallel to development of technologies, we must develop systems to reduce technology's harm to the environment and mechanisms to enforce rules for the production, use, and disposal of technology.

Chapter Summary

The rapid, far-reaching social change that the world is currently experiencing did not "just happen." It is the result of forces set into motion thousands of years ago. Transforming the course of human history, social change—the alteration of culture and societies over time— is a vital part of social life.

When technology changes, societies also change. The primary changes in human history are tied to the four social revolutions: domestication, agriculture, industrialization, and information. The change from *Gemeinschaft* societies to *Gesellschaft* societies, capitalism and industrialization, modernization, and global stratification are other examples of social change that have greatly affected our lives. Social movements, conflict, power, and global politics also contribute to social change.

Social change has fascinated theorists. Theories of social change include evolutionary theories (both unilinear and multilinear), cyclical theories, and conflict theories. Unilinear theories assume all societies follow the same path. Multilinear propose that different routes can lead to the same stage of development. Cyclical theories attempt to account for the rise of entire civilizations.

William Ogburn identified technology as the basic cause of social change. According to Ogburn, technology changes society through invention, discovery, and diffusion. Ogburn also coined the term "cultural lag" to describe how some elements of a culture typically lag behind the changes that come from invention, discovery, and diffusion. Changes in technology often have profound effects on social life. They can significantly change social organization, ideology, values, and social relationships.

Not all societal changes are necessarily good. The globalization of capitalism has significantly contributed to environmental problems. The environmental problems of the Most Industrialized Nations include smog, acid rain, the greenhouse effect, and global warming. As the Industrializing and Least Industrialized Nations rush to industrialize, they are also damaging the environment. In many cases, the Industrializing and Least Industrialized Nations have caused even greater damage to the environment than the Most Industrialized Nations. This is because they lack the pollution controls, anti-pollution laws, and experience in dealing with environmental issues that the Most Industrialized Nations possess. Concerns about the environment have sparked a worldwide environmental movement. This movement seeks to protect the environment through education, legislation, and political activism.

As a relatively recent specialty within sociology, environmental sociology examines how human activities affect the environment and how the environment affects human activities. Although many environmental sociologists are also environmental activists, the roles do not necessarily overlap. There is a mutual concern, however, for a sense of harmony to be developed between technology and the natural environment.

KEY TERMS
After studying the chapter, review the definition of each of the following terms.

acid rain: rain containing sulfuric and nitric acids (burning fossil fuels release sulfur dioxide and nitrogen oxide that become sulfuric and nitric acids when they react with moisture in the air) (647)

alienation: Marx's term for workers' lack of connection to the product of their labor; caused by their being assigned repetitive tasks on a small part of a product—this leads to a sense of powerlessness and normlessness; others use the term in the general sense of not feeling a part of something (638)

corporate welfare: the financial incentives (tax breaks, subsidies, and even land and stadiums) given to corporations in order to attract them to an area or induce them to remain (648)

cultural lag: Ogburn's term for human behavior lagging behind technological innovations (637)

dialectical process: (of history) each arrangement of power (a thesis) contains contradictions (antitheses) that make the arrangement unstable and that must be resolved; the new arrangement of power (a synthesis) contains its own contradictions; this process of balancing and unbalancing continues throughout history as groups struggle for power and other resources (635)

diffusion: the spread of invention or discovery from one area to another; identified by William Ogburn as one of three processes of social change (636)

discovery: a new way of seeing reality; identified by William Ogburn as one of three processes of social change (635)

ecosabotage: actions taken to sabotage the efforts of people who are thought to be legally harming the environment (651)

environmental injustice: refers to how minorities and the poor are harmed the most by environmental pollution (651)

environmental sociology: a specialty within sociology whose focus is how humans affect the environment and how the environment affects humans (652)

global warming: an increase in the Earth's temperature due to the greenhouse effect (648)

invention: the combination of existing elements and materials to form new ones; identified by William Ogburn as the first of three processes of social change (635)

modernization: the transformation of traditional societies into industrial societies (631)

postmodern society: another term for *postindustrial society*; its chief characteristic is the use of tools that extend the human abilities to gather and analyze information, to communicate, and to travel (638)

social change: the alteration of culture and societies over time (630)

sustainable environment: a world system that takes into account the limits of the environment, produces enough material goods for everyone's needs, and leaves a heritage of a sound environment for the next generation (646-647)

KEY PEOPLE

Review the major theoretical contributions or findings of these people.

James Flink: A historian who noted that the automobile changed women "from producers of food and clothing into consumers of national-brand canned goods, prepared foods, and ready-made clothes." (639-640)

Karl Marx: He noted that capitalism set in motion an antagonistic relationship between capitalists and workers that remain today. Marx developed the theory of dialectical materialism. (631, 635, 638)

Lewis Henry Morgan: Morgan's theory of social development once dominated Western thought. He suggested that societies pass through three stages: savagery, barbarism, and civilization. (634)

William Ogburn: Ogburn identified three processes of social change: invention, discovery, and diffusion. He also coined the term "cultural lag" to describe a situation in which some elements of culture adapt to an invention or discovery more rapidly than others. (634-637)

Oswald Spengler: Spengler wrote *The Decline of the West,* in which he proposed that Western civilization was declining. (634-635)

Arnold Toynbee: This historian suggested that each time a civilization successfully meets a challenge, oppositional forces are set up. Eventually, the oppositional forces are set loose and the fabric of society is ripped apart. (634)

Max Weber: Weber argued that capitalism grew out of the Protestant Reformation. (631-632)

SELF-TEST

MULTIPLE CHOICE QUESTIONS

1. The alteration of culture and society over time is (630)
   a. social transformation.
   b. social metamorphosis.
   c. social alternation.
   d. social change.

2. What does the author of your text identify as the fourth social revolution? (630)
   a. the invention of the steam engine
   b. the transformation from *Gemeinschaft* to *Gesellschaft*
   c. the invention of the microchip
   d. the development of capitalism

3. Weber identified _____ as the core reason for the development of capitalism. (631)
   a. religion
   b. industrialization
   c. politics
   d. none of the above

4. Which of the following statements about the second stage of the demographic transition is *incorrect*? (631)
   a. The population decreased.
   b. It upset the balance of family and property.
   c. It brought mass migration.
   d. It brought hunger.

5. What country is the newest member of the G8? (632)
   a. Russia
   b. China
   c. Egypt
   d. Mexico

6. What country does the author note is a threat to the G8? (632)
   a. Russia
   b. China
   c. Egypt
   d. Mexico

7. _____ theories assume that all societies follow the same path, evolving from simple to complex through uniform sequences. (634)

a. Cyclical
b. Uniformity
c. Unilinear evolution
d. Multilinear evolution

8. Today, evolutionary theories have been (634)
   a. accepted because history largely has proven this perspective to be correct.
   b. rejected because the assumption of progress has been cast aside.
   c. neither rejected nor accepted because these theories take into account the rich diversity of traditional cultures.
   d. none of the above

9. Which of the following attempt to account for the rise of entire civilizations, not a particular society? (634)
   a. multilinear evolutionary theory
   b. cyclical theory
   c. conflict theory
   d. epoch theory

10. According to Karl Marx, each _____ sows the seeds of its own destruction. (635)
    a. thesis
    b. ruling class
    c. epoch
    d. exploited class

11. Ogburn's analysis has been criticized because (636-637)
    a. it is too narrow in focus and not suitable for explaining the transformation of industrial into postindustrial societies.
    b. it does not recognize the importance of technology for social change.
    c. it places too great an emphasis on technology as the source for almost all social change.
    d. it predicts that material culture will change in response to symbolic culture, when in fact it is symbolic culture that changes in response to material culture.

12. As men were drawn out of their homes to work in factories, family relationships changed. This is an example of (638)
    a. changes in social organizations produced by technology.
    b. changes in social relationships produced by technology.
    c. changes in ideologies produced by technology.
    d. none of the above

13. Which of the following is *not* one of the ways that computers are transforming education? (642)
    a. They are making new areas of study available to students online.

b. They are changing the way that students learn.

c. They are increasing the opportunities for teachers and administrators to carry out surveillance on students.

d. They are expanding the gap in educational opportunities between wealthy school districts and poor school districts.

14. Which of the following is *not* one of the ways computers transform the workplace? (642-643)

a. changing the ways in which we do work

b. altering social relationships

c. increasing social interactions

d. reversing the location of where work is done

15. Which of the following will become a part of mainstream education? (642)

a. telecommunication

b. distance learning

c. teletransportation

d. all of the above

16. One concern about the expansion of the information superhighway is that (645)

a. interest in accessing it will outstrip capacity to carry so many users.

b. social inequalities will become greater, both on a national and global basis.

c. people will tie up the services with nonessential activities.

d. people will become even more alienated as they relate more and more through their computers and less and less face to face.

17. Which of the following is true about Star Wars? (645)

a. The Pentagon is building its own Internet.

b. Robots are being used in Iraq.

c. The Defense Department is planning to "weaponize space."

d. All of the above

18. According to the author of the text, which region of the world is considered the major polluter? (646)

a. the Most Industrialized Nations

b. the Industrializing Nations

c. the Least Industrialized Nations

d. the Most and Least Industrialized Nations

19. A consequence of burning fossil fuels is (647)

a. acid rain.

b. the greenhouse effect.

c. global warming.

d.   all of the above

20. Which of the following is the most prominent alternative source of energy for vehicles? (649)
   a.   fuel cells
   b.   internal combustion engines
   c.   gas-electric hybrids
   d.   converted hydrogen

21. Which groups in U.S. society are disproportionately exposed to environmental hazards? (651)
   a.   office workers and factory workers
   b.   racial minorities and the poor
   c.   farm workers and lumberjacks
   d.   racial and ethnic groups

22. The major source of pollution in the future is likely to be (653)
   a.   the Least Industrialized Nations.
   b.   the Industrializing Nations.
   c.   the Most Industrialized Nations.
   d.   none of the above

23. Which of the following presents the greatest threat to the survival of numerous plant and animal species? (649)
   a.   the continued burning of fossil fuels
   b.   the dumping of toxic waste in the least industrialized nations
   c.   the disappearance of the world's rain forests
   d.   the greenhouse effect

24. Environmental sociology (652-653)
   a.   examines how the physical environment affects human activities.
   b.   examines how human activities affect the physical environment.
   c.   has nine main assumptions.
   d.   all of the above

25. What is the goal of environmental sociologists? (653)
   a.   to stop pollution
   b.   to do research on the mutual impact that individuals and environments have on one another
   c.   to empower those who are disadvantaged by environmental threats so that the quality of their lives will be improved
   d.   to lobby for alternatives to fossil fuels

TRUE-FALSE QUESTIONS

1. _____ The assumption of evolutionary theories that all societies progress from a primitive state to a highly complex state has been proven. (634)
2. _____ Cyclical theories assume that civilizations are like organisms. (634)
3. _____ Some cyclical theories predict the decline of Western civilization. (635)
4. _____ Invention, discovery, and diffusion are Ogburn's three processes of social change. (635-636)
5. _____ Technology usually changes first, followed by culture. (637)
6. _____ Technology is not a very powerful force for social change. (638)
7. _____ Marx believed that the change to the factory system was a source of alienation. (638)
8. _____ The automobile confined women to the home since only men drove. (640-641)
9. _____ The use of computers in education will significantly reduce existing social inequalities between school districts. (642)
10. _____ Computers create the possibility for increased surveillance of workers and depersonalization. (642-643)

FILL-IN-THE-BLANK QUESTIONS

1. The sweeping changes ushered in by industrialization are called _____. (630)
2. _____ societies are small, rural, and slow to change. (630)
3. According to Marx's view, each ruling group sows the seeds of its own _____. (61)
4. _____ coined the phrase "cultural lag." (636)
5. All human groups make and use _____. (638)
6. _____ noted that technology also spurs ideology. (638)
7. Underlying today's environmental decay is the globalization of _____. (646)
8. As the rain forests disappear, so do the _____ tribes who live in them. (650)
9. _____ refers to actions taken to sabotage the efforts of people who are thought to be legally harming the environment. (651)
10. The goal of _____ sociology is to study how humans affect the physical environment and how the physical environment affects human activities. (653)

ESSAY QUESTIONS

1. The author of your text suggests that social movements reveal the cutting edge of change in a society or across the globe. In Chapter 21, you learned about different social movements, and in this chapter there is discussion of the environmental movement. Discuss a specific social movement in terms of what it reveals about social change.

2. Discuss Ogburn's three processes of social change, provide examples to illustrate each, and evaluate the theory.

3. Choose a particular technology, such as the computer, and discuss the impact that it has had on U.S. society.

4. Discuss the role of the automobile in changing cities, architecture, courtship, and women's roles.

5. Consider whether it is possible for us to achieve a sustainable environment.

CHAPTER 1

ANSWERS FOR THE MULTIPLE CHOICE QUESTIONS

1. **b** The sociological perspective is an approach to understanding human behavior by placing it within its broader social context.

2. **d** Sociologists consider occupation, income, education, gender, age, and race as dimensions of social location.

3. **d** All three statements reflect ways in which the social sciences are like the natural sciences. Both attempt to study and understand their subjects objectively; both attempt to undercover the relationships that create order in their respective worlds through controlled observation; and both are divided into many specialized fields.

4. **c** Generalization is one of the goals of scientific inquiry. It involves going beyond individual cases by making statements that apply to broader groups or situations.

5. **b** The Industrial Revolution, imperialism, and the development of the scientific method all contributed to the development of sociology. The fourth influence was the political revolutions in America and France—there was no political revolution in Britain at that time.

6. **d** Positivism is the application of the scientific approach to the social world.

7. **d** Of the four statements, the one that *best* reflects Herbert Spencer's views on charity is "The poor are the weakest members of society and if society intervenes to help them, it is interrupting the natural process of social evolution." While many contemporaries of Spencer were appalled by his views, the wealthy industrialists found them attractive.

8. **b** The proletariat is the large group of workers who are exploited by the small group of capitalists who own the means of production, according to Karl Marx.

9. **b** In his research on suicide rates, Durkheim found that individuals' integration into their social groups influences the overall patterns of suicide between groups. He called this concept *social integration.*

10. **c** Max Weber's research on the rise of capitalism identified religious beliefs as the key.

11. **a** Weber wanted objectivity to be the hallmark of social research.

12. **c** Social facts and *Verstehen* go hand in hand. Social facts are patterns of behavior that characterize a social group. By applying *Verstehen*—your understanding of what it means to be human and to face various situations in life—you gain an understanding of people's behavior.

13. **b** The statement, "Unlike the situation in Europe, many North American women found that there were few barriers and they were able to train in sociology and receive faculty appointments," is *incorrect.* In the early years of sociology, the situation of women in North America was similar to that of European women—they were largely excluded and their work ignored. As a result, many turned to social activism, especially working with the poor and immigrant groups. Many male sociologists who worked as professors denied female sociologists the title of sociologist, preferring to call them social workers.

14. **d** Jane Addams won the Nobel Prize for working on behalf of poor immigrants

15. **c** W. E. B. Du Bois was an African American sociologist who wrote extensively on race relations. He experienced prejudice and discrimination in both his personal and professional life. His commitment to racial equality led him to establish the NAACP.

16. **b** Using objective, systematic observations is *not* an accurate description of theory.

17. **b** Symbolic interactionism is the theoretical perspective that views society as composed of symbols that people use to establish meaning, develop their views of the world, and communicate with one another.

18. **d** According to Robert Merton, an unintended consequence that can hurt a system's equilibrium is a latent dysfunction.

19. **d** Industrialization and urbanization have undermined the traditional purposes of the family, according to theorists using functional analysis.

20. **a** Karl Marx first asserted that conflict is inherent in all relations that have authority.

21. **b** Conflict theorists might explain the high rate of divorce by looking at society's basic inequalities between males and females.

22. **a** Functionalists and conflict theorists focus on the macro level of sociological analysis.

23. **d** Since each theoretical perspective provides a different, often sharply contrasting picture of our world, no theory or level of analysis encompasses all of reality. By putting the contributions of each perspective and levels of analysis together, we gain a more comprehensive picture of social life.

24. **c** The first phase of sociology in the United States stretched from the founding of the first departments of sociology in the last decade of the nineteenth century into the 1940s. This phase was characterized by an interest in using sociological knowledge to improve social life and change society.

25. **d** The author of your text suggests that *globalization*—the breaking down of national boundaries because of communication, trade, and travel—is very likely going to transform sociology in the United States. As global issues intrude more into U.S. society, sociologists will have to broaden the scope and focus of their research.

ANSWERS FOR TRUE-FALSE QUESTIONS

1. *True.*
2. *True.*
3. *True.*
4. *True.*
5. *False.* Harriet Martineau's ground-breaking work on social life in Great Britain and the United States was largely ignored; she is remembered for her translations of Auguste Comte's work.
6. *True.*
7. *True.*
8. *False.* Although functionalists do believe the family has lost many of its traditional purposes, they do not believe they have all been lost. Some of the existing functions are presently under assault or are being eroded.
9. *False.* Some conflict theorists use this theory in a much broader sense.
10. *True.*

ANSWERS TO THE FILL-IN-THE-BLANK QUESTIONS

1. sociological perspective
2. generalized
3. scientific method
4. problems
5. replication
6. manifest
7. conflict
8. social interaction
9. social analysis
10. globalization

GUIDELINES FOR ANSWERING THE ESSAY QUESTIONS

1. *Explain what the sociological perspective encompasses and then, using that perspective, discuss the forces that shaped the discipline of sociology.*

There are two parts to this question. First, you are asked to define the sociological perspective. As you define this, you would want to mention the idea of social location, perhaps by bringing into your essay C. Wright Mills' observations on the connection between biography and history. Another way to explain the perspective would be to contrast sociology with other disciplines, talking about what sociology is and what it isn't.

The second part of the essay involves discussing the forces that shaped sociology and its early followers. You are being asked to think about what was going on in the social world in the early nineteenth century that might have led to the birth of this new discipline. Referring back to the book, you would want to identify three forces: (1) the Industrial Revolution; (2) the political revolutions of America and France; (3) imperialism; and (4) the emergence of the scientific method. You would conclude by discussing how each of the early sociologists—Auguste Comte, Herbert Spencer, Karl Marx, Emile Durkheim, and Max Weber—were influenced by these broader forces in making a contribution to sociology. You could also bring into the discussion some of the material on sexism in early sociology, noting how the ideas about the appropriate role for women in society functioned to exclude women like Harriet Martineau and Jane Addams from the discipline, or you could talk about the emergence of sociology in North America.

2. *Emile Durkheim studied European society at a time when it was undergoing major social upheaval as a result of the industrial revolution. In this first chapter, you are introduced to some of his major contributions—his work on suicide and his conclusions about social integration and anomie. Summarize what his contributions were and then consider how they are still useful for understanding social life today.*

You could begin by talking briefly about the research on suicide and how Durkheim analyzed how suicide rates varied for different types of social groups. You should also stress that Durkheim was trying to look beyond individual characteristics to locating social factors that underlie suicide; this was critically important to him as he tried to establish sociology as a separate academic discipline. In explaining this pattern, he identified *social integration*, or the degree to which individuals are tied to their social groups, as a key social factor in explaining suicide. At that time, the connections between individuals and many traditional social groups were weakening because of the growing individualism and impersonality of the emerging industrial society. Durkheim called for the creation of new social groups to stand between the state and the individual.

You then need to make the case as to why these concepts of social integration and anomie are still relevant. You should point out that the social conditions that Durkheim described still exist. If anything, the trends that he first identified have intensified. As examples, you could talk about how Durkheim's concepts could be applied to patterns of suicide among teenagers or the outbreaks of school violence in large, impersonal high schools.

3. *The textbook notes that Verstehen and social facts go hand in hand; explain how this is so. Assume that you have been asked to carry out research to find out more about why growing numbers of women and children are homeless and what particular problems they face. Discuss how you could use both Verstehen and social facts in your study.*

First, you would want to define what *Verstehen* and social facts are and how they are compatible in terms of arriving at a complete picture of a social pattern. Then you can argue that social facts would be most appropriate in trying to explain why growing numbers of women and children are homeless—you might look at the changing economic status of women in society, the increase in the number of female-headed households, and the decline in the amount of affordable housing. On the other hand, by applying *Verstehen*, you would be able to discover what particular problems they face. Through face-to-face interviews at shelter sites, you would be able to experience firsthand some of what they are experiencing.

4. *Explain why there has been a continuing tension between analyzing society and working toward reforming society since the very beginning of society.*

Referring to the work of such early sociologists as Auguste Comte and Emile Durkheim, you could begin by noting that sociology has had twin goals from its inception—the scientific study of society and the application of scientific knowledge to social reform. When sociology was transplanted to the United

States at the end of the nineteenth century, this society was undergoing significant changes, with industrialization, urbanization, and immigration among them. The earliest North American sociologists, like their European predecessors, defined the sociologist's role as both social scientist and social reformer. At the same time, the record suggests that the primary emphasis has generally been on the sociologist's work as social scientist. For example, women who had been trained as sociologists but then excluded from the universities, turned to social reform and were denied the title of sociologist; instead, they were called social workers by male sociologists working from within academic departments of universities.

At this point you could draw on material in the text about the development of North American sociology, as well as the discussion of the different phases it has passed through. From the 1920s through the early post–World War II era, the emphasis was on sociological research rather than social reform, as departments of sociology become more widely established. Sociologists like Talcott Parsons, whose work was primarily theoretical in nature, came to dominate the field. While the early part of this period was one of significant turmoil (with the Great Depression and World War II), at the end of this phase, social problems were largely "invisible," given the general prosperity of the immediate post–World War II era.

You could point out that people like C. Wright Mills kept the tradition of social reform alive during these years. And with the social upheavals of the 1950s and 1960s—the civil rights movement, the women's movement, and the anti-war movement to name a few—the focus once again shifted back to social reform.

You could conclude by talking about applied sociology, a recent development that attempts to blend these two traditions. While it has gained legitimacy within the discipline, there are still those on both sides of this debate who reject applied sociology. For those whose emphasis is on pure sociology, it smacks of social reform, while for those who believe sociology should be working to reform society, it doesn't go far enough. The debate over the appropriate focus of sociological inquiry is unlikely to be resolved any time soon, because it reflects traditions that go back to the very origins of the discipline. Both sides can find ample support for their positions within the work and writings of earlier sociologists.

5. Explain what Weber meant when he said that sociology should be value free. Do you think this is possible? How do values play a role in determining the purpose and use of sociology?

When Weber said that sociology should be value free, he meant that a sociologist's values—beliefs about what is good or worthwhile in life and the way the world ought to be—should not affect his or her research. You could discuss that this is an ideal given that sociologists are also people and they are influenced by the values of the time in history in which they live. Values play a role in determining the research that will be conducted because values may drive interests that sociologists have to pursue one line of research or another.

CHAPTER 2

ANSWERS FOR MULTIPLE CHOICE QUESTIONS

1. **b** Sociologists would use the term "nonmaterial culture" to refer to a group's ways of thinking and doing, including language and other forms of interaction.
2. **c** The value of individualism is not part of material culture.
3. **a** The one statement that is *not* true regarding culture is that "people generally are aware of the effects of their own culture."
4. **d** The disorientation that James Henslin experienced when he came into contact with the fundamentally different culture of Morocco is known as culture shock.
5. **c** An American who thinks citizens of another country are barbarians if they like to attend bullfights is demonstrating ethnocentrism.
6. **c** Robert Edgerton cautioned against blindly accepting other cultures on the basis of their cultures and values if those customs and values threaten the quality of people's lives. He advocated rating cultures according to their quality of life.
7. **d** Gestures can lead to misunderstandings and embarrassment when their meanings are not shared.
8. **a** It is possible for human experience to be cumulative and for people to share memories because of language.
9. **c** The example from Eviatar Zerubavel illustrates the Sapir-Whorf hypothesis, which suggests that language not only reflects a culture's way of thinking and perceiving the world, but also helps to shape thought and perception.
10. **c** A monetary reward, a prize, a hug, or a pat on the back are all examples of *positive sanctions*.
11. **d** You have violated a folkway; norms related to everyday behavior that are not strictly enforced.
12. **a** Mores are essential to our core values and require conformity.
13. **c** The author of your text cites eating human flesh as an example of a *taboo*, a norm that is so strongly ingrained that even the thought of its violation is greeted with revulsion.
14. **d** Subcultures are a world within a world, have values and related behaviors that distinguish its members from the dominant culture, and include occupational groups. Therefore, all of the above are correct.
15. **c** Sociologically speaking, the Hells Angels are an example of a counterculture.
16. **b** A sociologist would describe the United States as a pluralistic society because it is made up of many different groups.
17. **c** Henslin suggests that a new value cluster, made up of the values of leisure, self-fulfillment, physical fitness, and youthfulness, is now emerging in the United States.
18. **a** Value contradictions occur when a value, such as the one that stresses group superiority, comes into direct conflict with other values, such as democracy and equality.
19. **b** Ideal culture reflects the values and norms that a people attempt to follow; it is the goals held out for them.
20. **b** Discipline is *not* a cultural universal identified by George Murdock
21. **d** The perspective that views human behavior as the result of natural selection and considers biological characteristics to be the fundamental cause of human behavior is *sociobiology*.
22. **d** The printing press or the computer would be considered *new technologies* because both had a significant impact on social life following their invention.
23. **d** Continuing to visit physicians and to rely on their judgment about the diagnosis and treatment of illness, even when computer tests do a better job, is an example of cultural lag.
24. **c** The adoption of bagels, woks and hammocks by the United States illustrates the process of cultural diffusion.
25. **b** Exporting Coca-Cola around the globe has produced cultural leveling.

ANSWERS FOR TRUE-FALSE QUESTIONS

1. *True.*
2. *False.* Culture has a great deal to do with our ideas of right and wrong. For example, folkways and mores have sanctions attached to them to encourage people to do the right thing.
3. *True.*
4. *False.* Humans could not plan future events without language to convey meanings of past, present, and future points in time.
5. *False.* One society's folkways may be another society's mores.
6. *False.* Motorcycle enthusiasts who emphasize personal freedom and speed, while maintaining values of success, form part of a subculture, not a counterculture. Motorcycle gangs who commit crimes and use illegal drugs are an example of a counterculture.
7. *True.*
8. *False.* Concern for the environment has not always been a core value in U.S. society. It is one of the emergent values that is now increasing in importance.
9. *True.*
10. *True.*

ANSWERS TO THE FILL-IN-THE-BLANK QUESTIONS

1. culture shock
2. symbol
3. gestures
4. language
5. counterculture
6. value cluster
7. value
8. real culture
9. new technology
10. cultural leveling

GUIDELINES FOR ANSWERING THE ESSAY QUESTIONS

1. *Explain cultural relativism and discuss both the advantages and disadvantages of practicing it.*

You would begin your essay by defining cultural relativism and explaining that it developed in reaction to ethnocentrism. The primary advantage of this approach to looking at other cultures is that we are able to appreciate another way of life without making judgments, thereby reducing the possibilities for conflict between cultures. The primary disadvantage is that it can be used to justify any cultural practice and especially those that endanger people's health, happiness, and survival. You could conclude with a reference to Robert Edgerton's proposed "quality of life scale."

2. *As the author points out, the United States is a pluralistic society, made up of many different groups. Having read this chapter about culture, now discuss some of the things that are gained by living in such a society, as well as some of the problems that are created.*

The first thing to think about is how our national culture has been shaped by all of the different subcultures that exist within it You could consider aspects of both material culture and nonmaterial culture that have been influenced by youth subculture, by ethnic and racial subcultures, and by occupational subcultures, to name a few. At the same time, the presence of so many different subcultures creates the possibility for ethnocentrism and misunderstandings. Additionally, when the values of the subculture are too different from the mainstream culture, culture wars can develop.

3. *Consider the degree to which the real culture of the United States falls short of the ideal culture. Provide concrete examples to support your essay.*

Your first step is to define what real and ideal culture mean. Then you would want to refer to the core values that are identified in the text as reflective of the ideal culture and discuss the ways in which

Americans fall far short of upholding these values in their everyday lives. An interesting example of the difference between ideal and real culture would be the increasing value we place on leisure, and yet we are working more hours than ever before, or the value we place on physical fitness and yet we are more obese and less physically fit than ever.

4.   *Thinking about William Ogburn's term cultural lag, explain why college students still attend traditional classes in the classroom when the technology is available to take classes over the Internet.*
        William Ogburn would call this a cultural lag. By this he meant that a group's material culture uses changes first, with the nonmaterial culture lagging behind. You could discuss that college students are still more comfortable taking a class in the classroom rather than taking the course online. It is possible that some students don't have a computer at home or don't have access to a computer and this would make it difficult, if not impossible, to take a course over the Internet. Some students might never want to take a course over the Internet because they have certain beliefs about what it means to be a student.

CHAPTER 3

ANSWERS FOR MULTIPLE CHOICE QUESTIONS
1. **b** Feral children supposedly were abandoned or lost by their parents and raised by animals.
2. **a** From the case of Isabelle, we can conclude that humans have no natural language.
3. **c** On the basis of studies involving institutionalized children, psychologists H.M. Skeels and H. B. Dye concluded that the absence of stimulating social interaction was the basic cause of low intelligence among these children, not some biological incapacity.
4. **d** Studies of isolated rhesus monkeys demonstrated that the monkeys were not able to adjust to monkey life and did not instinctively know how to enter into "monkey interaction" with other monkeys or how to engage in sexual intercourse.
5. **d** Forming opinions about others based on our self-concept is not an element of the looking-glass self.
6. **c** According to Mead's theory, during the play stage children pretend to take the roles of specific people.
7. **a** According to Mead, the "I" is the self as subject.
8. **d** According to Mead, all three, language, the mind, and the self, are products of society.
9. **d** Using Piaget's theory, children are likely to become "young philosophers"—able to talk about abstract concepts, come to conclusions based on general principles, and use rules to solve abstract problems—during the formal operational stage.
10. **a** Freud's term for the inborn drives for self-gratification is the id.
11. **b** According to Lawrence Kohlberg, when a young child like Larry tries very hard to be nice to his younger sister in order to please his mother, he is in the preconventional stage of moral development.
12. **d** Most people are unlikely to ever reach the postconventional stage, according to Kohlberg. This is the stage in which people reflect on abstract principles of right and wrong and judge a behavior according to these principles.
13. **c** From her early research, Carol Gilligan concluded that women are more likely than men to evaluate morality in terms of personal relationships. On the other hand, men use abstract principles, a code of ethics that defines what is right and wrong.
14. **b** Although people around the world may share emotions, because emotions are in part due to biology, the way they express them varies considerably and this expression is learned through socialization. Therefore, the only statement that is *correct* is, "How we express emotions depends on our culture and our social location."
15. **c** According to this chapter, society sets up effective controls over our behavior by socializing us into self and emotions.
16. **d** Psychologists Susan Goldberg and Michael Lewis observed mothers with their six-month-old infants in a laboratory setting and concluded that the mothers unconsciously rewarded daughters for being passive and dependent.
17. **a** Research by Melissa Milkie indicates that young males actively used media images to help them understand what was expected of them as males in our society.
18. **b** Melvin Kohn suggests that the key to understanding social class differences in child rearing is the type of job the parents have.
19. **a** Religion is a key component to life. It is not a substitute for what parents teach.
20. **b** The research on the impact of day care demonstrated that the more hours per week a child spends in day care, the weaker the bond between mother and child.
21. **b** In schools, the corridor curriculum exists in which students teach each other behavior that may not always be appropriate.
22. **d** In terms of children's peer groups and academic achievement, research by Patricia and Peter Adler suggests that for boys, to do well academically is to lose popularity, while for girls, getting good grades increases social standing.

23. **d** Resocialization occurs when a person takes a new job, joins a cult, or goes to boot camp.
24. **b** The statement, "They are not very effective in stripping away people's personal freedom," is *incorrect*. In fact, total institutions are very effective in stripping away individuals' personal freedom because they are isolated from the public, they suppress pre-existing statuses, they suppress cultural norms, and they closely supervise the entire lives of their residents.
25. **a** For women between the ages of 30 and 49, it is a time of juggling many roles.

ANSWERS FOR TRUE-FALSE QUESTIONS

1. *False.* Studies of institutionalized children demonstrate that some of the characteristics that we take for granted as being "human" traits result not from basic instincts, but rather from early close relations with other humans.
2. *False.* Socialization has a great deal to do with how we feel. Because different individuals' socialization differs, they will actually experience different emotions.
3. *True.*
4. *False.* Advertising continues to reinforce gender stereotypes.
5. *False.* It is a *manifest* function of education, not a *latent* function, to transmit skills and values appropriate for earning a living.
6. *True.*
7. *True.*
8. *True.*
9. *True.*
10. *True.*

ANSWERS TO THE FILL-IN-THE-BLANK QUESTIONS

1. language
2. monkeys
3. looking-glass self
4. take the role of other
5. generalized other
6. preoperational stage
7. social class
8. religion
9. early middle years
10. behavior

GUIDELINES FOR ANSWERING THE ESSAY QUESTIONS

1. *Explain what is necessary in order for us to develop into full human beings.*

You might want to begin by stating that in order for us to become full human beings, we need language and intimate social connections to others. You could draw on the information presented in the previous chapter as to what language enables us to do: grasp relationships to others, think in terms of a shared past and future, and make shared plans. Our knowledge of language, and our ability to use it, develops out of social interaction, as the evidence of those children raised in isolation demonstrates. Furthermore, we learn how to get along with others only through close personal experiences with others. The experience of Isabelle and the children raised in institutionalized settings confirms this.

The importance of social interaction and close social contact for our development is underscored by the work of a number of social psychologists. Mead and Piaget suggest that our mind and our ability to reason develop out of social interactions, while Kohlberg and Gilligan argue that our sense of right and wrong develop in the same way. Finally, even our expression of emotion comes out of our contact with others in our society.

2. *Why do sociologists argue that socialization is a process and not a product?*

Sociologists would argue that socialization is a process rather than a product because there is no end to socialization. It begins at birth and continues throughout one's life whenever you take on a new role. Cooley was the first to note that we are continually modifying our sense of self depending on our reading of others' reactions to us. Mead's work on taking the role of the other in the development of the self also suggests that socialization is a process. Researchers have identified a series of stages through which we pass as we age; at each stage we are confronted by new demands and new challenges that need to be mastered.

3. *Having read about how the family, the media, and peers all influence our gender socialization, discuss why gender roles tend to remain unchanged from one generation to the next.*

You could begin your essay by defining gender socialization, the process of learning what is expected of us from society because we are born either male or female. You could then note that this socialization is so complete that, as adults, most of us act, think, and even feel according to our particular culture's guidelines of what is appropriate for our sex. We do not question the way in which gender roles are defined—we have come to see the way we behave as natural and normal. Consequently, when we have children, we set out to socialize them into the same set of gender roles. You could incorporate some discussion of the research by Susan Goldberg and Michael Lewis about child rearing, as well as the fact that children are generally provided with gender-appropriate toys and subject to different parental expectations.

The ways in which the media perpetuate traditional gender roles should also be noted. You could talk about gender stereotypes that show up in advertising, television, and video games. Include a reference to studies that show the more television people watch, the more they tend to have restrictive views about women's role in society. Milkie's research on peer groups also demonstrates how media images contribute to gender socialization; boys used the media images to discover who they are as males.

4. *As the text points out, the stages of the life course are influenced by the biological clock, but they also reflect broader social factors. Identify the stages of the life course and indicate how social factors have contributed to the definition of each of these stages.*

You should begin your essay by noting that the stages of the life course are shaped by both biological and social factors. Begin with childhood (from birth to age 12) and talk about how this stage extends over the earliest years as our bodies and minds are developing; at the same time, our understanding of childhood has been transformed by broader social factors like industrialization. The impact of social factors is even more apparent in the second stage, adolescence, which goes from ages 13 to 17. Our bodies are changing biologically, but this stage is a total social invention, the result of the Industrial Revolution and the growing importance of education.

It used to be that most people immediately assumed adult responsibilities upon graduation from high school: jobs, marriages and children. However, a growing number of young people today are postponing this next step as they acquire the additional education and training called for in our modern world. Consequently, we are witnessing the birth of a new stage: young adulthood. By the end of their 20s, most people are ready to launch their careers and their families, which leads to the next stage, the middle years. But because this is such a long stage, spanning the years from 30 to 65, it is generally divided into two stages—early and later. Although the life expectancy of people in U.S. society has been extended, during the later middle years issues of health and mortality are important. As their own parents die, there is a fundamental shift in their orientation to life. This stage ends at 65, at a time when most people are retiring, or have retired.

The final stage is the older years, again divided into early and later. A few generations ago, when life expectancy ran to the late 60s or early 70s, this was a relatively short stage, characterized by preparations for one's own death. Today, because we enjoy longer lives, the early part of this stage is often experienced as an extension of the middle years. People are unlikely to see themselves as old and they continue to be socially active. As health declines and friends and spouses die, they move into the final years.

5. *Are we prisoners of our socialization?*

While socialization is a very powerful force in our lives, we are more than an accumulation of our social experiences. As socialization influences our behavior, we, in turn, act on our environment. As humans, we also influence our own self-concept. It is this "self" that acts as a social agent and allows us to act on our environment. A major argument against humans as prisoners of socialization lies in the fact that human behavior is so unpredictable.

CHAPTER 4

ANSWERS FOR MULTIPLE CHOICE QUESTIONS

1. **a** Microsociology focuses on social interaction.
2. **d** Sociologists who study individuals would be using microsociology.
3. **a** As a budding sociologist who is interested in the best way to study different perceptions that different classes have of each other, you would use a macrosociological approach.
4. **c** "An individual's behaviors and attitudes are due to biology (one's race or sex, for instance) as much as it is due to his/her location in the social structure," is *incorrect*. As the author of your text points out, if you were to switch your social location, from being a college student to being a street person, you would still be the same person biologically, but because of the change, you would experience social life differently.
5. **d** Age is not part of the definition of social class.
6. **d** Sociologists use the term *status* to refer to the position that someone occupies.
7. **d** Positions you occupy are termed *status set*.
8. **a** A sociologist would use the term *ascribed status* to describe race, sex, and the social class of one's parents.
9. **d** Once you finish your education, you will move into some kind of occupation or profession, perhaps one that is based on your educational training. This job or career you will eventually hold is considered an achieved status.
10. **c** Wedding rings, military uniforms, and clerical collars are all examples of status symbols.
11. **c** The *incorrect* statement is "Status symbols are always positive signs or people would not wear them." Some social statuses are negative, and therefore, so are their status symbols (e.g., prison clothing issued to inmates).
12. **c** Master statuses are both ascribed and achieved.
13. **a** Status inconsistency most likely occurs when a contradiction or mismatch between statuses exists. For example, a college professor is accorded relatively high prestige while at the same time is generally not very well paid.
14. **d** The behaviors, obligations, and privileges attached to statuses are called roles.
15. **a** Education would be considered a social institution and therefore is formally, not informally, structured.
16. **d** "All of the above" is correct. Organic solidarity refers to a society with a highly specialized division of labor whose members are interdependent on one another and with a high degree of impersonal relationships.
17. **a** *Gemeinschaft* is the type of society in which everyone knows everyone else, people conform because they are very sensitive to the opinions of others and want to avoid being gossiped about, and people draw comfort from being part of an intimate group.
18. **b** The statement that "stereotypes are unlikely to be self-fulfilling" is *incorrect*. While stereotypes have no single, inevitable outcome, research by Mark Snyder found that college males immediately formed opinions about what women were like based only on photographs. In subsequent telephone conversations, they adjusted the way they talked to fit their stereotype of the woman. In response, the woman responded in a way that was consistent with the stereotype.
19. **d** Public distance zone marks the impersonal or formal relationship.
20. **d** Susan, a full-time student and a full-time worker, finds herself experiencing role conflict when her boss asks her to work during the same hours that she is expected to be in class.
21. **a** If you have ever been in the situation described, of being torn between answering the professor's question or showing up your peers, then you have experienced role strain.
22. **b** The social setting, appearance, and manner are all sign-vehicles used by individuals for managing impressions.

23. **d** Background assumptions are common understandings of how the world works; doctors do not cut hair so this would violate the belief of the role of doctors.
24. **c** The Thomas theorem would fall within symbolic interactionism.
25. **d** Research on the Saints and the Roughnecks demonstrated that in order to fully understand what happened to the boys in the study, William Chambliss needed to analyze both the social structure and the patterns of social interaction that characterized their lives.

ANSWERS FOR TRUE-FALSE QUESTIONS
1. *False.* Being a teenager is an example of an ascribed status.
2. *True.*
3. *False.* The amount and nature of control that a group has over you depends on the group. Some groups, like a stamp collecting club, don't have that much control over many aspects of our behavior, while other groups, like our family or friendship group, exert considerable control over a wide range of our behaviors.
4. *True.*
5. *False.* The Amish are an example of a *Gesellschaft* society.
6. *True.*
7. *True.*
8. *False.* The same setting will often serve as both a back and a front stage. When you are alone in your car it is a back stage, but when you are driving around with friends it becomes a front stage.
9. *True.* Studied nonobservance is a face-saving technique in which people give the impression that they are unaware of a flaw in someone's performance. Impression management describes people's efforts to control the impressions that others receive of them.
10. *True.*

ANSWERS TO FILL-IN-THE-BLANK QUESTIONS
1. social interaction
2. structure
3. social class
4. master status
5. roles
6. functionalists
7. division of labor
8. four
9. teamwork
10. face-saving behavior

GUIDELINES FOR ANSWERING THE ESSAY QUESTIONS
1. *Choose a research topic and discuss how you approach this topic using both macrosociological and microsociological approaches.*

The way to answer this question is to first think of a topic. I've chosen the topic of labor unions. Remember that the macrosociological level focuses on the broad features of society. So from this level, I might research the role that unions play within the economy or the political system, what types of workers are organized into unions, the level of union organization among workers, or the level of union activity. Shifting to a microsociological level of analysis, I would want to look at what happens within unions or between unions and management in terms of social interaction. From this perspective, I might want to investigate the behavior of union members and leaders at a union meeting, or the behavior of union and management negotiators at a bargaining session. By combining both perspectives, I have achieved a much broader understanding of the role of unions within society.

2. *The concept of a social structure is often difficult to grasp, yet social structure is a central organizing feature of social life. Identify the ways in which it takes shape in our society and in our lives.*

You will want to begin with the definition of social structure as the framework for society that establishes the typical patterns for the society. Then you can identify the major components of it: culture, social class, social status, roles, groups and social institutions. It is these components that give social structure shape and substance. The rest of your essay would focus on discussing the contribution that each of these components makes to the overall social structure. You can conclude with the observation that when we are born into a society, we are immediately located within the social structure based on the culture, the social class of our parents, and our ascribed statuses. As we grow and function within different groups and social institutions, we learn to perform roles that are consistent with our culture and our status. We may eventually acquire achieved statuses. All of this gives shape and meaning to our lives, which in turn gives shape and meaning to social life.

3. *Today we can see many examples of people wanting to recreate a simpler way of life. Using Tönnies' framework, analyze this tendency.*

You would want to begin by describing Tönnies' framework of *Gemeinschaft* and *Gesellschaft*, and discussing the characteristics of each. Using these concepts, you would indicate that individuals' search for community reflects a rejection of the ever-increasing impersonality and formality of modern society. In their actions, people are trying to recreate a social world where everyone knows each other within the context of intimate groups. Some sociologists have used the term "pseudo-*Gemeinschaft*" to describe the attractiveness of the past—people building colonial homes and decorating them with antiques.

4. *Assume that you have been asked to give a presentation to your sociology class on Goffman's dramaturgy approach. Describe what information you would want to include in such a presentation.*

You could begin by explaining how Goffman saw life as a drama that was acted out on a stage. This would lead you to making a distinction between front stage and back stage. You might even want to provide some examples. For instance, you are presenting on a front stage, but you practiced for this presentation in your bedroom without any audience. Because dramaturgy focuses on the performances we give when we assume different roles, you might also want to talk about the problems of role conflict and role strain and the fact that we tend to become the roles we play. An important contribution by Goffman was his insights into impression management, so you would want to explain what that is and how it involves the use of three different types of sign-vehicles: social setting, appearance, and manner. Finally, you could conclude with his concept of teamwork, especially as it relates to face-saving behavior, and remember to include examples of all of these concepts as you proceed.

5. *Differentiate between role conflict, role exit, and role strain and give examples.*

Role conflict is a situation in which one status (role) conflicts with another. For example, a student who is also a mom and wife might feel conflict in trying to juggle and balance all of those roles. Role conflict involves conflict between roles while role strain involves conflict within the same role. If you are a good student who is prepared and knows the answers, you may feel bad answering all of the questions when the teacher asks. You may feel that this makes the other students look bad. Role exit is leaving a role entirely. When people leave marriages or careers that they have been in for a long time, this is role exit. Some people feel that their identity is threatened because that role has been a part of their life for so long.

CHAPTER 5

ANSWERS FOR MULTIPLE CHOICE QUESTIONS

1. **b** A researcher interested in doing a macro level study would choose race relations as a topic. Waiting in public places, interactions between people on street corners, and meat packers at work are all topics that would interest a micro level researcher.

2. **d** "All of the above" is correct. Sociologists believe that research is necessary because common sense ideas may or may not be true, they want to move beyond guesswork, and researchers want to know what really is going on.

3. **c** Eight steps are involved in scientific research.

4. **c** Researchers review the literature in order to help them narrow down the problem by pinpointing particular areas to examine, to develop ideas about how to do their own research, and to determine whether the problem has been answered already. They are not trying to insure that their hypotheses are correct. That is why they will conduct the research.

5. **a** A relationship between or among variables is predicted by a hypothesis.

6. **b** Validity is important in the research process because the researcher wants to be sure that the operational definitions really measure what they are intended to measure.

7. **c** In analyzing data gathered by participant observation, a researcher is likely to choose qualitative analysis.

8. **d** All of the reasons stated in this question explain why computers are considered a valuable tool in quantitative analysis. They allow sociologists to analyze huge amounts of information and identify basic patterns; the software packages available for data analysis take much of the drudgery out of that work; and they make it possible for sociologists to try various statistical tests.

9. **a** Mean, median, and mode are ways to measure "average."

10. **a** Ethnomethodology is the study of how people use background assumptions to make sense of life and, thus, is a part of symbolic interactionism. Surveys, unobtrusive measures, and secondary analysis are research methods for gathering data.

11. **c** If you had carried out the procedure described, you would have selected a stratified random sample, defined as specific subgroups of the population in which everyone in the subgroup has an equal chance of being included in the study.

12. **c** This situation reflects interviewer bias. The respondent may feel uncomfortable voicing his or her true opinions directly to another person, but would be willing to reveal them in an anonymous situation.

13. **b** A researcher might "load the dice" in designing a research project because of a vested interest in the outcome of the research. He or she may be hired by business firms and is thus motivated to find results that are consistent with the interests of the firm.

14. **b** Given the time and cost factors, you are most likely to choose to use self-administered questionnaires, because this method allows a larger number of people to be sampled at a relatively low cost.

15. **b** The advantage of structured interviews is that they are faster to administer and make it easier for answers to be coded.

16. **d** Problems that must be dealt with in conducting participant observation include the researcher's personal characteristics, developing rapport with respondents, and generalizability. Therefore, "All of the above" is the correct response.

17. **b** Sources such as newspapers, diaries, bank records, police reports, household accounts and immigration files are documents that provide useful information for investigating social life.

18. **c** In order to study patterns of alcohol consumption in different neighborhoods, you decide to go through the recycling bins in your town and count the number of beer cans and wine and hard liquor bottles. This study would be using unobtrusive methods because you are making observations on people without their knowledge that they are being studied.

19. **a** A researcher who is trying to identify causal relationships is likely to use an experiment.
20. **b** In an experiment, the group not exposed to the independent variable in the study is the control group.
21. **b** The simultaneous occurrence of alcohol and physical abuse is known as a correlation.
22. **c** Surveys are more likely to be used by researchers trained in quantitative techniques.
23. **d** All of the reasons help explain why it is important to consider gender when planning and conducting research. Gender is a significant factor in social life; the gender of the interviewer could possibly contribute to interviewer bias; and because men and women experience the social world differently, both need to be studied in order to gain a complete picture.
24. **d** "All of the above" is correct. Research ethics require openness; that a researcher not falsify results or plagiarize someone else's work; and that research subjects should not be harmed by the research.
25. **b** Research and theory are both essential for sociology, since research without theory is simply a collection of facts, and theory without research is empty and abstract.

ANSWERS FOR TRUE-FALSE QUESTIONS
1. *True.*
2. *False.* Sociologists do not place one above the other. Rather, they take great care to assure that both are achieved.
3. *False.* In survey research, it is always desirable for respondents to express their own ideas.
4. *False.* Secondary analysis and use of documents are not the same thing. The data used in secondary analysis is gathered by other researchers while documents may be anything from diaries to police records.
5. *False.* It is not always unethical to observe behavior in people when they do not know they are being studied. However, there are circumstances when the issue of ethics should be raised.
6. *True.*
7. *True.*
8. *True.*
9. *True.*
10. *False.* Scully and Marolla's research demonstrates that it is possible to do research that contributes to our body of sociological knowledge under less than ideal conditions.

ANSWERS TO THE FILL-IN-THE-BLANK QUESTIONS
1. hypothesis
2. analyze
3. neutral
4. rapport
5. unobtrusive measures
6. independent variable
7. survey
8. interviewer
9. theory
10. common sense

GUIDELINES FOR ANSWERING THE ESSAY QUESTIONS
1. *Choose a topic and explain how you would go through the different steps in the research model.*

In order to answer this question, you must select a topic and then develop this from the beginning to the end of the research process, identifying all eight steps and explaining what tasks are carried out each step of the way. Your answer should make reference to variables, hypotheses, operational definitions, the different research methods, validity and reliability, different ways of analyzing the data, and replication.

2. *Discuss some of the things that can go wrong in the process of doing research and provide suggestions on how to overcome such problems.*

There are a number of problems that can arise if the researcher is not careful. Included would be: (1) deriving invalid and unreliable results because of inadequate operational definitions and inaccurate sampling procedures; (2) obtaining biased answers because biased questions were asked; (3) failing to establish rapport with research subjects because of personal qualities or characteristics; (4) failing to gain access to necessary documents because those who control the documents are unwilling to cooperate; and (5) failing to rule out possible spurious correlations. Each of these potential problems can be overcome if the researcher follows the steps in the research process carefully.

3. *The author of your text discusses six different research methods. Pick a research topic of interest to you and discuss how you might try to investigate this topic using these different methods. In your answer, consider how a particular method may or may not be suitable for the topic under consideration.*

To review, the different methods discussed in the text are (1) surveys; (2) participant observation; (3) secondary analysis; (4) documents; (5) unobtrusive measures; and (6) experiments. Your first step is to pick a potential research topic. Let's say you decide to research homeless women. You could do a survey, developing a questionnaire that would be either self-administered or completed through an interview. This would use either closed-ended or open-ended questions, or maybe a combination of both. You would need to discuss some of the problems that you might encounter in trying to define the homeless population or in attempting to draw a random sample. You could point out that while this method would allow you to sample a large number of people at a relatively low cost, you might have difficulties with rapport.

Participant observation might be more suitable for the topic under consideration. You could spend time in a homeless shelter getting to know the women who live there. Hopefully, over time you will have built some rapport with the clients and will be able to learn more about their lives and the reasons why they are homeless. You would want to make note that this method may make it difficult for you to generalize your findings.

As you proceed through the essay, you might consider the other methods. You could make an argument about using secondary analysis, documents, and unobtrusive measures. In all three instances, you would want to make note of how these could be used and the limitations that each presents. The only method you might find difficult to apply to this topic would be experiments.

Your conclusion would summarize what factors influence the researcher's choice of a method: available resources, degree of access to respondents, the purpose of the research, and the background of the researcher. You could also talk about the differences between quantitative and qualitative research.

4. *Explain why ethical guidelines are necessary when conducting social science research.*

Ethical guidelines are necessary for several reasons. First and foremost, the researcher is working with human subjects; there must be guidelines to protect these subjects from any undue physical or psychological harm. Secondly, the research is only valid and reliable if the subjects have honestly and accurately provided information to the researcher. For this reason, they must have confidence in the researcher and the research process; guidelines assure subjects that their identities will remain anonymous and their information will be confidential. Finally, an essential aspect of research is that it be shared with others in the research community and members of the wider society. Guidelines regarding falsification and plagiarism guarantee that all research will be carefully scrutinized, thereby assuring its validity and reliability.

5. *Discuss the relationship between research and theory and why commonsense is not enough.*

In this essay, you will want to begin with C. Wright Mills's observations about theory and research. He argued that research without theory is simply a collection of unrelated "facts," while theory without research is abstract and empty. Research tests theory and theory helps us explain unexpected or surprising findings. Both are essential for sociology, because both take us beyond commonsense.

Commonsense is not enough because problems and issues go well beyond what may sound logical. As sociologists do research, they often come up with surprising findings. You could conclude the essay by discussing the research by Scully and Marolla, which challenged common sense notions about rapists. They were not satisfied with the typical explanation that rapists were "sick." They found out that the motivating behavior in rape is power, not passion.

CHAPTER 6

ANSWERS FOR MULTIPLE CHOICE QUESTIONS

1. **b** The largest and most complex group that sociologists study is a society.
2. **c** Hunting and gathering societies consist of 25-40 members.
3. **a** Of all types of societies, the simplest is the hunting and gathering society.
4. **b** Pastoral societies are based on the pasturing of animals.
5. **d** "All of the above" is correct. The domestication revolution led to the human group becoming larger, the creation of a food surplus, and a more specialized division of labor.
6. **c** The society that emerged out of the invention of the plow was known as an agricultural society.
7. **d** "All of the above" is correct. Indicators of increasing equality include better housing, the abolition of slavery, and a move toward more representative political systems.
8. **a** Postindustrial society is based on information, services, and high technology.
9. **b** The United States was the first nation to have more than 50 percent of its workforce employed in service industries; it was followed quickly by Japan, Australia, New Zealand, and western Europe.
10. **d** "All of the above" is the correct answer. A *bioeconomic* society, in which the economy centers around the application of human genetics for medicine and plant genetics for the production of food, is associated with the identification of the double-helix structure of DNA and the decoding of the human genome in 2001. It may represent a new type of society or simply another aspect of postindustrial society.
11. **c** Emile Durkheim believed that small groups help prevent anomie, because, through their intimate relationships, they provide a sense of meaning and purpose to life.
12. **a** Cooley saw that primary groups are essential to an individual's psychological well-being.
13. **d** "All of the above" is correct. Secondary groups have members who are likely to interact on the basis of specific roles; are characteristic of industrial societies; and are essential to the functioning of contemporary societies.
14. **b** Groups that provide a sense of identification or belonging are referred to as in-groups.
15. **d** Because identification with a group generates not only a sense of belonging, but also loyalty and feelings of superiority, it can lead to rivalries with out-groups. Hence, the consequences of in-group membership can be all of the things mentioned: discrimination, hatred, and even killing.
16. **c** This would be her reference group. They are a group that you can compare yourself to and can provide you with standards even when you are not actually a member of the group.
17. **a** Sociologically speaking, the social ties radiating outward from the self, that link people together are social networks.
18. **a** Letters were sent to target people who then passed them on to people they knew on a first-name basis who would continue this pattern until it reached the final target person.
19. **d** "All of the above" is correct. Dyads are the most intense or intimate of human groups, require continuing active participation and commitment of both members, and are the most unstable of social groups.
20. **d** That the continuation of the triad depends on success of the arbitrator in settling disputes is *not* one of the characteristics of a triad; the other three are.
21. **c** A diffusion of responsibility occurs when a group is larger than a dyad and each member feels that someone else will act.
22. **c** An expressive leader increases harmony and minimizes conflict in a group.
23. **b** Research by Lippitt and White demonstrated that the authoritarian style of leader is most effective in emergency situations, and the laissez-faire style is generally ineffective. The one style that is best under most circumstances is the democratic style of leader.
24. **d** "All of the above" is correct. According to sociologists, leaders tend to have certain characteristics, including being more talking and able to express self-confidence, taller, and better-looking than others, and where they are sitting in a group.

25. **c** The Milgram experiment demonstrates how strongly people are influenced by authority.

ANSWERS FOR TRUE-FALSE QUESTIONS
1. *True.*
2. *False.* According to Elise Boulding, women's status fell rather than rose once metals were attached to plows. Plowing and the care of cows became associated with men, and their status rose even higher.
3. *True.*
4. *True.*
5. *True.*
6. *True.*
7. *True.*
8. *False.* Sociologically speaking, a leader does not have to be officially appointed or elected to be the "leader." A leader is someone who influences the behaviors of others.
9. *True.*
10. *True.*

ANSWERS TO THE FILL-IN-THE-BLANK QUESTIONS
1. horticultural societies
2. anomie
3. family
4. reference
5. faction
6. coalition
7. task
8. six
9. increases, decreases
10. groupthink

GUIDELINES FOR ANSWERING THE ESSAY QUESTIONS
1. *After summarizing the fundamental social changes that resulted from each of the different social revolutions, evaluate the degree to which the new technology of the microchip is contributing to a similar level of fundamental change.*

You would want to begin by summarizing characteristics of the first three social revolutions. The first social revolution was the domestication of animals and plants. This created a more dependable food supply, thereby allowing groups to grow larger in size, develop a more varied division of labor and increase trade between communities; it also led to the emergence of social inequality. The second social revolution was the agricultural revolution. The use of the plow contributed to higher crop yields using less labor, so that more people were freed to pursue other activities. Cities grew and "culture" developed. Inequality became a permanent feature of society. The third social revolution was the invention of machines powered by fuels instead of animals. Productivity was further enhanced and social inequality was initially greater than before, although over time the amount of inequality began to diminish.

Having done that, you should turn your attention to the current transformation of industrial society into a postindustrial society and the role of the microchip. You could mention the impact that computers are having on our lives, including everything from communications to the way we work. The earlier transformations contributed to increased division of labor, changes in the level of inequality within society, and relations between social groups. Your conclusion is based on your evaluation of whether you think this transformation is as profound as the earlier ones.

2. *Durkheim was among the first sociologists to argue that small groups stand as a buffer between the individual and the larger society. The author of your text notes that secondary groups today have become*

essential to our welfare, yet they fail to satisfy our deep needs for intimate association. In this essay, consider how it is possible that they are essential for our welfare if they fail to satisfy essential human needs.

The reason the author of your text claims that secondary groups are essential for our welfare has to do with the nature of industrial and postindustrial societies. These are societies with very large populations and a very complex division of labor. Given these changes in society, it is understandable why most of our activities are organized within secondary groups, since this type of group is defined as a large, relatively anonymous, formal organization devoted to a single interest or goal. Our daily lives would be chaotic and very unproductive without the work of secondary groups.

Durkheim was concerned about how our individual needs would be met within a large, relatively anonymous society and believed that we form small (primary) groups to serve as a buffer between us and society. Today we rely on this same type of group to serve as a buffer between us and the impersonality of the secondary group. Our essential human need for intimacy is provided by primary groups that tend to form within secondary groups. Without our friends at work and school and our families at home, our lives would be very alienating.

3.   *Explain the three different leadership styles and suggest reasons why the democratic leader is the best style of leader for most situations.*

You would want to begin by identifying the three styles of leadership and listing the characteristics of each. Then you should evaluate how characteristics of a democratic leader, like holding group discussions, outlining the steps necessary to reach the goals, suggesting alternatives, and allowing the group members to work at their own pace, all contributed to the outcomes like greater friendliness, group-mindedness, and mutual respect, and ability to work without supervision. Finally, consider why those qualities and outcomes were judged to be the best under most circumstances.

4.   *Explore the factors that influence the emergence of groupthink and consider strategies for minimizing the development of this collective tunnel vision.*

There are several factors you could discuss. First, you could bring in the findings of the Asch experiment about the influence of peer pressure in individual and group decision making. You could also include some reference to the Milgram experiment about obedience to authority. There is also strong pressure on members of a group to think alike, since voicing opposition can be viewed as a sign of disloyalty; your role as a "team player" may even be questioned. Within groups, there is also a tendency to put aside moral judgments for the sake of the group.

The author of your text suggests that groupthink develops when leaders and members of groups are isolated and become cut off from information sources that do not fit with their own views. His suggestion is for leaders to have the widest possible access to research findings of social scientists and information freely gathered by media sources. You could also discuss how groupthink might be reduced by being sensitive to the size of the group and the nature of leadership—two factors that play a role in overall group dynamics.

5.   *Discuss how the size of the group affects attitudes and behavior.*

You could start out by discussing the relationship between group size and what is known as the diffusion of responsibility. When people feel a sense of responsibility and are part of a small group (dyad or triad), they are more likely to help others than when they are a part of a larger group. When they are a part of a larger group, they feel less personally responsible for others because they know that others are available to help out. When the group grows larger, it becomes more formal and loses its intimacy. All of the members can no longer feel close and know one another. When a group grows too large, it will break into smaller, more intimate groups.

CHAPTER 7

ANSWERS FOR MULTIPLE CHOICE QUESTIONS

1.   **c**   Rationality is the acceptance of rules, efficiency, and practical results as the right way to approach human affairs.
2.   **a**   The idea that the past is the best guide for the present is the traditional orientation.
3.   **b**   One of the major obstacles to industrialization was a traditional orientation to life that led people to resist change.
4.   **c**   According to Karl Marx, the force behind rationality replacing the traditional orientation to life was capitalism.
5.   **d**   "All of the above" is correct. According to Max Weber, capitalism is the investment of capital in the hopes of producing profits. It became an outlet for the excess money of Calvinists, as well as producing success for many that was then interpreted as a sign of God's approval.
6.   **d**   Because sociologists have not been able to determine whose views are most accurate, the two views still remain side by side.
7.   **b**   A secondary group designed to achieve explicit objectives is the sociological definition of a formal organization.
8.   **b**   In a bureaucracy, assignments flow downward, not upward, and accountability flows upward, not downward.
9.   **c**   George Ritzer used the term "the McDonaldization of society" to refer to the increasing rationalization of daily living.
10. **b**   The force behind the "McDonaldization of society" is the increased efficiency that contributes to lower prices.
11. **b**   What Linda is feeling is referred to as alienation by sociologists.
12. **d**   "All of the above" is correct because workers resist alienation by forming primary groups, praising each other and expressing sympathy when something goes wrong, and putting pictures and personal items in their work areas.
13. **c**   According to your text, the alienated bureaucrat is not likely to do anything for the organization beyond what he or she is required to do.
14. **b**   The Peter principle states that each employee of a bureaucracy is promoted to his or her level of incompetence.
15. **c**   Goal displacement occurs when an organization adopts new goals.
16. **d**   The sociological significance of bureaucracy is that it represents a fundamental change in how people relate to one another.
17. **d**   "All of the above" is correct. Voluntary associations are groups made up of volunteers who organize on the basis of some mutual interest. They include political parties, unions, professional associations, and churches, and they have been an important part of American life.
18. **a**   Voluntary associations exist in the United States because they meet people's basic needs.
19. **a**   Pepsi is a company that has served as a positive example of diversity training.
20. **d**   Humanizing a work setting refers to organizing a workplace in such a way that human potential is developed rather than impeded. Among the characteristics of more humane bureaucracies are the availability of opportunities on the basis of ability and contributions, a more equal distribution of power, and less rigid rules and more open decision making.
21. **d**   Research on the costs and benefits of employer-financed day care demonstrates that such a benefit can save the employer money in terms of reducing employee turnover and absenteeism.
22. **a**   Quality circles are an excellent example of a business fad.
23. **c**   According to conflict theorists, the interests of workers and owners are fundamentally opposed and, in the final analysis, workers are always exploited.

24. **d** "All of the above" is correct. Computers in the workplace have reduced drudgery of the work, could lead to more surveillance of workers by managers, and may be the first step toward a society in which every move a citizen makes is recorded.

25. **c** Despite the myth that all Japanese workers are guaranteed lifetime job security, today only about one-third of that country's workforce actually attains it.

ANSWERS FOR TRUE-FALSE QUESTIONS

1. *True.*
2. *False.* Traditional orientation is *not* based on the idea that the present is the best guide for the future. It is based on the idea that the past is the best guide for the present.
3. *False.* Max Weber did not believe that the growth of capitalism contributed to the rise of the Protestant ethic but, rather, that the rise of the Protestant ethic as a result of Calvinism contributed to the growth of capitalism.
4. *True.*
5. *True.*
6. *True.*
7. *False.* The Peter principle has not been proven to be true. If it were generally true, bureaucracies would be staffed entirely by incompetents, and none of these organizations could succeed. In reality, bureaucracies are remarkably successful.
8. *True.*
9. *True.*
10. *False.* The Japanese system works better in theory than in reality. For example, only about one-third of Japanese workers find lifetime job security.

ANSWERS TO THE FILL-IN-THE-BLANK QUESTIONS

1. traditional
2. rationality
3. John Calvin
4. division
5. ideal
6. Peter principle
7. iron law of oligarchy
8. hidden
9. confrontational
10. myths

GUIDELINES FOR ANSWERING THE ESSAY QUESTIONS

1. *Explain what sociologists mean by the expression "rationalization of society" and discuss why this change has occurred.*

The first step is to talk about the shift from a traditional orientation to life to one based on the widespread acceptance of rationality. You could explore what the traditional orientation is—relationships are long-term and based on custom and history, change is viewed with suspicion and comes very slowly, and people are evaluated on how well they fulfill their traditional roles. You could then introduce the characteristics of social life based on rationality—efficiency, impersonality, concerns over the bottom line, and the explicit measurement of outcomes.

Once you have established the differences between these two orientations and forms of social organization, you would then want to talk about how Marx and Weber each explained the shift. Although both believed that capitalism could not function without rational organization, they differed on the source of the change. For Marx, capitalism was the driving force behind these changes. When people discovered that they could produce more and generate higher profits by organizing work and the wider society around these principles, their views on life changed. On the other hand, Weber believed that religion, and religious beliefs, were behind the shift. He pointed to the Protestant ethic, a combination of beliefs and values, as the source for the emergence of capitalism and rationalization.

2. *Explain "hidden values" within the workplace and why this continues in contemporary organizations.*

Rosabeth Moss Kanter stresses that the corporate culture contains "hidden values." These values create a self-fulfilling prophecy that affects people's corporate careers. For example, workers are often hired who reflect the bosses' background. These people are then given better access to information, networking opportunities and "fast track" positions. These people are then more committed and perform better. They receive promotions since they are meeting the stereotype that the boss had of them to begin with. Those workers who may not fit the stereotype that their boss had may not receive these opportunities. They may feel less committed to the organization and not perform as well. They also then meet the boss's stereotype of them. These "hidden values" are very difficult to detect and stay below the surface. As such, the hidden corporate culture and stereotypes are likely to eventually give way, but very slowly.

3. *Define the iron law of oligarchy and discuss why this problem occurs in voluntary associations.*

You would begin by explaining that the iron law of oligarchy is the tendency within organizations for the leadership to become self-perpetuating. Although this problem occurs in all types of organizations, it is particularly evident in voluntary associations. A major reason for this is the nature of membership in this type of organization; it tends to be passive, varying in its degree of commitment to and involvement in the organization. The elite keep themselves in power by passing leadership positions from one member of the clique to another. If the leadership is not responsive to the membership, it runs the risk of being removed from office by a grassroots rebellion.

4. *This chapter provides discussion of strategies to humanize the workplace. After identifying some of these strategies, consider the conflict perspective on these types of initiatives.*

Your essay should begin with a brief statement about what "humanizing the workplace" means. You could talk about how bureaucracies can contribute to alienation, and that this initiative is in response to that tendency toward dehumanization and alienation. From here, you would want to identify different strategies: quality circles, employee stock ownership plans, work teams, corporate day care, and even cooperatives. For each of these, you would provide a brief description of what aspect of dehumanization it is trying to address.

The second part of this essay is to consider the conflict perspective. Conflict theorists note that regardless of how the work is organized, the basic relationship between workers and owners is exploitative and confrontational. This is because they have conflicting interests: owners want to extract as much profit as they can so they exploit the workers and the workers want to find ways to resist the exploitation. That is the fundamental nature of capitalism, the "bottom line." Thus the conflict perspective sees such initiatives as just another way for the capitalists to exploit the workers.

5. *Evaluate whether the use of computer technology to control workers is an inevitable aspect of bureaucracy.*

You would want to begin by identifying the defining characteristics of bureaucracy—the presence of a hierarchy, a division of labor, written rules, written communications and records, and impersonality. You should then consider the ways in which computers are tied to these various characteristics. The computer's capacity to be accessed from remote sites means that managers can communicate with workers at any time and from any place and the workers' input on computers enable the managers to maintain records of their productivity (written communication and records); computers also promote impersonality. Your conclusion is to evaluate the degree to which such steps are inevitable.

CHAPTER 8

ANSWERS FOR MULTIPLE CHOICE QUESTIONS

1. **b** In sociology, the term deviance refers to all violations of social rules.
2. **b** Deviance is so often viewed as threatening because it undermines the predictability of social life that is established through the creation and observance of norms.
3. **c** Frowns, gossip, and crossing people off guest lists are examples of negative sanctions.
4. **c** Most negative sanctions are informal. At the same time, whether you consider the breaking of a norm simply an amusing matter that warrants no severe sanctions or a serious infraction that does, it depends on your perspective.
5. **c** The function of the stigma is to define or identify the person who violates the norm as deviant.
6. **a** A court-martial, in which the insignia of rank is publicly ripped off the uniforms of the officers found guilty, is an example of degradation ceremonies.
7. **c** Differential association theory is based on the symbolic interactionist perspective.
8. **d** According to differential association theory, an individual becomes a deviant because he has learned to deviate from society's norms. In particular, family, friends, neighborhoods and even subcultures will teach him to either conform to or deviate from the norms.
9. **c** All of the following are ways of neutralizing deviance: appeal to higher loyalties, denial of responsibility, and denial of injury and a victim. Denial of deviant labels is *not* one of the ways of neutralizing such behavior.
10. **b** William Chambliss' study of the Saints and Roughnecks suggests that people often live up to the labels that a community gives them.
11. **d** "All of the above" is correct. William Chambliss states that all of these are factors that influence whether people will be seen as deviant: social class, the visibility of offenders, and their styles of interaction.
12. **a** According to the functionalist perspective, deviance promotes social unity and social change.
13. **d** "All of the above" is the correct answer. Getting an education and then getting a good job and working hard are examples of what Merton meant by the term *institutionalized means*.
14. **d** Recidivism is not one of the responses to anomie identified by Merton.
15. **a** Steve's behavior reflects innovation. Steve is rejecting the institutionalized means, but wants to reach the cultural goal of wealth, so he finds a way to do it that is innovative.
16. **d** The illegitimate opportunity structures theory is based on the functionalist perspective.
17. **c** Crimes committed by people of respectable and high social status in the course of their occupations are called white-collar crimes.
18. **c** Sears defrauding the poor of more than $100 million is an example of corporate crime.
19. **c** Corporate crime costs us as a society several hundred billion dollars a year.
20. **b** The United States has the largest percentage of its population in prison; it also has more people in prison than any other country.
21. **b** The *correct* statement is that "about one-half of all recidivists have been convicted of a violent crime." There is no evidence that the "get-tough" policy has had a significant impact on lowering the rates of recidivism. Studies do show that individuals who have served time are likely to return to prison, but the statistic is that two-thirds will be rearrested within three years, not one year. Finally, approximately three-quarters of those in prison have served time before.
22. **b** Since the death penalty was reinstated in 1977, 37 percent of those executed have been African American.
23. **a** As a group, African Americans are more likely than other racial/ethnic groups to be victims of hate crimes.
24. **d** Hate crimes consist of all of the above.
25. **d** With deviance inevitable, Henslin suggests that one measure of a society is how it treats its deviants.

ANSWERS FOR TRUE-FALSE QUESTIONS

1. *False.* According to your text, a college student cheating on an exam and a mugger lurking on a dark street do have something in common: they are both engaged in deviant behavior, thus making them "deviants."

2. *False.* Symbolic interactionists stress that we are not destined by our group memberships to think and act as our groups dictate; we are not prisoners of our socialization. Rather, we help produce our own orientations to life.

3. *True.*

4. *True.*

5. *False.* According to strain theory, everyone does not have an equal chance to get ahead in society because of structural factors in the society (e.g., racism, sexism, and social class) that may deny them access to the approved ways of achieving cultural goals.

6. *True.*

7. *False.* White-collar crime often is more costly than street crime. Examples include the plundering of the U.S. savings and loan industry and other "crimes in the suites."

8. *False.* Conflict theorists believe that the criminal justice system functions for the well-being of the capitalist class.

9. *True.*

10. *False.* Official statistics are not always accurate counts of the crimes committed in our society. Both conflict theorists and symbolic interactionists believe that these statistics have bias built into them because of police discretion in arresting people, as well as many other factors.

ANSWERS TO THE FILL-IN-THE-BLANK QUESTIONS

1. outside
2. families
3. inner
4. neutralization
5. unity
6. accepts
7. anomie
8. white-collar
9. female
10. "Three Strikes and You're Out"

GUIDELINES FOR ANSWERING THE ESSAY QUESTIONS

1. *Discuss how the different sociological perspectives could be combined to provide a more complete picture of deviance.*

You would begin by identifying the strengths of each perspective. Symbolic interactionism focuses on group membership and interaction within and between groups, functionalism focuses on how deviance is a part of the social order, and conflict theory focuses on how social inequality affects definitions of and reactions to acts of deviance. An example of combining perspectives is reflected in the work of William Chambliss on the Saints and the Roughnecks; he looked at patterns of inequality and different interaction styles to explain the different treatment the two groups received. Another example would be Cloward and Ohlin's work on illegitimate opportunity structures; they added the concept of social class inequality to the notion of the strain between institutionalized means and cultural goals to explain patterns of lower class deviance.

2. *Explain how forms of deviance such as street gangs can be both functional and dysfunctional at the same time.*

You could begin your discussion by making reference to Durkheim's views on the functionality of deviance. In particular, the presence of street gangs may serve to affirm normative boundaries and to promote social unity, both within society and within the neighborhoods where gangs operate. Within this context, think about the dominant views we have of gang members and gang activity.

You would also want to make reference to Jankowski's research. Jankowski studied street gangs and discovered that gangs functioned within low-income neighborhoods as sources of employment (often the *only* source), recreation, and protection. In a few cases the gangs were involved in legitimate activities such as running small groceries and renovating and renting abandoned apartment buildings. All of these demonstrate the functional nature of gangs. At the same time, gangs generate most of their income through illegal activities, a dysfunctional aspect. Another dysfunctional aspect is the violence that accompanies gangs—violence that is not confined to gangs but often spills over into the neighborhood as a whole.

3. *Using any one of the different sociological perspectives, develop an explanation for why white-collar crime is generally treated as less serious crime in our society.*

First, you want to define what white-collar crime is. According to Edwin Sutherland, it is crime that people of respectable and high social status commit in the course of their occupations. You would then want to use the different perspectives to discuss why it is viewed as less serious than street crimes as a threat to our society. You could refer to labeling theory, especially the work of Sykes and Matza regarding techniques of neutralization. Given the nature of work and corporate life today, it is possible that not only do those responsible for the crimes not see themselves as deviant, but society as a whole does not see corporate employees as deviant. In addition, much of the crime that is committed is largely invisible and indirect—we may not even be aware that we have been victimized.

You could also write about the functionalist explanation for this type of crime. Specifically, you could begin with Merton's strain theory and then make reference to Cloward and Ohlin's discussion of illegitimate opportunity structures.

Perhaps it is easiest to apply conflict theory in trying to answer this question. White-collar crime is typically crime committed by those in power. As the conflict theorists point out, the law is an instrument of oppression. It does not operate impartially. It directs its energies against the violations of the law by the working class.

4. *Discuss the "get tough" policy that the United States has followed and how successful that has been.*

The United States has been following a get tough policy for about the last 20 years. One such example is the "three strikes and you're out" laws. This law gives a mandatory sentence, sometimes life imprisonment, for conviction of a third felony. While well intended, these laws have had unintended consequences. For example, a man was sentenced to 25 years for stealing a pizza. A man who stole nine videotapes from Kmart was sentenced to 50 years in prison without parole. The politicians in their haste to enact these laws did not limit the punishment to violent crimes. Also, they did not consider that some minor crimes are felonies. However, as a result of this as well as a few other changes, there has been a decline in crime. Judges have put more people in prison and reduced early releases of prisoners. Other sociologists disagree that these were the main reasons for the decrease in crime. Some believe that because of higher employment and a drop in drug use, the crime rate decreased.

5. *Obesity could be viewed as deviance because it is a condition that violates our cultural norms regarding appearance. Develop an explanation for how this type of deviance is increasingly subject to medicalization.*

Your textbook has a discussion of how certain types of deviance have been medicalized—redefined so that they are viewed as external symptoms of internal disorders. Subsequently, they become medical matters and subject to the care of physicians. For a long time, overweight people were considered weak and unable to control their eating; it was a commonly-held view that they were responsible for their condition. The standard treatment was for them to limit the intake of calories by going on a diet. In the

384

last several years, a different view of obesity has begun to emerge. No longer is the individual viewed as responsible for his or her deviant behavior. Their excess weight (the external symptom) is due to some medical problem (internal disorder). Today it is increasingly common for obese people to be treated with medications or medical procedures.

CHAPTER 9

ANSWERS FOR MULTIPLE CHOICE QUESTIONS

1. **b** The division of large numbers of people into layers according to their relative power, property, and prestige is social stratification.
2. **b** Slavery is a form of social stratification in which some people own other people.
3. **d** "All of the above" is correct. Slavery in the United States started as indentured service. When enough indentured servants could not be recruited, individuals were imported from Africa and turned into slaves. An ideology of racism justified these actions by asserting that the slaves were inferior, and perhaps not even fully human. Slavery became inheritable because if one's parents were slaves, the child also was considered to be a slave.
4. **c** India is the best example of a caste system.
5. **b** Caste systems practice endogamy, marriage within the group, and prohibit intermarriage.
6. **d** "All of the above" is correct. The South African system of social stratification known as apartheid was a caste system that contained four different racial categories: Europeans (whites), Africans (blacks), Coloureds (mixed races), and Asians. It was enforced by law and was finally dismantled following decades of international pressure and protest.
7. **c** Under the estate system that existed in Europe during the Middle Ages, the clergy made up the *second estate.*
8. **a** Class systems are characterized by social mobility, either upward or downward.
9. **b** It is true that about 60 percent of the world's illiterate are females. Of the other statements, in every society women's earnings are lower than men's, gender is still an important basis for stratifying people, and gender cuts across all systems of stratification.
10. **b** Marx concluded that social class depends upon the means of production.
11. **a** According to Max Weber, social class is determined by one's property, prestige, and power.
12. **d** According to the functionalist view, social stratification is not dysfunctional but an inevitable feature of social organization.
13. **d** Melvin Tumin's criticisms included (a) the measurement problems, (b) the reality that family background matters, and (c) the dysfunctional aspects of stratification. The one statement that does not reflect his criticisms is "d." In fact, what Tumin noted was that functionalists place too great an emphasis on income and ignore the fact that some people are motivated to take jobs for reasons of status or power.
14. **b** According to contemporary conflict theorists, the basis of social stratification is conflict over limited resources.
15. **a** According to Gerhard Lenski, the key to reconciling the different explanations for social stratification is whether a group has surpluses. The functionalists are correct when it comes to groups that do not accumulate any surplus, but once there is a surplus, groups compete with one another over who will control the extra; in these situations, conflict theory is more appropriate.
16. **d** "All of the above" is correct. The key to maintaining national stratification is having a strong police force and military to demand compliance, control of social institutions, and control of information.
17. **c** The British perpetuate their class system from one generation to the next by education.
18. **b** The former Soviet Union and its satellites in eastern Europe would be placed among the Industrializing Nations of the world.
19. **a** It's true that most people in the world live on less than $2000/year.
20. **c** It is difficult to know how to classify some nations into a global system of stratification because some nations have not yet industrialized but are still extremely wealthy.
21. **b** The colonialism of the United States usually involved planting corporate flags, thereby giving U.S. corporations ready access to the markets and raw materials of these colonies.

22. **d** According to Wallerstein, these groups of interconnected nations exist: core nations that are rich and powerful; nations on the semiperiphery that have become highly dependent on trade with core nations; nations on the periphery that sell cash crops to the core nations; and the external area, including most of Africa and Asia, that has been left out of the development of capitalism and have few, if any, economic connections with the core nations.

23. **d** The reason sociologists generally reject the culture of poverty theory in trying to explain global stratification is because it places the blame for poverty on the poor nations themselves, rather than focusing on the international arrangements that benefit some at the expense of others.

24. **d** "All of the above" is the correct answer. The reasons that the Least Industrialized Nations remain so poor is because their markets are controlled by the Most Industrialized Nations, who set prices and sell them goods on credit. The debt that they incur means that they will remain internal debtors, since their money must go to paying off the loans rather than developing their own infrastructure.

25. **b** With cheap telecommunications and the outsourcing of labor, workers in India and China are able to compete with their Western counterparts.

ANSWERS FOR TRUE-FALSE QUESTIONS

1. *False.* Your text notes that social stratification does not simply refer to individuals but rather to a way of ranking large groups of people into a hierarchy that shows their relative privileges.
2. *False.* Historically, slavery was based on defeat in battle, a criminal act, or a debt, but not some supposedly inherently inferior status such as race.
3. *True.*
4. *True.*
5. *True.*
6. *False.* Functionalists believe that society offers greater rewards for its more responsible, demanding, and accountable positions because society works better if its most qualified people hold its most important positions. From this standpoint, unique abilities would not be more important than the type of position held by the individual.
7. *True.*
8. *True.*
9. *True.*
10. *False.* Most sociologists find imperialism, world system theory and dependency theory preferable to an explanation based on the culture of poverty.

ANSWERS TO THE FILL-IN-THE-BLANK QUESTIONS

1. indentured
2. false consciousness
3. Most Industrialized Nation
4. education
5. colonialism
6. core
7. maquiladoras
8. culture
9. debt
10. elite

GUIDELINES FOR ANSWERING THE ESSAY QUESTIONS

1. *Compare and contrast Marx's theory of stratification with Weber's theory. Discuss why Weber's is more widely accepted by sociologists.*

Your first task is to summarize these two perspectives, pointing out the similarities and the differences between the two. Then you would want to consider the advantages offered by Weber's theory. You could mention that Weber's concept of property (or wealth) was broadened to include *control* over decision-making and ownership; that prestige and power can both be based on factors other than wealth; and that the three dimensions are interrelated but can, and do, operate independently. Your conclusion should be that Weber's theory offers sociologists a more complete framework for understanding and analyzing systems of stratification.

2. *Using the different theories presented in this chapter, answer the question, "Why is stratification universal?"*

There are two competing views on why stratification is universal. You would begin by discussing the Davis and Moore thesis that stratification is functional for society. You would want to elaborate on their argument, pointing out that society has certain important positions that need to be filled by the most qualified people; to motivate the most talented to fill these positions, society offers them greater rewards. You could provide some examples—college professors, military generals, doctors.

The alternative explanation is offered by the conflict theorists. Begin by noting that groups compete for control over society's resources. The "winners" use their position to keep other groups weak, thereby maintaining their own position. For conflict theorists, this arrangement is inevitable, once society begins to produce a surplus. You could also bring in Mosa's argument about the need for leadership that comes with social organization and how leadership creates inequalities.

Your concluding paragraph could focus on Lenski and his efforts to reconcile these two views. Lenski focused on the level of social development and found that functionalism made sense in societies without any surplus resources, but once a surplus emerges, then conflict theory is better at explaining why stratification emerges and persists.

3. *Consider why ideology is a more effective way of maintaining stratification than brute force.*

You should begin by considering why it is even necessary to "maintain stratification." On the surface, the idea that some people get more than other people should produce widespread instability—after all, isn't it natural for those without to want to do whatever they can to take some away from those with? However, this doesn't often happen because the elites have a number of methods for maintaining stratification, ranging from ideology to force. Without question, the most effective is ideology. Once a system of beliefs develops and people accept the idea in their minds that a particular system of stratification is right or just, then they will go along with the status quo.

4. *Compare and contrast the three theories of global stratification.*

You can start out by identifying the three theories of global stratification. They are colonialism, world system theory, and the culture of poverty. The theory of colonialism stresses that the countries that industrialized got a jump start on the rest of the world. These countries were able to invade weaker countries and make them into colonies. These countries were then able to exploit the people and resources in the weaker countries thereby establishing dominance. Immanuel Wallerstein proposed another theory known as world system theory. His theory was also based on industrialization that led to four groups of nations. The core group was the group that industrialized first and they became rich and powerful. Other nations industrialized less or were left out of the development of capitalism altogether. Unlike the other two explanations, the claim of the third theory was that the cultures of the Least Industrialized Nations are what held them back. Kenneth Galbraith argued that some countries have a culture of poverty or that their religion encourages them to accept their situation. Most sociologists prefer the first two theories because the third explanation puts the blame on the victim.

CHAPTER 10

ANSWERS FOR MULTIPLE CHOICE QUESTIONS

1. **c** According to your text, most sociologists agree with Max Weber that social class is best defined by employing three dimensions of social class.
2. **c** According to economist Paul Samuelson, if an income pyramid were made out of a child's blocks, most U.S. residents would be about 10 ft. off the ground.
3. **d** While it is true that the income distribution has not changed dramatically over the past 50 years, it is also true that the changes that have occurred have resulted in an increase in the percentage of income going to the top 20 percent of U.S. households and a decrease in the percentage going to the bottom 20 percent of households.
4. **c** Daniel Hellinger and Dennis Judd use the term *democratic facade* to describe the average citizen's belief that he/she exercises power when voting for Congressional representatives or the U.S. president.
5. **c** All of the following are true regarding jobs that have the most prestige: they pay more, require more education, and offer greater autonomy. They do not necessarily require special talent or skills.
6. **c** Gold discovered that the tenants did not like the fact that the janitors, as relatively low status workers, were earning more than themselves, so they reacted by being "snooty" to them.
7. **d** Wright responded to the criticism that Marx's categories were so broad that they did not accurately reflect the realities of people's lives by creating the concept of contradictory class location, which recognizes that some people can be members of more than one class simultaneously.
8. **b** Members of the upper middle class are the ones who owe their position to the achievement of a college and/or postgraduate degree.
9. **b** All of the following are characteristics of the working class: most are employed in relatively unskilled blue-collar and white-collar jobs; most hope to get ahead by achieving seniority on the job; and about thirty percent of the population belongs to this class. However, most have *not* attended college for one or two years.
10. **d** All of the statements describe the situation of homeless people in our society today.
11. **c** According to your text, the typical mechanic in a Ford dealership would be in the working class.
12. **d** Differential risks of dying because the U.S. has a two-tiered system of medical care, social class differences in lifestyles, and unequal access to medical care all help explain the social class differences in death rates.
13. **b** It is actually the poor who experience higher levels of stress because they live with less job security and lower incomes; the rich have the resources to cope with life's challenges.
14. **c** According to Melvin Kohn lower-class parents are concerned that their children be conformists; they want them to obey conventional norms and authority figures while middle class parents encourage their children to be creative and independent.
15. **a** Members of the capitalist class tend to bypass public schools entirely in favor of exclusive private schools.
16. **d** People in the working class are more likely to be more conservative on social issues and more liberal on economic issues.
17. **c** White-collar crimes committed by the more privileged classes are more likely to be dealt with outside the criminal justice system.
18. **d** A homeless person whose father was a physician has experienced downward mobility.
19. **c** Higginbotham and Weber studied women professionals from working class backgrounds and found parental encouragement for postponing marriage and getting an education.
20. **c** He found that people actually experienced pain when moving up the social class ladder because they were caught between two worlds.
21. **d** The cost of upward mobility is being caught in two worlds and for African Americans especially troubling is the sense of leaving one's racial-ethnic group.

22. **c** In the United States, 10 percent of the elderly population lives in poverty, compared to 13 percent for the total population.

23. **b** In trying to explain poverty, sociologists are most likely to stress features of the social structure that contribute to poverty rather than any individual characteristics.

24. **a** The reason most poor people do not defer gratification, giving up in the present for the sake of the future, is because they need whatever limited resources they have in order to simply survive.

25. **d** "All of the above" is correct. The Horatio Alger myth is beneficial to society, according to the functionalists, because it shifts the blame for failure away from the social system and onto the shoulders of the individual, thereby reducing pressures on the system. It also motivates people to try harder to succeed because "anything is possible."

ANSWERS FOR TRUE-FALSE QUESTIONS

1. *False.* While there is no one definition of social class on which all sociologists agree, most sociologists agree with Max Weber's conceptualization of social class as encompassing wealth, power and prestige.
2. *True.*
3. *True.*
4. *True.*
5. *True.*
6. *True.*
7. *True.*
8. *True.*
9. *False.* Research indicates that 59 percent of families studied lived in poverty for one year or less. Only 12 percent lived in poverty for five years or more.
10. *True.*

ANSWERS TO THE FILL-IN-THE-BLANK QUESTIONS

1. wealth
2. 10
3. power elite
4. 1
5. dying
6. divorce
7. intergenerational mobility
8. south
9. feminization
10. reserve labor force

GUIDELINES FOR ANSWERING THE ESSAY QUESTIONS

1. *Identify the three dimensions of social class and discuss some of the consequences of social class.*

You could begin your essay by discussing how sociologists define wealth and income, power, and privilege. You might also talk about how each is unevenly distributed within American society. Finally, you should talk about the consequences of this uneven distribution in terms of physical and mental health, family life, education, religion, politics, crime and the criminal justice system, and access to new technology.

2. *Discuss why you think women have been largely ignored in studies of mobility.*

You would want to point out that most studies of mobility have focused on occupational mobility. Until quite recently, most women did not have continuous occupational careers because of the nature of traditional gender roles. They derived their status from their fathers and their husbands. Therefore, in studies of intergenerational mobility, they were excluded because they did not have work histories that spanned their lifetime. As women's roles have changed, so has researchers' awareness of them as research subjects. Also, because of structural changes in the economy, employment opportunities for women have opened up; this reflects structural mobility.

3. *Describe which groups are at greater risks of poverty and then suggest ways in which poverty can be reduced by targeting these populations.*

You would want to begin by identifying those groups that are at greater risk—the rural poor, minorities, the undereducated, female heads of household, and children. You would then discuss specific ideas you have for overcoming some of the conditions that place these groups at greater risk; some possible programs would be improvements in education, including more funding for college and technical training, increases in minimum wage, increased number of jobs that pay a living wage, and more aggressive enforcement of anti-discrimination laws.

4. *Explore why individual explanations of poverty are easier for the average American to accept than structural explanations.*

When most Americans see or hear about poor people, their immediate response is that they are lazy and/or stupid. In trying to explain this response, you could refer back to the earlier discussion about American values, particularly the values of individualism and hard work. Given these values, it is understandable why people would draw this conclusion. Likewise, because we believe in the existence of a meritocracy, most people assume that they deserve the place they have earned in society. Therefore, if someone is poor, it must be because they don't deserve anything better.

You could also discuss the idea of the Horatio Alger myth. We grow up believing if we only work hard (a core value), we will be rewarded with success. Obviously, those who don't have success haven't tried hard enough. Finally, you would want to point out that it is much easier to connect individual decisions to outcomes than it is to see broader social forces that are at work.

5. *Discuss the Horatio Alger myth and whether or not it is functional for society.*

The Horatio Alger myth was formed in the late 1800s. He was an author whose stories told of fictional boy heroes going from rags-to-riches. Many people still hold the belief today that if they really try hard enough, they can get ahead. It is a statistical impossibility to believe that most Americans, including minorities and the poor, have an average or better-than-average chance of getting ahead. You could discuss that functionalists would certainly say that this belief system is functional for society. It encourages people to compete for higher positions. It also places blame on the individual because if someone doesn't make it, it's their fault and they didn't try hard enough. It also helps to stabilize society since there is individual rather than societal blame. Therefore, since the social arrangements and structure within society are sufficient, it reduces pressure to change the system.

CHAPTER 11

ANSWERS FOR MULTIPLE CHOICE QUESTIONS

1. **a** Gender stratification cuts across all aspects of social life and all social classes and it refers to men's and women's unequal access to power, prestige, and property on the basis of their sex. It is *not* a structured feature of society.

2. **a** The *incorrect* statement is, "There is not a lot of variation in gender roles around the world." In fact, expectations associated with gender vary so greatly that some sociologists suggest we replace the terms *masculinity* and *femininity* with *masculinities* and *femininities*.

3. **c** "All of the above" is correct. Patriarchy is a society in which men dominate women, it has existed throughout history, and it is universal.

4. **c** According to sociologists, if biology were the principal factor in human behavior, around the world we would find women to be one sort of person and men another.

5. **c** The study of Vietnam veterans has led sociologists to slowly consider biological factors.

6. **c** Women represent the largest minority group in the U.S.

7. **a** The major theory of the origin of patriarchy points to the social consequences of human reproduction. In earlier times, life was short and many children needed to be born in order for the group to survive. Consequently, women were pregnant or nursing young children for much of their adult lives. As a result of these biologically driven activities, women were limited in terms of alternatives and assumed tasks associated with the home and child care and men took up tasks that required more strength or longer absences from home.

8. **c** In regard to the prestige of work, greater prestige is given to male activities.

9. **b** The *incorrect* statement is the one that claims the U.S. leads the world in the number of women who hold public office. In fact, it is Norway, where 40 percent of the legislators are women; the U.S. percentage is 10, which is typical for most nations.

10. **d** All of the answers are true about female circumcision.

11. **d** All of the answers are correct. A "second wave" of protest and struggle against gender inequalities began in the 1960s when women began to compare their working conditions with those of men; it had as its goals everything from changing work roles to changing policies on violence against women.

12. **c** It is not yet clear if a "third wave" is emerging or not, but feminists point out that the values that currently underlie work and other social institutions—power, competition, emotional invulnerability, toughness, autonomy, and independence—represent "male" qualities. They need to be supplemented, if not replaced, with "female" values—cooperation, openness about vulnerability, gentleness, connection, and interdependence.

13. **c** Gender inequality in education is perpetuated by the use of sex to sort students into different academic disciplines.

14. **a** Research shows the largest gap in professional degrees obtained by men and women in 1970 was in the field of dentistry.

15. **c** The pay gap between men and women is found at all educational levels.

16. **c** The glass ceiling refers to the invisible barrier that keeps women from reaching the executive suite. Men who go into fields traditionally associated with women often encounter a glass escalator (they advance quickly) rather than a glass ceiling.

17. **b** Of the four statements, the one that says, "Women do not seek out opportunities for advancement and do not spend enough time networking with powerful executives" is the only one that is *not* a reason why more women are not found in core corporate positions; all the rest represent valid reasons as to why women are underrepresented in top corporate offices.

18. **c** Sexual harassment was first recognized as a problem in the 1970s.

19. **d** Sexual harassment, rooted in the structure of the workplace rather than individual relationships, involves a person in authority using the position to force unwanted sex on subordinates. Initially, it

was seen as a women's issue, but today it is no longer exclusively a female problem. The only statement that is *incorrect* is that "male victims of sexual harassment receive more sympathy than female victims."

20. **d** Date rape is not an isolated event; most go unreported and it is difficult to prosecute because of the pre-existing relationship.

21. **d** While women make up 51 percent of the U.S. population, 9 out of 10 murders are committed by men.

22. **a** Rather than higher testosterone levels in males, feminists would point to the association of strength and virility with violence, males' frustration at their loss of power and status, and cultural traditions that are patriarchal as sources for gender violence.

23. **c** Women are reluctant to get involved in politics because the demands of political life are in conflict with the demands of their roles as wives and mothers.

24. **d** "All of the above" is correct.

25. **c** Increased female participation in decision-making processes of social institutions is most likely going to result in breaking down the stereotypes that lock both males and females into traditional gender activities.

ANSWERS FOR TRUE-FALSE QUESTIONS
1. *True.*
2. *False.* Patriarchy, or male dominance, appears to be universal.
3. *False.* Female circumcision is still quite common in parts of Africa and Southeast Asia.
4. *True.*
5. *True.*
6. *True.*
7. *False.* While women have made gains in terms of the proportion of degrees earned and exceed men in earning Bachelor of Arts degrees, they still lag behind in postgraduate and professional degrees.
8. *False.* In 2008, men were more likely to obtain professional degrees in dentistry as well as medicine and law.
9. *True.*
10. *False.* In the U.S., males kill at a rate several times that of females.

ANSWERS TO THE FILL-IN-THE-BLANK QUESTIONS
1. master
2. group
3. patriarchy
4. nature
5. feminism
6. masculinity
7. 70
8. ceiling
9. power
10. thirty-eight

GUIDELINES FOR ANSWERING THE ESSAY QUESTIONS
1. *Summarize the sociobiological argument concerning behavioral differences between men and women. Explain which position most closely reflects your own: biological, sociological, or sociobiological.*

You would want to begin by stating how sociologists and biologists each explain the basis for differences in gendered behavior and then discuss how sociobiology tries to bridge the gap between these two disciplines' views. In discussing sociobiology you could refer to Alice Rossi's theory concerning the biological basis for mothering and the connection between biological predispositions and cultural norms.

As further evidence of the relationship between biology and social forces, you could discuss the two studies cited in the text: the case of the young boy whose sex was changed and the study of Vietnam veterans. Your final task would be to state which view you think is most consistent with what you have learned about gender inequality and explain why.

2. *Compare and contrast the two waves of the feminist movement in this country by identifying the forces that contributed to both waves.*

You could begin by noting that both waves of the feminist movement were committed to ending gender stratification and both met with strong opposition from both males and females. In both cases, there were two different branches that emerged—a liberal and a conservative branch—and within these branches, there were radical wings. The major difference between the two had to do with goals. The first wave was characterized by rather narrow goals. The movement focused on winning the vote for women, while the second wave was broader and wanted to address issues ranging from changing work roles to changing policies on violence against women.

3. *Discuss gender tracking and how that perpetuates inequality in education and the workforce.*

George Murdock found that in 324 societies around the world, activities are sex-typed. That is, every society associates certain activities with one sex or the other. You can discuss how this plays out both in the educational system and in the workforce. It is important to note that this also plays out globally, not just nationally. On a global level, two-thirds of women in the world cannot read. In every nation, women average less pay than men. In the U.S., until 1832 women were not allowed to attend college with men. Gender tracking occurs in which degrees tend to follow gender, which reinforces male-female distinctions. Men earn degrees in "masculine" fields while women earn degrees in "feminine" fields. This continues in graduate school where women are less likely to complete doctorates. The affect of gender tracking then plays out in the workforce where the average male college graduate can expect to earn more over the course of his lifetime as compared to the average female college graduate. You could also continue this discussion describing the research that has been done to discover why this difference persists.

4. *Discuss why women are so often the victims of violence.*

That women are often victims of violence is not only true in the United States, but globally. As your text points out, this has become a global human rights issue. Historically, women have been victims of foot binding (China), witch burning (Europe and the United States), and *suttee* (in India). Women around the globe continue to face the risk of rape, wife beating, female infanticide, and forced prostitution. In some areas of the world, young women are still being subjected to female genital mutilation.

In this country, women face the risk of becoming victims of rape, especially date rape, and of violence in the home. In trying to understand why this happens, you could use either symbolic interactionism or conflict theory. For symbolic interactionists, part of the explanation lies in the way in which our culture defines male and female roles. Men are expected to be strong and virile, while women are expected to be weak and submissive. Strength and virility are associated with violence, and both boys and girls learn this message as they grow up and are socialized into their respective gender roles.

For conflict theorists, the key lies in the changing nature of men's and women's roles in society. For the past century, women have slowly gained power and status in society. Because these are scarce and finite resources, women's gains translate into men's losses. For some men, the way to reassert their declining power and status is by becoming violent against women.

5. *As most of the legal barriers to women's full participation in society have been eliminated, it is commonly assumed that women have gained equality. Given what you have learned in this chapter, consider whether this is the case.*

Given the evidence that is presented throughout the chapter, it would be difficult to argue that women have gained equality. While they have made gains, as a group they continue to be subordinate to men. In answering this question, you could talk about continuing gender inequality they face in education, both as students and teachers. There is still the problem of gender inequality in everyday life, including the devaluation of things feminine and the patterns of conversations.

Most significantly, there is the experience of women employed outside the home. You would want to discuss the continuing gap in pay that exists across all occupations and at all educational levels. There are the issues of the glass ceiling and the glass escalator, as well as the problem of sexual harassment.

Finally, you could explore the area of politics. While women have made gains, they are still far from equal in terms of their representation in public office. You could talk about the factors that contribute to this pattern and the hopeful signs that change is happening.

CHAPTER 12

ANSWERS FOR MULTIPLE CHOICE QUESTIONS

1.   **b**   Race is inherited physical characteristics that distinguish one group from another.
2.   **b**   People often confuse race and ethnicity because of the cultural differences people see and the way they define race.
3.   **a**   A minority group is discriminated against because of physical or cultural differences.
4.   **a**   The dominant group in a society almost always considers its position to be due to its own innate superiority.
5.   **d**   A group's sense of ethnic identity is affected by the amount of power the group has, the size of the group, and the degree to which the group's physical appearance differs from the mainstream. Those groups with a heightened sense of ethnic identity generally have little power, are small in size, and stand out because of physical differences.
6.   **c**   Tracing family lines would be an example of ethnic work.
7.   **a**   A society in which groups quietly blend into a sort of ethnic stew is the best description of a melting pot. Many experts thought the United States would become a melting pot, but this notion is challenged by the fact that more people have a renewed interest in ethnic background.
8.   **c**   Prejudice and discrimination appear to characterize every society.
9.   **d**   "All of the above" is correct. Prejudice is an attitude; it may be positive or negative, and it often is the basis for discrimination.
10. **d**   From her interviews with women in the KKK and Aryan Nation, Kathleen Blee concluded that racism was a result of membership in the group not the cause of joining the group.
11. **d**   Discrimination that is woven into the fabric of society is referred to as institutional discrimination.
12. **d**   The research demonstrates that discrimination is built into the country's financial institutions; even when the credit histories were identical, African Americans and Latinos were 60 percent more likely to be rejected than whites.
13. **c**   The functionalists see prejudice as functional because it helps create solidarity within the group by fostering antagonisms directed against other groups; at the same time it can be dysfunctional because it has a negative impact on social relationships.
14. **d**   "All of the above" is correct. According to conflict theorists, prejudice benefits capitalists by splitting workers along racial or ethnic lines; contributes to the exploitation of workers, thus producing a split-labor market; and is a factor in keeping workers from demanding higher wages and better working conditions.
15. **a**   Symbolic interactionists stresses how labels create selective perception and self-fulfilling prophecies.
16. **d**   "All of the above" is correct. Genocide occurred when Hitler attempted to destroy all Jews. It is the systematic annihilation of a race or ethnic group, and it often requires the cooperation of ordinary citizens.
17. **c**   A society's policy of exploiting a minority group—using social institutions to deny the minority access to the society's full benefits—is referred to as internal colonialism.
18. **d**   Segregation is the separation of racial or ethnic groups, thereby allowing the dominant group to maintain social distance from the minority and yet continue to exploit them economically.
19. **d**   All of the above are true when trying to categorize into racial-ethnic groups.
20. **a**   WASPs (which stands for white Anglo Saxon Protestants whose ancestors came from England) were highly ethnocentric and viewed other immigrants as inferior. Because they were the ones who settled the colonies, they were able to take power and determine the national agenda, controlling the destiny of the nation. As white Europeans from other countries arrived in America, WASPs viewed them as inferior. Rather than being embraced by WASPs, they were typically greeted with negative stereotypes.

21. **a** According to your text, Latinos are distinguished from other ethnic minorities in the United States by the Spanish language.
22. **d** While African Americans who occupy a higher status receive less discrimination than those of lower status, the discrimination they receive is still as painful.
23. **c** While Asian Americans as a whole have been successful in this country, there are significant differences among Asian ethnic groups.
24. **a** The overarching issue for minorities is overcoming discrimination.
25. **b** Most immigrants who came over to the United States during the first wave of immigration were from Europe. In the current wave of immigration, immigrants are coming from many nations.

ANSWERS FOR TRUE-FALSE QUESTIONS
1. *True.*
2. *True.*
3. *False.* Psychological theories of prejudice stress the authoritarian personality and frustration displaced toward scapegoats.
4. *False.* In order to understand discrimination in the United States, it is necessary to explain the patterns of institutional discrimination.
5. *True.*
6. *True.*
7. *True.*
8. *True.*
9. *True.*
10. *False.* Affirmative action has been at the center of controversy for more than a decade.

ANSWERS TO THE FILL-IN-THE-BLANK QUESTIONS
1. homogenous
2. race
3. ethnic work
4. tossed salad
5. age
6. tripled
7. Asian Americans or Japanese
8. invisible minority
9. separatism
10. Proposition 209

GUIDELINES FOR ANSWERING THE ESSAY QUESTIONS
1. *Explain what the author means when he says that race is both a myth and a reality.*

You would begin by defining the concept of race. Then you would move on to talking about the myth of race, or how there is no universal agreement as to how many races there are and how a system of racial classification is more a reflection of the society in which one lives than any underlying biological bases. At the same time, race is a reality in terms of people's subjective feelings about race, the superiority of some and the inferiority of others. You should bring Thomas' observations into the essay; that is, if people believe something is real, then it is real in its consequences.

2. *Using the experiences of different racial and ethnic groups in the United States, identify and discuss the six patterns of intergroup relations.*

The book identifies six different types of intergroup relations—genocide, population transfer, internal colonialism, segregation, assimilation, and multiculturalism. You could begin by mentioning how these are arranged along a continuum from rejection and inhumanity to acceptance and humanity. Then, as you define each pattern, bring into your discussion an example, or examples, from the history of the United States. For example, in discussing genocide you could mention the treatment of Native Americans by the U.S. military. For population transfer you could bring up the movement of Native Americans to reservations or the relocation of Japanese Americans to internment camps during World War II. In discussing internal colonialism you could mention the economic exploitation of Latino farm workers. The example of segregation would be the Jim Crow South. The experiences of European immigrants would reflect assimilation. As the textbook notes, it is difficult to find an example of multiculturalism in the history of our nation; perhaps one example might be religious pluralism.

3. *Explore how both psychological and sociological theories can be used together to gain a deeper understanding of prejudice and discrimination.*

Your essay should discuss how psychological theories provide us with a deeper understanding of individual behavior, while sociological theories provide insights into the societal framework of prejudice and discrimination. You could discuss the work of Theodor Adorno on the authoritarian personality or Dollard's work on individual frustration and the role of scapegoats. However, without an understanding of the social environment, this work is incomplete. Bridging the two perspectives is symbolic interactionism and the analysis of the role of labels, selective perception, and the self-fulfilling prophecy in maintaining prejudice. But you should also include in your essay some reference to functionalist analysis and the work of Muzafer and Carolyn Sherif, as well as the conflict theorists and how the capitalist class exploits racial and ethnic strife to retain power and control in society.

4. *Discuss the difference between individual and institutional discrimination and give examples of both.*

Individual discrimination is the negative treatment of one person by another based on the physical characteristics. The discrimination is between the two people. For example, it could be a student excluding another classmate from a project because of his/her race. Institutional discrimination is negative treatment of a minority group that is built into the social system. This is also called systemic discrimination. You could discuss institutional discrimination in the issuing of home mortgages and car loans. African Americans and Latinos were 60 percent more likely to have their loan rejected than whites. Also, institutional discrimination has been found in health care. Whites are more likely to receive preventive care services than blacks. This preferential treatment is given both by black and white doctors.

5. *What would have to change in our society in order for us to truly be a multicultural society?*

Start by defining multiculturalism—the encouragement of racial and ethnic variation. In a pluralistic society, minority groups are able to maintain their separate identities, and still participate in their society's institutions. In a sense, minority groups no longer exist, since they would no longer be singled out for unequal treatment, nor would they regard themselves as objects of collective discrimination.

Before we can claim to be a multicultural society, we would have to attack the racism that continues. While we have eliminated many of the most blatant forms of racism, there is still much to be done. As the chapter points out, minorities still face prejudice and discrimination in terms of banking practices, real estate transactions, health care, employment, and education. Much of today's discrimination is institutionalized, which makes it much harder to see and to fight.

CHAPTER 13

ANSWERS FOR MULTIPLE CHOICE QUESTIONS

1. **b** The Abkhasians are an interesting example regarding age because they live such long lives.
2. **b** Today, 13 percent of Americans are age 65 or older.
3. **b** The process by which older persons make up an increasing proportion of the United States population is referred to as the graying of America.
4. **c** The number of years an individual is likely to live is referred to as his/her life expectancy.
5. **c** Gender age refers to the relative value that a culture places on men's and women's ages.
6. **d** "All of the above" is correct. Factors that may spur people to apply the label of old to themselves include personal history or biography, cultural signals about when a person is old, and biological factors.
7. **c** Symbolic interactionists stress that old age has no inherent meaning.
8. **a** Symbolic interactionism states that industrialization brought mass education and mass production, which eroded the meaning of aging and being elderly.
9. **b** It has been suggested that the baby boom generation will have a positive effect on U.S. social images of the elderly in the years to come, given the numbers and economic clout.
10. **d** "All of the above" is correct.
11. **b** Some researchers believe that the process of disengagement begins during middle age.
12. **d** "All of the above" is correct. The mass media communicate messages that reflect the currently devalued status of the elderly. They also tell us what people over age 65 should be like and often treat the elderly in discourteous and unflattering terms.
13. **b** Activity theory assumes that the more activities elderly people engage in, the more they find life satisfying.
14. **d** Continuity theory, the idea that we use strategies we have developed over a lifetime to cope with changes in old age, has been criticized because it is too broad; it is a collection of loosely connected ideas; and it has no specific application to the elderly.
15. **b** Conflict theorists believe that retirement benefits are the result of a struggle between competing interest groups.
16. **a** The requirement that workers retire at age 65 was protested for many years by the elderly, who felt the decision should be voluntary and not mandatory. Finally in 1986, Congress eliminated mandatory retirement at age 65.
17. **b** As the population of the United States grays, there is concern that the ratio of working people to retired people will become smaller, making it more difficult to support programs such as Social Security. This ratio is referred to as the dependency ratio.
18. **d** The first three are all problems currently associated with Social Security. The last is not. As your text points out, elderly poverty is actually lower than the overall rate of poverty in this country.
19. **b** The goal of the Gray Panthers, founded in the 1960s by Maggie Kuhn, is to encourage people of all ages to work for the welfare of both the old and the young.
20. **a** Isolation is a problem for many people over age 65, especially for women. This is because of differences in patterns of mortality between men and women. Because elderly women are more likely to live longer than their husbands, most elderly men are still living with their wives, and most elderly women are not.
21. **d** 90 percent of nursing homes are understaffed.
22. **b** Researchers have found that elder abuse is fairly extensive.
23. **c** Most abusers are not paid health-care staff, but family members who verbally and emotionally abuse, or financially exploit, their aged relatives. The *most* likely abuser is the spouse.
24. **b** a higher percent of elderly women are likely to be poor compared to elderly men.

25. **c** With industrialization, death was transformed into an event that is managed by professionals in hospitals. The result is that most of us have never seen anyone die. It is an event that is strange and alien to us.

ANSWERS FOR TRUE-FALSE QUESTIONS
1. *True.*
2. *True.*
3. *False.* In earlier times, because most people never reached old age, growing old was seen as an accomplishment. They were viewed as storehouses of knowledge about work skills and about how to live a long life. This view contrasts sharply with the more negative view our society has of old age today.
4. *True.*
5. *True.*
6. *True.*
7. *True.*
8. *False.* Elderly women are likely to live longer and experience the loneliness of widowhood.
9. *True.*
10. *True.*

ANSWERS TO THE FILL-IN-THE-BLANK QUESTIONS
1. age cohorts
2. more
3. broad
4. 65
5. dependency ratio
6. Gray Panthers
7. family members
8. less
9. acceptance
10. biomedical science

GUIDELINES FOR ANSWERING THE ESSAY QUESTIONS
1. *Explain why sociologists say that aging is socially constructed.*

You should begin your essay by explaining that "social construction of aging" means that there is nothing in the biological nature of aging that contributes to a particular set of attitudes, either in the person who is aging or in others who surround him/her. Rather, attitudes toward aging develop out of society and are shaped by the particular context of the society. Consequently, attitudes will vary from one social group to another. You could also talk about how the Industrial Revolution and the emergence of industrial societies affected the size of the aged population, social attitudes about aging, and the role of the aged in society.

In the context of this question it would be important to mention the symbolic interactionists' views on aging. In particular, you would want to discuss the fact that social factors influence individuals' perceptions about the aging process. These factors include biology, personal history, gender age, and timetables.

2. *Choose one of the three different perspectives and discuss how that perspective approaches the subject of aging. Consider both the strengths and weaknesses of the perspective you choose.*

In this question, you have the option of writing about symbolic interactionism, functionalism, or conflict theory. If you choose symbolic interactionism, you would want to talk about the process of labeling—both the cultural labels and factors that affect the individual's adoption of those labels. You would also want to bring up the concept of "ageism," the role of the media in defining images, and how the labels change over time. In particular, you could discuss how these labels changed with industrialization and how they are once again changing with the advent of a postindustrial society. The strength of this perspective is that it provides us with insights into the social nature of a biological process; a weakness would be that it does not consider the conflict that may surround the labeling process.

If you choose to write about functionalism, remember that this perspective focuses on how the different parts of society work together. Two important theories associated with this perspective are disengagement theory and activity theory. Strengths might be the focus on adjustment and the smooth transitioning from one generation to the next. Weaknesses are tied to the theories; disengagement theory overlooks the possibility that the elderly disengage from one set of roles (work-related) but may engage in another set of roles (friendship), while activity theory does not identify the key variables that underlie people's activities.

Finally, if you choose conflict theory, you would want to focus on the conflict that is generated between different age groups in society as they compete for scarce resources. As an example, you would want to discuss the controversy over social security, from its birth to the present time. A strength of this perspective is that it provides us with an understanding of why the elderly have reduced the level of poverty over time; a weakness might be that it tends to emphasize conflict to the extent that cooperation between generations is overlooked.

3. *Discuss the impact that industrialization and technology have had on aging as well as dying.*

You could begin the essay by talking about how technology and industrialization have brought improvements and new developments. You might want to refer to some of the discussion in this chapter on the cross-cultural variations in aging, such as with the Abkhasians, the Tiwi and Eskimo, or the Chinese. These were all preindustrial societies with various views on the elderly. To talk about the impact of industrialization, you should refer to the improvements in the quality of life and the changes in cultural views on aging. Finally, you would want to talk about how technology enables us to sustain life for longer periods, but that the quality of that life is often compromised.

4. *People who come here from other parts of the world are often very critical of families that place their elderly family members in nursing homes. Assume that a friend of yours who comes from another part of the world asks you about your family's decision to move your grandparent into a nursing home. Develop an explanation that draws on the material presented in this chapter.*

First, you should point out to your friend that most elderly are cared for by their families. It is only a small percentage of elderly who are in nursing homes at any one time. Also, those who are in nursing homes are generally there because they are very old and very likely do not have any family to care for them. Often, even when there is family to provide care, the elderly person is very ill; two-thirds of nursing home residents have memory loss or are disoriented.

You could also point out some of the broader changes that make it more difficult for families to provide care. Adult daughters or daughters-in-law are typically the ones who care for elderly parents. In the last few decades, more women are employed outside the home, which creates challenges for them if the elderly parent needs constant care. Also, families are more likely to be disrupted by divorce than in the past, which means there may not be a daughter-in-law who is available and the daughter may be a single mom who has to work to support her children.

Your friend should also know that being cared for in a nursing home does not necessarily mean that elderly family members are alienated from their children. One study found that the majority of residents of nursing homes reported good or improved relationships with adult children following their move to a nursing home. The researchers suggested that this was because having to provide care to an ailing parent can be extremely stressful. Once the parent is being cared for by professionals, the children are free to once again focus on the emotional needs of their parents.

5. *Discuss the five stages of death and what is being done to humanize the process of death and dying.*

You can review the five stages of the death process as described by psychologist Elizabeth Kübler-Ross. The first stage is denial—people have a difficult time believing they are going to die. The second stage is anger—they feel that their dying is unjust. In the third stage of negotiation, people start to bargain with God. The fourth stage is depression in which the death is grieved. The last stage is acceptance in which people come to terms with their impending death. Hospices have emerged as a way to humanize the dying process. Services are provided in the person's home for the purpose of giving comfort and dignity to the dying person. While medical needs are met, the hospice program is also concerned with the person's social and spiritual needs.

CHAPTER 14

ANSWERS FOR MULTIPLE CHOICE QUESTIONS

1. **b** An economy is a system of distributing goods and services.
2. **c** Hunting and gathering societies are characterized by a subsistence economy.
3. **b** In pastoral and horticultural economies a more dependable food supply led to the development of a surplus. This surplus was one of the most significant events in human history because it fundamentally altered people's basic relationships.
4. **d** Industrial economies are based on machines powered by fuels. Industrial economies also created a surplus unlike anything the world had seen, and these economies were based on the invention of the steam engine. Therefore, the *incorrect* statement is "A service sector developed and employed the majority of workers;" this is actually a characteristic of a *postindustrial society*.
5. **d** Thorstein Veblen used the term *conspicuous consumption* to describe the lavishly wasteful spending of goods in order to enhance social prestige.
6. **c** Postindustrial economies are characterized by a large surplus of goods, extensive trade among nations, and a "global village." While machines may still be powered by fuel, this is <u>not</u> a defining characteristic of this type of economy.
7. **c** The two forces that have combined to create this new society are biology and economics. Henslin identifies this new type as a *bioeconomic society*.
8. **d** In pastoral and horticultural societies, since there was little surplus bartering was a common medium of exchanging one item for another.
9. **a** Money was first used extensively in agricultural societies.
10. **c** The policy of only issuing as much paper money as there were gold reserves was known as the gold standard.
11. **a** The *gross domestic product* is the term used to describe the total goods and services produced by a nation.
12. **c** The debit card came into existence in the postindustrial economy.
13. **d** Private ownership of the means of production is an essential feature of capitalism.
14. **c** The possession of machines and factories by individuals who decide what shall be produced is referred to as private ownership of the means of production.
15. **b** An economic system characterized by the public ownership of the means of production, central planning, and the distribution of goods without a profit motive is socialism.
16. **b** According to Karl Marx, profits represent excess value that is extracted from workers. Because an item's value is derived from the work that goes into it, there can be no profit unless workers are paid less than the value of their labor.
17. **a** Protecting the welfare of the population is an element of welfare or state capitalism, not capitalism.
18. **b** Convergence theory states that capitalism and socialism will become more alike as they both develop industrially.
19. **a** Work binds us together, according to the functionalist perspective.
20. **b** As societies industrialize, they become based on organic solidarity.
21. **c** The joint ownership of a business enterprise whose liabilities and obligations are separate from those of its owners is a corporation.
22. **c** When stockholders are satisfied with the profits and their stock dividends, they generally just rubber-stamp whatever recommendations are made by management; a stockholders' revolt occurs when dissatisfaction with the overall level of performance leads to their refusal to approve management's recommendations.
23. **b** The statement that is *incorrect* is, "Relationships among members of the inner circle are always cooperative rather than competitive," since members often find themselves in competition with one another for business.

24. **d** Corporate capitalism is the domination of an economic system by giant corporations.
25. **c** The *correct* statement regarding wages today is "The buying power of today's wages is actually less than it was 30 years ago." Inflation has whittled away the value of the increased dollars workers are paid.

ANSWERS FOR TRUE-FALSE QUESTIONS
1. *False.* Pastoral and horticultural societies, not hunting and gathering societies, were the first economies to have a surplus.
2. *True.*
3. *False.* In agricultural societies, people bartering for goods and services is a common practice.
4. *False.* Postindustrial economies, not industrial economies, are based on information processing and providing services.
5. *True.*
6. *True.*
7. *False.* Credit cards and debit cards are not the same thing. A credit card allows its owner to purchase goods but to be billed later. A debit card allows its owner to purchase against his or her bank account.
8. *True.*
9. *False.* Industrialization decreased the amount of leisure time workers had.
10. *True.*

ANSWERS TO THE FILL-IN-THE-BLANK QUESTIONS
1. socialism
2. convergence theory
3. corporation
4. global superclass
5. conflict
6. two
7. undocumented workers
8. u-curve
9. telecommuting
10. Germany

GUIDELINES FOR ANSWERING THE ESSAY QUESTIONS
1. *Discuss the advantages and disadvantages of both capitalism and socialism as ideologies and as economic systems.*

This is a difficult question to answer because it is laden with social values. In this country we have been taught that capitalism is good and socialism is bad. Nevertheless, you should try to approach this from as objective a position as possible. You would want to begin by discussing the advantages and disadvantages of capitalism. For advantages, you could mention the idea of private ownership and the pursuit of profits, the motivation among workers to work hard, and the vast array of goods that are available in the marketplace. Among the disadvantages you could note the possibility for monopoly, the creation of constant discontent through advertising, and the violation of certain basic human rights like freedom from poverty. Turning to socialism, you could note that advantages include production for the general welfare rather than individual enrichment and the distribution of goods and services according to need rather than ability to pay. Critics point out that socialism violates basic human rights such as individual freedom of decision and opportunity.

2. *Explain why functionalists believe that work is functional for society.*

The first point to make is that work is functional for society because without work, society would collapse. This has always been the case, regardless of the type of society. In the earliest hunting and gathering societies, the work people did was mostly hunting and gathering. If they did not do this, they would starve. As societies became larger and more complex, the nature of work changed, but it was still essential for the continuation of society for people to engage in it.

Beyond that, functionalists as far back as Emile Durkheim have stressed that it is work that binds us together in a social group. It was Durkheim who identified two bases for social solidarity. In preindustrial societies, people do similar work and directly share most aspects of life; he called the sense of unity that develops out of doing similar activities mechanical solidarity. As societies undergo change with industrialization, the kind of work people do also changes. A more specialized division of labor emerges, with the result that people may not feel the connection with one another that comes from doing similar work. However, people begin to realize that they are contributing to the welfare of others as they do their specialized tasks and others are contributing to their welfare. Durkheim called this interdependence that comes out of the more specialized division of labor *organic solidarity*.

3. *Take the perspective of a conflict theorist and explain the goals of corporate leaders and the strategies they use to achieve these goals.*

The primary goal of corporate leaders is to make a profit for their corporation. There are a number of strategies they can use, or have used, in trying to achieve this goal. The first is the exploitation of workers. The corporation is interested in minimizing labor costs by hiring workers for the cheapest wage possible. In this country's past, that meant low wages and long working days. With the passage of minimum wage laws and regulated working hours, as well as the rise of unions, corporations sought business locations without these forces. In today's world, that means locating production facilities in the Least Industrialized Nations.

The conflict theorists also note that increasingly, these multinational corporations are headed by an inner circle, whose members are united by a mutual interest in preserving capitalism. They consult with high-level politicians in order to promote legislation that is favorable to big business. On a global level, they promote the ideology of capitalism and move capital from one nation to another in their search for greater and more immediate profits. You could also refer back to the discussion on neocolonialism in the chapter on global stratification for more information on the inner circle and local political elites.

Another strategy used by corporations is the attainment of monopoly control over an industry. In this way, they are able to set prices and make greater profits. As you now know from your reading, our government passed antimonopoly legislation in the wake of John D. Rockefeller's enormous success so it is very difficult for corporations to operate as a monopoly. Given this, they try for an oligopoly, where several large companies dominate a single industry. They can then divide up the market among themselves and dictate the quality and prices of their products. They can also use their combined power to cultivate political influence.

Finally, today corporate leaders are searching for merger partners globally. This not only reduces global competition but also enables them to dominate global markets. In the process, smaller competitors are driven out of business.

4. *Discuss what is meant by the underground economy and the extent to which it exists.*

The underground economy consists of the exchange of goods and services that are not reported to the government and escape taxation. These activities consist of legal and illegal activities. The largest source of illegal income is probably drug dealing. Billions of dollars flow from users to sellers each year. The million or so illegal immigrants who come to the U.S. each year are also a part of this underground economy. They work in restaurants, do housework, work in sweatshops, clean rooms in hotels, etc. The underground economy is estimated to be no less than 10 percent of the regular economy. It probably totals over $1 trillion a year.

5. *The chapter discusses several different economic trends that have been occurring in the second half of this century. Discuss the impact of each of the following: the movement of women into the economy,*

the underground economy, shrinking paychecks, changing patterns of work and leisure, and the emergence of the alternative office.

The first development you will want to talk about is women's increased participation in the paid workforce. This has transformed consumption patterns, relations at work, self-concepts, and relationships with significant others. The underground economy is another major force in our society today, generating about $1 trillion. What is significant is that its presence distorts official statistics on the nation's gross national product, income, and employment. It also means that the IRS loses more than $100 billion a year in taxes. The shrinking of workers' paychecks is connected to inflation—workers are finding that their buying power is less than it was 30 years ago. Finally, compared to a century ago, workers enjoy increased leisure, primarily because workers have organized and demanded greater leisure. At the same time, over the past 30 to 40 years, the trend toward greater leisure has been reversed, and workers today are working more than before.

CHAPTER 15

ANSWERS FOR MULTIPLE CHOICE QUESTIONS

1. **d** "All of the above" is correct. Power, as defined by Max Weber, is the ability to carry out one's will in spite of resistance from others; it is an inevitable part of everyday life.
2. **b** Governments, whether dictatorships or the elected forms, are examples of macropolitics.
3. **b** Coercion is the power people do not accept as just.
4. **c** Peter Berger considered violence to be the ultimate foundation of any political order.
5. **b** Revolutions are people's rejection of the government's claim to rule over them.
6. **d** "All of the above" is correct. Traditional authority, the hallmark of preliterate groups, is based on custom. With industrialization it declines, but does not totally disappear.
7. **b** Rational-legal authority comes from the position that someone holds. Because bureaucracies are based on written rules, rational-legal authority is sometimes called bureaucratic authority.
8. **c** Joan of Arc's authority to lead soldiers into battle is an example of charismatic authority. They followed her because they perceived that she was endowed by nature with exceptional qualities.
9. **d** "All of the above" is correct. John F. Kennedy was a rational-legal leader; was a charismatic leader; and is an example of a leader who is difficult to classify in terms of ideal types.
10. **c** The least stable type of authority is the charismatic.
11. **d** "All of the above" would be the correct answer. Representative democracy is a form of democracy in which citizens elect public officials to represent them in government. It is considered by many to be the greatest gift the United States has given the world. At the time it was first conceived, it was considered revolutionary.
12. **b** Universal citizenship is the principle that everyone has the same basic rights by virtue of being born in a country, or of immigrating to that country and becoming a naturalized citizen.
13. **b** An individual who seizes power and imposes his will onto the people is a dictator.
14. **c** A form of government that exerts almost total control is a totalitarian regime.
15. **a** The United States has centrist parties.
16. **b** The *incorrect* statement is the one that says, "members of Congress maintain strict party allegiances and will never cross party lines to vote for legislation proposed by a member of the other party."
17. **b** European systems of democracy, in which seats in the national legislatures are divided according to the proportion of votes each party receives (proportional representation), encourage the formation of minority parties.
18. **b** Studies of voting patterns in the United States show that voting varies by age, race/ethnicity, education, employment, income, and gender.
19. **d** According to research by Portes and Rumbaut, immigrants initially organize politically along lines of race and ethnicity. Once they have achieved a certain level of political power, attaining political representation roughly equivalent to their numbers in the population, then social class becomes more significant than race and ethnicity.
20. **b** In recent presidential elections, only about half of eligible voters actually cast a ballot.
21. **d** "All of the above" is correct. Lobbyists are people paid to influence legislation on behalf of their clients; are employed by special-interest groups; and are a major force in American politics.
22. **b** Functionalists believe that any one group is prevented from gaining control of the government because of the presence of checks and balances.
23. **a** Functionalists suggest that political conflict is minimized as special-interest groups negotiate with one another and reach compromise.
24. **d** Members of the power elite are drawn from all three arenas: the largest corporations, the armed services, and political office.
25. **c** According to conflict theorists, the ruling class is made up of people whose backgrounds and orientations to life are so similar that they automatically share the same goals.

ANSWERS FOR TRUE-FALSE QUESTIONS
1. *True.*
2. *False.* Authority, not coercion, refers to legitimate power.
3. *True.*
4. *True.* As societies industrialize, traditional authority is undermined; however, it never totally dies out. Parental authority provides an excellent example.
5. *False.* Most political action committees do not represent broad social interests but, rather, stand for narrow financial concerns, such as the dairy, oil, banking, and construction industries.
6. *True.*
7. *False.* Functionalists claim that no one group holds power in America; that the country's many competing interest groups balance each other.
8. *True.*
9. *False.* Because of technological advances in killing, the cost of war in terms of money spent and human lives lost has increased.
10. *True.*

ANSWERS TO THE FILL-IN-THE-BLANK QUESTIONS
1. Internet
2. totalitarianism
3. proportional representation
4. apathy
5. special interest group
6. money
7. checks and balances
8. power elite
9. ruling class
10. terrorism

GUIDELINES FOR ANSWERING THE ESSAY QUESTIONS
1. *Distinguish between macropolitics and micropolitics, explaining what each is and which perspectives are associated with each, and provide your own examples to illustrate each.*

You would begin by defining what each of these is—micropolitics is the exercise of power in everyday life, while macropolitics is the exercise of large-scale power over a large group. In general, symbolic interactionists focus more on micropolitics, because it is rooted in the social interactions that take place within social groups, although some conflict theorists could also take a micropolitical approach by focusing on the conflict that is generated by power inequalities. On the other hand, functionalists and conflict theorists are concerned with macropolitics, because they are concerned with the large-scale structures and patterns of a society. Finally, you would include some of your own examples of micropolitics (struggles between husbands and wives, parents and children) and macropolitics (struggles between political parties, between Congress and the President, between unions and elected officials).

2. *Compare and contrast the systems of democracy found in the United States and Europe and discuss how some of the problems associated with our system, such as voter apathy, the power of political action committees, and the concentration of power, are related to our system.*

For this essay you would want to point out that both systems are democratic, which means that the ultimate power resides in the people. Both are representative, rather than direct democracies, which means that citizens vote for representatives who actually make the decisions rather than the citizens themselves voting on each decision. Despite these similarities, the two systems have differences. You would want to mention the proportional representation of the European system versus the winner-takes-all outcomes of the American system, the encouragement of minority parties in the European system versus their discouragement in the American system, and the centrist parties of Europe versus the noncentrist parties of the United States.

Finally, you would want to consider how voter apathy, the power of political action committees, and the concentration of power are related to the specific features of the United States system. First, you might want to talk about how the winner-takes-all arrangement encourages the development of centrist parties which are forced to appeal to the middle of the voting population in order to receive the majority of the votes; because of this, many people come to feel that the political parties are too superficial and do not really represent their ideas or interests, so they decide to sit out the elections. The second problem, power of PACs, is also related to the particular feature of winner-takes-all systems. With so much riding on elections, candidates are pressured into spending excessive amounts of money in order to get their name and their message out to the voters. The cash requirements provide a perfect opportunity for PACs to donate and thereby influence not only the outcomes of elections but the voting behavior of the elected candidate. The final problem about the concentration of power is an outgrowth of the first two. You could go back to the discussion of the iron law of oligarchy and make the argument that the combination of voter apathy and the financial requirements of running for office produce a small elite that becomes committed to maintaining its power.

3. *Discuss the two major political parties in the United States. Explain differences and similarities.*

Even though numerous political parties emerged after the United States was founded, two parties dominate. The Democrats are typically associated with the working class and the Republicans with wealthier people. They each represent different philosophical principles and appeal to a broad membership. It is difficult, for example, to discern the difference between a conservative Democrat and a liberal Republican. The extremes of each party are easier to distinguish. The strongly Democratic support legislation that transfers money from the richer to the poorer or that controls wages, working conditions, and competition. Strong Republicans would not be supportive of this legislation. They are similar in that both parties support fundamentals such as free public education; a strong military; freedom of religion, speech, and assembly; and capitalism.

4. *Discuss why wars happen.*

As the book states, war is not universal. Rather, it is simply one option that groups may choose when dealing with disagreements. As the record indicates, not all societies choose this option. At the same time, it would appear that war is rather common, both across history and in our own time. The question is then, *why?*

In trying to answer this, you would want to bring up the work of Nicholas Timasheff. He identified three essential conditions of war: (1) cultural traditions; (2) an antagonistic situation; (3) a fuel that heats the situation to a boiling point. You could also discuss the different fuels and the fact that leaders often see war as an opportunity to achieve certain objectives.

Finally, there is the whole issue of dehumanization. You could argue that just as experience in war can lead those who are fighting to see the enemy as less than human, a history or culture of warfare can contribute to an entire society viewing its enemies as less than fully human. In addition, as sociologist Tamotsu Shibutani stresses, dehumanization is aided by the tendency for prolonged conflicts to be transformed into struggles between good and evil. In our own history, many of the wars we have fought have been framed exactly this way. Wars exalt killing and those who fight and kill are often given metals to glorify their actions.

CHAPTER 16

ANSWERS FOR MULTIPLE CHOICE QUESTIONS

1.   **a**   Polyandry is a marriage in which a woman has more than one husband.
2.   **d**   A household is the term used to describe the people who occupy the same housing unit or other living quarters. A family that lives together in the same house would be considered a household, but unrelated people who live together are not considered a family.
3.   **d**   family of orientation is the one in which a person grows up.
4.   **b**   Endogamy is the practice of marrying within one's own group.
5.   **a**   In a matrilineal system, descent is figured only on the mother's side.
6.   **c**   Although the roots of authority with U.S. families is patriarchal, today a growing number of families are egalitarian, sharing authority between men and women.
7.   **d**   "All of the above" is correct. The incest taboo is rules specifying the degrees of kinship that prohibit sex or marriage; helps families avoid role confusion; and facilitates the socialization of children.
8.   **c**   conflict theory.
9.   **d**   Conflict theorists focus on inequality in marriages, especially unequal power between husbands and wives.
10.   **b**   Most of the decisions made at home are by wives.
11.   **c**   According to research findings, there has been an increase in the time both husbands and wives spend caring for children.
12.   **a**   Research by Dutton and Aron found that love begins with a sexual attraction. This is followed by a cognitive awareness, as we attach a label to our feelings.
13.   **c**   The tendency of people with similar characteristics to marry one another is homogamy.
14.   **b**   Families of the same social class are likely to be similar, regardless of their race-ethnicity.
15.   **b**   In comparison to married couples, single mothers are much less likely to rely on the child's father for help.
16.   **d**   "None of the above" is correct. In regard to child rearing, Melvin Kohn concluded that parents of different social classes socialize their children differently. Working-class parents are more likely to use physical punishment than middle-class parents, who are more likely to withdraw privileges or affection.
17.   **d**   18% of 25- to 29-year-olds live with their parents. Some live with them during college and some return after college.
18.   **c**   According to your text, a major concern of upper-class African American families is the family background of those whom their children marry.
19.   **d**   "All of the above" is correct. Machismo distinguishes Latino families from other groups; is an emphasis on male strength and dominance; and is seen in some Chicano families where the husband-father plays a strong role in his family.
20.   **c**   One of the ways in which Native American families differ from most U.S. families is in terms of the participation of elders in their children's families. They not only provide childcare, but also play an active role in teaching and disciplining the children.
21.   **b**   Since 1970, the number of children in the United States who live with both parents has dropped from 85 percent to 66 percent.
22.   **a**   Children from one-parent families are more likely to drop out of school.
23.   **d**   Postponement of first marriage, an increase in cohabitation and an increase in caring for children and aging parents at the same time are the three major changes that characterize U.S. families today. An increase in interracial marriages is *not* one of the major changes.
24.   **c**   41 states prohibit same-sex marriages.
25.   **d**   "All of the above" is correct. Cohabitation, the condition of living together as an unmarried couple, has increased 12 times since the 1970s and has occurred before most couples marry.

ANSWERS FOR TRUE-FALSE QUESTIONS

1. *False.* Marriage and family are mechanisms for governing mate selection, reckoning descent, and establishing inheritance and authority.
2. *True.*
3. *False.* Laws of endogamy in the United States that prohibit interracial marriages have all been repealed.
4. *True.*
5. *True.*
6. *True.*
7. *True.*
8. *False.* Cohabitation and postponing marriage have both seen drastic increases since 1970.
9. *True.*
10. *True.*

ANSWERS TO THE FILL-IN-THE-BLANK QUESTIONS

1. Latino
2. fictive
3. poverty
4. blended families
5. marriage
6. commitment
7. aging parents
8. sexual morality
9. new chance
10. incest

GUIDELINES FOR ANSWERING THE ESSAY QUESTIONS

1. *Discuss whether the family still provides a useful function.*

This is a rather straightforward question. You would want to refer to the functionalist explanation regarding the functions that the family performs. These include (1) economic production, (2) socialization of children, (3) care of the sick and aged, (4) recreation, (5) sexual control, and (6) reproduction. Then, consider the degree to which families in this country still fulfill all of these functions. If they don't, which ones do they still fulfill? Are there other institutions that could do the job as well? Given your answers to these questions, construct an argument as to the continued usefulness of the family.

2. *Discuss what factors contribute to successful marriages and to happy families.*

You could discuss the research done by Jeanette and Robert Lauer. They interviewed 351 couples who had been married for at least 15 years. Three hundred of the couples reported being happily married. They identified eight factors that contributed to the success of their marriages. These were: (1) they think of their spouse as their best friend; (2) like their spouse as a person; (3) see marriage as a commitment; (4) believe marriage is sacred; (5) have similar aims and goals; (6) see spouse as more interesting over time; (7) want the relationship to succeed; and (8) laugh together. Sociologists have also found that those couples who get along with their in-laws and do enjoyable leisure activities are also happier. The research done on happy families shows the following to be important: (1) they spend a lot of time together; (2) express appreciation; (3) are committed to each other's welfare; (4) talk and listen to one another; (5) are religious; and (6) deal with crisis positively.

3. *Identify the stages in the family life cycle, discussing what tasks are accomplished in each stage and what event marks that transition from one stage to the next.*

You will want to discuss each of the several stages in sequence: love and courtship, marriage, childbirth, child rearing, the empty nest, and widowhood. For each stage, you should include the work that takes place and the events that mark the beginning and end of that stage. For example, the first stage is love and courtship. In our culture, this involves romantic love, with individuals being sexually attracted to one another and idealizing the other. Love actually has two components: one is emotion, related to feelings of sexual attraction, and the other is cognitive, attaching labels to our feelings. The stage begins with our meeting and being attracted to another person, and ends when we decide to get engaged to marry.

4. *Identify the trends among U.S. families today and explain the social forces that have contributed to each of them.*
    This chapter identifies five trends in U.S. families: postponement of marriage, cohabitation, unmarried mothers, and the sandwich generation and elder care. You should take each trend in turn, identifying and explaining the pattern. For example, for the first half of the twentieth century, the age at first marriage steadily declined, so that by 1950, women married at about age 20. For the next 20 years, this figure remained unchanged. Then, beginning in 1970, the average age began to climb. In 2000, women are waiting until they are almost 26 to marry. Now that you have described the pattern, you need to try and explain it. Here's where you want to apply what you have learned previously about changing norms (Chapter 2). You can talk about how women's roles have changed tremendously since 1970 (see Chapter 11); these changes have affected women's lives and decisions on when to marry. You could also talk about attitudes about premarital sex, which began to change in the 1960s and 1970s. More liberal attitudes about premarital sex and cohabitation have also affected young people's decisions about when to marry. Research on changes in marriage and cohabitation supports this. Once you have described and analyzed this first trend, you would then go on to do the same with the other three trends.

5. *Discuss the impact that divorce has on family members—men, women and children.*
    You would want to discuss each family role separately—children, wives and husbands. In your response, be sure to talk about the research on the impact on children, both short-term and long-term. In the short-term, this includes hostility, anxiety, nightmares, and poor school performance. In the long-term, it includes a loss of connection to parents and difficulties forming intimate relations.
    For spouses, there is anger, depression and anxiety following a divorce, but each also experiences unique problems related to their gender. For women, there is often a decrease in the standard of living, although the impact varies by social class. For men, there is a loss of connection to their children and the possible development of a series of families.

CHAPTER 17

ANSWERS FOR MULTIPLE CHOICE QUESTIONS

1. **b** In Japan, college admission is based on making a high score on a national test.
2. **c** Since the collapse of the Soviet Union, the educational system is being reinvented. Private, religious and even foreign-run schools are allowed. More importantly, teachers are allowed to encourage students to question and to think for themselves.
3. **a** Despite the fact that education is free at all levels, including college, children of the wealthy are several times as likely as children of the nonwealthy to continue their education beyond the basics.
4. **a** The use of diplomas and degrees to determine who is eligible for jobs, even though the diploma or degree may be irrelevant to the actual work, is known as a credential society.
5. **a** All of the following are manifest functions of education: transmitting cultural values; helping mold students into a more or less cohesive unit; and teaching patriotism. Helping to maintain social inequality is *not* one of the functions, according to the functionalists.
6. **c** Traditionally, the educational system in the United States has taught children the value of individualism, competition, and patriotism. Cooperation is less likely to be stressed.
7. **a** The policy that many schools now have of incorporating students with disabilities into regular school activities is called mainstreaming, or inclusion.
8. **a** Credentialing and tracking are two examples of gatekeeping.
9. **c** The hidden curriculum refers to the unwritten rules of behavior and attitudes that are taught in school.
10. **d** IQ tests have been criticized because they are culturally biased. Children from middle-class and upper-class backgrounds are more familiar with the concepts used in the test. Minorities and the poor often score lower on these tests, which results in them being assigned less demanding courses.
11. **c** Public schools are largely supported by local property taxes.
12. **b** The correspondence principle is the ways in which schools correspond to, or reflect the social structure.
13. **a** Bowles found that regardless of ability, students from affluent homes were more likely to go to college than were students from poor homes.
14. **a** Schools encourage competition rather than cooperation.
15. **c** The conflict perspective views education as reproducing the social structure.
16. **b** White and African Americans are the most likely to attend private colleges.
17. **b** Rist's research demonstrated the power of labels—the child's journey through school was essentially determined by the eighth day of kindergarten and was based on the teacher's somewhat biased assessment of ability.
18. **d** The Rosenthal/Jacobson experiment tended to confirm the concept of a self-fulfilling prophecy.
19. **d** Research by George Farkas focused on how teacher expectations affect students' grades.
20. **b** When compared to scores of twenty to thirty years ago, today's scores on tests such as the SAT are lower.
21. **b** The practice of passing students from one grade to the next even though they have not mastered basic materials is called social promotion.
22. **c** High-school graduates who have difficulty with basic reading and math are known as functional illiterates.
23. **b** An examination of the statistics published on page 495 of your text would lead you to conclude that the number of shooting deaths in schools at the end of the 1990s was half what it had been at the beginning of the decade.
24. **c** Coleman and Hoffer found that students attending Roman Catholic schools outperformed students attending public schools. They attributed this to the fact that higher standards were set by teachers at the Roman Catholic schools.

25. **d** "All of the above" is the correct answer. Social science is the only private industry reported to make less than public school teachers.

ANSWERS FOR TRUE-FALSE QUESTIONS

1. *False.* In earlier societies there was no separate social institution called education.
2. *True.*
3. *False.* College graduation in the United States is now much more common than high school graduation was in 1910.
4. *False.* In Japanese schools the value of cooperation rather than competition is stressed.
5. *True.*
6. *False.* Despite the fact that Egyptian education is free at all levels, children of the wealthy are more likely to get an education.
7. *True.*
8. *True.*
9. *False.* American schools encourage, rather than discourage, individualism and although teamwork is encouraged, individuals are singled out for praise when the team does well.
10. *True.*

ANSWERS TO THE FILL-IN-THE-BLANK QUESTIONS

1. acculturation
2. common
3. half
4. culture
5. one-third
6. hidden curriculum
7. grade inflation
8. higher
9. school administrators
10. technology

GUIDELINES FOR ANSWERING THE ESSAY QUESTIONS

1. *Explain the link between democracy, industrialization and universal education.*

For this question, there are two strains of thought that need to be developed. The first is the link between democracy and universal education. Here you will want to talk about the need for voters who are knowledgeable about the issues and are capable of making sound decisions; it is necessary that they read and understand news that is published in newspapers. In addition, the political culture is maintained through the educational system, as children learn patriotism and the facts of the political process.

The second strain is to connect industrialization and universal education. Here you would want to talk about the need for an educated workforce that is able to read instructions and learn how to use increasingly more complex machines. The workforce must also be able to move from job to job, learning new skills as the work requires. The most efficient way in which to train workers, both to have the specific skills needed for a particular job and the general skills needed to survive in a constantly changing workplace, is through universal education For these two reasons, universal education developed in the United States, as well as other industrialized nations.

2. *Compare the educational systems of Japan, Russia, and Egypt and discuss what is meant by the statement that education reflects culture.*

The education system is a reflection of the culture and economy of a country. The most industrialized nations tend to value education more and place higher standards on the level of education and ensuring that their populace receives an education. In Japan, education is a top priority. Their core education and cultural values include solidarity within the group and team-work and this is reflected in how students are taught in schools. The children work together in groups and use the same textbook throughout the country. However, the contradiction lies in that college admission is highly competitive and only the top scorers on a national exam go on to college. Russia represents education in the industrializing nations. In Russia, they made sure that socialist values dominated the schools. Students were discouraged from any critical thinking. After the change to a more capitalistic system, teachers had to be retrained and students taught how to be critical thinkers. Egypt represents education in the least industrialized nation. Many poor children do not receive any schooling, as they stay home to work the land. There is little emphasis placed on formal schooling. As such, significant portions of their population, especially women, are illiterate.

3. *Select one of the three perspectives and design a research project to test the claims of that perspective about the nature of education.*

In order to answer this question you must first choose one of the three perspectives. For example, you might choose the conflict perspective and decide to do a research project on the relationship between ethnicity and individual educational achievement and goals. Your research will involve an analysis of student choices of curricula, their grades, retention rates, and graduation from a large racially/ethnically diverse high school. You have access to student records and you collect data on students in one class as this class moves through the high school. You will compare white students' records to those of African American and Hispanic students in order to test whether the conflict theorists are correct in their assertion that the educational system reproduces the students' class background.

4. *In discussing solutions to educational problems, the author suggests that one direction schools should go is toward setting higher educational standards. The research by James Coleman and Thomas Hoffer support this. Discuss social factors that might explain why such a proposal has not been widely adopted by public schools across the country.*

In answering this question you will want to focus on obstacles to implementation. You could refer to some of the research on teacher expectations and student tracking to illustrate the status quo in the majority of schools. Henslin notes that one of the biggest obstacles is bureaucracy itself, where ritual often replaces performance. A routine becomes established and then difficult to change (refer to Chapter 7 for a complete discussion of bureaucracy).

CHAPTER 18

ANSWERS FOR MULTIPLE CHOICE QUESTIONS

1. **d** Durkheim wrote *The Elementary Forms of the Religious Life* in order to identify elements common to all religions.
2. **c** Durkheim was referring to aspects of life that are part of the ordinary, everyday life with the term *profane.*
3. **c** Durkheim used the word *church* in an unusual way to refer to a group of believers organized around a set of beliefs and practices regarding the sacred.
4. **a** All of the following are functions of religion: support for the government, social change, and social control. Encouraging wars for holy causes is a dysfunction of religion.
5. **b** In a review of the research, it was found that prayer (or meditation) changes people's brain activity and improves their immune response.
6. **c** War and religious persecution are dysfunctions of religion.
7. **b** A unified picture of the world, such as the belief in one God, creator of the universe, is called a cosmology.
8. **c** When some Protestants use the term *born again*, they are referring to a personal life-transforming religious experience.
9. **b** The *incorrect* statement is that "Family members are exempt from having to follow the practice when it involves one of their own." In fact, if the other family members want to remain in good standing in the congregation, they are expected to shun the person too.
10. **c** Marx felt that religion was like a drug and called it the opium of the people.
11. **d** "All of the above" is correct. These are all examples of the use of religion to legitimize social inequalities: the divine right of kings; a declaration that the pharaoh or emperor is god or divine; and the defense of slavery as being God's will.
12. **a** Weber believed that religion held the key to modernization.
13. **a** Weber analyzed how Protestantism gave rise to the Protestant ethic, which stimulated what he called the spirit of capitalism.
14. **a** Judaism was the first major religion to practice monotheism.
15. **b** Some groups believe that all objects in the world have spirits. This is known as animism.
16. **a** An unanticipated outcome of the Reformation was the splintering of Christianity into separate branches.
17. **c** The Shi'ites are the branch of Islam that are more conservative and inclined to fundamentalism.
18. **c** Polytheism is the belief that there are many gods.
19. **b** The religion with no specific founder is Hinduism.
20. **c** Reincarnation is the return of the soul after death in a different form.
21. **a** All religions began as cults.
22. **c** Although larger than a cult, a sect still feels tension from society.
23. **c** Rather than intolerance of differences, religion in the United States is characterized by tolerance.
24. **d** "All of the above" is correct. Secularization of religion occurs as a result of industrialization, urbanization, and mass education.
25. **b** An example of secularization of culture is that the influence of religion on public affairs has lessened today.

ANSWERS FOR TRUE-FALSE QUESTIONS

1. *True.*
2. *True.*
3. *True.*
4. *False.* Judaism, Christianity, and Islam are all monotheistic religions
5. *False.* Both cults and sects stress evangelism, or the active recruitment of new members.

6. *True.*
7. *True.*
8. *True.*
9. *False.* Many local ministers view the electronic church as a competitor for the attention of their members and for money that could go to their own good causes. Thus, they are not supportive of the electronic church.
10. *True.*

ANSWERS TO THE FILL-IN-THE-BLANK QUESTIONS
1. better
2. moral
3. functional
4. ritual
5. religious experience
6. shunned
7. modernization
8. Abraham
9. Christianity
10. Muslims

GUIDELINES FOR ANSWERING THE ESSAY QUESTIONS
1. *Assume that you have been asked to make a presentation about religion to a group of people who have absolutely no idea what religion is. Prepare a speech in which you define religion and explain why it exists.*

For this question, your first task is to explain what religion is. To do this you might want to refer to Durkheim's work on the elementary forms of religious life, talking about the differences between the sacred and profane, the presence of beliefs, practices, and a moral community. Once you have done this, your next task is to discuss why religion exists. Here you could talk about either the functionalist perspective or the conflict perspective or both. If you choose to focus only on the functionalist view, you would want to talk about how religion meets basic human needs; you might also want to refer to the symbolic interactionist views on community. If you want to focus only on conflict theory, or add that to your discussion of functionalism, you would want to talk about how, for Marx, religion is like a drug that helps the oppressed forget about their exploitation at the hands of the capitalists. Furthermore, conflict theorists point out that capitalists use religion to legitimize social inequalities and maintain the status quo.

2. *The functionalists point out the many functions of religion, but also note that it has certain dysfunctions. Discuss both the functions and dysfunctions and then consider whether it is possible for religion to fulfill its functions without producing dysfunctions.*

At the end of the chapter, Henslin notes that people have four major concerns. These are: (1) the existence of God; (2) the purpose of life; (3) the existence of an afterlife; and (4) morality. In his discussion of the functionalist perspective, Henslin outlines several important functions of religion that address these concerns. Religion provides answers to their questions about the ultimate meaning of life, which, in turn, comforts people. People find community among others who share their values and beliefs. Religion also sets out guidelines for everyday living—what we should and should not do, thereby setting limits and establishing morality. Having connections to a community and guidelines for living also help in adapting to new environments and social change.

Despite the fact that there are several major religions around the globe, people tend to see their religion as being the only true religion. This is understandable, given the nature of religion. At the same time, this orientation can produce dysfunctions. The author discusses two: (1) war and terrorism; and (2) religious persecution.

The final part of the essay is to consider whether religions can exist and be functional without producing dysfunctions. In answering this, you need to consider the nature of the world today. If contact between people of different religions could be minimized, these dysfunctions would not be problematic. However, today, people of different faiths are drawn even closer together because of globalization. If we are to avoid the dysfunctional side of religion, a way needs to be found for everyone with different belief systems to live together in harmony. So far, we have few examples of this but can think of many examples of war and religious persecution.

3. *Discuss the process by which a religion matures from a cult into a church.*
This is a pretty straightforward question. All you are asked to do is to discuss the process by which a religion moves from cult to sect to church. You would want to talk about what each is, how they range along a continuum, and what events mark the shift from one type to the next.

4. *Consider why fundamentalist Christian churches in the United States are currently undergoing a revival.*
Begin by thinking about the nature of social life today. With the continuing rationalization of society (see Chapter 7 for more on rationalization), more and more of our interactions are impersonal and formal, taking place with strangers who are employed by bureaucracies. Consequently, people may feel disconnected from one another. Because we work more, we spend less time at home. We don't know our neighbors and often don't even have enough time for family and friends. Families aren't what they once were. As our society continues to change at a rather rapid pace, we feel that the old norms no longer apply, but are not sure what are the new norms are.
Now go back to the different sociological perspectives on religion. First, there is the functionalist perspective. In response to the impersonality of our daily lives, religion provides connection and community. Religious teachings provide clear guidelines for everyday living, helping us find direction in the face of continuing social change. Henslin suggests that mainstream churches, which offer a more remote God and less emotional involvement, fail to meet basic religious needs of large numbers of Americans. In contrast, the different fundamentalist Christian churches, with their literal interpretation of the Bible, offer seekers comfort and direction.

5. *Discuss the major patterns of adaptation that occur when religion and culture conflict with one another.*
You should identify the three patterns that occur when people find themselves in conflict between the religion and culture. The first pattern is that members of the religion may have as little to do as possible with nonmembers of their religion. They may withdraw into closed communities. In the second pattern, only certain aspects of the culture are rejected while others are acceptable. For example, some clothing that may be immodest is unacceptable, but other appropriate clothing is OK. This pattern has some mild tension associated with it that is resolved either by following the religion or by participating in the forbidden acts on the "sly." The last pattern is that the society rejects the religious group. They may even try to destroy it in extreme cases.

CHAPTER 19

ANSWERS FOR MULTIPLE CHOICE QUESTIONS

1.   **d**   Sociologists focus on medicine as a profession, a bureaucracy, and a business; therefore, "all of the above" would be the correct answer.

2.   **c**   The healing specialist of a preliterate tribe who attempts to control the spirits thought to cause a disease or injury is a shaman.

3.   **a**   As practiced in the U.S., the primary characteristics of the social institution of medicine do not include personalization.

4.   **b**   When a person is unable to fulfill their normal obligations because they are sick or injured, they are said to be in the sick role.

5.   **b**   The individual's claim to the sick role is legitimized primarily by a doctor's excuse.

6.   **c**   According to research, women are more likely than men to claim the sick role when they feel poorly because they are socialized for greater dependency and self-disclosure.

7.   **c**   According to conflict theorists, health care is one of the scarce resources over which groups compete.

8.   **d**   "All of the above" is correct. Professionalization of medicine included rigorous education, a theoretical understanding of illness, and self-regulation.

9.   **a**   The *incorrect* statement is "While doctors were able to control women's access to medical schools, they were never very effective in keeping other minorities out." In fact, they were able to keep both women and minorities out of medical schools or to severely limit their enrollment.

10. **b**   The lower the social class, the more mental problems there are.

11. **a**   The study of disease and disability patterns in a population is called epidemiology.

12. **d**   Today the average American spends $8,000 annually; in 1960, the average was $150.

13. **b**   Medical care is considered a commodity, not a right. It is available to those who can pay either privately, through insurance, or a government assistance program.

14. **d**   Henslin suggests that the primary reason the practice of defensive medicine has grown is because it is in the doctors' best interest. They want to establish a paper trail to protect themselves in the event they are sued by a disgruntled patient.

15. **a**   Depersonalization is the practice of dealing with people as though they were objects, means treating patients as though they were merely cases and diseases, and occurs when an individual is treated as if he or she was not a person. The one statement that is *incorrect* is that "It is less common today because of all the reforms brought about by HMOs."

16. **c**   The continuing male dominance of medicine is what lies at the heart of sexism in medicine. While the number of women who graduate from medical schools has increased dramatically, only one in four U.S. physicians is a woman.

17. **b**   The transformation of something into a matter to be treated by physicians is referred to as medicalization.

18. **a**   Oregon allows for medically assisted suicide.

19. **c**   Medical costs have risen dramatically in the United States because of tests performed for defensive rather than medical reasons, an increase in the size of the elderly population, and because health care is seen as a commodity (and is operated for profit). People wanting doctors to do unnecessary tests to assure themselves they are healthy is *not* a factor in spiraling costs.

20. **b**   AIDS is known to be transmitted by exchange of blood and/or semen. The U.S. Centers for Disease Control and Prevention say that casual contact between a carrier and a noncarrier in which bodily fluids are exchanged will not result in the transmission of the virus.

21. **b**   African Americans are at greater risk of contracting AIDS. The risk differences are related to social factors such as rates of IV drug use and the use of condoms.

22. **b**   Obesity is more life-threatening than AIDS or alcohol abuse.

23. **b** Rather than the rate of cigarette smoking increasing, it has in fact declined. In less than two decades, cigarette smoking has been cut in half among U.S. men and by a third among U.S. women.

24. **b** The Tuskegee syphilis experiment is an example of the callous disregard of people's health by physicians and the U.S. government.

25. **d** In order to implement a national policy of "prevention, not intervention" it would be necessary for the medical establishment, the general public, and businesses to work together to eliminate disabling environments and reduce the use of harmful drugs.

ANSWERS FOR TRUE-FALSE QUESTIONS

1. *True.*
2. *False.* People who don't seek competent help when they are sick are not behaving according to the expectations of the sick role; in the sick role an individual is expected to seek help in order to get better and return to his/her normal routine. Someone who doesn't do this is denied the right to claim sympathy from others; they get the cold shoulder for wrongfully claiming the sick role.
3. *False.* There is often ambiguity between the well role and the sick role because the decision to claim the sick role is often more a social than a physical matter.
4. *True.*
5. *True.*
6. *True.*
7. *False.* There is a two-tiered system of medical care in which the wealthy receive superior treatment compared to the poor.
8. *True.*
9. *False.* While the health risks of some occupations are evident (lumberjacks, rodeo bull riders, lion tamers), in many occupations, people do not become aware of the risks until years after they were exposed.
10. *True.*

ANSWERS TO THE FILL-IN-THE-BLANK QUESTIONS

1. monopoly
2. gender
3. Alzheimer's disease
4. right
5. defensive
6. error
7. diagnosis-related groups (DRGs)
8. ration
9. AIDS
10. alternative

GUIDELINES FOR ANSWERING THE ESSAY QUESTIONS

1. *Describe the elements of the sick role and identify variations in the pattern of claiming this role.*

You should acknowledge Talcott Parsons' contribution to our understanding of the sick role and his work in identifying the elements in that role. In terms of variations in claiming that role, the text talks about gender differences, but you could expand beyond this to talk about other variations within our society. For instance, children and old people have an easier time claiming this role than do adults because they are seen as more vulnerable and more dependent.

2. *Discuss why medicine developed into a monopoly in this country and what the consequences of this development have been for the delivery of medical treatment.*

The key to the development of a medical monopoly was the professionalization of medicine. In the early 1900s, in reaction to the wide variations in medical training and practice, the Carnegie Foundation commissioned Abraham Flexner to investigate the state of medical education. He issued a report recommending that higher standards be set on the training of doctors and that training facilities in medical schools be significantly upgraded. As a result, doctors were increasingly subject to more rigorous education and licensing. In return, they were expected to regulate themselves and take control over their clients.

Given these changes, it was not long before doctors established a monopoly over the care of the sick and injured. In the interests of improved patient care, they were able to get laws passed that restricted medical licensing to graduates of approved schools. Given that only certain schools gained approval, they could control which philosophies of medicine were taught and who could acquire the education necessary to practice medicine. They were also able to set fees for services, and for more than half of the twentieth century, they were able to prevent any competition from government-funded medical care.

3. *Explain the pattern of the worldwide AIDS epidemic and suggest reasons why this threat to the health of the world's population has not been addressed more aggressively.*

You could immediately point out that the distribution of AIDS cases is not evenly balanced around the globe but heavily concentrated in Africa and Southeast Asia. Looking at AIDS globally, you would want to point out this maldistribution and note that those countries most directly affected have the least amount of money to spend. This reflects the global stratification of health care.

Looking at AIDS within the United States, you would want to point out that more than half of those with AIDS are members of minorities. Furthermore, the most common way in which to contract the disease is through behaviors that are stigmatized in our society—homosexual sex, promiscuous heterosexual sex, and IV drug users. You could point out that policymakers may have been slow to respond because of the character of those most directly affected by the epidemic.

4. *Define depersonalization and present evidence from the chapter as to its presence within medicine. Consider why it is present in a system that is supposed to care about the individual who is sick or injured.*

Begin with the definition; depersonalization is the practice of dealing with people as though they were cases and diseases, not individuals. Then you need to consider why this orientation exists. You could also talk about developments in the medical industry, such as the more than two million Medicare claims filed each day, the pressures to control costs, and the growing lack of confidence in doctors as reflected by increases in the number of malpractice suits. Finally, there are the examples of callous experiments. You could discuss the Tuskegee syphilis experiment and the Cold War nuclear experiments; to carry out such experiments on human subjects, doctors and medical researchers had to have seen them as less than fully human.

5. *Discuss a couple of threats to health either in the United States or worldwide.*

There are many threats to health that were identified in your textbook. HIV/AIDS is a serious health issue in the U.S. and most especially in Africa. You could also discuss obesity and thinness or alcohol and nicotine. Many work in disabling environments. Industrialization is threatening our basic environment worldwide. The burning of carbon fuels has led to the greenhouse effect, a warming of the Earth that may change its climate, melt the polar ice caps, and flood the earth's coastal shores. There have also been harmful medical experiments that have occurred throughout history that have been sanctioned by the U.S. government or other health officials. Lastly, you could choose to discuss the globalization of disease. As global travel has increased, so have the diseases that can be spread around the world.

CHAPTER 20

ANSWERS FOR MULTIPLE CHOICE QUESTIONS

1. **c** Studying the size, composition, growth, and distribution of human population is known as demography.

2. **b** The proposition that the population grows geometrically while the food supply increases arithmetically is known as the Malthus theorem.

3. **d** Anti-Malthusians believe that the demographic transition, an explanation of the shift from high birth and death rates to low ones that occurred previously in Europe, is an accurate picture of what will happen in the future in the Least Industrialized Nations of the world.

4. **b** The three-stage historical process of population growth is the demographic transition.

5. **c** The process by which a country's population becomes smaller because its birth rate and immigration are too low to replace those who die and emigrate is population shrinkage.

6. **b** Starvation does not occur because there is not enough fertile land, there are too many people, or people are not eating a well-balanced diet. Rather, experts argue that it occurs because some parts of the world lack food while other parts of the world produce more than they can consume.

7. **d** "All of the above" is correct. People in the Least Industrialized Nations have so many children because parenthood provides status, children are considered to be an economic asset, and the community encourages people to have children.

8. **c** For conflict theorists, the reason women in poor nations have so many children is that men control women's reproductive choices.

9. **b** Mexico's current population will continue to grow rapidly.

10. **b** Population pyramids are used to illustrate population dynamics.

11. **a** Factors that influence population growth (fertility, mortality, and net migration) are demographic variables.

12. **a** Fertility rate refers to the number of children that the average woman bears.

13. **a** The number of deaths per 1,000 population is the crude death rate.

14. **d** The factors pushing someone to emigrate include poverty, lack of religious and political freedoms, and political persecution.

15. **d** Around the globe, the flow of migration is from the Least Industrialized Nations to the Most Industrialized Nations. The United States is the world's number one choice of immigrants.

16. **a** According to your text, it is difficult to forecast population growth because of government programs that affect fertility.

17. **d** "All of the above" is the correct option. In the first place, China's practice of female infanticide is rooted in sexism; there is a general preference for males over females. In terms of economics, males will support parents in their old age and are in a better position to take advantage of economic opportunities. Finally, there are traditions, such as the traditional expenses associated with marrying off a daughter, which go back centuries and also contribute to female infanticide.

18. **d** Urbanization is when an increasing proportion of a population lives in cities.

19. **d** "All of the above" is correct. Today's urbanization means that more people live in cities, today's cities are larger, and cities will have a growing influence on U.S. culture.

20. **a** There are 274 MSAs, not 280.

21. **a** A megacity is a city of 10 million or more residents. Most megacities are located in the Least Industrialized Nations.

22. **d** "All of the above" is correct. Edge cities consist of a cluster of shopping malls, hotels, office parks, and residential areas near major highway intersections; overlap political boundaries and include parts of several cities or towns; and provide a sense of place to those living there.

23. **d** The pattern of a growing number of immigrants settling an area, with the consequence that those already living in the area move out because they are threatened by their presence, is referred to as an invasion-succession cycle.

24. **c** The model that is based on the idea that land use in cities is based on several centers, such as a clustering of restaurants or automobile dealerships is the multiple-nuclei model.

25. **c** Darley and Latané found that the more bystanders there are, the less likely people are to help. They referred to this as diffusion of responsibility.

ANSWERS FOR TRUE-FALSE QUESTIONS

1. *False.* Thomas Malthus was not a sociologist at the University of Chicago in the 1920s. He was an English economist who lived from 1766 to 1834.
2. *True.*
3. *False.* It is the New Malthusians, not the Anti-Malthusians, who believe that people breed like germs in a bucket.
4. *False.* There are three stages, not two, in the process of demographic transition, although some now recognize a fourth stage.
5. *False.* The main reason why there is starvation is because those countries that produce food surpluses have stable populations, while those with rapidly growing populations have food shortages.
6. *False.* The major reason why people in poor countries have so many children is not necessarily because they do not know how to prevent conception. The reason is more sociological in nature, including the status that is conferred on women for producing children, as well as the need for children to take care of elderly parents.
7. *True.*
8. *True.*
9. *False.* No one model is considered to be the most accurate because different cities develop and grow in different ways, especially if there are certain kinds of natural barriers such as rivers or mountains.
10. *False.* Urban renewal involves the destruction of deteriorated buildings and the building of stadiums, high-rise condos, luxury hotels, and expensive shops.

ANSWERS TO THE FILL-IN-THE-BLANK QUESTIONS

1. one couple, one child
2. zero population
3. urbanization
4. megalopolis
5. micropolis
6. nuclei
7. peripheral
8. alienation
9. cosmopolites
10. less

GUIDELINES FOR ANSWERING THE ESSAY QUESTIONS

1. *State the positions of the New Malthusians and the anti-Malthusians and discuss which view you think is more accurate, based on the information provided about each position.*

You should begin this essay by summarizing each side's arguments. For the New Malthusians you would want to include the idea of the exponential growth curve, while for the anti-Malthusians, you would want to refer to the concepts of the demographic transition and population shrinkage. For both, you would want to include some of the facts such as how world population growth does seem to reflect the exponential growth curve (New Malthusians), while the Least Industrialized Nations reflect the second stage of the demographic transition and the population of European countries is shrinking (anti-Malthusians). Finally, you need to draw conclusions about which view you think is more accurate.

2. *Identify some of the population challenges that affect the Most Industrialized and the Least Industrialized Nations and provide explanations for these problems.*

First, for some of the Most Industrialized Nations, populations are shrinking. Of the 42 nations of Europe, 40 are in this situation. As the author notes, they fill more coffins than cradles. The reason for this is a declining birth rate—couples are having fewer children and are not replacing themselves A second challenge that the Most Industrialized Nations face is the migration of people from the Least Industrialized Nations. As immigrants move into these nations, there is some question about whether they contribute to the economy or are a drain. Regardless, as they immigrate, they create pressures on the receiving society to provide employment and services for them.

For the Least Industrialized Nations, the first challenge is how to feed people. People in many of these nations are starving because the country cannot produce enough food. In some cases, there is famine caused by drought, inefficient farming, and wars. In other cases, because of globalization, the major share of agricultural land is committed to producing crops for export rather than for indigenous consumption. A second challenge is to slow population growth. Some nations have successfully reduced the number of children a couple has, but the population continues to grow. The explanation lies in social and cultural factors. In these traditional societies, cultural values encourage couples to have large families, having children confers a status on the parents, and children will provide for parents in their old age. These factors are strong barriers to effective population control.

3. *Identify the problems that are associated with forecasting population growth.*

Your first step is to define the basic demographic equation—that is, the calculation used to project population growth. Then you need to identify problems that make the demographer's job more difficult. These would include natural phenomena (famines and plagues), economic factors (short-term booms and busts as well as longer-term industrialization), political factors (wars and government policy), and social factors (educational levels). In your essay you need to not only identify these, but also discuss the ways in which they make forecasting a challenge.

4. *Discuss the five types of urban dwellers that Gans describes and how life in the city is different for each of these groups.*

Gans discusses five groups that live in the city. Three of those groups live there by choice because of the opportunities and conveniences that the city offers. The cosmopolites are drawn to the city because of the conveniences and cultural benefits. The singles come to the city to seek jobs and entertainment. The ethnic villagers create their own close-knit neighborhoods in which they are united by ethnicity. The next two groups have little choice about where they live. The deprived are the poor and emotionally disturbed. Their neighborhoods are like urban jungles rather than urban villages. The trapped are those who have nowhere else to turn and cannot afford to move out. These include the unwanted elderly and drug and alcohol abusers.

5. *Discuss the factors that fueled suburbanization and consider the impact that this population shift had on cities.*

The trend in suburbanization began in the early decades of the twentieth century, but really accelerated after World War II. One of the major factors in this shift of population from cities to surrounding communities was the automobile. As more cars were sold, and more highways were built, people had the means to live a distance from where they worked. The rate of suburbanization increased in the 1950s and 1960s, as racial integration of both city schools and neighborhoods increased. Driven by racism, many whites sought to escape these changes by moving to all-white suburbs.

The cities were deeply affected by this shift in population. As more people left, businesses and jobs soon followed. This contributed to a shrinking tax base, with the result that city governments found it harder to maintain city services. Banks began to redline certain deteriorating, and changing, neighborhoods; people in those neighborhoods found it harder to obtain loans for housing or business purposes. You might also point out how these population changes also contribute to the development of metropolises and megalopolises. This, in turn, leads to increased environmental problems like air pollution.

CHAPTER 21

ANSWERS FOR MULTIPLE CHOICE QUESTIONS

1. **c** The *incorrect* statement is that "He proposed that a collective mind develops once a group of people congregate." It was Gustave LeBon, not Charles Mackay, who suggested that the crowd develops a collective mind.

2. **d** Gustave LeBon's term for the tendency of people in a crowd to feel, think, and act in extraordinary ways is collective mind.

3. **c** Social unrest is the condition most conducive to the emergence of collective behavior.

4. **a** A back-and-forth communication between the members of a crowd whereby a collective impulse is transmitted is a circular reaction.

5. **d** "All of the above" is correct. *Acting crowd,* a term coined by Herbert Blumer, is an excited group that collectively moves toward a goal, and is the end result of the five stages of collective behavior.

6. **b** Richard Berk used the term *minimax strategy* to describe the tendency for humans to minimize costs and maximize rewards. This is true regardless of whether an individual is deciding what card(s) to discard in a poker game or what store to loot in an urban riot.

7. **a** The development of new norms to cope with a new situation is emergent norms.

8. **a** The ego-involved has the most important role. Because this individual feels a personal stake in the unusual event, he/she may step forward to make suggestions about what should be done or will simply take action.

9. **d** The ego-involved, the insecure, and the exploiters are all participants in a crowd.

10. **c** Sociologists refer to unfounded information spread among people as rumor.

11. **c** It doesn't occur often, but rumors can lead to the destruction of entire communities.

12. **b** Sociologists have found that when a disaster such as a fire occurs, some people continue to perform their roles.

13. **b** Moral panics are generally fed by rumor, information for which there is no discernible source and which is usually unfounded.

14. **d** The bungalow house, the miniskirt, and the use of the word "cool" are all examples of fashion. We tend to think that the term fashion applies only to clothing, but it call also refer to furniture, hairstyles, and even the design and colors of buildings. Sociologist John Lofland points out that fashion also applies to language.

15. **a** The Women's Christian Temperance Union, a powerful social movement in the late nineteenth and early twentieth centuries, is an example of an alterative social movement. Its goal was to alter the drinking behavior of individuals.

16. **c** A millenarian movement is based on the prophecy of coming social upheaval.

17. **c** This new type of social movement that has developed because many issues of concern today cross national boundaries is called a transnational social movement. Examples are the women's movement, labor movement, environmental movement, and the animal rights movement.

18. **d** The public that social movements face can really be divided into sympathetic public, hostile public, and disinterested people.

19. **d** "All of the above" is correct. In deciding on what tactics to use, the inner core is influenced by its own predispositions and background, as well as its relationship to authorities. Research by Ellen Scott demonstrates that factors like friendship, race/ethnicity, and even the size of the town are important in determining tactics.

20. **b** How people think about some issue is public opinion.

21. **b** The statement "propaganda generally involves negative images" is *incorrect.*

22. **d** All of the answers are correct. The mass media are the gatekeepers to social movements; they engage in biased reporting, controlled and influenced by people who have an agenda to get across

and they are sympathetic to some social movements, while ignoring others; it all depends on their individual biases.

23. **c** Multiple realities refers to the notion that on any topic there are competing points of view that represent different realities based on different people's experiences.

24. **b** Deprivation theory claims people feel deprived of money, justice, status, or privilege. Therefore, they join social movements in hopes of solving their grievances.

25. **b** In order to turn a group of people who are upset about a social condition into a social movement, there must be resource mobilization. The resources that must be mobilized include time, money, people's skills, technologies such as direct mailings and fax machines, attention by the mass media, and even legitimacy among the public and authorities.

ANSWERS FOR TRUE-FALSE QUESTIONS

1. *True.*
2. *True.*
3. *True.*
4. *True.*
5. *False.* Urban legends are not just another kind of rumor. According to Jan Brunvand, they are passed on by people who think that the event happened to "a friend of a friend"; he sees them as modern morality stories, teaching us moral lessons about life.
6. *False.* A social movement that promotes some social change is known as a proactive social movement.
7. *True.*
8. *True.*
9. *False.* Propaganda and advertising are not quite different from one another. In essence, advertising is a type of propaganda because it fits both the broad and the narrow definition of propaganda perfectly.
10. *False.* Deprivation theory and relative deprivation theory are not identical perspectives. Deprivation theory is based on the idea that people who are deprived of things deemed valuable in society join social movements with the hope of redressing their grievances. Relative deprivation theory asserts that it is not people's actual negative conditions that matter but, rather, it is what people think they should have relative to what others have, or even compared with their own past or perceived future.

ANSWERS TO THE FILL-IN-THE-BLANK QUESTIONS

1. fads
2. social movement
3. prophecies
4. metaformative
5. institutionalized
6. propaganda
7. ideological commitment
8. moral
9. agent provocateur
10. decline and death

GUIDELINES FOR ANSWERING THE ESSAY QUESTIONS

1. *Compare and contrast the early explanations of collective behavior, as advanced by Charles Mackay, Gustave LeBon, Robert Park and Herbert Blumer, with more contemporary explanations developed by Richard Berk, Ralph Turner and Lewis Killian.*

You must first discuss the elements that these different theories have in common and then move on to the elements that separate them. First, they are all trying to explain why people act differently when they are swept up into a crowd of people. That is probably the single point on which there is agreement. The early explanations focused on the individual and how he or she was affected by forces outside themselves. Mackay talked about the herd, LeBon the collective mind, and Park the collective impulse. While Blumer developed a more systematic explanation, he also focused on events outside of the individual that impacted his or her behavior. In contrast, the more contemporary explanations focus on the individual as a rational actor. Berk depicts humans as calculating, weighing the costs against the benefits before taking any action. Turner and Killian also see humans as rational; in their work they argue that people develop new norms when confronted with new and unfamiliar situations. They also suggest that there are different kinds of participants, with different motives for being involved.

2. *Develop an explanation as to why panics, rumors, and urban legends thrive in society.*

You could begin this essay by defining what each of these different forms of collective behavior is. A panic is when people are so fearful of something that they cannot function normally and may even flee. A rumor is information for which there is no discernible source and which is usually unfounded. An urban legend is a story with an ironic twist that sounds realistic but is false. What all three of these have in common is that they develop when people are anxious about changes that are occurring in their environment and where there is a certain degree of ambiguity.

One reason why these thrive in society is because of social change. In times of change, when the old, established and comfortable ways are disappearing, people are often susceptible to rumors and urban legends that restore some degree of certainty in their lives. Conditions of change can also produce fear of the unknown future in people, which leaves them open to panic when something unforeseen occurs.

3. *Discuss the different theories about why people join social movements and consider how they could all be accurate.*

The text presents three different theories about why most people get involved in social movements: mass society theory, deprivation theory, and ideological commitment theory. Each provides us with an understanding of why some people get involved, but no one theory explains why all people become involved in social movements. One theory may be more appropriate at explaining why some people get involved in some social movements but not others. By using all three, we come away with a better understanding of the process by which individuals are drawn into social movements. You might also want to tie this discussion to that of the different types of social movements and the different types of members. For example, those people at the core of the movement may be connected for moral or ideological reasons, while those further out, such as the committed or less committed, may be involved because they feel isolated or alienated by modern society. Finally, a small number of people become involved in order to spy on the movement and sabotage its activities. You should mention the special case of the agent provocateur.

4. *Explain what propaganda is and why it is so important in the development of social movements.*

Begin by referring to the resource mobilization theory of social movements. As sociologists have noted, a crucial factor in enabling a social movement to move beyond the first stage is resource mobilization—finding time, money, and skilled individuals for the movement, as well as gaining the attention of the mass media. There may be many people who are upset about a situation or condition, but they need to be mobilized. One of the primary ways in which this is accomplished is through propaganda.

Propaganda is simply the presentation of information in an attempt to influence people. In particular, the movement will want to use propaganda in order to attract members of the sympathetic public to its cause. It may also be important to try to reach members of the disinterested public with propaganda. Because these people do not care about the issue, or may even be unaware of the issue, propaganda can be a critically important tool in trying to win them to the cause.

The mass media is important to the social movement. Because of this, they are often referred to as the gatekeepers to the social movement. Depending on the type of connection to the media that develops, media propaganda will be sympathetic to or unfavorable toward the social movement. Either way, the success of the movement in getting its message across will hinge on the type of propaganda the media put forth.

5. *Discuss the difference between fads and fashion and provide examples.*

A fad is a novel form of behavior that catches people's attention. It appears quickly and the media helps to spread the fad. Very short, intense fads are called crazes. Examples include Beanie Babies and the "Tickle Me Elmo" dolls. Organizations can also get caught up in fads. Quality circles at one time were a fad. Fads can involve millions of people and still die out quickly. Fads can affect child rearing, food, and diets. Fads that die out can make a comeback, such as the hula hoop. Fads that last are known as fashions. Fashions can be certain hairstyles, clothing or furniture. Fashion can also apply to common expressions. For example: "awesome" in the 1980s, "bad" in the 1990s and "sweet" in the early 2000s.

CHAPTER 22

ANSWERS FOR MULTIPLE CHOICE QUESTIONS

1. **d** The alteration in the characteristics of culture and society over time is social change.
2. **c** Henslin identifies the invention of the microchip as the fourth social revolution.
3. **a** Max Weber identified religion as the core reason for the development of capitalism.
4. **a** During the second stage of the demographic transition, the population increased not decreased.
5. **a** Russia recently became part of the G8.
6. **b** China
7. **c** Unilinear evolution theories assume that all societies follow the same path, evolving from simple to complex through uniform sequences.
8. **b** Today, evolutionary theories have been rejected because the assumption of progress has been cast aside.
9. **b** Cyclical theory attempts to account for the rise of entire civilizations, rather than a particular society.
10. **b** According to Karl Marx, each ruling class sows the seeds of its own destruction.
11. **c** Ogburn's analysis has been criticized because it places too great an emphasis on technology as the source for almost all social change. Technology and social change actually form a two-way street: technology leads to social change and social change leads to technology.
12. **b** The fact that as men were drawn out of their homes to work in factories, family relationships changed, is an example of how technology contributes to changes in social relationships.
13. **c** Henslin suggests that computers are allowing students to study new subjects because they can access courses online. Computers are also changing the way students learn and widening the gap between wealthy and poor school districts. The one thing that he does not mention is that computers are increasing the opportunities for teachers and administrators to carry out surveillance against students.
14. **c** Henslin suggests that computers are altering social relationships, changing the way we do work, and reversing the location of where work is done—not increasing social interaction.
15. **b** Distance learning is becoming a mainstream part of the educational system.
16. **b** One concern about the expansion of the information superhighway is social inequalities will become greater, both on a national and global basis.
17. **d** All of the above answers are true. The Pentagon is building its own Internet, robots are being used in Iraq, and the Defense Department plans to "weaponize" space.
18. **a** While all regions of the world contribute to the world's environmental problems, the Most Industrialized Nations are considered the major polluters.
19. **d** Acid rain, the greenhouse effect, and global warming are all consequences of burning fossil fuels.
20. **c** Of the technologies being developed, the most prominent alternative source of energy in vehicles are gas-electric hybrids.
21. **b** Racial minorities and the poor are disproportionately exposed to environmental hazards.
22. **a** The major source of pollution is likely to become the Least Industrialized Nations.
23. **c** The disappearance of the world's rain forests presents the greatest threat to the survival of numerous plant and animal species.
24. **d** "All of the above" is correct. Environmental sociology examines how the physical environment affects human activities; how human activities affect the physical environment; and has nine main assumptions.
25. **b** The goal of environmental sociologists is to do research on the mutual impact that individuals and environments have on one another.

ANSWERS FOR TRUE-FALSE QUESTIONS

1. *False.* The assumption of evolutionary theories that all societies progress from a primitive state to a highly complex state has not been proven. With Western culture in crisis, it is no longer assumed that it holds the answers to human happiness; consequently, the assumption of progress has been cast aside and evolutionary theories have been rejected.
2. *True.*
3. *True.*
4. *True.*
5. *True.*
6. *False.* Technology is a very powerful force for social change because it alters the ways in which those tools are used.
7. *True.*
8. *False.* The automobile actually gave women freedom outside of the home.
9. *False.* The use of computers in education is likely to increase, rather than decrease, the social inequality between school districts, because poor districts will not be able to afford the hardware.
10. *True.*

ANSWERS TO THE FILL-IN-THE-BLANK QUESTIONS

1. modernization
2. Gemeinschaft
3. destruction
4. William Ogburn
5. technology
6. Karl Marx
7. capitalism
8. Indian
9. ecosabotage
10. environmental

GUIDELINES FOR ANSWERING THE ESSAY QUESTIONS

1. *The author of your text suggests that social movements reveal the cutting edge of change in a society or across the globe. In Chapter 21, you learned about different social movements and in this chapter there is discussion of the environmental movement. Discuss a specific social movement in terms of what it reveals about social change.*

Let's use the discussion of abortion that is presented at the end of Chapter 21. The fact that there are opposing groups that have organized around this issue suggests that this is an extremely controversial one. The question you need to answer is "what does this suggest about our society and change?" First, you need to consider the history of this struggle. Until 1973, abortions were illegal in this country. In the decade immediately preceding *Roe v. Wade*, a revitalized women's movement made abortion rights one of its issues. Bear in mind that this was a period in which our understanding of, and expectations about, women's role in society was changing. The Supreme Court ruling was considered a major victory for the champions of the pro-choice side.

In the aftermath of that decision, an opposing movement emerged. This prolife group was reacting not only to the decision by the Supreme Court, but also to the broader changes that were occurring in the context of women's roles. Many of the supporters of this view believe that if a woman becomes pregnant, it is her duty to have the child. They see women who advocate for the right to control their own reproductive rights as potential murderers—too self-centered to put the lives of their unborn child ahead of their own desires for school or career. If you stop and think about this, what they are reflecting is a traditional view of womanhood as wife and mother.

In most instances, it is possible to look beyond the surface arguments to see how a social movement is advocating or resisting a change in society. You just need to use your sociological imagination to do that.

2. *Discuss Ogburn's three processes of social change, provide examples to illustrate each, and evaluate the theory.*

This is a fairly straightforward essay question. What you need to do is discuss each of Ogburn's processes—invention, discovery, and diffusion—and provide examples for each. Your conclusion would be an evaluation of the theory. How accurately do you think it explains the process of social change? Do you agree with the critics or do you think Ogburn is basically correct in his assumption that the material changes first and that the symbolic culture follows?

3. *Choose a particular technology, such as the computer or another technology, and discuss what impact it has had on U.S. society.*

The author presents four different ways in which technology can transform society: changes in social organization, changes in ideology, transformation of values, and transformation of social relationships. The first part of your essay should include some discussion of these four. Then you would want to discuss how one particular technology affects these four different aspects of social life. The book provides information on computers but you could choose another one, such as the automobile, television, airplanes, and the telephone, to name a few significant ones. Remember to provide examples to illustrate each aspect.

4. *Discuss the role of the automobile in changing cities, architecture, courtship, and women's roles.*

As your textbook notes, the automobile was the new technology within the last 100 years that had the greatest impact on social life. The automobile changed the shape of U.S. cities and stimulated urbanization. By the 1920s, Americans had begun to leave the city. Commercial architecture changed from the huge parking lots that surrounded shopping malls to the drive-up windows at banks and fast food restaurants. The architecture of homes also changed as garages were built to accommodate these automobiles. The automobile was used extensively for dating and removed children from the watchful eye of their parents. This invention may also lie at the heart of the changed role of women within society. It gave women the freedom to leave the confines of the home. They shopped for pre-made food and with the electric refrigerator, shopping became a weekly rather than daily activity. It changed the relationship women had with their spouses. Essentially, the automobile allowed women to participate in social life not connected with the home.

5. *Consider whether it is possible for us to achieve a sustainable environment.*

Begin with a definition of a sustainable environment—a world system in which we use our physical environment to meet our needs without destroying humanity's future. As the author notes, we cannot continue to trash the earth or to rape the environment for the sake of profits. In this chapter, you have learned that much of the problem lies with industrialization and a capitalist economic system. For most of the industrialized world, the message has been "growth at any cost." And now, as the Industrializing Nations and the Least Industrialized Nations make an attempt to catch up with the Most Industrialized Nations, they too are forsaking the environment in the name of industrialization.

It is the goal of capitalism to produce in order to make a profit and this has two consequences for the environment. First, as capitalist enterprises seek new ways to lower costs, they are increasingly locating production facilities in countries with few environmental regulations, since having to comply with the environmental standards imposed by the Most Industrialized Nations often increases the cost of production and lowers the profit margin. Second, capitalist enterprises have got to sustain a market for their products so consumers have got to consume at a high level in order to maximize sales. We, like other industrialized nations, have become a disposable economy; the time before a product becomes obsolete has shrunk and we throw away our outdated products rather than recycle or reuse. This has produced enormous problems around garbage disposal.

The question then is "can we control the growth machine?" Here's where you can use all the knowledge you have gained over the semester about stratification and inequality, as well as the power of social movements to bring about change. Consider the issues of capitalism, of global stratification, and the global environmental movement, as you frame your conclusions.